A GRAMMAR OF THE HINDUSTANI OR URDU LANGUAGE

A GRAMMAR OF THE HINDUSTANI OR URDU LANGUAGE.

BY

JOHN T. PLATTS

GYAN

Published by

Gyan Publishing House
5, Ansari Road
Daryaganj, New Delhi-110002
Phone: 011-47034999, 9811692060
E-mail: books@gyanbooks.com

Distribution Network
gyanbooks.com
India, USA, Canada, UK, Australia

ISBN: 978-93-6280-125-8 (HB)
First Published, 1874

2nd Impression 2024

Printed at: Gyan Press, Delhi.

A GRAMMAR OF THE HINDUSTANI OR URDU LANGUAGE
Author: JOHN T. PLATTS

A GRAMMAR

OF THE

HINDŪSTĀNĪ OR URDŪ LANGUAGE.

A GRAMMAR OF THE HINDŪSTĀNĪ OR URDŪ LANGUAGE.

BY

JOHN T. PLATTS,

LATE AN INSPECTOR OF PUBLIC INSTRUCTION IN THE CENTRAL PROVINCES OF INDIA.

LONDON:

Wm. H. ALLEN & CO., 13, WATERLOO PLACE, S.W.

PUBLISHERS TO THE INDIA OFFICE,

1874.

PREFACE.

The Grammar now offered to the public was begun in India many years ago; but its progress was so retarded by illness, press of official work, and other causes, that on my return to England about eighteen months ago, scarcely a third of it was in a form ready for the press.

It owes its origin to certain Indian friends, whose arguments, backed by the results of my own reading and observation, led me to conclude—(1) that, much as had been achieved in the field of Urdū Grammar by Europeans (and especially by Englishmen), that field had not been so thoroughly worked but that a great deal more might be won from it; (2) that no small portion of the work which had been done was of a kind that afforded room for improvement.

In justification of the first of these opinions, I would refer my readers to the large quantity of what is believed to be absolutely new matter that is to be found in almost every part of this work, and especially in the sections which treat of—(1) gender; (2) numerals; (3) Persian and Arabic constructions; (4) causal verbs; (5) compound verbs; (6) particles; (7) derivation of words; and in almost every chapter of the Syntax. In support of the second, I would point to the sections which treat of the construction—(1) of verbs and adjectives in connection with the broken plurals of the Arabic; (2) of nominal and frequentative verbs; (3) of the accusative case; (4) of predicative adjectives in construction with factitive verbs; (5) of the participles; and also to the sections which notice the different uses of the fragmentary verbs *hai* and *thā*, and the tenses of the subjunctive mood. In respect of some of these, the views propounded are so directly opposed to those maintained by preceding grammarians, that I have felt constrained to support them by foot-notes, remarks, citations from native grammars, and the opinions of native scholars; and thus the work has to some extent assumed a polemical character, for which I consider that some apology is due. This I offer the more readily, as I am conscious of being actuated by no motive beyond the simple desire to establish what, supported by the best native authorities, I hold to be correct views of the constructions in question.

Besides the additions and changes referred to above, I may also, I believe, claim to have succeeded in reducing to rule some constructions which have hitherto been regarded as arbitrary. And here I may be permitted to observe that there is little in the structure of Urdū of the loose and arbitrary character which some recent writers on the grammar of the language impute to it. It may be difficult to discover the rules for certain constructions; and, in many instances, native scholars, no doubt, are unable to assign a satisfactory reason for the forms they use; but it is surely inconsequent to conclude from these facts that rules in such cases cannot be discovered, and that native scholars cannot be trusted to compose correctly in their own tongue. That "writers are guided by usage rather than by rule, and test the accuracy of a passage by the ear rather than by any recognized law," is, in the main, true. But this practice is by no means confined to Urdū writers; nor are they a whit more liable to err in following the guidance of usage and the ear than the many excellent speakers and writers in other living tongues who follow the same guides. Indeed, as far as constructions which constitute the marked peculiarities of the language are concerned, it may be safely affirmed that Urdū writers of even ordinary ability are scarcely likely to make a slip. When therefore a form or expression occurs in one or more standard authors which appears to violate some well-known rule, a foreigner would do well to pause ere he condemns it as a "transgression"; for it is infinitely more probable that he has not understood the construction, than that the authors have committed a palpable solecism.

One of the features peculiar to this Grammar which I would notice here are the remarks and notes that touch upon the derivation and origin of words, and the formation of the cases and tenses—a subject upon which so much light has been thrown of late years by the study of comparative grammar. Students of Urdū and Hindī in the schools of India especially will, I trust, find this portion of the work both interesting and instructive;—and not only students, but those also who speak and write Urdū with perfect facility and accuracy. For it is notorious that Urdū scholars (and especially Moḥammadans) are grossly ignorant of the origin of such words and inflexions in their language as are not derived from the Persian and Arabic. And the general restriction of their studies to these languages alone puts it out of their power to acquire a knowledge of the linguistic discoveries of modern philologists in fields lying apart from them.

The arrangement and nomenclature of the work differ somewhat from those of preceding grammars. The declensions have been reduced to *two*; the numerals are noticed immediately after the attributive adjective; and the sections on Persian and Arabic constructions, treating as they do of substantives, adjectives, and numerals, it has been judged advisable to introduce immediately after the Urdū (Hindī) numerals, with the view of keeping the same parts of speech as much as possible together. These sections are, as has been already hinted, fuller and more complete than any notice of Persian and Arabic inflexions that has hitherto appeared in a grammar of Hindūstānī. Full as they are however, it would be presumptuous to say that they comprise all the constructions that occur in the language. But I trust I may say that they contain few that do *not* occur. The student will find it to his advantage to read these sections through—without dwelling on them at first; but more carefully on a second perusal, after he has made some acquaintance with Urdū literature; for Persian and Arabic, although not the back-bone, so to speak, form very important members of Urdū, and hence a knowledge of some of the principal facts of their inflexion is indispensable to a correct understanding and use of the language.

The examples under the more important rules of the Syntax are numerous and varied. In their selection I have not confined myself to the Bāg o Bahār and a few other works compiled about the same comparatively remote period—works which, however excellent they may be, can hardly be supposed to furnish examples of all the constructions and idioms current even in their day, much less of those now in use; and which may certainly be supposed to contain not a little that is now obsolete or rare—but have also drawn from more modern works, such as the Fasāna'ĕ 'Ajā'ib, the Urdū Reader (a work published under the authority of the Government of the N.W. Provinces of India), etc., and also from some of the best native newspapers; *e.g.* the Shŏ'la'ĕ Ṭūr of Kānhpūr, and the 'Alīgaṛh Institute Gazette. Should the examples under some of the rules be regarded as too copious, I would urge the importance of the rules themselves in such cases, or the misconception that has hitherto prevailed respecting the constructions exemplified; and also that, while the copiousness of the examples is calculated to impress the rules on the student's mind, their generally varied character and full propositional form will have the advantage of introducing him to diversities both of idiom and style.

In the preparation of the work I have made free, but not, I trust, unfair, use of the Grammars of my predecessors, and especially of those published in recent years by native scholars: *e.g.* the Urdū Grammar of M. Imām Bakhsh of the Dehlī College; the Ḳawā'idu'l-mubtadī of M. Karīmu'd-dīn; the Ḳawā'idĕ Urdū (a work published under the authority of the Government of the North-West Provinces of India). I have also obtained much assistance from the following works: (1) the Prākṛita-Prakāśa of Professor Cowell; (2) the Sindhī Grammar of Dr. Trumpp (a work to which I am greatly indebted for direct help as well as numerous hints touching the derivation of Hindī words); (3) the Grammatica Linguae Persicae of Dr. Vullers; (4) the Arabic Grammar of Professor Wright. And, lastly, I have at various times obtained much valuable information from several native scholars in India, and especially from Maulavīs Shaikh ʻAbdullāh of Kānhpūr, Moḥammad Riẓā of Ilāhābād, ʻAlī Asgar of Ajmer, and Ṣafdar ʻAlī of Jabalpūr, to whom I take this opportunity of offering my grateful thanks for the aid they were always so ready to afford me in my Oriental studies.

In spite of the greatest possible care in preparing the MS. and correcting the press, some omissions and errors have been discovered in the work, and it is probable that others of a not very serious character (as, for example, the omission of dots and vowel marks) have escaped detection. It must not be imagined, however, that every instance of omission of a long vowel mark is an oversight. The Persian numeral *dū*, for example, is generally written *du*, because the vowel is pronounced short; and the long vowel of the Arabic words *fī*, *z̤ū*, etc., being always shortened in pronunciation before the conjunctive *alif*, is of course not marked long. A list of such errors as have been discovered is given further on, and the reader is requested to correct them in the text before perusing it.

JOHN T. PLATTS.

London,
1st *November*, 1873.

CONTENTS.

SYNTAX.

HINDŪSTĀNĪ GRAMMAR.

PART I.—ORTHOGRAPHY.

CHAPTER I.

I. THE ALPHABET.

1. Urdū, or Hindūstānī, though a composite language, is derived mainly from the Hindī. The Persian and Arabic languages have contributed largely, but Hindī is the chief source. Like Persian and Arabic it is written and read from right to left, and books written in it begin at the page which, in an English book, would be the last. The letters (حُرُوفُ ٱلتَّہَجِّي *ḥurūfu 'ttahajjī*) are thirty-five in number, and are all consonants, though three of them are also used as vowels. When grouped into words, they are (with nine exceptions) connected with one another, and several of the letters assume somewhat different shapes according as they stand at the beginning, in the middle, or at the end of a connected group. The following Table exhibits the several forms of the letters, along with their names and numerical values.

Name.	Power.	Unconnected Form.	Connected Form: Final.	Medial.	Initial.	Exemplification of Final.	Medial.	Initial.	Numerical Value.
الف *alif*	.....	ا	ـا	ـا	ا	تا	بار	آب	1
بے *be*	*b*	ب	ـب	ـبـ	بـ	جَب	خَبَر	بَد	2
پے *pe*	*p*	پ	ـپ	ـپـ	پـ	تَپ	سِپَر	پَس	[2][2]
تے *te*	*t*	ت	ـت	ـتـ	تـ	مَت	لَتَرہ	تب	400
ٹے *ṭe*, or ٹہ *ṭa*	*ṭ*	ٹ[1]	ـٹ	ـٹـ	ٹـ	ہَٹ	مَٹَر	ٹیپ	[400]
ثے *se*	*s̤*	ث	ـث	ـثـ	ثـ	بَحْث	کثر	ثنا	500
جیم *jīm*	*j*	ج	ـج	ـجـ	جـ	لج	فجر	جب	3
چے *che*	*ch*	چ	ـچ	ـچـ	چـ	سچ	بچہ	چُپ	[3]
حے *ḥe*	*ḥ*	ح	ـح	ـحـ	حـ	صبح	بحْث	حرف	8
خے *khe*	*kh*	خ	ـخ	ـخـ	خـ	میخ	بخش	خال	600
دال *dāl*	*d*	د	ـد	ـد	د	بد	فِدا	دست	4
ڈہ *ḍa*	*ḍ*	ڈ	ـڈ	ـڈ	ڈ	مُنڈ	نِڈر	ڈال	[4]
ذال *zāl*	*z̲*	ذ	ـذ	ـذ	ذ	کاغذ	نذر	ذات	700
ري *re*	*r*	ر	ـر	ـر	ر	جر	برد	راد	200
ڑہ *ṛa*	*ṛ*	ڑ	ـڑ	ـڑ	ڑ	جڑ	بڑا	ڑوڑا	[200]
زي *ze*	*z*	ز	ـز	ـز	ز	گز	بزم	زر	7
ژي *zhe*	*zh*	ژ	ـژ	ـژ	ژ	پُژ	مُژدہ	ژرف	[7]
سين *sīn*	*s*	س	ـس	ـسـ	سـ	بس	نسب	سر	60
شين *shīn*	*sh*	ش	ـش	ـشـ	شـ	غش	حشر	شب	300

[1] Instead of ٹ, ڑ, etc., the forms ٹ (with ط), ڑ (with ط), etc., are commonly used in books printed and lithographed in India. The form ٹ is peculiar to books printed in England.

[2] The brackets are intended to show that these letters had originally no value, but afterwards received the same value as the cognate Arabic letters

Name.	Power.	Unconnected Form.	Connected Form: Final.	Medial.	Initial.	Exemplification of Final.	Medial.	Initial.	Numerical Value.
صاد *ṣād*	*ṣ*	ص	ـص	ـصـ	صـ	خلص	قصب	صاف	90
ضاد *ẓād*	*ẓ*	ض	ـض	ـضـ	ضـ	بعض	حضر	ضبر	800
طوي *ṭoe*	*ṭ*	ط	ـط	ـطـ	طـ	خط	خطا	طاق	9
ظوي *ẓoe*	*ẓ*	ظ	ـظ	ـظـ	ظـ	حفظ	نظر	ظفر	900
عين *ʿain*	*ʿa*	ع	ـع	ـعـ	عـ	صنع	بعد	عسل	70
غين *gain*	*g*	غ	ـغ	ـغـ	غـ	تيغ	بغل	غسل	1000
فے *fe*	*f*	ف	ـف	ـفـ	فـ	سلف	سفر	فرح	80
قاف *ḳāf*	*ḳ*	ق	ـق	ـقـ	قـ	طبق	نقل	قمر	100
كاف *kāf*	*k*	ك	ـك	ـكـ	كـ	نيك	بكر	كام	20
گاف *gāf*	*g*	گ	ـگ	ـگـ	گـ	الگ	مگس	گل	[20]
لام *lām*	*l*	ل	ـل	ـلـ	لـ	حمل	طلب	لعل	30
ميم *mīm*	*m*	م	ـم	ـمـ ـمـ	مـ	قلم	قمر / قمر	مال	40
نون *nūn*	*n*	ن	ـن	ـنـ	نـ	من	منع	نعل	50
واو *wāʾo*	*w*	و	ـو	ـو	و	بو	پور	وحل	6
هے *he*	*h*	ه	ـه	ـهـ ـهـ	هـ	نه	كها / كها	هنر	5
يے *ye*	*y*	ى	ـي / ـے	ـيـ	يـ	بي / بے	بيد	ياد	10

Rem. a. The form ـيـ is used for the letters *b, p, t, ṭ, s̤, n, y,* before ج *j,* چ *ch,* ح *ḥ,* and خ *kh,* as in the words تخت *takht,* بچ *bach.*

Rem. b. ا in connection with a preceding ل forms the figures لا, لا. This combination is generally reckoned a letter of the alphabet, and inserted before ي, to the perplexity of many grammarians, who, ignorant of the reason why it is placed there, erroneously call it *lām-*

alif, whereas it is nothing else than tne name of the *alif* of prolongation (see § 11, *Rem. c.*) written at full length. It must not be confounded with the *consonant* ا (or the *hamzated alif,* or *hamza,* as it is commonly called), the first letter of the alphabet.

2. To the above letters should be added the aspirated letters of the Devanāgarī, or Alphabet of the Sanskrit, viz. भ *bha,* फ *pha,* थ *tha,* ठ *ṭha,* झ *jha,* छ *chha,* ध *dha,* ढ *ḍha,* ख *kha,* घ *gha.* The aspirate in these letters is said to be مخلوط *ma<u>kh</u>lūṭ,* or 'blended' (with the preceding letter). They are represented in Urdū by the combinations بھ, پھ, تھ, ٹھ, جھ, چھ, دھ, ڈھ, کھ, گھ, the 'butterfly- or spectacle-shaped' *h* (*du-chashmī he*) being conventionally used with all except د and ڈ, which letters are not (except, optionally, in the case of a final *h*, see *Rem. a,* § 3) connected with a following letter, and therefore take the initial form of the *h* after them.

Rem. a. The letters ا, ب, پ, ث, ج, ح, خ, د, ذ, ر, ز, س, ش, ص, ض, ط, ظ, ع, غ, ف, ق, ک, ل, م, ن, و, ہ, ي are borrowed from the Arabic; پ, چ, گ and ژ from the Persian (they are called بائے فارسي *bā'ĕ Fārsī,* 'the Persian *b*,' etc.); and the remaining letters are conventionally used as the equivalents of certain Hindī letters.

Rem. b. The letters ث, ح, ص, ض, ط, ظ, ع, ق are peculiar to Arabic words. ص is to be met with in a few Persian words (*e.g.* صد *ṣad,* 'a hundred'), but in every such instance an original س *s* has been changed to ص *ṣ*. The letters خ, ذ, ز and غ are common to both Arabic and Persian words; but خ and غ occur in a few Hindī words in place of کھ and گھ. The letter ژ occurs in Persian words alone. پ, چ and گ may occur in Persian or Hindī words, but never in those derived from the Arabic. ٹ, ڈ, ڑ, and the ten aspirated letters بھ, پھ, etc., can occur in Hindī words alone. The remaining letters are common to Hindī, Persian, and Arabic words.

3. The letters ا, د, ڈ, ذ, ر, ڑ, ز, ژ and و, are joined to a preceding letter, provided it be not one of their own number, but not generally to a following one. The letters ط and ظ are connected with both a preceding and a following letter, but their form remains unchanged.

Rem. The above rule is strictly true only of the printed character. In writing and in lithographed books these letters, with the exception of ا, are frequently joined to a following *h*, if it be final: *e.g.* دیده *dīda.*

4. The correct pronunciation of some of the letters, as, for example, ح and ع, it is scarcely possible for a European to acquire. Most of them, however, are sufficiently represented by the corresponding English characters, as may be seen from the following remarks:

ا *alif*, or *hamza* (as it is commonly called, to distinguish it from the *alif* of prolongation), is the *spiritus lenis* of the Greeks. It may be compared with *h* in the English *hour*.

ب and پ are our *b* and *p*.

ت is much softer and more dental than the English *t*. In pronouncing it, the tip of the tongue should be placed against the edge or the back of the upper teeth.

ٹ has a heavier[1] sound than our *t*, but it represents it more closely than ت does. In pronouncing it the tip of the tongue is applied to the back part of the mouth.

[1] This *t* is termed تاي مثقّله *tā'ĕ mus̤aḳḳala* 'the heavy *t*,' and the same epithet is applied to the letters ڈ and ڑ.

ث, س, ص are all sounded alike, like our hard *s* in *sit.*[1]

ج has the sound of *j* in the English *jail.*

چ is the English *ch*, as in *church.*

ح is a very sharp, but smooth guttural aspirate, stronger than ہ, but not rough like خ. Its sound approximates to that of our *h* in *huge.*

د is softer and more dental than our *d*. It is pronounced in the same way as our ت, by placing the tongue against the back of the upper teeth.

ڈ has a sound resembling the English *d* in *dame;* but it is generally heavier. It is pronounced by applying the tip of the tongue to the back part of the roof of the mouth.

ذ, ز, ض and ظ have all one sound in Urdū, viz. that of our *z* in *zeal.*[1]

ر is, in all positions, a distinctly uttered lingual *r*, as pronounced by the French and Germans.

ڑ is a heavy sounding *r*, uttered by turning the tip of the tongue towards the roof of the mouth, as in the case of ڈ, with which letter it is interchangeable.

ژ has the sound of our *z* in *azure.*

ش is represented by our *sh*, as in *shut.*

ط is a strongly palatal *t*; but by all except, perhaps, the educated Musalmān, it is pronounced like ت.

ع has a strong guttural sound, pronounced by a smart compression of the upper part of the wind-pipe, and forcible emission of the breath. Its correct pronunciation is rarely heard in India, and is scarcely to be acquired by a European.

غ is a guttural *g*, accompanied by a grating or rattling sound as in

[1] In reading the Ḳor'ān, however, the true sound is given to these letters; *i.e.* ث is pronounced like our *th* in *thing*; س like *s* in *sit*; ص somewhat like *ss* in *hiss*; ذ like *th* in *this*; ز as the common English *z*; ض like a strongly articulated palatal *d*; and ظ, either like ض, or as a strongly articulated palatal *z*.

gargling, of which English affords no example. The Northumbrian *r*, and the French *r* in *grasseye*, are approximations to it.

ف is our *f*.

ق is a strongly articulated guttural *k*, of which we have no example in English. It closely resembles the sound uttered by a crow in its *caw*.

ک is our *k*.

گ has the sound of our *g* in *get*, *give*; never that of *g* in *gem*, *gaol*, *gibe*.

ل, م are exactly equivalent to the English *l*, *m*.

ن has three distinct sounds: it has the sound of the English *n* in *not*—1) When it occurs at the beginning of a word or syllable, as نام *nām*; 2) at the end of a word or syllable, when preceded by a short vowel, as بن *ban*; 3) in all Arabic words in which it is not immediately followed by ب *b*. It is *nasal* (غنّہ *gunna*), or *indistinct* (خفا *khafā*), like the French *n* in *bon*—1) When it is quiescent (*i.e.* not movent), and immediately preceded by a long vowel; *e.g.* دِرختاں *dirakhtāṅ*, برسوں *barsoṅ*, سانپ *sāṅp*, آندھی *āṅdhī*, اینٹ *īṅṭ*, اونٹ *ūṅṭ*: (2) when it is quiescent, and is immediately followed by a quiescent letter; *e.g.* انتری *aṅtrī*, پھنسنا *phaṅsnā*, منہ *muṅh*. It has the sound of *m* in all Persian and Arabic words in which it is immediately followed by ب *b* or پ *p*; and generally[1] in Hindī words also, if a short vowel precede it; *e.g.* انبوہ *amboh*, تنبیہ *tambīh*, عنبر *'ambar*,

[1] There are numerous exceptions to the rule in the case of Hindī words; a good test, perhaps, is the method of writing: if a word can be written with either *n* or *m* (before *b* or *p*), the *n* invariably has the sound of *m*: *e.g.* لنبا or لمبا *lambā*; چنپا or چمپا *champā*: if *n* cannot be replaced by *m* in writing, then it has a nasal or obscure sound; as چنبیلی *chaṅbelī*. To say, as all the grammarians do, that "*n* immediately preceding *b* or *p* always has the sound of *m*," is quite wrong; for if a long vowel precede the *n*, it almost invariably has a *nasal* sound: *e.g.* سانپ *sāṅp*, تانبا *tāṅbā*, کانپنا *kāṅpnā*, سونپنا *sauṅpnā*; and the instances of its having a nasal sound, even when preceded by a short vowel, are by no means few. The rule really applies to Persian and Arabic words alone.

چنْپا *champā*, لنْبا *lambā*.—In these pages nasal *n*, when final, will be printed without the dot, thus ں; and in the Roman character it will, in all positions, be indicated by *n* with a dot (*ṅ*).

ه is an aspirate like our *h* in *hand*. At the end of most words, however, when preceded by the short vowel *a* (*fatḥa*, § 5), it is not sounded: *e.g.* خانه *khāna*, 'house,' بنده *banda*, 'servant,' 'slave.' It is then termed هائے مُختَفي *hā'ĕ mukhtafī*, 'the imperceptible *h*,' in contradistinction to the perceptible *h* (هائے ظاهِر *hā'ĕ ẓāhir*), in such words as راه *rāh*, 'road,' بادشاه *bādshāh*, 'king.' Final *h*, when not sounded, is omitted in the Roman character. In a few Arabic words *h* final occurs with two points over it, thus ة: it is then sounded like ت *t*, into which letter it is sometimes changed.

Rem. a. Final *h* can only be silent when it is not an original letter. It is found chiefly in Persian and Arabic words, in the latter of which it is a servile letter forming (originally) feminine nouns: *e.g.* مَلِكه *malika*, 'queen,' from مَلِك *malik*, 'king;' مُحَاوَره *muḥāwara*, 'idiom,' from the Arabic fem. مُحاورة *muḥāwarat*: in the former it is used simply to convey the sound of the preceding short vowel (*fatḥa*).

Rem. b. Of the medial forms of *h*, ھ is conventionally used to aspirate the letters ب *b*, پ *p*, etc., as has been shown in § 2, the form ﮩ being employed when it is to be pronounced as a separate letter; but this distinction is not generally regarded in India.

و and ي generally have the sound of our *w* and *y*; but in most Persian words و is pronounced like *v*. In a few Persian words, moreover, و preceded by خ *kh* is scarcely, if at all, audible: *e.g.* خواه *khwāh*, 'whether,' 'or;' خود *khwud*, 'self;' خوراك *khwurāk*, 'food;' خويش *khwesh*, 'own,' which are pronounced as though written *khāh*, *khud*, *khurāk*, *khesh*. This و is termed 'distorted' (معدُوله *ma'dūla*): in the Roman character it will be represented by *w* with a dot (*ẉ*).

The aspirated letters بھ *bh*, پھ *ph*, etc., are uttered with a greater effort of breath than usual, and by one action of the vocal organ; there is no pause between the *b*, *p*, etc., and the *h*. The only one of these letters which has an English equivalent is ثہ, which is sounded like *th* in our *thick*. The sounds of *ph*, *ṭh*, etc., are said by grammarians to resemble those of the same combinations in our words, *up-hill*, *hot-house*, etc.; but this is scarcely correct.

II. THE VOWELS AND OTHER ORTHOGRAPHIC SIGNS.

5. The following signs are used to indicate the short vowels:

1) ـَ (called فَتحَہ *fatḥa*, or زَبَر *zabar*).[1] It is written *above* the consonant after which it is sounded, and is invariably pronounced like our *a* in *cedar*, or our *u* in *bun*: *e.g.* بَن *ban*, 'a forest.'

2) ـِ (called کَسرَہ *kasra*, or زیر *zer*). It is written *beneath* the consonant after which it is pronounced, and has the sound of our *i* in *pin*: *e.g.* بِن *bin*, 'without.'

3) ـُ (called ضَمَّہ *ẓamma*, or پیش *pesh*). It is written *over* the consonant to which it belongs, and has the sound of *u* in *pull*: *e.g.* پُل *pul*, 'a bridge.'

Rem. a. The short vowels *kasra* and *ẓamma*, when immediately followed by ہ, or by the harsh gutturals ح and ع, are generally pronounced like obscure *e* and *o* respectively; as یِہ *yĕh*, 'this,' وُہ *wŏh*, 'that,' مِحنَت *mĕḥnat*, 'toil,' 'trouble,' مُحَمَّد *Mŏhammad*, فِعل *fĕ'l*, 'action.' So also *ẓamma* preceded by the guttural *k* (ق) has the sound of *ŏ*; as قُرآن *ḳŏr'ān*.

Rem. b. The three short vowels are collectively termed حَرَکات *ḥarakāt*, 'motions;' and the letter which is accompanied by one of them is said to be مُتَحَرِّک *mutaḥarrik*, or 'movent.'

[1] *Fatḥa*, *kasra*, *ẓamma*, are the Arabic names for the short vowels; *zabar*, *zer*, *pesh*, the Persian: both are commonly used by the native grammarians.

TANWĪN.

6. The marks of the short vowels when doubled are pronounced with the addition of the sound *n*, as ـً *an̲*, ـٍ *in̲*, ـٌ *un̲*. This is called تَنوِين *tanwīn*, or 'nūnation' (from the name of the letter *nūn*), and takes place only at the end of an Arabic word: *e.g.* فَوراً *fauran̲*, 'instantly,' مَثَلاً *mas̤alan̲*, 'for example,' دَفعَةً *daf'atan̲*, 'all at once,' مُشَارٌ اِلَيه *mushārun̲ ilaih*, 'the aforesaid.' The *tanwīn* of *fatḥa* (ـً) takes an ا after all the consonants except ة; but the *tanwīn* should always be written over the letter preceding the *alif*, and not over the *alif* itself. This *alif* in no way affects the quantity of the vowel, which is always short.

Rem. a. If a word end in ا, the *tanwīn* with *hamza* (§ 13) is written after it; *e.g.* اِبتِدَاءً *ibtidā'an̲*, 'firstly,' 'originally.'

Rem. b. The *tanwīn* of *z̤amma* rarely occurs in Urdū; that of *kasra* perhaps never.

JAZM OR SUKŪN.

7. When a consonant is not accompanied by one of the three short vowels *fatḥa*, *kasra*, and *z̤amma*, that is to say, when it occurs at the end of a shut syllable (and is therefore not مُتَحَرِّك *mutaḥarrik*, or 'movent'), it is termed مَجزُوم *majzūm*, 'amputated,' or سَاكِن *sākin*, 'resting' or 'quiescent,'[1] and is then marked with the orthographic sign ـْ, called جَزم *jazm*, 'amputation,' or سُكُون *sukūn*, 'rest,' which serves, when another syllable follows, to separate the two, *e.g.* مارْنا *mārnā*, 'to beat,' مَسْجِد *masjid*, 'a mosque.'

[1] The word *quiescent* is to be understood in its original signification of *not moving*, and not in the secondary sense of 'not sounded,' that it has in English grammar.

Rem. a. When two or more quiescent letters occur together in a word, the first alone is termed سَاكِن *sākin*, and the others are termed مَوقُوف *mauḳūf*, 'supported,' or 'dependent on;' *e.g.* in the word دوست *dost*, 'friend,' the و is termed *sākin*, but the س and ت are said to be *mauḳūf*.

Rem. b. The *jazm* is not written over the last letter of a word, although that letter is, in all but a very few cases, quiescent.

Rem. c. A few words begin with two consonants, the first having no vowel; *e.g.* كيا *kyā*, 'what,' كيوں *kyoṅ*, 'why,' بَراهْمَن *brāhman*, 'a Brāhman.' It is not customary to write *jazm* over the first letter in these words, since a quiescent consonant is not supposed to occur at the beginning of a word. When the second of the two letters is *r*, the first is not unfrequently pronounced with *kasra*, e.g *birāhman*. Sometimes the *r* is elided, as in بَاهْمَن.

TASHDĪD.

8. A consonant that is to be doubled, or 'strengthened,' (مُشَدَّد *mushaddad*) is written only once, but marked with the ـّ, called تَشْدِيد *tashdīd*, 'strengthening,' *e.g.* ٹَٹّی *taṭṭī*, 'a screen,' تَصَرُّف *taṣarruf*, 'use,' قُوَّت *ḳuwwat* (not *ḳūwat*), 'power.' The first of the double letters ends the preceding syllable, and the second begins the following, as *taṣar-ruf*; and each of them must be distinctly pronounced, and not slurred over as the double letters are in the English words *manner*, *mummy*.

Rem. The *tashdīd* is not generally used in the case of infinitives, the roots of which end in ن; *e.g.* جَانْنَا *jānnā*, 'to know,' سُنْنَا *sunnā*, 'to hear,' not جانَّا and سُنَّا.

LONG VOWELS AND DIPHTHONGS.

9. The long vowels (*ā*, *ī*, *ū*) are indicated by placing the marks of the short vowels before the corresponding

letters ا, و, and ي respectively, as in the words بَار *bār*, نُور *nūr*, بِيس *bīs*. Long *a* (*ā*) is pronounced like our *a* in *far*, never like *a* in *ball*; long *u* (*ū*) is sounded like our *u* in *rule*, or our *oo* in *fool*; long *i* (*ī*) has the sound of our *i* in the words *police*, *caprice*. But the sounds of the long vowels endure much longer in Urdū than in English, especially when they occur in the first part, or in the middle of words.

10. The combinations ـُو and ـِي also often form sounds like our *o* in *mole*, and the French *e* in *fête* (or the English *a* in *fate*), *e.g.* مول *mol*, 'price,' پيٹ *pet*, 'belly.' As these sounds are unknown to the Arabic, they are termed مَجْهُول *maj-hūl*, 'unknown,' in contradistinction to the sounds of *ū* and *ī*, which are termed مَعْرُوف *ma'rūf*, 'known.'

11. The short vowel *fatḥa* before ي and و forms the diphthongs *ai* and *au*, as exemplified in the English *aisle*, and the German *haus*, (or in the English *house*): *e.g.* حَيْف *ḥaif*, 'pity,' حَوْض *ḥauẓ*, 'reservoir.'

Rem. a. ا, و and ي, when they form vowels, are termed *letters of prolongation* (حُرُوفُ ٱلْمَدّ *ḥurūfu 'l madd*), because they have the effect of lengthening the preceding short vowels; and حُرُوفُ ٱلْإِشْبَاع *ḥurūfu 'l ishbā'*, 'the letters added to give fullness of sound' (to the preceding homogeneous short vowels). They are merely sounds of prolongation after the short vowels, and cannot have a vowel (that is to say, are quiescent), wherefore they cannot commence a word or syllable. Thus they are distinguished from the consonants ا, و, ي. If و and ي be preceded by *kasra* and *ẓamma* respectively, they must have a vowel, and are therefore consonants, *e.g.* سِوَا *siwā*, 'more,' 'except,' مُيَسَّر *mu-yassar*, 'attained.'

Rem. b. The letters of prolongation, though they are quiescent, are not generally marked with *jazm*; but in certain works printed in England, و and ي, when they have the *majhūl* sound, are marked with that sign—or rather with a complete circle, thus كوْ *ko*, تيْل *tel*; and when they form diphthongs (in which case they might be marked with *jazm*), with the sign ^; *e.g.* اَوْر *aur*, فَوْرًا *fauran*.

Rem. c. The *alif* of prolongation is, by some grammarians, regarded as a letter of the alphabet, and named لا *lā*, the ل with *fatḥa* being prefixed to it because it cannot be pronounced at the beginning of its own name, as every other letter can (see § 1, *Rem. b*).

12. The *alif* of prolongation is omitted in some Arabic words, but the omission is indicated by the preceding *fatḥa* being written perpendicularly: *e.g.* رَحْمٰن (for رَحْمَان) *raḥmān*, 'most merciful,' هٰذا (for هاذا) *hāẕā*, 'that.' The perpendicular *fatḥa* represents a small *alif*.

Rem. a. In a few Arabic words the perpendicular *fatḥa* is followed by و or ي; in such cases these letters are sounded like the *alif* of prolongation; *e.g.* صَلٰوة *ṣalāt*, 'prayer,' اَولٰيتَر (or اولَيتَر) *aulātar*, 'better.'

Rem. b. ي at the end of a word after *fatḥa* is pronounced like ا, which is generally written over it, *e.g.* دَعْوىٰ or دَعْوىٰ *da'wā*, 'claim,' عُقْبىٰ *ukbā*, 'the next world.' This ي is termed اَلِفُ ٱلْمَقْصُورَة *alifu'l maksūra*, 'the abbreviated *alif*,' in contradistinction to 'the lengthened *alif*' (§ 17). It is so named because, when it comes in contact with 'the conjunctive *alif*' (اَلِفُ ٱلْوَصْل *alifu'l waṣl*, § 15), it is shortened in pronunciation before the following consonant. The Persians generally change this ى into ا.

THE HAMZATED ALIF, OR HAMZA.

13. *Alif*, when it is not a mere letter of prolongation, but a consonant, pronounced like the *spiritus lenis*, is distinguished by the mark ء *hamza* (هَمْزَة), either expressed or implied, and is commonly called *hamza*. When it

occurs at the beginning of a word, the form assumed by the 'soft breathing' is ا alone (*hamza* being understood), *e.g.* آب *ab*, اِس *is*, اُن *un*, اِيكهہ *īkh*, اِيرِي *erī*, اُون *ūn*, اُوتْ *ot*, اَي *ai*, اَور *aur*. At the beginning of a syllable not the first in a word, the soft breathing may be represented by ـٔ alone, or by *alif* alone, or by و or ي accompanied by *hamza* (see § 14).

Rem. a. According to Arabic grammarians, a syllable cannot begin with a vowel; but every vowel must be preceded by a symbol indicating the movement of the vocal organ whereby the emission of the breath is produced. Now, in uttering what *we* regard as an initial vowel, there takes place (in the fauces), according to this theory, a sudden emission of the voice after a total suppression; and this is represented by the symbol أ or ـٔ *hamza*, which signifies 'prick,' 'impulse.' This effort of utterance (which, not being a vowel, comes to be ranked as a consonant) the Greeks represented by the mark ('). In the pronunciation of an Arab the *hamza* is a very perceptible articulation, especially at the commencement of a syllable in the middle of a word, preceding a shut syllable; *e.g.* قُرْآن *ḳŏr'ān*, جُرْأَت *jur'at* (not *ḳŏ-rān*, and *ju-rat*).

14. When *hamza* occurs at the beginning of a syllable not the first in a word, the following cases arise:

1). If it be pronounced with *fatha*, it generally appears in the form of *alif* with *hamza*: *e.g* سُؤَر *sū'ar*, 'pig,' جُرْأَت *jur'at*, 'daring,' تَوْأَم *tau'am*, 'twin.'

2). If it be accompanied by *ẓamma*, and preceded by one of the letters of prolongation, it generally takes the form of *hamza* alone (ـٔ): *e.g.* جاؤُں *jā'ūṅ*, 'shall, or should, I go?' پاؤں *pā'oṅ*, 'foot,' آنْسُوؤں *ānsū'oṅ*, 'tears,' جِيؤُں *jī'ūṅ*, '(if) I live.' If it be moved by *kasra*, and followed by the *majhūl* ـي, *hamza* alone may be written, or ئ may be used, but the former is the more common: *e.g.* پائي or پائے *pā'e*, 'foot,' هوئي or هوئے *hū'e*, 'been.'

3). If it is pronounced with *kasra*, and preceded by a letter of prolongation, or by *fatha*, it generally passes into ئ (in which case it is correct to omit the two points of the letter ي): *e.g.* جُدائِي *judā'ī*, 'separation,' فَائِدَه *fā'ida*, 'advantage,' گُنجائِش *gunjā'ish*, 'capacity,' 'room,' هُوئِي *hū'ī*, 'been, كوئِي *ko'ī*, 'some,' كَئِي *ka'ī*, 'several.'

Rem. a. أ sometimes passes into ؤ: *e.g.* مُؤَنَّث *mu'annaṣ*, 'feminine,' طاؤوس *ṭā'ūs*, 'peacock.' The first of these words calls for no comment, as the law by which its change is effected does not operate in Urdū: it is taken from the Arabic, as given above. As regards the second, it may be observed that it is a more correct, though less common, form than طاؤس. Similarly جَاؤوں, پاؤوں, though they never occur, are, strictly speaking, more correct than جَاؤں, etc. But so far are the natives of India from being particular in such matters, that they commonly write the *hamza* over the letter of prolongation itself: *e.g.* جَاؤں, طاؤس, هُوئِي.

Rem. b. *Hamza* is often found at the end of a syllable in Arabic words: *e.g.* تأثير, مُؤْمِن. In such cases the *hamza* is changed (in Urdū) into the letter of prolongation corresponding to the preceding short vowel: *e.g.* تَاثِير *tāṣīr*, 'effect,' مُومِن *mūmin*, 'believer.'

Rem. c. The letters ا, و and ي are termed حُرُوفِ عِلَّت *ḥurūf-i 'illat*, 'weak letters,' on account of the changes to which they are subject among themselves.

Rem. d. *Hamza*, as its character indicates, is the abbreviation of ع, which is in fact but an aggravation of the *spiritus lenis*. This may guide the student to some extent in pronouncing the ع; but as we have observed before, it is almost impossible for an Englishman to acquire the true pronunciation of this letter; and it is quite impossible to explain the true sound in writing: it must be learned by the ear alone. A Hindū makes scarcely any distinction between the sounds عَب *'ab*,

عِب *'ib,* عُب *'ub,* and those of آب *ab,* اِب *ib,* اُب *ub;* but in the mouth of an educated Mohammadan they are very different sounds. When we have occasion to write Hindūstānī in the Roman character, *hamza* in the middle of a word will be represented by the Greek symbol ('), and ع by that symbol inverted: *e.g. pā'on* (پاؤں), *'alam* (عَلَم). *Hamza* at the beginning of a word will be omitted.

WASL.

15. The mark (ٱ), called وَصْل *waṣl*, 'union,' occurs in Urdū only over the consonant ا of the Arabic article ال, in phrases from the Arabic, *e.g.* أَمِيرُ ٱلْمُؤمِنِين *amīru 'l mūminīn*, 'Commander of the Faithful,' أَشْرَفُ ٱلْأَشْرَاف *ashrafu 'l ashrāf*, 'the noblest of the noble,' بِٱلْكُلّ *bi'lkull* (pronounced *bil-kull*), 'in the totality,' 'completely.' In such phrases the ا at the commencement of the article is absorbed by the final vowel of the preceding word and the mark ٱ written over the *alif* indicates the elision of the *spiritus lenis*. The و and ي of prolongation, as also 'the abbreviated *alif*' (*alifĕ maksūra*, ـَي or ـَىٰ, § 12, Rem. *b.*), are shortened in pronunciation before an *alif* with *waṣl*: *e.g.* فِي ٱلْفَوْر *fi 'l faur*, 'on the instant,' 'instantly,' بُو ٱلْهَوَس *bu 'l hawas*, 'possessed of desire,' 'desirous,' دَعْوَي ٱلْمُتَأَخِّرِين *da'wa 'l muta'akhkhirīn*, 'the claim, or assertion, of the moderns.' These words are invariably pronounced as though they were written فِلْفَور *filfaur*, بُلْهَوَس *bulhawas*, دَعْولْمُتَأَخِّرِين *da'walmuta'akhkhirīn*.

Rem. *Alif* with *waṣl* (ٱ) is altogether omitted in the first word of the introductory formula بِسْمِ ٱللّٰه (for بِاسْمِ ٱللّٰه) *bismillāh*, 'in the name of God,' and also after the Arabic preposition لِ *li*, 'to': *e.g.* لِلْعَالَمِين *li'l'ālamīn* 'to the worlds.'

16. If the first letter of the word to which the Arabic article is prefixed be one of the following fourteen—ت, ث, د, ذ, ر, ز, س, ش, ص, ض, ط, ظ, ل, ن, the *l* of the article, though written, is for the sake of euphony passed over in pronunciation, and assimilated to the following consonant, which is then marked with *tashdīd*, and the *jazm* of the ل is omitted: *e.g.* دارُ ٱلسَّلْطَنَت *dāru 'ssaltanat*, 'the abode of sovereignty,' 'the royal city,' إِخْوَانُ ٱلصَّفَا *ikhwānu 'ṣṣafā*, 'the Brethren of Purity,' عَوَامُّ ٱلنَّاس *'awāmmu 'nnās*, 'the mass of men,' 'the common people.'

Rem. The letters ت, ث, etc., mentioned above, are called حُرُوفُ ٱلشَّمْسِيَّة *ḥurūfu 'shshamsīya*, or 'the solar letters,' because the word شَمْس *shams*, 'sun,' happens to begin with one of them; and the other letters of the Arabic alphabet are termed حُرُوفُ ٱلْقَمَرِيَّة *ḥurūfu 'l ḳamarīya*, or 'the lunar letters,' because قَمَر *ḳamar*, 'moon,' commences with one of them.

MADD.

17. At the beginning of a word or syllable the sound of long *a* (*ā*) is represented by the *alif* of prolongation preceded by the inaudible consonant ا. The two *alifs* are commonly represented in writing by one with the sign of prolongation, ـٓ, *madd* (مدّ i.e. *lengthening, extension*), placed over it: *e.g.* آج *āj*, 'to-day' (for اَاج), آب *āb*, 'water,' قُرْآن *ḳor'ān*. *Alif* with *madd* can only occur at the beginning of a syllable.

Rem. آ is called اَلِفِ مَمْدُودَه *alifĕ mamdūda*, 'the lengthened *alif*,' in contradistinction to 'the abbreviated or short *alif*' (اَلِفِ مَقْصُورَه *alifĕ maḳṣūra*, § 12, *Rem. b.*).

18. The attainment of a correct pronunciation will be materially facilitated by a strict attention to the rule for

dividing a word correctly into syllables. Every syllable begins with a movable consonant, and every word has just as many syllables as it has vowels. Hence a syllable consists of a consonant and a vowel, or a consonant, a vowel, and any following *quiescent* consonants: *e.g.* بھُوکھا *bhū-khā*, 'hungry.' حَرَکَت *ḥa-ra-kat*, 'motion,' دِرَخْت *di-rakht*, 'tree,' تَبَسُّم *ta-bas-sum*, 'smile.'

Rem. The short vowels, and other orthographical signs, are rarely to be met with in MSS. and books printed in India, and the points of the final ي are frequently dispensed with. However necessary then the aid of the orthographical marks may be to a European student, he should not fail to accustom himself to their omission. In these pages an attempt has been made to mark all the most necessary signs. The short vowel *fatḥa* is generally omitted, as also the *kasra* and *ẓamma* when they help to form the *majhūl* sounds *e* and *o*. When the *majhūl* sound *e* occurs at the end of a word it is written ے, with 'the reversed *ye*' (یائے مَعکُوسِي *yā'ĕ ma'kūsī*), provided the preceding letter is one which admits of its being connected with it.[1] The letter غ is represented by *g*, instead of the usual *gh*, since the aspirate in the latter is calculated to mislead the student as to the true sound of the letter.

19. The letters of the alphabet are also used for the purpose of numerical computation—chiefly, if not exclusively, in recording the date of important events: *e.g.* پادْشاهٔ شعرا بُود اهْلِي *pādshāhĕ shu'arā būd ahlī*, 'Ahlī was the king of poets,' wherein the sum of the letters پ, ا, د, etc., amounts to 942 (A.H.), the date of the death of the poet *Ahlī*; باغ و بهار *bāg o bahār*, where the sum of the numerical values of the letters ب, ا, etc., amounts to 1217 A.H., the year in which the work called the *Bāg o bahār* was completed. The arrangement of the letters of

[1] The *yā'ĕ ma'kūsī*, or 'reversed *ye*,' can only be employed, *in the Arabic character*, when connected with a preceding letter.

the alphabet according to their numerical values is called the *abjad*, and is contained in the following eight unmeaning words:

اَبْجد هوز حُطِي كلَمَن صعْفص قُرِشت ثخَذ ضظَغ

The value of each letter will be found in the Table of the Alphabet.

20. The special numerical figures are

١	٢	٣	۴	٥	٦	٧	٨	٩	٠
1	2	3	4	5	6	7	8	9	0

which are compounded in exactly the same way as our numerals: *e.g.* ١٨٧٣ 1873.

21. The following passage, with the transcript in English letters, will serve as a useful exercise in reading for the student, and also to exemplify the most important of the remarks in the preceding paragraphs.

سِنْدْباد جهازِي كا پہْلا سفر *

سِنْدْباد نے کہا ۔ مَیْں نے جو دَوْلت اَوْر جائْداد اپْنے باپ کے تَرِکے
سے پائِي تِھي عالمِ شباب میں عَیّاشِي کرْکے سب خرْچ کر ڈالِي ۔
اور پِھر اپْنِي حماقت اَوْر نادانِي پر مُطّلِع هوکر کمال نادِم اَوْر پشیمان
هُوْا ۔ اَوْر اُس دَوْلتِ کثِیر اَوْر مال و اسْباب کے ضائِع کرْنیکا بہُت افسوس
کِیَا ۔ دانِشْمنْدوں کا یِہہ قَوْل کِہ "مُفْلِسِي سے مرْجانا بِہْترهَي" یاد کرْتا
اور اُسْکو اپْنے حسْبِ حال پاتا ۔ اور میری باپ کا بِھي یِہِي قَوْل تھا *
آخِرُ الْاَمْر مِیراث کا بچا بچایَا جو میرِي فضُول خرْچِیوں سے باقِي رہ گیَا
تھا سب جمْع کرْکے بیچا ۔ اَوْر تاجِرانِ بحْرِي سے اپْنے باب میں مشْوَرہ
کِیَا ۔ اُنھوں نے مُجھْکو اِچّھي صلاح بتْلائِي ۔ مَیْں نے اُس رُوپَي کو تجارت

میں لگادِیا - اَور تِجارت کا اسباب خرِید کر اُن تاجِروں کے ہمراہ بندر
بانسرا کو گیا - اَور وہاں سے - بااِتفاق اُن سبکے - جہاز کِرایَہ کرکے
سوار ہُوا *

Sindbād jahāzī-kā pahlā safar.

Sindbād-ne kahā, maiṅ-ne jo daulat aur jā'edād apne bāp-ke tarike-se pā'ī thī, ʻālamĕ shabāb-meṅ ʻaiyāshī-karke sab kharch kar ḍālī, aur phir apnī ḥamāḳat aur nā-dānī-par muṭṭaliʻ-hokar kamāl nādim aur pashemān hū'ā, aur us daulatĕ kaṣīr aur māl o asbāb-ke ẓā'ĕʻ karne-kā bahut afsos kiyā; dānishmandoṅ-kā yĕh ḳaul ki "muflisī-se mar-jānā bĕhtar hai" yād-kartā, aur usko apne ḥasbĕ ḥāl pātā, aur mere bāp-kā bhī yĕhī ḳaul thā. Ākhiru 'lamr mīrāṣ-kā bachā bachāyā jo merī faẓūl-kharchiyoṅ-se bāḳī rah-gayā thā, sab jamʻ-karke bechā, aur tājirānĕ baḥrī-se apne bāb-meṅ mashwara kiyā; unhoṅ-ne mujh-ko achchhī ṣalāḥ batlā'ī; maiṅ-ne us rūpai-ko tijārat-meṅ lagā-diyā, aur tijārat-kā asbāb kharīd-kar, un tājiroṅ-ke ham-rāh bandar bāṅsrā-ko gayā, aur wahāṅ-se, ba-ittifāḳ un sab-ke, jahāz kirāya-kar-ke sawār hū'ā.

TRANSLATION.

Sindbād the Sailor's First Voyage.

Sindbād said: Whatever wealth and property I inherited from my father's estate, I spent all in debauchery in the season of youth; and then, perceiving my folly and stupidity, became extremely ashamed and sorry, and much regretted having squandered that vast wealth and property; I used to call to mind the saying of the wise, 'Death is better than poverty,' and to find it in accordance with my predicament; this saying moreover was my father's also. Ultimately, collecting all the remnants of my inheritance, which had escaped my extravagances, I sold (them), and consulted some merchants (*lit.* sea-traders) respecting myself; they gave me good counsel: I invested that money in commerce, and purchasing trading commodities, accompanied those merchants to the sea-port of Baṣrā, and thence, conjointly with them all, hired a ship, and embarked.

PART II.—ETYMOLOGY.

CHAPTER II.

THE PARTS OF SPEECH.

22. Urdū grammarians, using the grammatical terminology of the Arabic, class all the parts of speech under the three general heads of *Verbs* (فِعْل *fĕ'l*), *Nouns* (إِسْم *ism*), and *Particles* (حَرْف *ḥarf*). Under the verb they class what we call the Conjunctive Participle (فِعْلِ مَعْطُوف *fĕ'lĕ ma'ṭūf*). The *Noun* includes—

1°. The Substantive (إِسْمِ مَوصُوف *ismĕ mauṣūf*, or simply إِسم *ism*, 'the noun which is described or qualified').

2°. The Adjective (إِسْمِ صِفت *ismĕ ṣifat*, 'the noun indicating a quality').

3°. The Numerical Adjective (إِسْمِ عدد *ismĕ 'adad*, 'the noun of number').

4°. The Personal Pronoun (ضمِير *ẓamīr*, 'the noun that is kept in mind').

5°. The Demonstrative Pronoun (إِسْمِ إشارہ *ismĕ ishāra*, 'the noun of indication, or by which something is pointed out').

6°. The Relative Pronoun [إِسْمِ مَوصُول *ismĕ mauṣūl*, 'the noun that is connected' (with a relative clause)].

7°. The Interrogative Pronoun (اِسْم اِسْتِفْهام *ismĕ istifhām*, 'the noun that seeks information,' or 'the noun of questioning').

8°. The Indefinite Pronoun (اِسْم مُبْهم *ismĕ mubham*, 'the indeterminate or indefinite noun').

9°. The Infinitive, or Verbal Noun (مصْدر *maṣdar*, 'the source whence the different forms of the verb originate').

10°. The Deverbal Nouns, as the Noun of Agency (اِسْم فاعِل *ismĕ fā'il*), the Perfect, or Passive Participle (ماضِي or اِسْم مفْعول *māẓī*, or *ismĕ maf'ūl*), and the Imperfect Participle (اِسْم حالِيَه *ismĕ ḥāliya*, 'the noun of state or circumstance' of the subject or object).

Under the term *Particles* are comprised—1°. *Adverbs*;[1] 2°. *Prepositions* (حُرُوفِ جر *ḥurūfĕ jarr*, 'particles of attraction'); 3°. *Conjunctions* (حُرُوفِ عطْف *ḥurūfĕ 'aṭf*, 'conjunctive particles,' or حُرُوفِ شرْط *ḥurūfĕ sharṭ*, 'conditional particles,' etc.); 4°. Interjections (حُرُوفِ نِدا *ḥurūfĕ nidā*, 'particles of calling').

I. THE ARTICLE.

23. It will be perceived from the above classification that the Article finds no place among the parts of speech in Urdū. The context alone can determine whether a noun is definite or indefinite. The force of the definite article is, however, often conveyed by the demonstrative pronouns يِہ *yĕh*, 'this,' and وُہ *wŏh*, 'that'; and that of the

[1] There is no special name for an *adverb* in Urdū; it is termed تمِيز *tamīz*, 'the specification,' ظرْف *ẓarf*, 'the vessel, or that *in* which the act is done,' or نفِي *nafī*, 'the particle of negation,' according to the sense in which it is used.

indefinite article by the numeral ایک *ek*, 'one,' or by the indefinite pronoun کوئي *ko'ī*, 'some.' A fuller notice of this will be found in the Syntax.

II. THE SUBSTANTIVE (إِسْم).

1. GENDER (جِنْس *jins*).

24. In respect of gender, Urdū nouns are divisible into *two* classes: 1) those which are *masculine* (مُذَكَّر *muzakkar*); 2) those which are *feminine* (مُؤَنَّث *mu'annas*).

Rem. Most nouns are masculine or feminine merely by *usage* (سماعِي *samā'ī*); the gender of a large number, however, is based on rule (قِيَاسِي *kiyāsī*): it is with these chiefly that we have to deal

25. That a noun is of the *masculine* or *feminine* gender may be ascertained either: 1) from its *signification*; or 2) from its *form*.

26. All common nouns and proper names that denote males are masculine by signification, and those that denote females are feminine: *e.g.* باپ *bāp*, 'father,' شَوْهر *shauhar*, 'husband,' لوهار *lohār*, 'blacksmith,' موهن *Mohan*, are masculine; and ماں *māṅ*, 'mother,' جورو *jorū*, 'wife,' چهوچهو *chhochho*, 'nurse,' بنّو *Bannū*, are feminine by signification.

Rem. There is one exception even to this rule. The word قبيله *kabīla*, 'family,' 'tribe,' is used euphemistically to signify *wife*, and treated as a masculine; and the masculine terms خاندان *khāndān*, 'family,' گهرانه *gharāna*, 'household,' گهر کے آدمِياں *ghar ke ādmiyāṅ*, 'people of the house,' are still more commonly used in the sense of 'wife.'

27. Masculine by form are:

1). Hindī nouns ending in ـا *ā*, as آٹا *āṭā*, 'flour,' گھڑا *ghaṛā*, 'an earthen vessel,' ہیرا *hīrā*, 'diamond.'[1]

Rem. The exceptions (though numerous in the Hindī dialect) are not numerous in Urdū.[2] The chief exception to the rule is a class of feminine diminutives ending in ـیا *iyā*: *e.g.* چڑیا *chiṛiyā*, 'a bird,' پھڑیا *phuṛiyā*, 'a small boil,' ڈبیا *ḍibiyā*, 'a tiny box.'

2). Nouns ending in ـو *ū* or *o*, and especially those ending in *ā'o*: *e.g.* آلو *ālū*, 'potato,' اُلّو *ullū*, 'owl,' بچھو *bichchhū*, 'scorpion,' پہلو *pahlū*, 'side,' جادو *jādū*, 'magic,' حشو *ḥasho*, 'stuffing' (a pillow, etc.), بھاو *bhā'o*, 'price,' چھڑکاو *chhiṛkā'o*, 'sprinkling.' Abstract nouns, like the last of the examples, are without exception masculine.

Rem. Hindī and Arabic words furnish a few exceptions, as بالو *bālū*, 'sand,' دارو *dārū*, 'liquor,' روہو *rohū*, 'a kind of fish,' ناو *nā'o*, 'a boat,' ہجو *hajo*, 'satire,' and perhaps one or two more. The chief exceptions are Persian words, as ابرو *abrū*, 'eyebrow,' آبرو *ābrū*, 'honour,' آرزو *ārzū*, 'wish,' بو *bū* or *bo*, 'smell,' ترازو *tarāzū*, 'a pair of scales,' دارو *dārū*, 'medicine,' جو *jo*, 'a stream,' خو *kho*, 'habit,' and a few more.

3). Nouns ending in ـہ *a*: *e.g.* بندہ *banda*, 'a slave,' پردہ *parda*, 'a curtain,' غصّہ *guṣṣa*, 'anger,' قصّہ *ḳiṣṣa*, 'a tale.'

Rem. a. بنفشہ *banafsha*, 'a violet,' توبہ *tauba*, 'repentance,' دفعہ *dafa*, 'time,' 'a class,' صرفہ *ṣarfa*, 'expenditure,' فاختہ *fākhta*, 'a

[1] I use the term *Hindī* advisedly; for Sanskrit, not having been a spoken language when Urdū sprung into existence, could only have furnished words to it through the Hindī.

[2] Words like *mansā*, *dayā*, *jachā*, *kirpā*, *sobhā*, etc., belong, not to Urdū, but to Hindī. Such words were commonly used by the older writers, but are rarely found in modern authors; and even the older writers generally used them under peculiar circumstances, just as an English novelist, the scene of whose novel is laid in Cornwall, for example, might introduce something of the Cornish dialect into his work.

dove,' لاشه *lāsha*, 'a corpse,' and a few more, are exceptions; as are also all such Arabic nouns as have ه affixed to the masculine to form the feminine, ملكه *malika*, 'queen,' from ملک *malik*, 'king,' والده *wālida*, 'mother,' from والد *wālid*, 'father.'

Rem. b. Final ه (masculine) is frequently changed into ا, and *vice versâ*: *e.g.* راجه *rāja*, for راجا *rājā*, 'a king;' آگره *āgra*, for آگرا *āgrā*, 'Agra.'

4). All nouns terminating in the syllable پن *pan*: *e.g.* اُلّوپن *ullū-pan*, 'owlishness,' کمینہ‌پن *kamīnapan*, 'meanness,' لڑکپن *larak-pan*, 'childishness,' 'childhood.' Such words are all abstract substantives.

5). Arabic verbal nouns of the measure اِفْعال *if'āl*, in which the two *alifs* (the first and fourth letters) are servile and constant: *e.g.* اِحْسان *ĕhsān*, 'a kindness,' اِقْبال *ikbāl*, 'good fortune,' اِقْرار *ikrār*, 'avowal,' اِنْکار *inkār*, 'denial.'

Rem. The few exceptions are اِجْلاس *ijlās*, 'a sitting,' اِدْبار *idbār*, 'turning back,' اِصْلاح *iṣlāḥ*, 'correction,' اِکْراه *ikrāh*, 'aversion,' اِلْحاح *ilḥāḥ*, 'solicitation,' اِمْداد *imdād*, 'assisting,' اِيراد *īrād*, 'adducing,' and a few more words that end in ت *t* or ا *ā*, which are common feminine terminations in Arabic nouns.

6). Arabic verbal nouns of the measure تَفَعُّل *tafa''ul*, in which the first letter (ت *t*) is servile and characteristic, and the third is marked with *tashdīd*: *e.g.* تردُّد *taraddud*, 'vacillation,' تکبُّر *takabbur*, 'haughtiness.'

Rem. The exceptions are تَوَجُّه *tawajjuh*, 'regard,' تَوَضُّو *tawazzū*, 'performing ablution before prayer,' تَوَقُّع *tawakku'*, 'expectation,' تَمَنّا *tamannā*, 'wish,' and all nouns ending in ي *ī*, as تَسَلّي *tasallī*, 'consolation,' تَرَقّي *tarakkī*, 'advancement.'

7). Arabic verbal nouns of the measure تَفاعُل *tafā'ul*, in which the first and third letters are servile and constant:

e.g. تدارك *tadāruk*, 'calling to account,' تفاوت *tafāwut*, 'difference.'

Rem. تواضع *tawāzu'*, 'civility,' is an exception; so also are all nouns ending in ي ـِ *ī*, as تحاشي *taḥāshī*, 'exception.'

8). All Arabic verbal nouns of the measure اِنفِعال *infi'āl*, in which the first, second, and fifth letters are servile and constant: *e.g.* اِنصِرام *inṣirām*, 'ending,' 'ceasing,' اِنفِصال *infiṣāl*, 'decision.'

9). Arabic verbal nouns of the measure اِفتِعال *ifti'āl*, in which the first, third, and fifth letters are servile and constant: *e.g.* اِختِصار *ikhtiṣār*, 'abridgment,' اِلتِماس *iltimās*, 'petition.'

Rem. There are a few exceptions, as اِحتِياج *iḥtiyāj*, 'necessity,' اِحتِياط *iḥtiyāṭ*, 'careful guarding,' اِصطِلاح *iṣṭilāḥ*, 'a conventional term,' اِطِّلاع *iṭṭilā'*, 'announcement' (in which word, as also in that preceding it, the characteristic ت is assimilated to the preceding letter; see § 105, viii. *Rem.*), اِعتِراض *i'tirāẓ*, 'objection,' and a few words ending in *ā* or *t*, as اِبتِدا *ibtidā*, 'beginning,' اِلتِفات *iltifāt*, 'attention.'

10). Arabic verbal nouns of the measure اِستِفعال *istif'āl*, in which the first three letters are servile and characteristic, and the sixth letter also is servile: *e.g.* اِستِغفار *istigfār*, 'begging forgiveness,' اِستِعمال *istĕ'māl*, 'use.'

Rem. The exceptions are اِستِعداد *istĕ'dād*, 'capacity,' اِستِكراه *istikrāh*, 'aversion,' اِستِمداد *istimdād*, 'begging help,' اِستِدعا *istid'ā*, 'supplication,' اِسترضا *istirẓā*, 'seeking to please.'

11). Arabic nouns of place and time of the measures مَفعَل *maf'al* and مَفعِل *maf'il*, in which the first letter is characteristic: *e.g.* مصدر *maṣdar*, 'the source' (of any thing), مسكن *maskan*, 'habitation,' مقام *maḳām* and مكان

makān, 'halting, or dwelling place,' مشرِق *mashrik*, 'rising place' (of the sun), مغرِب *magrib*, 'setting place' (of the sun).

Rem. The principal exceptions are: مجال *majāl*, 'scope,' 'power,' محشر *maḥshar*, 'a place of gathering,' محضر *maḥẓar*, 'royal presence,' محفِل *maḥfil*, 'a place of meeting,' مجلِس *majlis*, 'a place of sitting,' مسجِد *masjid*, 'a mosque,' منزِل *manzil*, 'a halting place.'

12). Arabic *nomina instrumenti* of the measure مِفعَل *mif'al*, in which the first letter is characteristic, *e.g.* مِنبر *mimbar*, 'a pulpit,' مِصقل *miṣḳal*, 'a furbishing instrument.'

Rem. مِنخر *minkhar*, 'a nostril,' is perhaps the only exception.

28. Feminine by form are:

1). Arabic nouns ending in *ā*: *e.g.* بقا *baḳā*, 'duration,' بلا *balā*, 'evil'; and all Hindī diminutives ending in ـِيا *iyā*, as چڑيا *chiṛyā*, 'a bird,' پھڑيا *phuṛiyā*, 'a pimple.'

Rem. Not a few Arabic nouns ending in *ā* are masculine, but those that are feminine are far more numerous.

2). Arabic nouns ending in ت *t*: *e.g.* اُلفت *ulfat*, 'familiarity,' عِزّت *'izzat*, 'honour;' as also Persian abstract nouns formed by dropping the final ن of the Infinitive: *e.g.* رفت *raft* (from رفتن) 'going,' گفت *guft* (from گفتن), 'speaking.'

Rem. The exceptions in the first case are very few: *e.g.* ثُبوت *ṣubūt*, 'confirmation,' شربت *sharbat*, 'a drink,' وقت *waḳt*, 'time,' خِلعت *khil'at*, 'a robe of honour,' ياقوت *yāḳūt*, 'a ruby,' and perhaps a few more. The rule does not apply to Hindī nouns, nor indeed to any other Persian nouns than the class mentioned.

3). All nouns terminating in the syllable ہٹ *haṭ* or

وٹ, *wat*, preceded by the long vowel *ā*: *e.g.* گھبراھٹ *ghabrāhaṭ*, 'perturbation,' بناوٹ *banāwaṭ*, 'invention,' 'fabrication.'

Rem. The affixes *āhaṭ* and *āwaṭ* help to form a large class of abstract substantives. In the Dakhinī dialect these affixes take the form *āṭ*: *e.g.* گھبراٹ *ghabrāṭ*.

4). Persian nouns (chiefly, if not all, abstract substantives) ending in the syllable ـِش *ish*; as دانِش *dānish*, 'wisdom,' نالِش *nālish*, 'complaint.'

Rem. بالِش *bālish*, 'a pillow,' is perhaps the solitary exception. It may here be observed that *sh*, simply, is not a feminine termination in Urdū.

5) Nouns ending in ـِي *ī*: *e.g.* روٹي *roṭī*, 'bread,' صُراحِي *ṣurāḥī*, 'a gugglet,' ھڈّي *haḍḍī*, 'a bone.'

Rem. پانِي *pānī*, 'water,' جِي *jī*, 'life,' دھِي *dahī*, 'curdled milk,' گھِي *ghī*, 'clarified butter,' موتِي *motī*, 'a pearl,' ھاتھِي *hāthī*, 'an elephant,' and a few other words are exceptions.[1] Relative adjectives, as دھوبِي *dhobī*, 'a washerman,' خزانچِي *khazānchī*, 'a treasurer,' are of course masculine by signification.

6). Abstract nouns formed by dropping the characteristic

[1] These words are masculine or neuter in Sanskrit, and, as a general rule, such words are masculine in Hindī. There are numerous exceptions though: *e.g.* *āg*, 'fire,' *tārā*, 'star,' *bhāph*, 'steam,' 'vapour' (=S. *vāshpa*, m.), *deh*, 'the body,' etc. Mr. Dowson, however (Urdū Grammar, p. 22), writes as though the rule were of *universal application*, and applied equally to words derived from the Arabic also. He says, "Sanskrit and Arabic scholars should bear in mind that words borrowed from those languages retain their original gender; masculines and neuters being masculine, and feminines remain (*sic*) feminine in Hindūstānī." We were not aware before of there being a neuter gender in Arabic; and as regards the derivatives from that language we can adduce examples by the score in which Arabic feminines have been changed to masculines in Urdū and *vice versâ*; here are a few: *af'a*, 'viper,' *jahannam*, 'hell,' *khamr*, 'wine,' *shams*, 'the sun,' *ṣaḥrā*, 'desert,' *'aṣā*, 'staff,' *nafs*, 'soul,' etc., not to speak of the long list of verbal nouns in which Urdū changes the feminine termination ة of the Arabic into the masculine ـه *a*; as *muḥāwara*, 'idiom.'

syllable نا *nā* of the Infinitive; *e.g.* مار *mār* (from مارنا *mārnā*), 'beating,' لوٹ *lūṭ* (from لوٹنا *lūṭnā*), 'plunder,' چھاپ *chhāp*, 'printing,' 'impression,' سمجھ *samajh*, 'understanding,' رگڑ *ragaṛ*, 'rubbing,' 'friction.'

Rem. The exceptions are کھیل *khel*, 'play,' نوچ *noch*, 'scratch,' ڈھکیل *ḍhakel*, 'shove,' نچوڑ *nichoṛ*, 'extract,' ناچ *nāch*, 'dance,' رنگ, *rang*, 'colour,' and a few more.

7). Arabic verbal nouns of the measure تَفْعِيل *taf'īl*, in which the first and fourth letters are servile and characteristic; *e.g.* تَرْغِيب *targīb*, 'exciting desire,' تَسْكِين *taskīn*, 'consolation,' تَعْمِيل *ta'mīl*, 'execution' (of an order).

Rem. تَعْوِيذ *ta'wīẕ*, 'an amulet,' is perhaps the only exception.

8). Arabic *nomina instrumenti* of the measure مِفْعَال *mif'āl*, in which the first and fourth letters are servile and characteristic: *e.g.* مِقْرَاض *miḳrāẓ*, 'scissors,' مِنْكَار *minkār*, 'a bird's beak,' مِيزَان *mīzān*, 'a balance.'

Rem. a. The exceptions are مِنْشَار *minshār*, 'a hand-saw,' مِسْمَار *mismār*, 'a peg or nail,' مِعْيَار *mi'yār*, 'a touchstone,' 'an assay-balance.'

Rem. b. The following twenty-one letters of the alphabet are feminine, viz. ب, پ, ت, ٹ, ث, ج, چ, خ, د, ڈ, ذ, ر, ڑ, ز, ژ, ط, ظ, ف, و, ہ, ی.

Rem. c. The words بُلْبُل *bulbul*, جان *jān*, 'life,' فِکر *fikr*, 'thought,' are masculine or feminine, but the latter is generally considered correct in Northern India.

Rem. d. Generic nouns (اِسْمِ جِنْس *ismĕ jins*) are either masculine or feminine, and apply equally to both sexes; *e.g.* چیل *chīl*, 'a kite,' is feminine; ھرن *haran* or *hiran*, is masculine. In some cases, however, the terminations *ā*, *ī* are added to such nouns to distinguish the sex: *e.g.* ھرنا *harnā*, 'a buck,' ھرنی *harnī*, 'a doe.' The word آدمی *ādmī*, 'a human being,' though properly a generic noun, and hence applicable to females as well as males, is rarely treated as a feminine by Mohammadans; where a Hindū might say اچّھي آدمِي *achchhī ādmī*, 'a good woman,' a Musalmān would say, اچّھي عَورت *achchhī 'aurat.*

29. The gender of compounds is generally determined by the latter part of the compound: *e.g.* شِکارگاه *shikār-gāh*, 'a hunting-ground,' شہرپناه *shahr-panāh*, 'a wall of defence round a town,' are feminine, because the words گاه *gāh* and پناه *panāh* are feminine. There are exceptions however; as پائےگاه *pā'e-gāh*, 'dignity,' قِبلهگاه *kibla-gāh*, 'an object of reverence,' 'father,' نوشدارُو *nosh-dārū*, 'medicine,' 'a draught.'

FORMATION OF FEMININES FROM MASCULINES.

30. The most common termination used to form feminines from masculines is ـِي *ī*. If the masculine end in a consonant, this termination is merely added to it; as

براهمن *brāhman*, 'a Brāhman,	براهمِني *brāhmanī*, 'a Brāhman woman.'
اهير *ahīr*, 'a cowherd,'	اهِيرِي *ahīrī*, 'a woman of the Ahīr caste.'
پٹھان *paṭhān*, 'a Paṭhān,'	پٹھانِي *paṭhānī*, 'a woman of the Paṭhān race.'

If the masculine end in *ā* or *a* (ـَه), these terminations are changed into *ī* for the feminine: *e.g.*

لڑکا *laṛkā*, 'a boy,'	لڑکي *laṛkī*, 'a girl.'
گھوڑا *ghoṛā*, 'a horse,'	گھوڑي *ghoṛī*, 'a mare.'
بندہ *banda*, 'a male slave,'	بندِي *bandī*, 'a female slave.'
شاهزاده *shāh-zāda*, 'a prince,'	شاهزادِي *shāh-zādī*, 'a princess.'

31. Other common feminine affixes are ـَن an or in, نِي nī, and ـَانِي ānī, which are all used in the case of rational beings (chiefly with nouns denoting *caste*, *trade*, *occupation*, etc.), and the last two in the case of irrational animals also. In the application of these the following rules are to be observed:

1). If the masculine end in a consonant, the affixes are merely added: *e.g.*

سُنار *sunār*, 'a goldsmith,' { سُنارن *sunāran*, / سُنارْنِي *sunārnī*, } 'a goldsmith's wife.'

کُمّهار *kumhār*, 'a potter,' { کُمهارن *kumhāran*, / کُمهارْنِي *kumhārnī*, } 'a potter's wife.'

شير *sher*, 'a tiger,' شيرْنِي *shernī*, 'a tigress.'

أُونْٹ *ūnṭ*, 'a male camel,' أُونْٹْنِي *ūnṭnī*, 'a female camel.'

مِہتر *mĕhtar*, 'a sweeper or scavenger.' مِہترانِي *mĕhtarānī* (vulg. *mĕhtrānī*), 'a *mĕhtar's* wife.'

2). If the masculine end in a long vowel preceded by any consonant except ي *y*, the vowel is generally dropped before the affixes are added, and a long *ma'ruf* vowel in a monosyllabic masculine noun shortened: *e.g.*

دُلْها *dulhā*, 'a bridegroom,' دُلْهن *dulhan*, 'a bride.'

بريٹها *bareṭhā*, 'a washerman,' بريٹهن *bareṭhan*, 'a washerwoman.'

کُنجرا *kuṅjrā*, 'a greengrocer,' کُنجرن *kuṅjran*, 'a greengrocer's wife.'

دهوبِي *dhobī*, 'a washerman,' دهوبِن *dhobin* or *dhoban*, 'a washerwoman.'

مالِي *mālī*, 'a gardener,' مالِن *mālin*, 'a gardener's wife.'

هاتهِي *hāthī*, 'a male elephant,' هتّهنِي *hathnī*, 'a female elephant.'

کهتّرِي *khatrī*, 'a man of the Khatrī caste,' کهتّرانِي *khatrānī*, 'a Khatrī's wife or daughter.'

مامو *māmū*, 'a maternal uncle,' — مُمانی *mumānī*, 'a maternal uncle's wife.'

مُلّا *mullā*, 'a doctor or school-master,' — مُلّانی *mullānī*, 'a *mullā's* wife.'

Rem. In the word *mumānī* (for *mamānī*) the influence of final *ū* in the masculine is sufficient to change the first vowel from *a* into *u*. In some instances final *ū* of the masculine is not dropped in the feminine: *e.g.* ٹٹّوانی *ṭaṭwānī* (for *ṭaṭū'ānī*), from ٹٹّو *ṭaṭṭū*, 'a stallion pony.'

3). If the termination of the masculine be *ā* preceded by *y* (یا *yā*), or *ī* preceded by *hamza* (ئی *'ī*, in which case a long vowel precedes), *ā* in the first is not dropped, and in both cases the affix *an* or *in* is changed to یَن *yan* or ئِن *'in*: *e.g.*

بنیا *baniyā*, 'a corn-seller,' — { بنیایَن *baniyāyan*, بنیائِن *baniyā'in*, } 'a *baniyā's* wife.'

نائی *nā'ī*, 'a barber.' — { نایَن *nāyan*, نائِن *nā'in*, } 'a barber's wife.'

Rem. The above affixes are all derived from the Sanskrit affix आनी *ānī*, (*e.g.* इन्द्राणी *indrāṇī*, 'the wife of Indra'). Of the two forms *an* and *in* of the first affix, the latter is more commonly used in towns, and by Musalmāns. This affix is also added to Arabic nouns to form the names of women; *e.g.* امیرن *Amīran*, نصیبن *Naṣīban*, which are generally, though incorrectly, written امیرًا *Amīraṉ*, نصیبًا *Naṣībaṉ*.

32. Other masculines and feminines are:

راجا *rājā*, 'a king,' — رانی *rānī*, 'queen.'

{ نایک *nāyak*, نائک *nā'ik*, } 'a youth,' etc. — { نایکا *nāyikā*, نائکا *nā'ikā*, } 'a damsel,' etc.

بھائی *bhā'ī*, 'brother,' — بہن *bahin*, 'sister.'

خالو *k͟hālū*, 'a maternal uncle,' — خالہ *k͟hāla*, 'aunt.'

بیگ *beg*, 'lord,' 'prince,' — بیگم *begam*, 'lady,' 'princess.'

خاں *k͟hāṉ*, 'lord,' 'prince,' — خانم *k͟hānam*, 'lady,' 'princess.'

The first of these is derived, through the Prākrit, from the Sanskrit *rājnī*, by elision of *j*; the second is taken intact from the Sanskrit, and is perhaps the only example in Urdū of a feminine so formed; the third is derived through the Prākrit from the Sanskrit *bhaginī*; the fourth is the regular Arabic feminine of *khāl*, which is also in use, and of which *khālū* is probably a corruption; the two last are borrowed (through the Persian) from the Turkish.

33. In many cases distinct words are used for the feminine: *e.g.*

باپ *bāp*, 'father,'	ماں *māṅ*, 'mother.'
سانڈ *sāṅḍ*, 'bull,'	گائے *gā'e*, 'cow.'

And the distinction of sex is occasionally indicated, as in Persian, by means of the words نر *nar*, 'male,' مادہ *māda*, 'female': *e.g.* شیرِ نر *sherĕ nar*, or نر شیر *nar sher*, 'a male tiger,' شیرِ مادہ *sherĕ māda*, 'a female tiger.'

Rem. The formation of Arabic feminines will be treated separately in the section on Persian and Arabic constructions.

2. Number (عدد *'adad*).

34. Nouns have *two* numbers, the singular (واحد, *wāḥid*), and the plural (جمع *jam'*). The nominative singular has no case-sign, but is always identical with the crude form of the noun. The formation of the plural depends on the termination and gender of the singular. The following rules may be laid down respecting it.

1). Masculines ending in a consonant, or in one of the long vowels ـُو *ū* or *o*, ـِي *ī*, as also a few Hindī masculines ending in ـَا *ā*, that are *proper names*, or nouns denoting *relationship*, *titles*, *professions*, etc., and Persian and

Arabic words with the same termination, remain unchanged in the nominative plural: *e.g.*

گهر *ghar*, 'a house,'	plural	گهر *ghar*.	
بچّهو *bichchhū*, 'a scorpion,'	,,	بچّهو *bichchhū*.	
موتي *motī*, 'a pearl,'	,,	موتي *motī*.	
چچا *chachā*, 'a paternal uncle,'	,,	چچا *chachā*.	
لالا *lālā*, 'master,'	,,	لالا *lālā*.	
راجا *rājā*, 'king,'	,,	راجا *rājā*.	
دريا *daryā*, 'a river' (Pers.),	,,	دريا *daryā*.	
صحرا *ṣaḥrā*, 'a desert' (Arabic),	,,	صحرا *ṣaḥrā*.	

Rem. A few Arabic words ending in *ā* are exceptions: *e.g.* ماجرا *mājarā*, which is treated like Hindī masculines ending in *ā*, and has for its nom. plural ماجري *mājare*.

2). Masculines ending in ـا *ā* (with the exceptions noticed above), or ـه *a* (which is interchangeable with *ā*), form the nominative plural by changing *ā*, or *a*, into ي—*e*: *e.g.* لڑکے *laṛke*, 'boys,' from لڑکا *laṛkā*, 'a boy;' پردي *parde*, 'curtains,' from پرده *parda*, 'a curtain or screen.'

Rem. a. One Hindī noun of relationship, namely, دادا *dādā*, 'a paternal grandfather,' and a few Arabic nouns; as ماجرا *mājarā*, 'state,' 'incident,' also come under this rule. And as regards nouns ending in ـه *a*, it may be observed that the custom now appears to be to retain the final *h* in *writing*, but to *pronounce* it like *e*: *e.g.* پرده (pronounced *parde*) 'curtains.'

Rem. b. The plural termination *e* corresponds to the plural termination *e* of the Prākrit, *vide* Lassen's Instit. Ling. Prāk. p. 430.

3). Feminines ending in ـي *ī* form the nominative plural by adding ـاں *āṅ* to the singular, the *fatḥa* of the affix changing the letter of prolongation ي into the consonant *y*: *e.g.*

لڑکي *laṛkī*, 'a girl,' plural لڑکِيَاں *laṛkiyāṅ*, 'girls.'

Rem. The termination *āṅ* corresponds to the Prākrit plural increment *o*, which is changed to *ā* and nasalized.

4). Feminines ending in any letter except ـِي *ī* form the nominative plural by adding the termination ـيں *eṅ* to the singular; as

عَوْرَت *'aurat*, 'a woman,' plural عَوْرَتيں *'aurateṅ*.
كِتاب *kitāb*, 'a book,' „ كِتابيں *kitābeṅ*.

If the singular end in one of the long vowels ـَا *ā*, ـو *ū* or *o*, *hamza* is employed to enounce the initial vowel of the termination: *e.g.*

دَوَا *dawā*, 'medicine,' plural دوائِيں or دوائيں *dawā'eṅ*.
بو *bū* or *bo*, 'smell,' „ بوئِيں *bū'eṅ*.
جورُو *jorū*, 'wife,' „ جورُوئِيں *jorū'eṅ*.
ناؤ *nā'o*, 'a boat,' „ ناويں *nā'o'eṅ* or *nāweṅ*.

If, however, the singular end in ـَه *a*, or ـئے *e*, these terminations are dropped before the plural affix is added: *e.g.*

فاخْتَه *fāḵẖta*, 'a dove,' plural فاخْتيں *fāḵẖteṅ*.
دفْعَه *daf'a*, 'time,' 'class,' „ دفْعيں *daf'eṅ*.
گائے *gā'e*, 'a cow,' „ گائِيں or گائيں *gā'eṅ*.
رائے *rā'e*, 'opinion,' „ رائِيں or رائيں *rā'eṅ*.

Rem. a. The word *jorū* has for its plural جورُوٓاں *jorū'āṅ* as well as the regular *jorū'eṅ*; and a few other words ending in *ū* or *o* perhaps never occur in the plural: *e.g.* بالُو *bālū*, 'sand,' دارُو *dārū*, 'liquor,' كو *kū*, 'a street,' سُو *sū*, 'direction,' هجو *hajo*, 'satire,' ترازُو *tarāzū*, 'a pair of scales.' As exceptions to the rule we may note the class of feminine diminutives which end in ـِيا *iyā*; as چڑِيا *chiṛiyā*, 'a bird,' بڑھیا *buṛhiyā*, 'an old woman,' پھڑِیا *phuṛiyā*, 'a pimple;' these take the plural forms of the feminines from which they are derived: *e.g.* چڑِیاں *chiṛiyāṅ* (= pl. of *chiṛī*), بڑھیاں *buṛhiyāṅ* (= pl. of *buṛhī*).

Rem. b. The plural affix *eṅ*, like the preceding affix *āṅ*, corresponds to the Prākrit affix *o*, which is frequently changed to *e* in the Prākrit dialects.

Rem. c. Dissyllables with a short vowel in the first syllable, and *fatḥa* (*a*) in the second, generally drop the *fatḥa* when, in the course of inflection or derivation, a syllable is added beginning with a vowel: *e.g.* جگہیں *jagheṅ*, plural of جگہ *jagah*, 'a place.'

3. Declension (تصرِيف *taṣrīf*, or گردان *gardāṅ*).

35. Strictly speaking there is no such thing as declension in Urdū; the cases are formed by means of certain adverbs (called حُرُوفِ معنوي *ḥurūfĕ ma'nawī*, 'significant particles,' by the native grammarians), which are placed *after* the noun, and hence termed postpositions.

36. The cases (حالات *ḥālāt*), as generally given in Hindūstānī grammars, are eight in number; namely, the Nominative, Agent, Genitive, Dative, Accusative, Ablative, Locative, and Vocative. In reality, however, there are but *two* cases; viz. the crude form or *Nominative*, and the oblique form, or that to which the postpositions are added, and which Dr. Caldwell happily terms the *Formative*.

Rem. Most Urdū grammarians, ignoring all grammatical forms save those of the Arabic and Persian, recognise but *three* cases; viz. the Nominative and Agent (حالتِ فاعِلي *ḥālatĕ fā'ilī*, or فاعِل *fā'il*), the Genitive (حالتِ إضافت *ḥālatĕ iẓāfat*), and the Dative-Accusative (حالتِ مفعُولي *ḥālatĕ maf'ūlī*, or مفعُول بِہ *maf'ūl bih*). The Ablative and Locative they term مجرور و جار *majrūr o jārr*, 'the attracted and the attracting' (*i.e.* the *object attracted* and the *preposition attracting it*); and the Vocative they call ندا و منادیٰ *nidā o munādā*, 'the calling and the called.'

37. The postpositions which are used in lieu of case-endings are:

نے *ne*, 'by,'	for the	Agent,	sing. and plural.
کا *kā*, 'of,' etc.	,,	Genitive,	,,
کو *ko*, 'to,' 'for,'	,,	Dative,	,,
سے *se*, 'from,' 'with,' 'by,'	,,	Ablative,	,,
میں - پر or پہ *meṅ*, *par* or *pa*, 'in,' 'on,'	,,	Locative	,,

38. The singular nominative, as we have already observed, has no postposition added to it, but is always identical with the crude form of the noun.

The postposition of the agent case is derived from the affix *na*[1] of the Sanskrit instrumental case (singular), to which it was no doubt at first understood to correspond in use and signification; but according to the conception of those who now employ it, it is nothing more than a mere sign to distinguish the subject or agent of a transitive verb in the tenses formed with the passive participle (§§ 183, 188).

The genitive case is simply an adjective, formed by means of an adjective affix (see § 42).

The accusative case, strictly speaking, does not exist in Hindī and Urdū; its place is supplied by the nominative (which we shall call *the direct object*), or by the dative, in which case the postposition *ko* is not to be translated into English.

The vocative case takes no postposition. but a variety of interjections may be prefixed to it.

[1] For the derivation of the other postpositions see the section on Prepositions and Postpositions.

Rem. a. The force of the dative is occasionally expressed by the postpositions تئيں *ta'īn*, 'to,' and ليئے *lī'e* or واسطے *wāsṭe*, 'for the sake of,' 'for,' together with the genitive they govern: *e.g.* باپ كے تئيں *bāp-ke ta'īn* (= باپ كو *bāp ko*), 'to the father;' بهائي كے لِيئے *bhā'ī-ke lī'e*, 'for (my) brother.' Other obsolete forms of the ablative postpositions, which occur in the older writings, are سيں *sen*, سوں *son*, سِتي *sitī*; and in some grammars تک *tak* (تلک *talak*) also is given as a postposition of the locative case, but as this particle never signifies 'in,' 'on,' but simply indicates motion towards and arrival at an object, the Urdū grammarians rightly regard it as a distinct postposition governing the inflected form of a noun. Instead of تک *tak* the postpositions توڑي *toṛī* and تئيں *ta'īn*, 'till,' 'up to,' are occasionally found in the older writings, but are now obsolete.

Rem. b. Two postpositions (generally those of the ablative and locative cases) are frequently used together: *e.g.* گهرميں سے *ghar-meṅ-se*, 'from within the house,' بَيّل پر سے *bail-par-se*, 'from upon the ox.' In such cases the first is regarded by some of the native grammarians as a noun governing the preceding noun in the genitive.

39. The form assumed by a noun before it takes a postposition after it (whether that postposition be expressed or understood) is generally termed the *oblique form.* We prefer calling it, with Dr. Caldwell, the *Formative.* In constructing the Formative the following cases arise:

1). If the nominative singular end in any letter except the masculine terminations ـَا *ā* and ـَه *a* (§ 33, 2), the Formative singular is identical with the nominative, and the Formative plural is obtained by *adding* the termination ـوں *oṅ* to the singular: *e.g.* nom. sing. گهر *ghar*, 'a house,' Formative singular گهر *ghar*, Formative plural گهروں *gharoṅ*. In the vocative plural the nasal *n* of the termination *oṅ* is dropped, *e.g.* گهرو *gharo*, 'O houses.'

2). If the nom. sing. end in ا‎ـَ *ā* or ہ‎ـَ *a* (§ 33, 2), the Formatives are obtained by *changing* these letters into ي‎— *e* for the singular, and وں‎— *oṅ* for the plural: *e.g.* nom. sing. گهوڑا‎ *ghoṛā*, 'a horse,' singular Formative گهوڑي‎ *ghoṛe*, plural Formative گهوڑوں‎ *ghoṛoṅ*; nom. sing. غصّه‎ *guṣṣa*, 'anger,' sing. Form. غُصّے‎ *guṣṣe*, plural Form. غُصّوں‎ *guṣṣoṅ*. But nouns which are the names of living beings do not inflect: *e.g.* گهسيٹا‎ *Ghasīṭā*, Formative گهسيٹا‎ *Ghasīṭā*.

Rem. a. According to some native grammarians *no proper name* should be inflected; hence we find in the *Ḳawā'idĕ Urdū*, Part III., جمّنا كے كہنے سے وُہ درّيا سمّجها جائيگا جو دِهّلي مٿهرا آگرہ كے نِيچے بہتّا هَي‎ *jamnā-ke kahne-se wŏh daryā samjhā-jā'egā jo dĕhlī mathurā āgra-ke nīche bahtā hai*, 'By mentioning the Jamnā that river will be understood which flows by (*lit.* under) Dehlī, Mathurā, and Āgra.'

Rem. b. The Formative is originally, as Dr. Trumpp suggests (Sindhī Gram. p. 123), the Prākrit Genitive. This is not very clear in the singular, but the termination *oṅ* of the Formative plural is evidently the termination *āṇa* or *ūṇa* of the Prākrit genitive plural, and in the case of the pronouns the identity is unmistakeable.

40. All nouns then may be arranged in two classes or declensions, corresponding to the two forms of the Formative.

The First Declension.

41. The first declension comprises *all* feminines, and masculines terminating in any letter except (original) ہ‎ـَ *a*; those ending in ا‎ـَ *ā*, however, are Persian or Arabic words, or Hindī nouns of relationship, etc. (§ 33, 1); *e.g.*

1). گھر *ghar*, 'a house' (masc.).

	SINGULAR.	PLURAL.
Nom.	گھر *ghar*, 'a house.'	گھر *ghar*, 'houses.'
Formative	گھر *ghar*.	گھروں *gharoṅ*.
Agent.	گھرنے *ghar-ne*, 'by a house.'	گھروں نے *gharoṅ-ne*, 'by houses.'
Gen.	گھرکا *ghar-kā*, 'of a house.'	گھروں کا *gharoṅ-kā*, 'of houses.'
Dat.	گھرکو *ghar-ko*, 'to a house.'	گھروں کو *gharoṅ-ko*, 'to houses.'
Acc.	{ گھر *ghar*, گھرکو *ghar-ko*, } 'a house.'	{ گھر *ghar*, گھروں کو *gharoṅ-ko*, } 'houses.'
Abl.	گھرسے *ghar-se*, 'from, with, by, a house.'	گھروں سے *gharoṅ-se*, 'from houses.'
Loc.	گھرمیں - پر *ghar-meṅ*, *-par*, 'in, on, a house.'	گھروں میں *gharoṅ-meṅ*, 'in houses.'
Voc.	اَي گھر *ai ghar*, 'O house.'	اَي گھرو *ai gharo*, 'O houses.'

2). چچا *chachā*, 'a paternal uncle.'

	SINGULAR.	PLURAL.
Nom.	چچا *chachā*, 'an uncle.'	چچا *chachā*, 'uncles.'
Form.	چچا *chachā*.	چچاؤں *chachā'oṅ*.
Agent	چچانے *chachā-ne*, 'by an uncle.'	چچاؤں نے *chachā'oṅ-ne*, 'by uncles.'
Gen.	چچا کا *chachā-kā*, 'of an uncle.'	چچاؤں کا *chachā'oṅ-kā*, 'of uncles.'
	etc. etc. etc.	etc. etc. etc.

Rem. Like *chachā* are declined such Hindī nouns as راجا *rājā*, 'a king,' لالا *lālā*, 'a master,' as also Persian and Arabic nouns (masc.); *e.g.* دریا *daryā*, 'a river,' صحرا *ṣaḥrā*, 'a desert.'

3.) موتي *motī*, 'a pearl' (masc.).

	SINGULAR.	PLURAL.
Nom.	موتي *motī*, 'a pearl.'	موتي *motī*, 'pearls.'
Form.	موتي *motī*.	موتيوں *motiyoṅ* or *motī'oṅ*.
Gen.	موتي کا *motī-kā*, 'of pearl.'	موتيوں کا *motiyoṅ-kā*, 'of pearls.'
	etc. etc.	etc. etc.

4). بچھو *bichchhū*, 'a scorpion' (masc.).

	SINGULAR.	PLURAL.
Nom.	بچھو *bichchhū*, 'a scorpion.'	بچھو *bichchhū*, 'scorpions.'
Form.	بچھو *bichchhū*.	بچھوؤں *bichchhū'on*.
Agent	بچھو نے *bichchhū-ne*, 'by a scorpion.'	بچھوؤں نے *bichchhū'on-ne*, 'by scorpions.'

Rem. Final *ū* is occasionally shortened before the termination *on* of the Formative plural is added; as آنسُوں *ānsu'on* (for آنسُوؤں *ānsū'on*); and if final ـُو *ū* or *o* be preceded by ـَا *ā*, it is frequently dropped in the Formative plural: *e.g.* گھاؤں *ghā'on*, from گھاو *ghā'o*, 'a wound or sore.' On the same principle final *w* in such words as پانو *pānw*, 'a foot,' گانو *gānw*, 'a village,' etc., is frequently dropped in the Formative plural, and occasionally the preceding nasal also: *e.g.* پانوں *pān'on* and پاؤں *pā'on*, for پانووں *pānwon*. In the singular of such words moreover final *w* is often transposed and changed to *o*, and hence the singular form پاؤں *pā'on*, 'a foot,' گاؤں *ga'on*, 'a village,' the Formative plural of which has the same form by contraction.

5). رات *rāt*, 'night' (fem.).

Nom.	رات *rāt*, 'night.'	راتیں *rāten*, 'nights.'
Form.	رات *rāt*.	راتوں *rāton*.
Gen.	رات کا *rāt-kā*, 'of night.' etc. etc. etc.	راتوں کا *rāton-kā*, 'of nights.' etc. etc. etc.

6). دوا *dawā*, 'medicine' (fem.).

Nom.	دوا *dawā*, 'medicine.'	دوائیں *dawā'en*, 'medicines.'
Form.	دوا *dawā*.	دواؤں *dawā'on*.
Agent	دوا نے *dawā-ne*, 'by the medicine.' etc. etc. etc.	دواؤں نے *dawā'on-ne*, 'by medicines.' etc. etc. etc.

7). بو *bo* or *bū*, 'smell' (fem.).

SINGULAR.	PLURAL.
Nom. بو *bo* or *bū*, 'smell.'	بوئیں *bo'eṅ* or *bū'eṅ*, 'smells.'
Form. بو *bo* or *bū*.	بوؤں *bū'oṅ*.

Rem. The few feminines ending in *e* and *a* (ـَہ) not only drop those letters in the nominative plural, but also in the Formative plural: *e.g.* گاؤں *gā'oṅ*, from گائے *gā'e*, 'a cow;' فاختوں *fā<u>kh</u>toṅ*, from فاختہ *fā<u>kh</u>ta*, 'a dove.'

8). لڑکي *laṛkī*, 'a girl.'

Nom. لڑکي *laṛkī*, 'a girl.'	لڑکیاں *laṛkiyāṅ*, 'girls.'
Form. لڑکي *laṛkī*.	لڑکیوں *laṛkiyoṅ* or *laṛkī'oṅ*.

Rem. a. Feminine diminutives, such as چڑیا *chiṛiyā*, 'a bird,' پھڑیا *phuṛiyā*, 'a small boil,' drop the final *ā* in the Formative plural (as in the plur. nom.), and so have the same plural forms as feminines ending in *ī*: *e.g.* nom. pl. چڑیاں *chiṛiyāṅ*, 'birds,' Form. pl. چڑیوں *chiṛiyoṅ*.

Rem. b. A noun terminating in nasal *n* is declined in the singular just as if the nasal were not present, but the nasal is dropped in the plural.

THE SECOND DECLENSION.

42. The second declension comprises all masculine (Hindī) nouns ending in ـَا *ā* (except such as denote *relationship*, *titles*, *professions*, etc.) and all masculines ending, in ـَہ *a*: *e.g.*

1). لڑکا *laṛkā*, 'a boy.'

	Singular	Plural
Nom.	لڑکا *laṛkā*, 'a boy.'	لڑکے *laṛke*, 'boys.'
Form.	لڑکے *laṛke*.	لڑکوں *laṛkoṅ*.
Agent	لڑکے نے *laṛke-ne*, 'by a boy.'	لڑکوں نے *laṛkoṅ-ne*, 'by boys.'
Voc.	لڑکے *laṛke*, 'boy!' اَي لڑکے *ai laṛke*, 'O boy!'	لڑکو *laṛko*, 'boys!' اَي لڑکو *ai laṛko*, 'O boys!'

2). پردہ *parda*. 'a curtain.'

	SINGULAR.	PLURAL.
Nom.	پردہ *parda*, 'a curtain.'	پردے *parde*, 'curtains.'
Form.	پردے *parde*	پردوں *pardoṅ*.

Rem. a. According to the present custom of writing such words as end in ہ *a*, the Formative singular is identical, in writing, with the nominative: *e.g.* پردہ, pronounced *parde*.

Rem. b. A few masc. Arabic nouns also, as ماجرا *mājarā*, 'incident,' 'circumstance,' نشا *nashā*, 'intoxication,' belong to this declension.

Rem. c. Nasal *n* at the end of words is retained in the singular, as also in the nominative plural, but dropped in the Formative plural: *e.g.* nom. sing. بنیاں *baniyāṅ*, 'a merchant,' Form. sing. بنییں *baniyeṅ*, nom. pl. بنییں *baniyeṅ*, Form. pl. بنیوں *baniyoṅ*.

Rem. d. Words ending in یہ *ya*, as پایہ *pāya*, 'the foot or leg' (of a thing), کرایہ *kirāya*, 'hire,' 'rent,' may follow the general rule, or change ی *y* into *hamsa* in the Form. sing.: *e.g.* پایے *pāye* or پائے *pā'e*, کرایے *kirāye* or کرائے *kirā'e*. In the plural, however, the rule is generally observed. Similarly from روپیہ *rūpaya* are formed روپئے *rūpa'e* or روپی *rūpai*; and from رپیہ *rupaya* the forms رپئے *rupa'e* or رپی *rupai*. It is a mistake to derive these forms from روپیہ *rūpiya*, and call them irregular.

The Genitive (مُضاف إلیہ).

43. The Genitive, as has been remarked before, is formed by means of an *adjective affix* (کا *kā* = Prākrit को *ko* = Sanskrit क *ka*), and is a real adjective, changing its termination so as to agree with its governing noun (the مُضاف), just as the Hindī adjective ending in ا *ā* does.

Rem. The Persian genitive construction is also used in Urdū, and it is a noteworthy fact that the relation of the governed to the governing noun is expressed in the same manner as that of a noun to the adjective qualifying it (see *Persian Constructions*, § 76).

III. THE ADJECTIVE (اِسْم صِفت).

44. The adjective generally precedes the noun it qualifies, and, unless it end in ـَا *ā*, and be derived from the Hindī, is indeclinable: *e.g.* سفيد گهوڑا *safed ghoṛā*, 'a white horse;' سفيد گهوڑِي *safed ghoṛī*, 'a white mare;' سفيد گهوڑے *safed ghoṛe*, 'white horses.'

45. Adjectives (not Persian or Arabic) which end in ـَا *ā* (the masc. termination), are declined in the singular like nouns of the Second Declension, and form the nom. pl. in the same way; but the Formative pl. is identical with that of the singular. The feminine is formed by changing the termination ـَا *ā*, of the masc. into ـِي *ī*, and is not altered for case or number: *e.g.*

SINGULAR.

	Masculine.	Feminine.
Nom.	اچّها *achchhā*, 'good.'	اچّهِي *achchhī*.
Form.	اچّهے *achchhe*.	اچّهِي *achchhī*.

PLURAL.

	Masculine.	Feminine.
Nom.	اچّهے *achchhe*.	اچّهِي *achchhī*.
Form.	اچّهے *achchhe*.	اچّهِي *achchhī*.

The genitive is similarly declined: *e.g.*

SINGULAR.

	Masculine.	Feminine.
Nom.	گهرکا *ghar-kā*, 'of the house,' 'household.'	گهرکِي *ghar-kī*.
Form.	گهرکے *ghar-ke*.	گهرکِي *ghar-kī*.

PLURAL.

	Masculine.	Feminine.
Nom.	گهرکے *ghar-ke*.	گهرکِي *ghar-kī*.
Form.	گهرکے *gkar-ke*.	گهرکِي *ghar-kī*.

Examples: اچّھا آدمي *achchhā ādmī*, 'a good man,' dat. sing. اچّھے آدمي کو *achchhe ādmī ko*, 'to a good man;' nom. pl. اچّھے آدمي *achchhe ādmī*, 'good men,' abl. pl. اچّھے آدميوں سے *achchhe ādmiyoṅ se*, 'from good men:' اچّھي عَورت *achchhī 'aurat*, 'a good woman,' dat. sing. اچّھي عَورت کو *achchhī 'aurat ko*, 'to a good woman,' nom. pl. اچّھي عَورتيں *achchhī 'auraten*, 'good women;' موهن کا گھوڑا *mohan-kā ghoṛā*, 'Mohan's horse,' loc. sing. موهن کے گھوڑے پر *mohan-ke ghoṛe par*, 'on Mohan's horse,' nom. pl. موهن کے گھوڑے *mohan-ke ghoṛe*, 'Mohan's horses,' dat. pl. موهن کے گھوڑوں کو *mohan-ke ghoṛon ko*, 'to Mohan's horses.'

Rem. a. One Persian adjective ending in ـا *ā*, viz. جُدا *judā*, 'separate,' and one Arabic, فُلانا *fulānā* (for فُلانه), 'certain,' are similarly declined.

Rem. b. If a masculine noun is qualified by several adjectives capable of inflection, they are all declined in the same way: *e.g.* بڑے کالے گھوڑے *baṛe kāle ghoṛe*, 'large black horses.' And if the adjective be a compound word, the latter part of which is itself an adjective or participle determining a preceding substantive, this last is declined so as to agree with the noun qualified by the compound adjective: *e.g.* ٹوپے پھٹے لڑکے *topī-phaṭe laṛke*, 'the boys with torn caps' (*lit.* 'the cap-torn boys'), دوپٹّا پھٹي لڑکي *dupaṭṭā-phaṭī laṛkī*, 'the girl with a torn veil or mantle.'

Rem. c. If final *ā* of an adjective be nasalized, the nasal does not affect its declension, but is retained in all the cases: *e.g.* باياں هاتھ *bāyāṅ hāth*, 'the left hand,' بايیں (or بائيں) هاتھ کو *bāyeṅ* (or *bā'eṅ*) *hāth-ko*, 'to the left hand,' بائيں طرف *bā'īṅ ṭaraf*, 'the left side.'

Rem. d. The adjective occasionally follows the noun it qualifies. This is especially the case if the attribute is to be emphasized or brought prominently to notice. In the older writings, moreover, feminine adjectives following the nouns they qualify sometimes take the plural termination of substantives; as راتیں بھارِیاں *rāteṅ bhāriyāṅ*, 'heavy or wearisome nights;' کوٹھرِیاں بہُت اُونچِیاں *koṭhriyāṅ bahut ūṅchiyāṅ*, 'very lofty rooms;' but this construction is now obsolete.

46. A few Persian adjectives ending in ـَه *a* are declined like Hindī adjectives ending in *ā*; but as a rule such adjectives are indeclinable. The following are the most important of those that inflect: بیچارہ *be-chāra*, 'helpless,' 'poor,' تازہ *tāza*, 'fresh,' حرامزادہ *ḥarām-zāda*, 'base-born,' 'rascally,' دِیوانہ *dīwāna*, 'mad,' 'insane,' رانده *rāṅda*, 'rejected,' شرمِندہ *sharminda*, 'ashamed,' 'bashful,' کمینہ *kamīna*, 'mean,' گندہ *ganda*, 'fetid,' 'rotten,' ماندہ *māṅda*, 'tired,' 'indisposed,' نادِیدہ *nā-dīda*, 'unseen,' ناکارہ *nā-kāra*, 'useless.'

Rem. a. To these some grammarians add عُمدہ *'umda*, 'exalted,' یک سالہ *yak-sāla*, 'annual,' دوسالہ *dū-sāla*, 'biennial,' etc., but these are not inflected by writers of the present day: *e.g.* عُمدہ بات *'umda bāt*, 'an excellent matter,' not عُمدِي بات.

Rem. b. Adjectives, when used as concrete nouns, are declined like nouns: *e.g.* دانا *dānā*, 'a wise man,' داناؤں سے *dānā'oṅ-se*, 'from the wise.'

Comparison of Adjectives.

47. Adjectives undergo no change of form to express the comparative and superlative degrees. When two objects are compared, that with which the comparison is made generally takes the form of the ablative, the adjective itself remaining in the positive and following it: *e.g.* موہن زَید سے بڑا هَي *mohan zaid-se baṛā hai*, 'Mohan is bigger than Zaid.' The superlative is, strictly speaking, nothing more than a comparative involving the pronominal adjective

سب *sab*, 'all,' (prefixed to the ablative, either expressed or understood) as its complement: *e.g.* موهن سب لڑکوں سے اچّها هَي *mohan sab laṛkoṅ-se achchhā hai*, 'Mohan is better than (the best of) all the boys;' وُه سب سے بڑا هَي *wŏh sab-se baṛā hai*, 'he is bigger than (the biggest of) all.'

Rem. a. The particle سے signifies the *difference between* two objects that are compared with each other, and hence its use in forming the comparative degree. It is a remarkable fact that this method of forming the comparative and superlative is borrowed from the Semitic languages. The only trace of the Sanskrit method that exists in Urdū is found in the forms borrowed from the Persian, as بِہ *bĕh*, 'good,' بِہتر *bĕh-tar*, 'better,' بِہترِین *bĕhtarīn*, 'best' (see Persian Constructions, § 78).

Rem. b. Instead of the ablative, however, we occasionally meet with the genitive or the locative; as موهن سب کا بڑا هَي *mohan sab-kā baṛā hai*, 'Mohan is biggest of all;' سب طالِبعِلموں میں زَید اچّها هَي *sab ṭālib-'ilmoṅ meṅ zaid achchhā hai*, 'Zaid is the best among all the students.' The comparative is also frequently expressed by using the word بِنِسبت *ba-nisbat*, 'in relation to,' 'in comparison with,' with the genitive of the noun with which the comparison is made; as زَید کا قد بِنِسبت موهن کے بُلند هَي *zaid-kā ḳadd banisbat mohan-ke buland hai*, 'Zaid's stature is tall in comparison with Mohan's.'

48. An intensive signification is given to an adjective, in either the positive or comparative degree: 1) by repeating it; as اچّها اچّها *achchhā achchhā*, 'very good,' بِہتر بِہتر *bĕhtar bĕhtar*, 'much better:' 2) by prefixing to it an adverb, or a noun or adjective used adverbially, as بڑا بهارِی *baṛā bhārī*, 'very heavy;' بہُت اچّها *bahut achchhā*, 'very good' (which is still more intensified by the addition of the emphatic particle هِي *hī* to the adverb, as

بہت هي اچّها *bahut-hī achchhā*, 'exceedingly good'); نِہايت خُوبصُورت *nihāyat khūb-ṣūrat*, 'extremely handsome;' آور كالا *aur kālā*, 'more black,' and آور بهي كالا *aur bhī kālā*, 'even, or still, blacker;' زِيادہ حسين *ziyāda ḥasīn*, 'more beautiful,' or 'exceedingly beautiful;' بدرّجه بِہتر *ba-darja bĕhtar*, or بدرّجها بِہتر *ba-darjahā bĕhtar*, 'by degrees, or many degrees, better,' 'far better;' كہيں بِہتر *kahīṅ bĕhtar*, 'anywhere better,' 'ever so much, or incomparably, better:' 3) by adding to the adjective the termination سا *sā*; كالا سا *kālā-sā*, 'very black,' or 'blackish,' بہت سا *bahut-sā*, 'a large quantity,' 'very much'; تهوڑا سا *thoṛā-sā*, 'just a little,' 'a very little.'

49. With the intensive affix سا *sā* must not be confounded the *adjective of similitude* سا *sā*, سار *sār*, or سان *sāṅ* 'like.' This may be added to substantives or adjectives to form adjectives corresponding (when subjoined to substantives) to those which in English have the termination *ish*; as لڑكاسا *laṛkā-sā*, 'boyish,' كالاسا *kālā-sā*, 'black-like,' ايكسان *ek-sāṅ*, or يكسان *yak-sāṅ*, 'one-like,' 'similar.'

50. Whether the adjunct سا be employed as an intensive, or as an adjective of similitude, it is declinable like Hindī adjectives ending in ـا *ā*, and the noun to which it is added inflects just as it would do without it: *e.g.* بہت سے گهوڑے *bahut-se ghoṛe*, 'a great many horses;' كالِي سِي گهوڑِياں *kālī-sī ghoṛiyāṅ*, 'very black (or blackish) mares.'[1]

Rem. سا *sā* or سان *sāṅ*, 'like,' 'resembling,' is most probably the

[1] The use of *sā* after the genitive appears to have perplexed the grammarians greatly. The matter belongs properly to Syntax; but we may observe here, that the construction in such cases is precisely similar to that of the English; the *muẓāf*, or noun which governs the genitive, is invariably understood, and it is to this that the adjunct of similitude is attached: *e.g.* in the phrase *sher-kī-sī ṣūrat*, the word *ṣūrat* (to which the adjunct *sā* pertains) is understood after *kī*, just as, in the English equivalent, 'a form like a tiger's,' the word 'form' is understood after 'tiger's' (Cf. also § 362).

Prākrit form of the Sanskrit समान *like*; whereas the intensive particle سا is derived from the Sanskrit शस् *śas*, 'fold,' etc.

IV. NUMERAL ADJECTIVES (إسم عدد).

51. The Urdū numerals are the same as those of the Hindī, and are derived from the Sanskrit through the medium of the Prākrit.[1] Like other adjectives they

[1] In deriving its words from the Prākrit, the Hindī generally drops final short vowels, elides one or both the letters of conjuncts, and lengthens medial short vowels, especially where a conjunct, or one of the consonants, is elided. Thus we have:—*One*, Sanskrit *eka*, Prākrit, *ĕkka*, Hindī *ek*:—*Two*, S. *dvi*, P. *do*, H. *do*:—*Three*, S. *tri*, P. *tiṇṇi*, H. *tīn*:—*Four*, S. *chatur*, P. *chattāri*, H. *chār*, by elision of the conjunct:—*Five*, S. *pañchan*, P. *pañcha*, H. *pāñch*:—*Six*, S. *shash*, P. *chha*, H. *chha* (the cerebral sibilant of the Sanskrit being changed in Prākrit into *chh*: occasionally this sibilant is changed into *h*, very commonly into *s*, as is also the palatal sibilant *ś* of the Sanskrit, since Prākrit has no palatal or cerebral sibilant):—*Seven*, S. *saptan*, P. *satta*, H. *sāt*:—*Eight*, S. *ashṭan*, P. *aṭṭha*, H. *āṭh*:—*Nine*, S. *navan*, P. *naä*, H. *nau*:—*Ten*, S. *daśan*, P. *dasa*, H. *das*.

From *ten* upwards the numbers are formed by prefixing the units to the tens, which, however, previously undergo a change of form: *e.g.* the Prākrit *dasa* is changed, first to *daha*, and then to *raha*; as *Eleven*, S. *ekādaśan*, P. *eäraha*, H. *igārah* (not eliding the *k* of the Sanskrit, but changing it into the soft *g*, and changing the diphthong *e* into the short vowel *i*), whence, by transposition of vowel, *giärah*, whence *gyārah*:—*Twelve*, S. *dvādaśan*, P. *vāraha*, H. *bārah*:—*Thirteen*, S. *trayodaśan*, P. *terah*, H. *terah*:—*Fourteen*, S. *chaturdaśan*, P. *chaüdah*, H. *chaudah*:—*Fifteen*, S. *pañchadaśan*, P. *paṇṇaraha*, H. *pandrah*, for *pandarah*, by change of conjunct to *nd* before the liquid *r*:—*Sixteen*, S. *shoḍaśan*, P. *sorah* or *solah* (?), H. *sorah* or *solah*:—*Seventeen*, S. *saptadaśan*, P. *sattaraha*, H. *satrah* for *sattarah*:—*Eighteen*, S. *ashṭadaśan*, P. *aṭṭharaha*, H. *aṭhārah*:—*Twenty*, S. *viṁśati*, P. *vīsaï*, H. *bīs*.

The numbers 19, 29, 39, etc. are formed by prefixing to the *following* decades the word *un* (Sanskrit *ūna*, 'diminished'), and making certain changes in the initial letters of some of the decades: *e.g.* the *v* of the Prākrit *vīsaï*, is elided; as, *Nineteen* (*i.e.* 20 diminished by 1) is *un-īs*: so also in the other compounds, *ekīs*, 'twenty-one,' and so on.

Thirty, S. *triṁśat*, P. *tīsaä*, H. *tīs*, whence *Twenty-nine*, *untīs*.

Forty, S. *chatvariṁśat*, P. *chattārisa* (?), H. *chālīs*, by elision of the conjunct *tt*, and change of *r* to *l*. In compounds, *chālīs* is changed into *tālīs*, before which the vowels *a*, *i*, *ī* of the units are changed to *e*, *eṅ*, or *aiṅ*. In *forty-two* and *forty-six*, *ch* is elided.

Fifty, S. *pañchāśat*, P. *paṇṇāsa*, H. *pachās* (which is closer to the Sanskrit than to the Prākrit); whence, *Forty-nine*, *unchās*, the *first* syllable of *pachās* being elided. In the numbers 50 to 58, the *last* syllable is dropped and original *n* restored; as *pachpan*. In 51, 52, 54, 57, 58, the *p* of *pan* is, for the sake of euphony, softened into *b*, and thence into *v* or *w*.

From the Sanskrit *shashṭi* is derived the Hindī *sāṭh*, whence *un-saṭh*, 'fifty-nine,' *iksaṭh*, 'sixty-one,' etc.

generally precede the noun, which may be in the singular or plural.

THE CARDINAL NUMBERS.

FIGURES.			NAMES.	FIGURES.			NAMES.
	ARABIC.	DEVA-NAGARI.			ARABIC.	DEVA-NAGARI.	
1	١	१	ایک *ek.*	12	١٢	१२	بارہ *bārah.*
2	٢	२	دو *do.*	13	١٣	१३	تیرہ *terah.*
3	٣	३	تِین *tīn.*	14	١٤	१४	چَودہ *chaudah.*
4	٤	४	چار *chār.*	15	١٥	१५	پنّدرہ *pandrah.*
5	٥	५	پانْچ *pāṅch.*	16	١٦	१६	سولہ *solah.*
6	٦	६	چھہ *chha.*	17	١٧	१७	ستّرہ *satrah.*
7	٧	७	سات *sāt.*	18	١٨	१८	اٹھارہ *aṭhārah.* اٹھارا *aṭhārā.*
8	٨	८	آٹھ *āṭh.*				
9	٩	९	نَو *nau.*	19	١٩	१९	اُنیس *unīs* and *unnīs.*
10	١٠	१०	دس *das.*	20	٢٠	२०	بِیس *bīs.*
11	١١	११	اِگارہ *igārah.* گیارہ *gyārah.*	21	٢١	२१	ایِکّیس *ekīs.* اِکّیس *ikkīs.*

In *sattar*, 'seventy,' the *p* of the Sanskrit *saptati* is assimilated to *t*, and final *t* changed into *r*; and in the compounds, initial *s* is, for the sake of euphony, changed into *ḥ*; as *unhattar*, 'sixty-nine;' *ikhattar*, 'seventy-one.'

Assī, 'eighty,' is from the Sanskrit *aśīti*, the final *t* being elided, and the sibilant doubled. In the compounds, however, the doubling of the sibilant does not take place, while the conjunctive vowel *ā* is added to the units; as *unāsī*, 'seventy-nine;' *ikāsī*, 'eighty-one;' . . . . . *nawāsī*, 'eighty-nine,' instead of *unānawe*, as might have been expected.

Nawe, or *nawwe*, 'ninety,' is derived from the Sanskrit *navati*. In the compounds formed therewith, the conjunctive vowel *ā* is added to the units: *e.g. ikānawe*, 'ninety-one.'

The word *sau*, or *sai*, 'one hundred,' is derived from the Sanskrit *śata*, Prākrit *saä*.

FIGURES.			NAMES.	FIGURES.			NAMES.
	ARABIC.	DEVA-NAGARI.			ARABIC.	DEVA-NAGARI.	
22	۲۲	२२	بائِیس *bā'īs.*	40	۴۰	४०	چالِیس *chālīs.*
23	۲۳	२३	تیئِیش *te'īs.*	41	۴۱	४१	ایکتالِیس *ĕktālīs.* / اِکتالِیس *iktālīs.*
24	۲۴	२४	چَوبِیس *chaubīs.*	42	۴۲	४२	بیالِیس *be'ālīs.*
25	۲۵	२५	پچِیس *pachīs.*	43	۴۳	४३	تینتالِیس *teṅtālīs.*
26	۲۶	२६	چھبِّیس *chhabbīs.*	44	۴۴	४४	چَوالِیس *chau'ālīs.*
27	۲۷	२७	ستائِیس *satā'īs.*	45	۴۵	४५	پَینتالِیس *paiṅtālīs.*
28	۲۸	२८	اٹھائِیس *aṭhā'īs.*	46	۴۶	४६	چھیالِیس *chhe'ālīs.*
29	۲۹	२९	اُنتِیس *untīs.*	47	۴۷	४७	سَینتالِیس *saiṅtālīs.*
30	۳۰	३०	تِیس *tīs.*	48	۴۸	४८	اڑتالِیس *aṛtālīs.* / اٹھتالِیس *aṭhtālīs.*
31	۳۱	३१	ایکتِیس *ĕktīs.* / اِکتِیس *iktīs.*	49	۴۹	४९	اُنچاس *unchās.*
32	۳۲	३२	بتِّیس *battīs.*	50	۵۰	५०	پچاس *pachās.*
33	۳۳	३३	تینتِیس *teṅtīs.*	51	۵۱	५१	ایکاون *ĕkāwan.* / اِکاون *ikāwan.*
34	۳۴	३४	چَونتِیس *chauṅtīs.*	52	۵۲	५२	باون *bāwan.*
35	۳۵	३५	پَینتِیس *paiṅtīs.*	53	۵۳	५३	تِرپن *trĕpan* or *tirpan.*
36	۳۶	३६	چھتِّیس *chhattīs.*	54	۵۴	५४	چَوّن *chauwan.*
37	۳۷	३७	سَینتِیس *saiṅtīs.*	55	۵۵	५५	پچپن *pachpan.*
38	۳۸	३८	اٹھتِیس *aṭhtīs.* / اڑتِیس *aṛtīs.*	56	۵۶	५६	چھپّن *chhappan.*
39	۳۹	३९	اُنتالِیس *untālīs.* / اُنچالِیس *unchālīs.*	57	۵۷	५७	ستاون *sattāwan.*

	FIGURES.		NAMES.		FIGURES.		NAMES.
	ARABIC.	DEVA-NAGARI.			ARABIC.	DEVA-NAGARI.	
58	٥٨	५८	اٹھاون *aṭhāwan.*	75	٧٥	७५	پچہتّر *pachhattar.*
59	٥٩	५९	اُنسٹھ *unsaṭh.*	76	٧٦	७६	چِھہتّر *chhihattar.*
60	٦٠	६०	ساٹھ *sāṭh.*	77	٧٧	७७	ستْہتّر *sathattar.*
61	٦١	६१	ایکسٹھ *ěksaṭh.* اِکسٹھ *iksaṭh.*	78 79	٧٨ ٧٩	७८ ७९	اٹھہتّر *aṭhattar.* اُناسی *unāsī.*
62	٦٢	६२	باسٹھ *bāsaṭh.*	80	٨٠	८०	اسّی *assī.*
63	٦٣	६३	تِرْسٹھ *tresaṭh* or *tirsaṭh.*	81	٨١	८१	ایکاسی *ěkāsī.* اِکاسی *ikāsī.*
64	٦۴	६४	چَونْسٹھ *chaunsaṭh.*	82	٨٢	८२	بیاسی *be'āsī.*
65	٦٥	६५	پَینْسٹھ *painsaṭh.*	83	٨٣	८३	تِراسی *tirāsī.*
66	٦٦	६६	چھیاسٹھ *chhe'āsaṭh.*	84	٨۴	८४	چَوراسی *chaurāsī.*
67	٦٧	६७	سڑْسٹھ *sarsaṭh.*	85	٨٥	८५	پچاسی *pachāsī.*
68	٦٨	६८	اَڑْسٹھ *aṛsaṭh.* اٹھْسٹھ *aṭhsaṭh.*	86 87	٨٦ ٨٧	८६ ८७	چھیاسی *chhe'āsī.* ستاسی *satāsī.*
69	٦٩	६९	اُنہتّر *unhattar.*	88	٨٨	८८	اٹھاسی *aṭhāsī.*
70	٧٠	७०	ستّر *sattar.*	89	٨٩	८९	نَواسی *nawāsī.*
71	٧١	७१	ایکہتّر *ěkhattar.* اِکہتّر *ikhattar.*	90	٩٠	९०	نوے *nawe* or *nawwe.*
72	٧٢	७२	بہتّر *bahattar.*	91	٩١	९१	ایکانوے *ěkānawe.* اکانوے *ikānawe.*
73	٧٣	७३	تِہتّر *tihattar.*	92	٩٢	९२	بانوے *bānawe.*
74	٧۴	७४	چَوہتّر *chauhattar.*	93	٩٣	९३	تِرانوے *tirānawe.*

FIGURES.			NAMES.	FIGURES.			NAMES.
	ARABIC.	DEVA-NAGARI.			ARABIC.	DEVA-NAGARI.	
94	٩٤	९४	چورانوي *chaurānawe*	98	٩٨	९८	اٹھانوي *aṭhānawe.*
95	٩٥	९५	پانچانوي *pañchānawe* پچانوي *pachānawe*	99	٩٩	९९	ننانوي *ninānawe.* نوانوي *navānawe.*
96	٩٦	९६	چهيانوي *chhe'ānawe.*	100	١٠٠	१००	سَو *sau.* سَي *sai.*
97	٩٧	९७	ستانوي *satānawe.*				

Rem. In the compounds, *nawe* is generally contracted to *nwe,* as *ikānwe, bānwe,* or the vowel of *n* is pronounced very rapidly. In *Hindī* it also takes the form *nawwe.*

52. The numbers above one hundred are formed as in English,[1] but the conjunction 'and' is not expressed: *e.g.* ايک سَو ايک *ek sau ek,* 'one hundred (and) one;' ايک سَو دو *ek sau do,* 'one hundred (and) two' ...... دوسَو *do sau,* 'two hundred;' دو سَو ايک *do sau ek,* and so on to 1000, which may be expressed by دس سَو *das sau,* 'ten hundred,' or by a distinct word هزار *hazār,* borrowed from the Persian. Similarly 1873 may be expressed by اٹھارہ سَو تِہتّر *aṭhārah sau tihattar,* 'eighteen hundred (and) seventy-three,' or ايک هزار آٹھ سَو تِہتّر *ek hazār āṭh sau tihattar,* 'one thousand eight hundred and seventy-three.' 'Ninety-nine thou-

[1] In Hindī, the numbers between 100 and 200 are also expressed in two other ways: 1) by placing the smaller number with the adjective termination *ā* added to it, before the word سَو *sau*: *e.g.* بيسا سَو *bīsā sau,* 'a hundred and twenty,' literally, 'one hundred having or possessing twenty:' 2) by adding to the numeral adjective the noun *utar* (Sanskrit *uttar,* 'over,' 'above'), the initial vowel of which coalesces with the termination *a* of the numeral into *o*: *e.g.* اٹھوتر سَو *aṭhotar sau* 'one hundred (and) eight,' literally 'eight over a hundred.' Such forms are, however, only used in counting, and in the Multiplication Table.

sand' is نِنانوي هزار *ninānawe hazār*; but 'a hundred thousand' is expressed by a distinct word لاکھ *lākh* (Sanskrit *laksha*); a hundred lacs, or 'ten millions,' by the word کروڑ *karoṛ*; a hundred *karoṛs*, or 'a thousand millions,' by the word اَرْب *arb*; a hundred *arbs*, or 'a hundred thousand millions,' by the word کھَرْب *kharb*.

Rem. The numerals سَو, هزار, لاکھ, کروڑ, اَرْب, and کھَرْب, are properly collective substantives, and are frequently used as such; *arb* and *kharb* do not occur as numeral adjectives in Urdū, but they are used in Numeration.

53. By adding to a cardinal number the particle ایک *ek*, signifying 'about,' 'or so,' the idea of indefiniteness is given to it: *e.g.* بِیس ایک *bīs ek*, 'about twenty;' سَو ایک *sau ek*, 'a hundred or so.' When so used, the numeral generally follows the noun it qualifies; as برس چار ایک *baras chār ek*, 'about four years.'

Rem. This ایک is called حرفِ تنکِیر *ḥarfĕ tankīr*, 'the indefinite particle.' It is occasionally prefixed to nouns, and then has the signification of the English indefinite article.

54. The numeral ایک *ek*, 'one,' is rendered indefinite by placing after it the word آد *ād* (said to be the contraction of the word *ādhā*, 'half,' but more probably the Sanskrit *ādi*, 'beginning'); as ایک آد *ek ād*, 'beginning with one' 'one or more,' 'a few.'

55. Two numerals (not generally consecutive), when combined, often convey the idea of indefiniteness: *e.g.* دو چار *do chār* (lit. two four), 'two or three,' 'a few;' دس بِیس *das bīs*, 'ten or twenty.'

The Ordinal Numbers.

پہلا *pahilā* or *pahlā*, 'first.'	چھٹواں *chhaṭwāṅ*, } 'sixth.'
	چھٹها *chhaṭhā*, }
دُوسْرا *dūsrā*, 'second.'	ساتْواں *sātwāṅ*, 'seventh.'
تِيسْرا *tīsrā*, 'third.'	آٹھواں *āṭhwāṅ*, 'eighth.'
چَوتها *chauthā*, 'fourth.'	نَواں *nauwāṅ* or *navāṅ*, 'ninth.'
پانْچْواں *pāṅchwāṅ*, 'fifth.'	دسْواں *daswāṅ*, 'tenth.'

The first four of the series are regularly derived from the Prākrit. The remaining ordinals are formed from the cardinals, by adding the termination *wāṅ* (corresponding to the Sanskrit *tama*). As in English, in numbers above a hundred, the last part of the compound takes the form of the ordinal; as ايکْ سَو بِيسْواں *ek sau bīswāṅ*, 'the one hundred (and) twentieth.'

56. The ordinals are regularly inflected like adjectives ending in ـا *ā*: *e.g.* پانْچْواں *pāṅchwāṅ*, 'the fifth,' Fem. پانْچْوِيں *pāṅchwīṅ*, Formative masc. پانْچْويں *pāṅchweṅ*.

Collective Numbers.

57. Collective numerals may be formed by adding to the cardinals the adjective terminations ـا *ā*, ـِي *ī*; as بِيسا *bīsā*, 'a score;' چالِيسا *chālīsā*, 'an aggregate of forty;' بَتِّيسِي *battīsī*, 'an aggregate of thirty-two.'

58. The following nouns are used as collective numerals:

جوڑا *joṛā*, } 'a pair,' 'couple.'	گاهِي *gāhī*, 'an aggregate of five.'
جوڑِي *joṛī*, }	کوڑِي *koṛī*, 'a score.'
گَنْڈا *ganḍā*, 'a quaternion,' mostly applied to four cowries.	سَيکْڑا *saikṛā*, 'a hundred.'

They are used as substantives, taking the noun after them in the genitive case, or in apposition.—The word سَيكڙا is always used in lieu of سَو *sau*; *a*) in Numeration; as ايکائِي *ĕkā'ī*, 'units,' دهائِي *dahā'ī*, 'tens,' سَيکڙي *saikṛe*, 'hundreds,' هزار *hazār*, 'thousands:' *b*) in speaking of Interest; *e.g.* پانچ رُپئے سَيکڙي *pāṅch rupa'e saikṛe*, 'five rupees per cent.'

Rem. The phrase 'per cent.' is also very generally expressed by the Persian phrase في صد *fī ṣad*, or في صدِي *fī ṣadī*.

59. The cardinal numbers, especially the tens, may also be used as collective numerals; as چار بِيس *chār bīs*, 'four twenties.' More commonly, however, the cardinal number is put in the Formative plural, and is then used to convey the idea of 1) *inclusiveness* or *totality*; as دونوں *donoṅ*, 'the two together,' 'both' (the medial *n* of *donoṅ* is inserted for euphony); تِينوں *tīnoṅ*, 'the three together,' 'all the three;' and in some cases, to add force to the form, the crude form of the numeral is added to the Formative; as آٹھوں آٹھ *āṭhoṅ āṭh*, 'the whole eight,' *lit.* 'the eight of the eight:' 2) *indefiniteness* or *numerousness*, in which case the higher numerals are of course used, and the word سَيکڙا *saikṛā* is employed in lieu of سَو *sau*: *e.g.* سَيکڙوں گهر *saikṛoṅ ghar*, 'hundreds of houses,' *lit.* 'houses in hundreds;' هزاروں آدمِي *hazāroṅ ādmī*, 'thousands of men,' 'men in thousands;' لاکهوں رُپئے *lākhoṅ rupa'e*, 'lacs of rupees.'

Rem. a. It would appear from the current usage of the cognate dialects, that this form originally expressed *collectiveness* alone, and hence may be assumed by the lower numbers also; *e.g.* Sindhī وِيهين *vīhen*, 'in twenties.'

Rem. b. By adding to the numeral ایک the *affix of intensity*, ـیلا *elā*, we have the form اکیلا *akelā*, 'one by itself,' 'alone,' corresponding to the series دونوں *donoṅ*, تینوں *tīnoṅ*, etc.

Distributive Numerals.

60. The distributives are expressed by repeating the cardinal numbers once: *e.g.* ایک ایک *ek ek*, 'one at a time,' 'singly,' 'one apiece;' دو دو *do do*, 'by twos,' 'two apiece.'

Multiplicative Numerals.

61. The multiplicatives are formed from the cardinals: 1) by adding to them the word گُنا *gunā* (fem. گُنِي *gunī*), 'time,' 'fold;' as دوگُنا *dogunā*, or *dugunā*, (whence by contraction, دُگْنا *dugnā*, and, by elision of *g*, the more common دُونا *dūnā*), 'two-fold;' تِگُنا *tigunā*, 'threefold;' چَوگُنا *chaugunā*, 'fourfold:' 2) by adding the termination هرا *harā* or *ahrā*; as ایکہرا *ĕkahrā*, 'single;' دوهرا *doharā* or *dohrā*, 'double,' 'twofold;' تِہرا *tiharā* or *tihrā*, 'triple,' 'threefold.'

Rem. a. The Persian and Arabic multiplicatives are also frequently used: the construction of these is given in §§ 103, 133.

Rem. b. The word گُنا *gunā* is derived from the Sanskrit *guṇa*, 'quality,' etc; the affix هرا *harā* (contracted from هارا *hārā*) from the Sanskrit *vāra*, by elision of *v*, and insertion of a euphonic *h*.

Numeral Adverbs.

62. The numeral adverbs *once*, *twice*, *thrice*, etc. are expressed by adding to the cardinals the word بار *bār*, or بارا *bārā*, 'time' (Sanskrit *vāra*), or one of the synonymous Arabic words دفعه *daf'a*, مرتبه *martaba*: as ایک بار *ek bār* or

ایک دفعہ *ek daf'a* or ایک مرتبہ *ek martaba*, 'once;' دو بار *do bār*, دو بارا *dŏbārā*, دو مرتبہ *do martaba*, etc., 'twice;' تین بار *tīn bār*, تبارا *tibārā*, or تین دفعہ *tīn daf'a*, etc., 'thrice.'

Rem. The same affixes (with the change of بارا *bārā* into بارہ *bāra*) are used with the Persian cardinal numbers (§ 104).

63. Numeral adverbs showing in what order certain facts are treated, are expressed by employing the ordinals in the Formative singular: *e.g.* پہلے *pahle*, 'firstly;' دوسری *dūsre*, 'secondly;' تیسری *tīsre*, 'thirdly,' etc.; or by using the Persian ordinals; as اوّل *avval*, 'firstly,' دُوُم *duwum*, 'secondly,' etc. (§ 104).

Fractional Numbers.

64. The fractional numbers are: *a*) Substantives; as

پاؤ *pā'o*,[1] چوتھائی *chauthā'ī*, } 'a quarter.'	آدھا *ādhā*, 'a half.'
تہائی *tihā'ī*, 'a third.'	سوائی *sawā'ī*, 'one and a quarter.'

Rem. The fractional numbers of the Arabic are also of frequent occurrence: *e.g.* نِصف *niṣf*, 'a half,' ثُلث *ṡulṡ*, 'a third,' etc. (§ 134); and the Persian نِیم *nīm*, 'half,' is occasionally used.

b) Adjectives; as

پون *paun*, پونے *paune*, } 'one quarter less.'	ساڑھے *sāṛhe*, 'one half more.'
	ڈیڑہ *ḍeṛh*, 'one and a half.'
آدھا *ādhā*, آدہ *ādh*, ادہ *adh*, 'half.'	اڑھائی *aṛhā'ī*, ڈھائی *ḍhā'ī*, } 'two and a half.'
سوا *sawā*, 'a quarter more.'	

[1] پاؤ is derived from the Sanskrit *pāda*; تہائی from the Sanskrit *tṛitīyāṁśa*, پون and پونے from the S. adj. *pādona*; آدھا from the S. *arddha*; سوا from the S. *sapāda* (*sa* + *pāda*), 'with a quarter,' ساڑھے from the S. *sārddha* (*sa* + *arddha*), 'with a half.'

65. These fractions always precede the numeral or the noun with which they are used; and the unit employed in using them is 1, from 1 to 99 inclusive; 100, from 100 to 999 inclusive, and so on: *e.g.* پَونے بِيس *paune bīs* = 20—¼ of 1 = 19¾; سوَا اُنِيس *sawā unīs* = 19 + ¼ = 19¼; but پَونے سَو *paune sau* = 100—¼ of 100 = 75; سوا دو سَو *sawā do sau* = 200 + ¼ of 100 = 225; سوا هزار *sawā hazār* = 1000 + ¼ of 1000 = 1250; پَونے دو هزار *paune do hazār* = 2000—¼ of 1000 = 1750.

66. پَون *paun*, differs from پَونے *paune*, inasmuch as it is generally used with units only; as پَون رُوپَيَا *paun rūpayā*, 'a rupee *minus* a quarter,' *i.e.* '¾ of a rupee;' پَون گز *paun gaz*, '¾ of a yard.'

آدها *ādhā*, 'half,' is an ordinary adjective, and is used accordingly.

ساڑھے *sāṛhe*, is used in the same manner as پَونے and سوا, but only with numerals after 2; *e.g.* ساڑھے تِين *sāṛhe tīn*, 'three and a half;' ساڑھے چار *sāṛhe chār*, 'four and a half,' etc. Similarly ساڑھے تِين سَو *sāṛhe tīn sau*, 'three hundred and fifty,' ساڑھے چار سَو *sāṛhe chār sau*, 'four hundred and fifty,' etc.; and ساڑھے تِين هزار *sāṛhe tīn hazār*, 'three thousand five hundred,' and so on.

ڈيڑھ *ḍeṛh* is used with units of measure, quantity, etc. (as *one yard, one maund*), and with the collective numerals سَو *sau*, هزار *hazār*, etc.: *e.g.* ڈيڑھ گز *ḍeṛh gaz*, 'one yard and a half;' ڈيڑھ من *ḍeṛh man*, 'one maund and a half;' ڈيڑھ سَو *ḍeṛh sau*, 'one hundred and fifty;' ڈيڑھ هزار *ḍeṛh hāzār*, 'one thousand five hundred.'

اڑھائِي *aṛhā'ī* also is used with collective numerals and nouns denoting measure, quantity, etc., which may be in the singular or the plural, as in the case of the integers:

e.g. اڑھائي سَو *aṛhā'ī sau*, 'two hundred and fifty;' اڑھائي ہزار *aṛhā'ī hazār*, 'two thousand five hundred;' اڑھائي گز *aṛhā'ī gaz*, 'two yards and a half;' اڑھائي رُوپيَه *aṛhā'ī rūpiya*, 'two rupees and a half.'

Rem. From these fractions are derived other nouns and adjectives signifying 'consisting of,' 'containing,' 'at the rate of,' etc. *e.g.* پَوّا *pauwā*, 'consisting of, or containing, one *pā'o*:' سوايا *sawāyā* and سوَيّا *sawaiyā*, 'consisting of one and a quarter,' or 'at the rate of $1\frac{1}{4}$;' ڈيوڑھا *ḍe'oṛhā*, 'half as much again.'

67. Other fractional numbers are: *a*) those which are formed from the integers, or from the fractions, adjectives or substantives; as

آدھ پاو *ādh pā'o* = $\frac{1}{2}$ of $\frac{1}{4}$ = $\frac{1}{8}$.	دو تِہائي *do tihā'ī* = $\frac{2}{3}$.
ڈيڑھ پاو *ḍeṛh pā'o* = $1\frac{1}{2}$ of $\frac{1}{4}$ = $\frac{3}{8}$.	تِين پاو *tīn pa'o*, } = $\frac{3}{4}$.
اڑھائي پاو *aṛhā'ī pā'o* = $2\frac{1}{2}$ of $\frac{1}{4}$ = $\frac{5}{8}$.	تِين چوتھائي *tīn chauthā'ī*, }

b) those which have a special application, and are formed by adding to the fractions پاو *pā'o* and ادھ *adh* the suffix ـيلا *elā*, or لا *lā*; as پاؤلا *pā'olā*, 'a quarter of any coin;' ادھيلا *adhelā*, 'half a pice' (*paisā*); ادھيلي *adhelī*, 'half a rupee.'

RAḲAM (رقم).

68. Distinct from the system of notation noticed above is that called رقم *raḳam* (an Arabic word signifying 'writing, or price-mark' on a thing), which is always used in recording pecuniary transactions, or computations involving *weight*, *measure* (of land), such as *maunds*, *bīghās*, etc. (as shown in the Plate adjoining). It is taken, for the most part, from the initial letters of the names of the Arabic numerals: *e.g.* عدم *one* is a contraction of the Arabic عدد

Table of Rakm.

رقم	تعداد	رقم	تعداد	رقم	تعداد	رقم	تعداد	رقم	تعداد	رقم	تعداد
		81 to	100	61 to	80	41 to	60	21 to	40	1 to	20
[illegible]	۲۰۰	[illegible]	۸۱	[illegible]	۶۱	[illegible]	۴۱	[illegible]	۲۱	[illegible]	۱
[illegible]	۳۰۰	[illegible]	۸۲	[illegible]	۶۲	[illegible]	۴۲	[illegible]	۲۲	[illegible]	۲
[illegible]	۴۰۰	[illegible]	۸۳	[illegible]	۶۳	[illegible]	۴۳	[illegible]	۲۳	[illegible]	۳
[illegible]	۵۰۰	[illegible]	۸۴	[illegible]	۶۴	[illegible]	۴۴	[illegible]	۲۴	[illegible]	۴
[illegible]	۶۰۰	[illegible]	۸۵	[illegible]	۶۵	[illegible]	۴۵	[illegible]	۲۵	[illegible]	۵
[illegible]	۷۰۰	[illegible]	۸۶	[illegible]	۶۶	[illegible]	۴۶	[illegible]	۲۶	[illegible]	۶
[illegible]	۸۰۰	[illegible]	۸۷	[illegible]	۶۷	[illegible]	۴۷	[illegible]	۲۷	[illegible]	۷
[illegible]	۹۰۰	[illegible]	۸۸	[illegible]	۶۸	[illegible]	۴۸	[illegible]	۲۸	[illegible]	۸
[illegible]	۱۰۰۰	[illegible]	۸۹	[illegible]	۶۹	[illegible]	۴۹	[illegible]	۲۹	[illegible]	۹
[illegible]	۲۰۰۰	[illegible]	۹۰	[illegible]	۷۰	[illegible]	۵۰	[illegible]	۳۰	[illegible]	۱۰
[illegible]	۳۰۰۰	[illegible]	۹۱	[illegible]	۷۱	[illegible]	۵۱	[illegible]	۳۱	[illegible]	۱۱
[illegible]	۴۰۰۰	[illegible]	۹۲	[illegible]	۷۲	[illegible]	۵۲	[illegible]	۳۲	[illegible]	۱۲
[illegible]	۵۰۰۰	[illegible]	۹۳	[illegible]	۷۳	[illegible]	۵۳	[illegible]	۳۳	[illegible]	۱۳
[illegible]	۶۰۰۰	[illegible]	۹۴	[illegible]	۷۴	[illegible]	۵۴	[illegible]	۳۴	[illegible]	۱۴
[illegible]	۷۰۰۰	[illegible]	۹۵	[illegible]	۷۵	[illegible]	۵۵	[illegible]	۳۵	[illegible]	۱۵
[illegible]	۸۰۰۰	[illegible]	۹۶	[illegible]	۷۶	[illegible]	۵۶	[illegible]	۳۶	[illegible]	۱۶
[illegible]	۹۰۰۰	[illegible]	۹۷	[illegible]	۷۷	[illegible]	۵۷	[illegible]	۳۷	[illegible]	۱۷
[illegible]	۱۰۰۰۰	[illegible]	۹۸	[illegible]	۷۸	[illegible]	۵۸	[illegible]	۳۸	[illegible]	۱۸
[illegible]	۱۱۰۰۰	[illegible]	۹۹	[illegible]	۷۹	[illegible]	۵۹	[illegible]	۳۹	[illegible]	۱۹
لدکھ	۱۰۰۰۰۰	[illegible]	۱۰۰	[illegible]	۸۰	[illegible]	۶۰	[illegible]	۴۰	[illegible]	۲۰

[illegible] = ¼ of an ānā; [illegible] = ½ an ānā; [illegible] = ¾ of an ānā; [illegible] = one ānā

Rs. As. Pāi
[illegible] = 1125, 11, 8¾,

Rs. As.
[illegible] = 795. 11¾

'adad; عددا *two*, of the Arabic dual, عددان *'adadān*; ثلاث *three*, from the Arabic ثلاثة *s̤alās̤a*, and so on (See Arabic numerals, § 129).

PERSIAN AND ARABIC CONSTRUCTIONS.

69. The Urdū borrows largely from the Persian and Arabic languages, and the words borrowed are frequently treated according to the rules of inflection peculiar to the language from which they are taken. A knowledge of some of the most important facts of Persian and Arabic inflection is therefore indispensably necessary to the student of Urdū.

PERSIAN CONSTRUCTIONS.

70. *Gender.*—There is no distinction of genders in Persian. The distinction of sex is indicated, as in English, by the use of different words; as مرد *man*, زن *woman*; or by the aid of the words نر *nar*, 'male,' ماده *māda*, 'female;' as شیرِ نر *sherĕ nar*, 'a male tiger,' شیرِ ماده *sherĕ māda*, 'a female tiger.'

71. *Declension.*—In the declension of nouns, the cases, with the exception of the genitive, accusative, and vocative, are formed by means of prepositions, as in English. The only cases which demand notice in connection with Urdū are the genitive and the vocative.

The Genitive.

72. The 'relation of the genitive case' (إضافت *iẓāfat*) is indicated by placing the *determined* or *governing* noun first, with the vowel *kasra* (called كسرۂ إضافت *the kasra of annexation*) attached to its final letter; as عِلمِ طِبّ *'ilmĕ*

tibb, 'the science, or art, of medicine;' شہرِ بغداد *shahrĕ bagdād*, 'the city of Bagdād.' If the governing noun end in ـَہ *a*, or ـِي *ī*, *hamza* must be employed to enounce the *kasra* (which need not then be written, since *hamza* can occur in such a position for no other purpose); *e.g.* ملکۂ ہند or ملکۂ ہند *malika'ĕ hind*, 'the Queen of India;' ماہئِ دريا *māhī'ĕ daryā*, 'the fish of the sea.' When the first, or governing word, ends in either of the long vowels ـَا *ā*, ـُو *ū* or *o*, the *hamza* is followed by ي (the *majhūl ye*); as پائے تخت *pā'ĕ takht*, 'the foot of the throne;' روي زمين *rū'ĕ zamīn*, 'the face of the earth.'

Rem. a. In employing this construction in Urdū, a Hindī proper name may stand in the place of the *governed* noun, but the *governing* noun must be Persian or Arabic: *e.g.* شہرِ بريلي *shahrĕ barelī*, 'the city of Barelī' (Bareilly).

Rem. b. Whatever be the sign of the *iẓāfat*, its sound in Urdū is always that of short *e* (*ĕ*), between the *kasra* and the *yā'ĕ majhūl*.

73. The genitive may also be formed by reversing the order of the words and placing the governed noun first, in which case the *iẓāfat* is not used: *e.g.* شہرپناہ *shahr panāh* = پناہِ شہر *panāhĕ shahr*, 'the protection of the city,' 'a wall of defence round a city;' جہاں پناہ *jahāṅ panāh* = پناہِ جہاں *panāhe jahāṅ*, 'the refuge of the world,' 'His Majesty.' But the more common result of this construction is either an *attributive compound* (corresponding to the *Bahuvrīhi* of the Sanskrit); as سنگ دل *sang-dil*, 'possessing a heart of stone,' 'hard-hearted;' فيلتن *fīl-tan*, 'elephant-bodied;' پري روي *parī-rū*, 'fairy-faced;' or a *determinative compound* (corresponding to the *Tatpurusha* of the Sanskrit); *e.g.* پندنامہ *pand-nāma*, 'the book of counsels;' شبگاہ *shab-gāh*, 'night-time.'

The Vocative.

74. The vocative case may be formed as in English, by prefixing an interjection to the nominative: *e.g.* اَي دوسْت *ai dost*, 'O friend;' but another common way of forming it is to add the termination ـَا *ā* to the nominative; as دِلا *dilā*, 'O heart;' دوسْتا *dostā*, 'O friend.' If the nominative end in *ā*, a euphonic *y* is inserted between it and the affix; *e.g.* خُدايا *khudā-yā*, 'O God.'

The Plural.

75. The terminations of the plural are two; namely ـَان *āṅ* for things animate, and ها *hā* for things inanimate: *e.g.* مرْد *mard*, 'a man,' pl. مرْدان *mardāṅ*; ساقِي *sāḳī*, 'a cup-bearer,' pl. ساقِيَان *sāḳiyāṅ*; بار *bār*, 'a time,' pl. بارْها *bārhā*; سال *sāl*, 'a year,' pl. سالْها *sālhā*. There are exceptions however, chiefly in the use of the plural affix *hā* (which in Persia would appear to be now used generally to form the pl. of all nouns): *e.g.* چراغان *chirāgāṅ*, 'lamps,' اسْپْها *asphā*, 'horses.' If the singular end in ـَه *a*, this letter is changed into گ *g* before the termination *āṅ* is added, and dropped before the addition of *hā*: *e.g.* بنْدگان *bandagāṅ*, 'slaves,' 'servants,' from بنْده *banda*; خانها *khānahā*, 'houses,' from خانه *khāna*. And if the singular end in *ā*, a euphonic ي *y* is inserted between it and the affix *āṅ*; as پارْسايان *pārsā-yāṅ*, 'the devout,' from پارْسا *pārsā*, 'devout.'

76. The Persian plural of nouns denoting inanimate things is also formed, in imitation of the Arabic, by the addition of the termination ـَات *āt* to the singular: *e.g.* دِهات *dĕh-āt*, 'villages,' 'the country' (in contradistinction to 'the town'), from دِه *dĕh*, 'a village;' زيوَرات *zewar-āt*, 'ornaments,' 'jewels,' from زيور *zewar*; كاغذات *kāgaz̤-āt*,

'papers,' 'documents,' from كاغذ *kāgaẕ*. If ﮧ *a* be the final letter of the singular, it is changed into ج *j* before the pl. affix is added: *e.g.* نامجات *nāmajāt*, 'letters,' from نامه *nāma*.

The Adjective.

77. The construction of the genitive case is also that of the noun and its qualifying adjective, the adjective being generally placed after the noun: *e.g.* مردِ نیک *mardĕ nek*, 'a good man,' زبانِ شیرین *zabānĕ shīrīn*, 'a sweet tongue.'

78. The adjective however often precedes the substantive, and in that case the *iẕāfat* is dispensed with: *e.g.* نیک مرد *nek mard*, 'a good man.' But more generally in this construction, the adjective and noun together form either a *determinative compound* (corresponding to the *Karmadhāraya* of the Sanskrit); as رخشنده روز *rakhshinda-roz*, 'shining day,' خوش نویس *khwush navīs*, 'a neat writer;' or an *attributive compound* (similar to the *Bahuvrīhi* of the Sanskrit): *e.g.* خوبصورت *khūb-ṣūrat*, 'handsome-faced,' 'handsome;' بد خوي *bad-kho*, 'ill-behaved,' 'having a bad disposition;' نیک نام *nek-nām*, 'having a good name,' 'celebrated.'

Comparison of Adjectives.

79. The comparative of an adjective is formed by adding to the positive the termination تر *tar*; the superlative, by adding ترین *tarīn*: *e.g.*

بہ *bĕh*, 'good,'	بہتر *bĕh-tar*, 'better,'	بہترین *bĕh-tarīn*, 'best,'
بد *bad*, 'bad,'	بدتر *bad-tar* (or بتر *bat-tar*), 'worse,'	بدترین *bad-tarīn* / بترین *bat-tarīn* 'worst,'
فاضل *fāẕil*, 'learned,'	فاضلتر *fāẕil-tar*, 'more learned,'	فاضلترین *fāẕil-tarīn*, 'most learned.'

Rem. a. The suffixes تر and ترین are frequently added to the Arabic superlative (§ 106); *e.g.* اَوْلٰی تر *aulā-tar*, 'better,' اَوْلٰی ترین *aulā-tarīn*, 'best.' Such forms may be regarded as double comparatives and superlatives.

Rem. b. The suffix اَ *ā* adds the idea of intensiveness to the signification of an adjective; as خُوشا *khwushā*, 'very happy,' from خُوش 'happy.'

THE INFINITIVE AND VERBAL NOUN.

80. Persian infinitives are of rare occurrence in Urdū, but derivatives from them, as also from the verbal root, are frequently met with.

81. The infinitive always ends in one of the syllables دن *dan* or تن *tan*; as دِیدن *dīdan*, 'to see;' گُفتن *guftan*, 'to speak.'

82. The root (which is also the form of the singular imperative) is commonly used as a noun of action or abstract substantive. To obtain the root from the infinitive, it is sufficient, occasionally, to simply drop the characteristic termination of the latter: *e.g.* پرور *parwar*, from پرورْدن 'to protect;' کن *kan*, from کندن 'to dig.' But, generally, the letter immediately preceding the termination is either dropped as well, or changed into some other letter or letters; *e.g.* دان *dān*, from دانِستن 'to know;' دار *dār*, from داشتن 'to have or possess;' باز *bāz*, from بازِیدن 'to play,' etc.; ساز *sāz*, from ساختن 'to make;' کُن *kun*, from کَردن 'to do or act;' بنْد *band*, from بستن 'to bind or fasten;' گو and گوی *go*, from گُفتن 'to speak.'

VERBAL ADJECTIVES.

83. *Past Participles* are formed from infinitives, by changing the final ن into silent ہ. They may have both an

active and a passive signification (though more commonly the latter), and may be used either as adjectives or substantives: *e.g.* دِیدہ *dīda*, 'seeing,' 'seen,' 'the eye' (from دِیدن 'to see'); پرورْدہ *parwarda*, 'protected,' 'a protégé.' The past participles of some neuter verbs generally have the signification of the present part.; as خُفْتہ *khufta*, 'sleeping,' 'asleep' (from خُفْتن 'to sleep'); شایِسْتہ *shāyista*, 'decent,' 'proper,' 'becoming' (from شایِسْتن 'to become,' 'to be worth').

84. Passive participles are of frequent occurrence in composition with nouns, forming therewith *determinative* compounds (like the *Tatpurusha* of the Sanskrit): *e.g.* سال خُورْدہ *sāl-khwurda*, 'old in years;' سایہ پرورْدہ *sāya-parwarda*, 'brought up in the shade,' 'delicately reared.' Occasionally the final ہ of participles ending in دہ is dropped; as زنْگ آلود *zang-ālūd* (= زنْگ آلودہ), 'covered with rust,' 'rusty.'

Rem. The participle ending in تہ *ta* does not appear to be so used; but it seems probable that many words, as دوسْت 'a friend,' بخْت 'fortune,' مسْت 'intoxicated' (= Sanskrit मत्त), which are now used as substantives and adjectives, were originally past participles.

85. *Active Participles*, adjectives, and nouns of agency, are formed:—*a*) By adding to the roots of verbs the terminations:

1) ا— *ā*; as دانا *dānā*, 'knowing,' 'learned,' 'wise,' 'a sage' (from the root of دانِسْتن 'to know'); بینا *bīnā*, 'seeing,' 'seer' (from بِین *bīn*, the root of دِیدن 'to see'); گویا *goyā*, 'speaking,' 'speaker,' 'an orator' (from the root of گُفْتن 'to speak'); تُوانا *tuwānā*, 'powerful' (from the root of تُوانِسْتن 'to be able'). Participles so formed sometimes

have a *passive*, as well as an *active*, signification; *e.g.* پذیرا *pazīrā*, 'accepting,' and 'accepted' (from the root of پذیرفتن 'to accept').

2) ان– *ān*; as جویان *joyān*, 'seeking,' 'seeker' (from the root of جُستن 'to seek'); روان *rawān*, 'going' (from the root of رفتن 'to go'); باران *bārān*, 'raining,' 'rain' (from the root of باریدن 'to rain'); گویان *goyān*, 'speaking,' 'speaker,' 'an orator' (from the root of گفتن 'to speak').

3) نده– *anda* (or *inda*); as رونده *ravanda*, 'going,' 'goer' (from the root of رفتن 'to go'); کُنِنده *kuninda*, 'doing,' 'doer' (from the root of کردن 'to do'); جوینده *joyanda*, 'seeking,' 'seeker' (from the root of جُستن 'to seek').

Rem. This suffix may be attached to the root of any verb, and, like the preceding suffix *ān*, often forms appellatives as well as present participles. Like the corresponding suffix والا *wālā*, of the Hindī, it is sometimes added to nouns also; *e.g.* شرمِنده *sharminda*, 'ashamed,' 'bashful' (from شرم 'shame'). It sometimes takes the form ند–; as پرند *parand* (= پرنده), 'flying,' 'a bird,' چرند *charand* (= چرنده), 'grazing,' 'an animal.' Occasionally, too, it would appear to take the form ُنده–; as فرخُنده *farkhunda*, 'happy,' 'fortunate.' The original suffix appears to have been the same as the Sanskrit अन्त् *ant*.

b) By adding the root of a verb to a noun, and thus forming a *determinative* compound (corresponding to the *Tatpurusha* of the Sanskrit). The root governs the noun:

1) In the *accusative*; as کاردان *kār-dān*, 'knowing work,' 'skilful;' زمِیندار *zamīn-dār*, 'holding or possessing land,' 'a landholder;' مالگذار *māl-guzār*, 'paying revenue,' 'one who pays revenue,' 'a tenant;' نعلبند *na'l-band*, 'fastening or fixing a shoe' (on a horse, etc.), 'a farrier.'

2) In the *ablative*; as شمشیرزن *shamsher-zan*, 'striking with the sword,' 'a swordsman' (from the root of زدن 'to strike').

3) In the *locative*; as تخت نِشِين *takht-nishīn*, 'sitting on a throne,' 'a king' (from the root of نِشستن 'to sit'); صُبح خيز *subh-khez*, 'rising in the early morning,' 'one who so rises,' and thence, 'a morning-thief' (from the root of خيزِيدن 'to rise').

Rem. a. The root in the same construction often gives the signification of the *passive* participle: *e.g.* خانه ساز *khāna-sāz*, 'made in the house,' 'home-made;' خُدا بخش *Khudā bakhsh*, 'given by God' (from the root of بخشِيدن 'to bestow'); رُوشِناس *rū-shinās*, 'known by the face,' 'an acquaintance' (from the root of شِناختن 'to know,' etc.).

Rem. b. In Urdū a Persian root is occasionally joined to a Hindī word, which, if it end in *ā*, is inflected: *e.g.* گهڑِي ساز 'a watch-maker;' سونٹے بردار 'a mace-bearer' (بردار being the root of برداشتن 'to carry,' etc.); ٹهٹهے باز 'one who repeatedly plays jokes,' 'a jester;' کوڑي باز 'one who plies the whip,' 'a whipper.'

c) By adding a passive participle to a noun; as جهان دِيده *jahān-dīda*, 'one who has seen the world,' 'experienced;' غم خُورده *gam-khwurda*, 'one who has suffered sorrow.'

d) By adding the suffixes تار *tār* and دار *dār* to apocopated infinitives (the former to those ending in تن, and the latter to those ending in دن), and eliding the ت or د of the infinitive termination; *e.g.* خواستار *khwāstār* (for خواست تار), 'one who makes a request,' 'a petitioner' (from خواستن 'to wish,' etc.); خرِيدار *kharīdār* (for خرِيددار), 'a purchaser' (from خرِيدن 'to purchase').

Rem. These suffixes sometimes form adjectives with a *passive* signification; as گِرِفتار *giriftār*, 'taken captive,' 'captive' (from گِرِفتن 'to take or seize'). They are also used to form abstract substantives (§ 97).

Suffixes Forming Nouns of Agency.

86. Nouns of agency, and adjectives, are also formed by adding to substantives the following suffixes:

1) کار *kār*; دستکار *dast-kār*, 'a handicraftsman,' 'an artificer' (from دست 'hand'); جفاکار *jafā-kār*, 'an oppressor' (from جفا 'oppression'); پیشکار *pesh-kār*, 'an assistant,' 'an agent' (from پیش 'before').

2) گار *gār*; as خدمتگار *khidmat-gār*, 'a servant' (from خدمت 'service'); پرهیزگار *parhez-gār*, 'abstinent,' 'a devout man' (from پرهیز 'abstinence'); گناه گار *gunāh-gār*, 'an offender,' 'a sinner' (from گناه 'sin'); ستم گار *sitam-gār*, 'unjust,' 'an oppressor' (from ستم 'oppression'); یادگار *yādgār*, 'a memorial,' 'a monument' (from یاد 'remembrance').

Rem. The idea of agency is sometimes not very prominent: *e.g.* روزگار *roz-gār*, 'time,' 'the world,' 'fortune' (from روز 'day').

3) گر *gar*; as آهنگر *āhan-gar*, 'a blacksmith' (from آهن 'iron') جلدگر *jild-gar*, 'a book-binder' (from جلد 'a skin,' 'a volume'); زرگر *zar-gar*, 'a gold-smith' (from زر 'gold'); شیشه گر *shīsha-gar*, 'a glass-blower' (from شیشه 'glass'); ستم گر *sitam-gar*, 'an oppressor' (from ستم 'oppression').

Rem. کار *kār* is, originally, a *noun*, signifying 'work,' 'action;' but it is commonly used as a suffix, denoting 'work,' or 'the doing, or doer of, a work.' In گار the ک of کار is softened into گ, these letters being interchangeable. The suffix گر is simply a contraction of گار; it most frequently indicates 'a worker,' 'a maker,' but it is interchangeable with both کار and گار. Occasionally گر has the signification of 'possessor;' *e.g.* توانگر *tuwāngar*, 'one possessing power,' 'rich.' These affixes correspond to the Sanskrit कार and कर at the end of compounds; *e.g.* अन्धकार, दन्तकार, दिनकर, दुष्कर.

4) چي *chī*; as باورچي *bāwar-chī* (*lit.* 'one possessing trust or confidence'), 'a cook' (from باور 'trust, confidence'); مشعلچي *mash'al-chī*, 'a torch-bearer' (and, in India) 'a cook's mate' (from مشعل 'a torch'). If the final letter of the noun be ة (silent), it is dropped before the termination is added; as خزانچي *khazān-chī*, 'a treasurer' (from خزانه 'treasure').

Rem. This suffix is derived from the Turkish.

5) بان *bān*, or وان *wān*, signifying 'keeping, watching, or guarding;' as باغبان *bāg-bān*, 'a gardener' (from باغ 'a garden'); دربان *dar-bān*, and دروان *dar-wān*, 'a gatekeeper,' 'a porter' (from در 'a gate'); گريبان *girebān*, 'the collar of a garment' (*lit.* 'that which protects the گري or 'neck'); مهربان *mihrbān*, 'benevolent,' 'affectionate,' 'kind' (*lit.* 'guarding or keeping مهر, or affection').

Rem. This suffix is occasionally attached to Hindī words also: *e.g.* گاڑي وان *gāṛī-wān*, or گاڑي بان *gāṛī-bān* (= گاڑي والا) 'a cart man, or carter.' The original suffix is doubtless وان (related to the Sanskrit वन्त् *vant*), the letters ب and و being interchangeable.

87. Possessive Adjectives and substantives are formed by adding to substantives the following suffixes, denoting 'possession,' 'affection,' or 'fullness':

1) آور or اور *āwar*; as زبان آور *zabān-āwar*, 'possessing speech,' 'eloquent' (from زبان 'speech'); زوراور *zor-āwar*, 'possessing strength,' 'strong,' 'an athlete' (from زور 'strength'); دلاور *dil-āwar*, 'possessing heart,' 'brave,' 'warlike' (from دل 'heart'); بختاور *bakht-āwar*, 'fortunate' (from بخت 'fortune'). This affix is sometimes contracted

to ـار *ār*; *e.g.* سالار *sāl-ār* (*lit.* 'possessed of years,' 'old,' and thence,) 'a chief, or leader'; دِيوار *dīw-ār*, 'a wall' (*lit.* 'possessing a stratum, or foundation,' from دِيو, for داو, by *imāla*, or change of vowel).

Rem. In some words the suffix *ār* is redundant: *e.g.* زنگار *zang-ār* (= زنگ), 'rust,' also written زنگال *zang-āl*, the letters ر and ل being interchangeable. So also دِيوال for دِيوار 'a wall.'

2) ور *war*; as جانور 'possessing life,' 'an animal' (from جان 'life'); سرور *sar-war*, 'a chief, or leader' (from سر 'head'); كِينه ور *kīna-war*, 'rancorous,' 'malevolent' (from كِينه 'rancour'); هُنروَر *hunar-war*, 'possessing virtue or merit,' 'skilful,' 'accomplished' (from هُنر 'virtue,' 'merit'). This suffix occasionally takes the form ـور *ūr*; *e.g.* دستُور *dastūr*, 'a prime-minister,' etc. (from دست 'hand,' 'power,' etc.); رنجُور *ranjūr*, 'vexed,' 'afflicted' (from رنج 'vexation,' 'sorrow'); مزدُور *muzdūr* (but, in India, *mazdur*), 'a hireling' (from مُزد 'hire').

3) وار *wār*; as اُميدوار *umed-wār*, 'having hope,' 'hopeful' (from اُميد 'hope'); سوگوار *sog-wār*, 'having grief,' 'mourning,' 'afflicted' (from سوگ 'grief,' 'sorrow').

4) يار *yār*; as بختيار *bakht-yār*, 'fortunate' (from بخت 'fortune'); شہريار *shahr-yār*, 'possessor, or lord of the city,' 'a king' (from شہر 'city'); هوشيار *hosh-yār*, 'possessing sense,' 'sensible,' 'prudent' (from هوش 'sense,' etc.). In a few words this suffix is contracted to ـير *er*: *e.g.* دِلير *diler*, 'possessing heart,' 'bold,' 'valiant,' = دلاور *dil-āwar*.

Rem. The suffix آور or ـاور *āwar* is properly (though not used as) the root of the verb آوردن 'to bring;' and to this is related the suffix ور, for بر, the root of the verb بُردن 'to bear or carry,' which, when compounded with the preposition آ, becomes آوَرْدن, ب and و being interchangeable. From ور again, by lengthening the vowel, is formed the suffix وار. The suffix يار is but another form of وار or ور.

5) سار *sār*; as شرمْسار *sharm-sār*, 'bashful,' 'modest' (from شرم 'shame').

6) منْد *mand*; دانِشمنْد *dānishmand*, 'possessing learning, or wisdom,' 'learned,' 'wise' (from دانِش 'knowledge,' etc.); دَولتمنْد *daulat-mand*, 'wealthy' (from دَولت 'wealth'); عقلمنْد *akl-mand*, 'sensible,' 'wise' (from عقل 'understanding'). This suffix sometimes takes the forms ـُومنْد *ūmand*, and ـُمنْد *umand*: *e.g.* برُومنْد *barūmand*, 'fruitful,' 'fertile,' 'successful,' 'happy' (from بر 'fruit'); ارجُمنْد *arjumand* (and ارْجمنْد *arjmand*), 'precious,' 'esteemed' (from ارْج 'price').

Rem. منْد corresponds to the Sanskrit मन्त् *mant.* It occasionally also takes the form وَنْد, the Sanskrit वन्त् *want.*

7) گِين *gīn*; as شرمْگِين *sharm-gīn*, 'abashed,' 'bashful;' خِشمْگِين *khishm-gīn*, 'inflamed with anger,' 'irate' (from خِشم 'anger'); غمْگِين *gam-gīn*, 'sorrowful' (from غم 'sorrow').

Rem. The original form of گِين is آگِين *āgīn*, derived from the verb آگنْدن, and signifies 'filled.' Added to nouns it sometimes serves to express a *quality*, as well as to form a possessive.

8) ناک *nāk*; as غضبْناک *gazab-nāk*, 'inflamed with wrath,' 'enraged' (from غضب 'rage,' 'violence'); دردْناک *dard-nak*, 'painful' (from درْد 'pain'); هَولْناک *haul-nāk*, 'terrible,' 'fearful' (from هَول 'fear,' 'terror').

Rem. ناک more commonly forms adjectives of *quality*. It would appear to be related to the Sanskrit नश् *naj.* It is occasionally added to verbal roots and adjectives also.

88. Possessive Adjectives are also formed by prefixing to a substantive:

1) با *bā*, signifying 'possessed of,' 'according to;' as با آبرو *bā-ābrū*, 'honourable' (from آبرو 'honour'); باتمیز *bā-tamīz*, 'discriminating,' 'judicious' (from تمیز 'discrimination,' 'judgment'); باقاعده *bā-ḳā'ida*, 'regular' (from قاعده 'a rule'); باوفا *bā-wafā*, 'faithful' (from وفا, 'faith').

2) صاحب *ṣāḥib* (an Arabic noun, signifying 'possessor,' 'owner'); as صاحب دل *ṣāḥib-dil*, 'pious,' 'godly' (*lit.* 'possessor of the heart'); صاحب جمال *ṣāḥib-jamāl*, 'beautiful,' 'handsome' (from جمال 'beauty'); صاحب نصیب *ṣāḥib-naṣīb*, 'fortunate' (from نصیب 'destiny,' 'fortune').

89. Negative Adjectives, denoting privation, or the absence of a quality, are formed by prefixing to a noun one of the following prepositions or adverbs, corresponding in signification to the English *un*, *in*, *dis*, *less*, etc.:

1) بے *be*, 'without' (always prefixed to substantives); as بے پروا *be-parwā*, 'fearless,' 'careless;' بے اِنصاف *be-inṣāf*, 'unjust;' بے وفا *be-wafā*, 'faithless.'

2) کم *kam*, 'less,' 'lacking' (prefixed to substantives); as کم بخت *kam-bakht*, 'luckless;' کم زور *kam-zor*, 'powerless,' 'feeble;' کم ہمّت *kam-himmat*, 'spiritless,' 'unaspiring.'

3) نا *nā*, 'not' (prefixed, originally, to adjectives alone, but, at the present time, to substantives also); as نا أمید *nā-umed*, 'hopeless,' 'despairing;' نا پاک *nā-pāk*, 'unclean;' نا خوش *na-khwush*, 'displeased;' نا اہل *nā-ahl*, 'unworthy.'

4) غیر *gair*, 'other,' 'different,' 'opposite' (borrowed from the Arabic, and used before substantives and adjectives); as غیر اِنصاف *gair-inṣāf*, 'unjust;' غیر حاضِر *gair-ḥāẓir*, 'not present,' 'absent;' غیر مُمکِن *gair-mumkin*, 'impossible.'

5) لا *lā*, 'not' (also borrowed from the Arabic, and prefixed chiefly to substantives, or adjectives employed as substantives); as لاچار *lā-chār*, 'helpless,' 'remediless;' لاجواب *lā-jawāb*, 'answerless;' لاوارِث *lā-wāriṣ*, 'heirless,' 'unclaimed.'

90. Adjectives of Similitude are formed by adding to substantives the suffixes:

1) آسا *āsā*, سا *sā*, or سان *sān*; *e.g.* شیرآسا *sher-āsā*, or شیرسا *sher-sā*, or شیرسان *sher-sān*, 'like a tiger,' 'tigrish;' مَردآسا *mard-āsā*, 'like a man,' 'manly;' فِرِشتہ سان *firishta-sān*, 'angelic.'

Rem. The origin of these suffixes is the verb سُودن, whence by prefixing the preposition آ, the verb آسودن is derived.

2) سار *sār*; as خاکسار *khāk-sār*, 'like dust,' 'humble;' سگسار *sag-sār*, 'dog-like,' 'miserly,' 'a miser.'

Rem. سار affixed to substantives and adjectives is occasionally synonymous with سر 'head;' *e.g.* سگسار *sag-sār*, 'dog-headed,' 'an inhabitant of a region where the inhabitants have heads like dogs;' سبُکسار *sabuk-sār* (= سبُکسر), 'light-headed,' 'unsteady,' 'foolish.'

3) وار *wār*: as بُزُرگوار *buzurg-wār*, 'like the great,' 'great,' 'excellent;' ذرّہ وار *zarra-wār*, 'atom-like,' 'humble.'

4) گان *gān*; as خُدایگان *khudā'egān*, 'like God' (a title of kings and great men), 'most excellent,' 'omnipotent.'

Rem. The signification of 'similitude,' in the case of both وار and گان, often passes into that of 'fitness,' 'worthiness' (see § 91, 2, 3).

5) مان *mān*; as آسمان *āsmān*, 'like a mill-stone' (revolving), 'heaven' (from آس 'a mill-stone').[1]

[1] Such is the derivation of *āsmān* according to native scholars. The Zend form of the word is *ashman*, the Sanskrit अश्मन् *aśman*.

Rem. ماں is used in some Persian words with the signification of 'possessing,' but is not found in Urdū. In the word شادماں it does not signify 'possession,' as Professors Monier Williams and Dowson affirm, but is *redundant*. It never can signify 'possession' when joined to an adjective.

6) وش *wash*; as ماہوش *māh-wash*, 'like the moon.'

7) وند *wand*; as خداوند *khudā-wand*, 'like God,' 'lord,' 'possessor;' whence, by contraction, خاوند, also signifying 'lord,' 'master,' 'husband.'

91. Adjectives denoting *fitness* or *worthiness* are formed by attaching to substantives the suffixes:

1) ـانہ *āna*; as شاہانہ *shāhāna*, 'befitting a king,' 'royal,' 'splendid;' مردانہ *mardāna*, 'becoming a man,' 'manly.'

Rem. a. Such is the teaching of the native grammarians; but it appears far more probable that in these words, as also in دیوانہ ـ بزرگانہ عاشقانہ ـ شاگردانہ, and many more, the *relative* suffix ـہ (§ 92, 6) is added to the *plurals* شاہاں ـ مرداں, etc.: ـانہ also occurs as a relative suffix.

Rem. b. From the signification of 'fitness,' arises that of 'manner,' which is also common to this suffix, and hence its use in forming adverbs: *e.g.* شاہانہ 'royally,' مردانہ 'in a manly manner;' غرضانہ 'interestedly.'

2) گاں *gāṅ*; as شایگاں *shā'e-gāṅ* (for شاہگاں), 'worthy of a king;' رایگاں *rā'e-gāṅ* (for راہگاں), 'fit to throw on the road,' 'a thing found on the road,' hence, 'a thing obtained, or lost, for nothing,' 'anything worthless.'

3) وار *wār*, or وارہ *wāra*; as شاہوار *shāh-wār*, 'worthy of a king,' 'princely,' 'royal;' بزرگوار *buzurg-wār*, 'worthy of the great,' 'great,' 'excellent;' گوشوار *gosh-wār*, or گوشوارہ

gosh-wāra, 'suitable to the ear,' 'an earring;' ماهوار *māh-wār*, or ماهواره *māhwāra*, 'adapted to a month,' 'monthly stipend,' etc., 'monthly.'

Rem. From the signification of 'fitness,' etc., arises that of 'measure,' 'quantity;' as جامه وار *jāma-wār*, ('*fit* to make,' or) '*sufficient* to make a garment' = جامه بهر *jāma-bhar*. The original form of this suffix is بر, corresponding to the Sanskrit and Hindī भर् *bhar*.

4) ـي *ī*, added to infinitives only; as خوردني *khwur-danī*, 'fit to eat,' 'eatable' (from خوردن 'to eat'); گفتني *guftanī*, 'fit to utter;' شدني *shudanı*, 'fit to be.'

92. Relative Adjectives and Substantives are formed by adding to substantives the suffixes:

1) ـال *āl*, (used to form substantives); as چنگال *chang-āl*, 'a claw' (from چنگ 'bent, curved'); دنبال *dumb-al*, 'the extremity of a thing,' 'a tail' (from دنب = دم 'a tail').

2) ـان *ān*; as بيابان *biyābān*, 'a desert' (from بےآب 'without water'); پايان *pāyān*, 'end' (of the foot), 'extremity' (from پاي 'foot'); پيشان *peshan*, 'the front or foremost part' (from پيش 'before;' from پيشان is derived پيشاني *peshanī*, 'the forehead').

Rem. The suffix ـان also forms *patronymics* and *relative nouns of place*: *e.g.* ايران *Īrān* and توران *Tūrān* (from Īr and Tūr, sons of Farīdūn); اسپهان *ispahān*, Ispahān (for سپاهان *sipāhān*, from سپاه 'an army'). It is sometimes redundant: *e.g.* آبادان = آباد 'inhabited,' 'peopled.'

3) ـانه *āna*; as دستانه *dast-āna*, 'a glove' (from دست 'hand'); مردانه *mard-āna* 'pertaining to man;' كاشانه *kāsh-āna*, 'a glass-house,' thence generally, 'a house;' سالانه *sāl-una*, 'pertaining to a year,' 'yearly.'

4) گاں *gāṅ*; as گِرْدگاں *gird-gāṅ*, 'a walnut' (from گِرْد 'round'); دِہْگاں *dih-gāṅ* = دِہْقاں 'pertaining to a village,' 'a villager' (دِہْقاں is the Arabic form of the word); بازرگاں *bāzar-gāṅ* (from بازارگاں), 'a merchant.'

5) واں *wāṅ*, and وں *wan* (but in Urdū generally occurring under the form ـُوں *ūṅ*); as ہمایُوں *humāyūṅ*, 'fortunate,' 'happy' (from ہُماي 'a bird of happy omen,' 'Humāy'); گرْدُوں *gardūṅ*, 'the celestial orb,' 'a wheel' (from گرد 'revolving'); واژُوں *wāzhūṅ*, 'inverted,' 'unfortunate' (from واژ 'inverted').

Rem. The suffixes وَنْد and ـاوَنْد are also *relative*, and are common in Persian, although not frequently occurring in Urdū: *e.g.* خُداوَنْد 'pertaining to God,' 'a lord;' خويشاوَنْد 'pertaining, or related, to self,' 'a kinsman.' These suffixes are all no doubt derived from the Sanskrit वन्त् *vant*, nom. वान् *vān*.

6) ـه *a*; as أُسْتُرَه *ustura*, 'a razor' (from أُسْتُر the root of أُسْتُرْدن 'to shave'); دسْتَه *dasta*, 'a handle' (from دسْت 'hand'); زبانه *zabāna*, 'flame' (of fire, etc.), from زباں 'tongue;' دهانه *dahāna*, 'the bit of a bridle' (from دهاں 'mouth'); روزه *roza*, 'pertaining to a day' (from روز 'day'); ساله *sāla*, 'pertaining to a year;' يكْ طرْفه *yak-ṭarfa*, 'pertaining to one side,' 'one-sided' (from يكْ طرف 'one side').

Rem. The suffix ـه is sometimes redundant, as in چارہ *chāra*, كِينه *kīna*, آوازه *āwāza*.

7) ـِيں *īṅ*, denoting, besides *relation*, the *material* of which a thing is made; as زرِيں *zarīṅ*, 'golden' (from زر 'gold'); رنْگِيں *rangīṅ*, 'coloured' (from رنْگ 'colour'); سنْگِيں *sangīṅ*, 'of stone;' نمكِيں *namakīṅ*, 'salty;' پوسْتِيں *postīṅ*, 'a cloak or jacket made of a skin' (پوسْت).

Rem. In lieu of ـِین the form ـِینه sometimes occurs: *e.g.* پشمینه *pashmīna*, 'made of wool,' 'woollen;' گنجینه *ganjīna*, 'that which is obtained from a repository of treasure,' 'a treasury.' The suffix ـِین is also used in forming the superlative degree, and is added to many words to form degrees of comparison: as پیشین *peshīn*, 'anterior;' پسین *pasīn*, 'posterior.' It is sometimes redundant: *e.g.* اوّلین *awwalīn* = اول 'first.'

8) ـِي *ī*, forming *patronymics* and other *relative* adjectives; as پارسي *pārsī*, 'of Persia,' 'Persian;' هِنْدِي *hindī*, 'of India,' 'Indian;' شاهِي *shāhī*, 'pertaining to a king,' 'royal;' آتِشِي *ātishī*, 'of fire,' 'fiery;' خونِي *khūnī*, 'sanguinary,' 'bloody,' 'a murderer.' If the final letter of the noun be ـَه *a*, it is changed into گ before the suffix; *e.g.* خانگِي *khānagī* (or *khāngī*) 'pertaining to the house,' 'domestic.'

Rem. ـِي is occasionally redundant, chiefly at the end of Arabic words: *e.g.* اِعْتِقادِي *'itikādī* = اِعْتِقاد 'to believe firmly;' زِيادتِي *ziyādatī* = زِيادت 'increase,' 'excess.'

93. Adjectives denoting *colour*, or similitude of colour, are formed by means of the suffixes فام *fām*, and گُون *gūn*, as سِياه فام *siyāh-fām*, 'blackish;' لَعْل فام *la'l-fām*, 'ruby-coloured;' گُلگون *gul-gūn*, 'rose-coloured;' لاله گون *lāla-gūn*, 'tulip-coloured.'

Rem. فام may also take the forms وام *wām*, پام *pām*, and بام *bām*; and in place of گون the form گُونه is occasionally found.

94. Adjectives and substantives denoting *fellowship*, *companionship*, *equality*, etc., are formed by prefixing to a substantive the adverb هم *ham*, signifying 'together,' 'same,' and corresponding to the English 'fellow,' 'mate,'

'con-,' 'co-;' as هم درد *ham-dard*, 'fellow-sufferer,' 'sympathetic' (from درد 'pain'); هم جنس *ham-jins*, 'of the same genus, or class,' 'congener,' 'homogeneous;' هم عمر *ham-'umr*, 'of the same age,' 'coeval;' هم سبق *ham-sabak*, 'a class-fellow' (from سبق 'a lesson').

Rem. هم may also occur as the latter part of a compound, a preposition being prefixed to it: *e.g.* باهم *bāham*, 'together,' 'along with;' برهم *bar-ham*, 'upon one another,' 'confused' 'jumbled,' 'angry,' درهم *dar-ham*, 'one under another,' 'higgledy-piggledy,' 'confused,' 'angry.'

95. Nouns of Place, or اسمائے مکان *asmā'ĕ makān*, called also اسمائے ظروف *asmā'ĕ ẕurūf* ('nouns that express the *vessels* which contain things'), are formed: *a*) by placing after a noun one of the following nouns:

1) آباد *ābād*, 'populated by,' 'city;' as اِلٰہ آباد *ilāh-ābād*, 'the city of God,' (Anglice) 'Allahabad;' اکبر آباد *akbar-ābād*, 'the city of Akbar,' 'Agra;' شاہ جہان آباد *shāh-jahān-ābād*, 'the city of Shāh-jahān,' 'Dehli.'

2) گاہ *gāh*, 'place;' as شِکارگاہ *shikār-gāh*, 'hunting-ground;' عِبادت گاہ *'ibādat-gāh*, 'place of worship;' خواب گاہ *khwāb-gāh*, 'sleeping-place,' 'bed-chamber.'

Rem. گاہ also signifies 'time,' and is used to form *nouns of time* (اسمائے زمان *asmā'ĕ zamān*); as سحرگاہ *sahar-gāh*, 'morning' (from سحر 'dawn'); شام گاہ *shām gāh*, 'eventide' (from شام 'evening').

3) خانہ *khāna*, 'house;' as کارخانہ *kār-khāna*, 'a workshop;' کُتُب خانہ *kutub-khāna*, 'a library' (from کُتُب pl. of کِتاب 'a book'); قَید خانہ *kaid-khāna*, 'a prison' (from قید 'imprisonment:' in India the compound جیل خانہ, from the English 'jail,' is also commonly used).

Rem. The words آباد, گاہ, and خانہ must not be regarded as suffixes.

The construction is that of the inverted genitive (§ 73), and forms determinative compounds.

b) By adding the following suffixes to nouns:

1) ـِستان *istān* (the Sanskrit स्थान *sthāna*); as گُلِستان *gul-istān*, 'a rose-garden;' کوهِستان *koh-istān*, 'a mountainous region;' ریگِستان *reg-istān*, 'a sandy place.' If the noun end in a vowel, the initial vowel of the suffix is dropped: *e.g.* بُوستان *būstān*, 'a place of fragrance,' 'a garden.'

2) شن *shan*; as گُلشن *gul-shan*, 'a rose-bed, or rose-garden.'

3) نا *nā*, or نائے *nā'e*; as آبنائے *'āb-nā'e* 'a strait;' تنگنائے *tang-nā'e*, 'a narrow place,' 'a defile,' 'a strait' (also تنگنا *tangnā*).

A variety of the noun of place is the *noun of multitude* (اِسمِ کثرت *ismĕ kaṣrat*), which designates the place where the object signified by the noun to which the suffix is added, is found in large numbers or quantities. It is formed by means of the following suffixes:

1) زار *zār*; as گُلزار *gul-zār*, 'a place where roses abound,' 'a rose-garden;' سبزه زار *sabza-zār*, 'a place where verdure abounds,' 'a meadow;' بازار *bā-zār* (contracted from ابازار), 'a place where provisions (ابا) abound,' 'a market.'

2) سار *sār*; شاخسار *shā<u>kh</u>-sār*, 'abounding in branches,' 'a place where branchy trees abound;' نمکسار *namak-sār*, 'abounding in salt,' 'salty,' 'a salt-mine;' رُخسار *ru<u>kh</u>-sār*, 'the cheek,' 'the face.'

3) بار *bār*; as سنگبار *sang-bār*, 'a place abounding in stone,' 'a stone-pit;' جویبار *jo'e-bār*, 'a place abounding in streams;' زنگبار *zang-bār*, 'the country inhabited by the Ethiopians;' 'Zanguebar.'

Rem. بار is related to the Sanskrit वार *vāra*, 'a multitude.' It has other significations also; *e.g.* *a*) 'permission,' 'approach to royalty,' as in دربار *darbār*, 'the court or levee of a prince:' *b*) 'time,' 'turn,' as in يكبار *yak-bār*, 'one-time,' 'once.' With the suffix بار must not be confounded the root of the verb باريدن 'to rain,' which occurs in compounds: *e.g.* گوهربار *gauhar-bār*, 'raining or scattering pearls.'

4) لاخ *lākh*; as سنگلاخ *sang-lākh*, 'a place abounding in stone;' ديولاخ *dev-lākh* (or *de'o-lākh*), 'a place abounding in demons.'

96. Connected with the *noun of place* is the 'noun which is the *vessel* or *receptacle* (ظرف) of a thing,' and which is formed by means of the suffix دان *dān*; *e.g.* نمكدان *namak-dān*, 'a salt-cellar;' شمعدان *shama'-dān*, 'a candle-stick;' قلمدان *kalam-dān*, 'a pen-case.'

Rem. This suffix is added to Hindī nouns also, and may take the form داني; *e.g.* اگالدان *ugāl-dān*, (or اگالداني *ugāl-dānī*), 'a spit-box;' پيكدان *pīk-dān* (or پيكداني *pīk-dānī*), 'a spittoon'—properly, 'a vessel for receiving the *ugāl* or *pīk*, *i.e.* the juice of the betel-leaf which is spit out.' Nouns (masc.) ending in *ā* are inflected before the affix is added: *e.g.* چوهے دان *chūhe-dān*, 'a mouse-trap, or rat-trap.'

97. Abstract Nouns are of two kinds: *a*) those which denote *states* or *acts*, and are *verbal*, being derived from infinitives, or roots of verbs:

1) By dropping the final ن of infinitives; as خريد *kharīd*, 'purchase,' from خريدن 'to buy;' درخواست *dar-khwāst*, 'request,' from درخواستن 'to desire or request;' فروخت *farokht*, 'sale,' from فروختن 'to sell.'

2) By adding the suffixes تار *tār* and دار *dār* to apocopated infinitives; the former to those which end in تن *tan*,

and the latter to those ending in دن *dan*; *e.g.* گُفتار *guftār*, 'saying,' 'speech;' رفتار *raftār*, 'gait,' 'procedure;' ديدار *dīdār*, 'seeing,' 'sight.'

3) By adding to the roots of verbs the suffix ـَاك *āk*; as تپاك *tapāk*, 'agitation;' خُوراك *khwurāk*, 'food;' سوزاك *sozāk*, 'inflammation,' 'strangury.'

4) By adding the suffix ـَان *ān* to verbal roots; as فرمان *farmān*, 'command' (the Sanskrit प्रमाण *pramāṇa*); باران *bārān*, 'rain.'

5) By adding the suffix ـِش *ish* to verbal roots; as خواهِش *khwāhish*, 'desire,' 'wish;' پرورِش *parwarish*, 'nurture,' 'support;' بينِش *bīnish*, 'seeing,' 'discernment;' دانِش *dānish*, 'knowledge,' 'wisdom.'

Rem. This suffix often forms abstract nouns of *quality* also.

6) By adding the suffix ـَه *a* to verbal roots; as لرزه *larza* = لرزِش 'tremor;' ناله *nāla* = نالِش 'lamentation;' سُفَيده *sufaida* = سُفَيدِي 'whiteness.'

b) Those which denote *qualities*: they are formed by means of the suffixes:

1) ـَا *ā*, added to adjectives; as گرما *garmā*, 'heat,' 'summer;' سرما *sarmā*, 'cold,' 'winter.'

2) ـِي *ī*, added chiefly to adjectives, primitive and verbal; as دوستي *dostī*, 'friendship;' نيكِي *nekī*, 'goodness;' سُفَيدِي *sufaidī*, 'whiteness;' دانائِي *dānā'ī*, 'wisdom;' خِدمتگارِي *khidmatgārī*, 'service;' عقلمندِي *'aklmandī*, 'sense,' 'wisdom.' If the final letter of a Persian adjective be ـَه *a*, it is changed into گ *g* before the termination is added; *e.g.* بندگِي *bandagī*, 'service;' تازگِي *tāzagī*, 'freshness;' چسپيدگِي *chaspīdagī*, 'adhesiveness,' 'attachment' (from

چسپیده the pass. part. of چسپیدن 'to stick'); but if the adjective be an Arabic word, the final *h* is changed to *t* (or rather the original ة *t*, which on account of the loss of the final vowel became ه *h*, is restored); *e.g.* زِيَادتي *ziyā-datī*, 'excess,' from زِيَاده *ziyāda*, 'more,' 'excessive.'

98. The Diminutive is formed by means of the following suffixes:

1) ـَک *ak* (used chiefly with nouns denoting animate things); as مردک *mardak*, 'a manikin,' 'a contemptible man;' طِفلک *tiflak*, 'a little child;' اسپک *aspak*, 'a small horse,' 'a pony;' دستک *dastak*, 'a small hand,' 'a tap at a door;' زنبورک *zambūrak*, 'a small gun or swivel.'

2) چه *cha*, or ـِیچه *īcha*, or زه *za*, or ـِیزه *īza* (چ being interchangeable with ج, ز, and ژ); as باغچه *bāgcha*, and باغِیچه *bāgīcha*, 'a small garden;' چمچه *chamcha*, 'a spoon;' دیگچه *degcha*, 'a small caldron,' 'a pot;' کُوچه *kūcha*, 'a lane;' جوزه *chūza*, 'a young bird,' 'a chicken;' دوشِیزه *doshīza*, 'a virgin;' مشکِیزه *mashkīza*, 'a small leather bottle.'

Rem. a. ه being interchangeable with ا in Urdū, this suffix sometimes takes the form چا; *e.g.* دیگچا *degchā*; whence, by forming the Hindī diminutive thereof, دیگچی *degchī*.

Rem. b. Diminutive forms are commonly used in Persian and Urdū to express *contempt*, *endearment*, *regard*, etc.

99. Compounds occur in great variety of forms in Persian, and many such are borrowed by the Urdū. The most important of these—the Determinative and the Attributive—have been noticed in treating of the genitive case, and the adjective (§§ 73, 78). There remains:

THE COPULATIVE COMPOUND.

This may be composed: 1) of two verbal roots or imperatives: *a*) either one and the same verb repeated, and the last a negative; as دارمدار *dār-ma-dār* (and داروىدار), 'hold, hold not,' 'adjustment of a dispute;' کش مکش *kash-ma-kash* (and کش و مکش), 'pull, pull not,' 'pulling backwards and forwards,' 'distraction,' 'tumult;' *b*) or of two different verbs; as دارگیر *dār-gīr* (and داروگیر), 'seizing,' 'pomp,' 'tumult.'

2) of an apocopated infinitive and the root of the same verb; as گفتگو *guft-gū* (and گفت وگو), 'conversation;' جُسْت جو *just-jū* (and جُسْت وجو), 'search,' 'quest.'

3) of two apocopated infinitives; as آمد رفت *āmad-raft* (and آمد ورفت), 'coming and going,' 'intercourse;' گفت و شنود *guft o shanūd*, 'speaking and hearing,' 'colloquy,' 'altercation.'

4) of two nouns of different signification, as پاي و پر *pa'e-o-par*, 'power;' or of the same signification, as جو جو *jau jau*, 'grain, grain,' 'grain by grain;' قِیل وقال *ḳīl o ḳāl*, 'speech and response,' 'discourse.'

Rem. To this class also belong those compounds in which the last word (which is used merely to rhyme or jingle with the first) is called the تابع *tābi'* or *appositive*, by the native grammarians: *e.g.* هرج مرج *harj-marj*, 'confusion,' 'tumult.'

Two words, whether the same or different, are often connected by means of the letter ا, which may have the signification: *a*) of و 'and;' *e.g.* کشاکش *kashā-kash*, 'pulling one way and the other,' 'distraction,' 'tumult;' رستاخیز *rastā-khez*, 'escaping and rising,' 'the day of resurrection;'

تگاپو *tagāpū*, 'running and running,' 'diligent search,' 'bustle,' 'toil.'

b) *of close proximity*; as برابر *barā-bar*, 'breast to breast,' 'on a level with,' 'equal;' لبالب *labā-lab*, 'lip to lip,' 'brimful;' دمادم *damā-dam*, 'moment to moment,' 'each moment,' 'continually.'

c) *totality* or *completeness*; *e.g.* سراسر *sarā-sar*, 'from end to end,' 'throughout,' 'altogether;' سراپا *sarā-pā*, 'from head to foot,' 'completely.'

Rem. Similarly two members of a compound are often connected by the preposition بہ *ba* 'to,' etc., *e.g.* دم بدم *dam-ba-dam*, 'from moment to moment,' 'each instant;' جابجا *jā-ba-jā*, 'from place to place,' 'one place after another;' یک بیک *yak-ba-yak*, 'one by one;' دست بدست *dast-ba-dast* 'hand in hand,' 'from hand to hand,' 'quick,' 'prompt.'

Numerals.

100. The following Table gives the leading Cardinal Numbers:

یک *yak*	1	دُوَازْدہ *duwāzdah* . . .	12
دُو *du*	2	سِیزْدہ *sīzdah*.	13
سِہ *sih*	3	چہارْدہ *chahārdah* . .	14
چہار *chahār*	4	پانْزْدہ *pānzdah*. . .	15
پنْج *panj*	5	شانْزْدہ *shānzdah* . . .	16
شش *shash*	6	هفْدہ *hafdah*	17
هفْت *haft*.	7	هشْدہ *hashdah*. . . .	18
هشْت *hasht*	8	نوزْدہ *nūzdah*	19
نُہ *nuh*.	9	بیست *bīst*	20
دہ *dah*	10	بِیست و یک *bīst-o-yak*. . .	21
یازْدہ *yāzdah*	11	بیست و دُو *bīst-o-du* . . .	22

سِي *sī*	30	سِصد *si-ṣad* . . .	300
چهل *chihal* . . .	40	چهارصد *chahār-ṣad*	400
پنجاه *panjāh* . .	50	پانصد *pān-ṣad* . .	500
شصت *shaṣt* . . .	60	ششصد *shash-ṣad* .	600
هفتاد *haftād* . .	70	هفتصد *haft-ṣad* . .	700
هشتاد *hashtād* . .	80	هشتصد *hasht-ṣad* .	800
نوَد *nuvad* . . .	90	نُهصد *nuh-ṣad* . .	900
صد *ṣad*	100	هزار *hazār* . . .	1000
صد و یک *ṣad-o-yak* .	101	ده هزار *dah hāzār*.	10,000
دُوصد *dū-ṣad* . .	200	لک *lak*	100,000

Ordinal Numbers.

101. The ordinal numbers are formed by adding the termination ـُم *um* to the corresponding cardinals, but in the *third* and the *ninth* (optionally) the final ه is changed into و before the termination is added; *e.g.* یکُم *yakum*, 'first;' دُوُم *duwum*, 'second;' سِوُم *siwum*, 'third,' etc.; نُهُم *nuhum*, or نُوُم *nuwum*, 'ninth;' دَهُم *dahum*, 'tenth,' and so on. If the number lie between the *decades* (as بیست و دُو), the termination is added to the last word; *e.g.* بیست و دُوُم *bīst-o-duwum*, 'twenty-second.'

Distributive Numerals.

102. The distributives are formed, as in Hindī and Urdū, by repeating the cardinals: *e.g.* یک یک *yak yak*, 'one at a time,' 'singly,' 'one apiece;' دُو دُو *dū dū*, 'two at a time,' 'by twos,' 'two apiece.'

Multiplicatives.

103. Multiplicatives are formed by adding to the cardinals: 1) the adverb چند *chand*, 'so many:' *e.g.* دُوچند

du-chand, 'twofold;' 2) the suffix تا *tā*; as یکتا *yak-tā*, 'single,' دُوتا *du-tā*, 'double:' 3) the suffix گانه *gāna* (corresponding to the Hindī affix گُنا *gunā*): *e.g.* یگانه *yagāna*, 'single' (for یک گانه, by contraction); دُوگانه *du-gāna*, 'double.'

Numeral Adverbs.

104. The numeral adverbs 'once,' 'twice,' etc., are expressed by adding to the cardinals the word بار *bār*, or باره *bāra*, 'time,' or one of the synonymous Arabic words نَوبت *naubat*, مرتبه *martaba*, or دفعه *dafʻa*: *e.g.* یکبار *yak-bār*, or یکباره *yak-bāra*, یک نَوبت *yak-naubat*, etc., 'once;' دُوبار *du-bār*, دُوباره *du-bāra*, دُونَوبت *du-naubat*, etc., 'twice.' The adverbs 'firstly,' 'secondly,' etc., are expressed by the ordinals: *e.g.* یکم *yakum*, 'firstly,' دُوُم *duwum*, 'secondly,' etc.

ARABIC CONSTRUCTIONS.

105. Nearly all Arabic words are derived from some verbal root, consisting for the most part of *three* letters, with the help of one or more of the seven letters of augmentation (or, as they are commonly termed, *servile* letters) *y*, *t*, *s*, *m*, *n*, *ū*, *ā*, or *a*, which are comprised in the word يَتَسَمَّنُوا *yatasammanū*. A large number of verbal nouns are derived from the ground form of the triliteral verb, but it is not necessary to notice more of these than occur in Urdū; the models (or, as they are technically termed, the *measures*) of such are given below with examples. In these measures, as in those of all the derived forms to be noticed, the letters ف, ع, ل, of the root فعل 'acting,' are employed to indicate *radical* letters, and the servile ة to represent final ه and ت of the Urdū.

MEASURE.	EXAMPLE.	MEASURE.	EXAMPLE.
1. فَعْل	قَتْل *ḳatl*, 'killing.'	17. فُعَال	دُعَا *du'ā*, 'praying.'[1]
2. فِعْل	عِلْم *'ilm*, 'knowing.'	18. فَعُول	قَبُول *ḳabūl*, 'accepting.'
3. فُعْل	حُكْم *ḥukm*, 'ordering.'	19. فُعُول	حُصُول *ḥuṣūl*, 'acquiring.'
4. فَعَل	طَلَب *ṭalab*, 'seeking.'	20. فِعْلَان	حِرْمَان *ḥirmān*, 'repelling.'
5. فِعَل	صِغَر *ṣigar*, 'being small.'	21. فُعْلَان	غُفْرَان *gufrān*, 'forgiving.'
6. فُعَل	هُدىٰ *hudā*, 'guiding aright.'	22. فَعَلَان	خَفَقَان *khafaḳān*, 'palpitating.'
7. فَعْلَة	رَحْمَت *raḥmat*, 'pitying.'	23. فَعَالَة	سَعَادَت *sa'ādat*, 'being happy.'
8. فِعْلَة	رِحْلَت *riḥlat*, 'travelling.'	24. فِعَالَة	كِتَابَت *kitābat*, 'writing.'
9. فُعْلَة	قُدْرَت *ḳudrat*, 'being able.'	25. فُعَالَة	بُغَايَت *bugāyat*, 'rebelling.'
10. فَعَلَة	حَرَكَت *ḥarakat*, 'moving.'	26. فُعُولَة	صُعُوبَت *ṣu'ūbat*, 'being difficult.'
11. فَعِلَة	سَرِقَه *sariḳa*, 'stealing.'	27. فَعَلِيَة	رَفَاهِيَت *rafāhiyat*, 'being ample.'
12. فَعْلَى	دَعْوىٰ *da'wā*, 'asserting.'	28. مَفْعَل	مَرْجَع *marja'*, 'returning.'
13. فِعْلَى	ذِكْرىٰ *ẕikrā*, 'remembering.'	29. مَفْعَلَة	مَرْحَمَت *marḥamat*, 'pitying.'
14. فُعْلَى	بُشْرىٰ *bushrā*, 'communicating goodness.'	30. مَفْعُلَة	مَمْلُكَت *mamlukat*, 'having dominion.'
15. فَعَال	سَلَام *salām*, 'being safe.'		
16. فِعَال	قِيَام *ḳiyām*, 'standing.'		

All these forms cannot be derived from *one* verbal root; very few verbs have more than two or three, and the majority admit of but one form. Some of the measures (for example Nos. 10, 11, 18) offer very few examples in Urdū.

[1] دُعَا *du'ā* was originally دُعَاو (from the root دعو). In verbal nouns of the measures of Nos. 15, 16, 17, final و or ي is in Arabic changed into *hamza* (as generally happens when they follow the *alif* of prolongation), but the Persians and Indians drop the *hamza*, unless the noun is in the *status constructus*, and the *iẓāfat* is used.

VERBAL ADJECTIVES.

106. Other important derivatives are the *verbal* adjectives. The *measures* of those which commonly occur in Urdū are:

1) فَاعِل—the Active Participle, or Noun of Agency: *e.g.* عالِم *'ālim*, 'a learned man' (from علم 'to know'); حاكِم *ḥākim*, 'a judge,' etc. (from حكم 'to judge'); صابِر *ṣābir*, 'patient' (from صبر 'to be patient'); غافِل *gāfil*, 'negligent' (from غفل 'to neglect').

Rem. If the second radical of the verbal root be و or ي, it is changed into *hamza* (ء) in the active participle; *e.g.* قائِم *ḳā'im*, 'standing' (from قوم 'to stand'). If the second and third radicals be identical, the second rejects its vowel and unites with the third so as to form a double letter, which is marked with *tashdīd*: *e.g.* خاصّ *khāṣṣ*, 'special' (from خصص); as however *tashdīd* over a final (vowelless) letter is useless, it is dropped in Urdū: *e.g.* خاص *khāṣ*. If the third radical be *hamza* (أ), or و, it is changed into ي: *e.g.* خالِي *khālī*, 'empty' (from خلو).

2) مَفْعُول—the Passive Participle: *e.g.* مَعْلُوم *ma'lūm*, 'known' (from علم 'to know'); مَنْظُور *manẓūr*, 'seen,' 'approved' (from نظر 'to see').

Rem. If the second radical letter be و, it is elided in the pass. part., but throws back its *ẓamma* upon the preceding vowelless letter: مَقُول *maḳūl*, 'said' (from قول 'to say'). If the second radical be ي, the same thing takes place, but, to indicate the elision of radical ي, the *ẓamma* is changed into *kasra*, and the servile و is in consequence changed into ي: *e.g.* مبِيع *mabī'*, 'sold' (from بيع 'to sell'). If the third radical be و, it is elided: *e.g.* مدْعُو *mad'ū*, 'called,' 'invited' (from دعو 'to call').

3) فَعِيل—a form expressing either an inherent or permanent quality, or a degree of intensity: *e.g.* حكِيم *ḥakīm*, 'a sage' (from حكم 'to judge,' etc.); رحِيم *raḥīm*, 'very compassionate' (from رحم 'to have mercy').

Rem. Adjectives of the three measures noticed above are commonly used as substantives also.

4) فَعُول—a form with the same signification as the preceding: *e.g.* صبُور *ṣabūr*, 'very patient' (from صبر 'to be patient'); غفُور *gafūr*, 'very forgiving' (from غفر 'to forgive').

Rem. Verbal adjectives of the measures فَعِيل and فَعُول, derived from verbs of which the third radical is و, or ي, are subject to the same changes as those of the form مَفْعُول: *e.g.* نبِي *nabī*, 'a prophet' (from نبو).

5) اَفْعَل—the measure of *the noun of preeminence* (اِسْمِ تفْضِيل *ismĕ tafẓīl*). It has the signification of the English comparative and superlative, and is formed from verbal adjectives with three radicals, or with three radicals and a letter of prolongation: *e.g.* احْسن *aḥsan*, 'more or most beautiful' (from حسن *ḥasan*, 'beautiful'); افْضل *afẓal*, 'more or most excellent' (from فاضِل *fāẓil*, 'excellent'); اكْبر *akbar*, 'greater,' 'greatest' (from كبِير *kabīr*, 'great'). This measure is also used for adjectives denoting *colour*, or *deformity*, derived from neuter triliteral verbs: *e.g.* احْمر *aḥmar*, 'red;' اصْفر *aṣfar*, 'yellow;' اعْرج *a'raj*, 'lame' (by nature); اعْمىٰ *a'mā*, 'blind.'

6) فَعَّال—the measure of *the noun of intensiveness* (اِسْمِ مُبالغہ *ismĕ mubālaga*). Its signification approaches very nearly to that of the measures فَعِيل and فَعُول: *e.g.* كذّاب *kazzāb*, 'a great, or habitual, liar;' ظلّام *zallām*, 'very tyrannical;' علّام *'allām*, 'very learned.' The same form is commonly used for nouns which indicate *professions and trades*: *e.g.* بزّاز *bazzāz*, 'a cloth-merchant;' بقّال *bakkāl*, 'a greengrocer' (but, in India), 'a grain-merchant' (= بنِيا *baniyā*); صرّاف *sarrāf*, 'a money-changer,' 'a banker.' By adding the termination ـَہ *a* to this form with the first signification, still greater intensiveness is given to the meaning; as علّامہ *'allāma*, 'exceedingly learned.'

Rem. Other adjectives of the measures فَعْل - فِعْل - فُعْل - فَعَل - فَعِل - فَعَال - فُعَال - فَعْلَان - فُعْلَان, also occur in Urdū: *e.g.* صعْب *sa'b*, 'difficult,' صِفْر *sifr*, 'empty,' 'a cypher,' صُلْب *sulb*, 'hard,' حسن *hasan*, 'good,' 'beautiful,' خشِن *khashin*, 'rough' جبان *jabān*, 'cowardly,' شُجاع *shujā'*, 'brave,' عطْشان *'atshān*, 'thirsty,' عُرْيان *'uryān*, 'naked;' but as these are not to be distinguished by their forms from verbal nouns, they can only be learned by reading.

107. From triliteral roots are derived other forms of verbal nouns also, which, since two or more of the servile letters occur in them, are termed *augmented infinitives* (مصْدرِ مزِيد *masdarĕ mazīd*) by the native grammarians. It will be more convenient to speak of them as verbal nouns of the *second*, *third*, etc., derived forms. These

verbal nouns moreover have corresponding adjectives, similar to the فَاعِل and مفْعُول of the *first* or ground form of the triliteral verb. The measures of both are given below, with examples.

a) VERBAL NOUNS OF THE DERIVED FORMS.

II. تَفْعِيل / تَفْعِلَة — *e.g.* تفْرِيح *tafrīḥ*, 'gladdening' (from فرح 'being glad'); تعْلِيم *taʿlīm*, 'teaching' (from علم 'to know'); تذكِرة *tazkira*, 'reminding' (from ذكر 'to remember'); تفْرِقة *tafrika*, 'scattering,' 'distributing' (from فرق 'to separate'). Of the two measures, the first is the more common, the last is used chiefly where the third radical letter is و or ي.

III. مُفَاعَلَة / فِعَال — *e.g.* مُقابله *mukābala*, 'facing,' 'confronting' (from قبل 'being opposite,' 'coming towards'); مُقاتله *mukātala*, and قِتال *kitāl*, 'fighting' (from قتل 'killing'); مُجادله *mujādala*, and جِدال *jidāl*, 'contending,' 'disputing' (from جدل 'contending'); مُحافظت *muḥāfazat*, 'guarding' (from حفظ 'to preserve'). The first of the two measures is of more frequent occurrence than the second.

Rem. If the third radical of the verb be و or ي, it is changed into ا: *e.g.* مُلاقات *mulākāt*, 'meeting,' from لقي 'to meet.'

IV. إِفْعَال—*e.g.* إِجْرا *ijrā*, 'causing to flow' (from جري 'to flow'); إِخْراج *ikhrāj*, 'causing to go out,' 'issuing' (from خرج 'to go out'); إنكار *inkār*, 'denying' (from نكر 'not knowing or acknowledging').

Rem. If the *first* of the radical letters be و, it is changed into ي: *e.g.* إيفا (for إوفا), *īfā*, 'performing a promise' (from وفي). If the *second* radical be و or ي, it is elided, but throws back its vowel upon the vowelless first radical, and the termination ت *t* is added by way of compensation: *e.g.* إعانت *ĕ'ānat*, 'helping' (for إعوان, from عون). If the *third* radical be و or ي, it is changed into *hamza*: *e.g.* إعفاء *ĕ'fā*, 'granting freedom, or pardon' (from عفو); in Persian and Urdū however the *hamza* is dropped, unless the noun is in the *status constructus*, and the *izāfat* is used.

V. تَفَعُّل—*e.g.* تكبّر *takabbur*, 'making oneself great,' 'being proud' (from تكبير *takbīr*, 'making great'); تصوّر *taṣawwur*, 'picturing to oneself,' 'conceiving' (from تصوير *taṣwīr*, 'making a picture').

Rem. If the third radical be و or ي (و is always changed into ي, and), the influence of the ي changes the *zamma* of the penult syllable into *kasra*: *e.g.* تسلّي *tasallī*, 'becoming comforted' (from سلي).

VI. تفاعُل—*e.g.* تناسُب *tanāsub*, 'resembling,' 'being related' (from مُناسبت *munāsabat*, 'being related to'); تقارُب *taḳārub*, 'approaching' (one another), from مُقاربت *muḳārabat*, 'approaching.'

Rem. If the third radical be و or ي, the same change is made as in the *fifth* form: *e.g.* تداوي *tadāwī*, 'treating oneself medically' (from دوي). The Persians frequently change the final ي of such words into ا‍ـَ; as تمنّا *tamannā*, 'desire,' تماشا *tamāshā*, 'spectacle,' 'recreation,' 'fun.'

VII. اِنْفِعَال—*e.g.* اِنْفِصال *infiṣāl*, 'being decided' (from فصل 'to decide'); اِنْكِشاف *inkishāf*, 'being uncovered, or revealed' (from كشف 'to open or reveal').

Rem. If the third radical be و or ي, it is changed into *hamza*, which however is, as usual, dropped in Urdū: *e.g.* اِنْطِفا (for اِنْطِفاء), *inṭifā*, 'being extinguished' (from طفي).

VIII. اِفْتِعَال—*e.g.* اِجْتِماع *ijtimā'*, 'becoming collected,' 'assembling' (from جمع 'to collect'); اِعْتِراض *i'tirāẓ*, 'putting oneself in the way,' 'opposing' (from عرض 'to place'—before one); اِقْتِدار *iḳtidār*, 'becoming powerful' (from قدر 'to make powerful,' etc.).

Rem. If the first radical letter be ت *t*, the characteristic ت of this form unites with it into تّ; as اِتّباع *ittibā'*, 'following' (from تبع). So also, if the first radical be و, it is changed into ت, which unites with the characteristic ت of the form into تّ: *e.g.* اِتّفاق *ittifāḳ*, 'agreeing' (from وفق). If the first radical be د or ز, the characteristic ت of the form is changed into د, which unites with an initial د into دّ: *e.g.* اِدّعا *iddi'ā*, 'claiming one's rights' (from دعو); اِزْدِحام *izdiḥām*, 'pressing,' 'crowding' (from زحم). If the first radical be ص ض, or ط the characteristic ت of the form is changed into ط, which unites with initial ط, into طّ: *e.g.* اِصْطِلاح *iṣṭilāḥ*, 'a technical term' (from صلح); اِضْطِراب *iẓṭirāb*, 'being agitated' (from ضرب); اِطّلاع *iṭṭilā'*, 'becoming informed' (from طلع).

IX.—This form does not occur in Urdū.

x. إِسْتِفْعَال—*e.g.* إِسْتِعْدَاد *isti'dād*, 'getting oneself ready,' 'being ready' (from عَدّ, the verbal noun of the *fourth* form of which, viz. إِعْدَاد *i'dād*, signifies 'making ready'); إِسْتِغْفَار *istigfār*, 'seeking forgiveness' (from غفر 'to forgive').

Rem. a. The changes which take place in this form are precisely similar to those which take place in the *fourth* form.

Rem. b. The following brief observations will throw light on the signification of these various forms:

The *second* (تَفْعِيل), and the *fourth* (إِفْعَال), are usually *causative* or *factitive*. Verbs that are *intransitive* in the first form become *transitive* in these, and those that are *transitive* become *doubly transitive*, or *causative*. But in some instances the two forms have different meanings: *e.g.* I. عِلْم *'ilm*, 'knowing,' 'knowledge,' II. تَعْلِيم *ta'līm*, 'teaching,' IV. إِعْلَام *i'lām*, 'informing one of a thing.'

The *third* (مُفَاعَلَة), and the *sixth* (تَفَاعُل), commonly convey the idea of *reciprocity*, the latter necessarily so. When the first form is *transitive*, the third expresses *the effort* or *attempt to perform that act upon the object*; *e.g.* قَتْل *ḳatl*, 'killing,' مُقَاتَلَة *muḳātala*, ('trying to kill, or) fighting with.' In the *sixth* form the idea of effort or attempt becomes *reflexive*: *e.g.* تَجَاهُل *tajāhul*, 'feigning ignorance.'

The *fifth* form (تَفَعُّل) is the reflexive of the *second*; but it is more commonly used with the *effective* signification, implying that an act is done to a person, or a state produced in him, whether caused by *another* or by *himself*: *e.g.* عِلْم *'ilm*, 'knowledge,' تَعْلِيم *ta'līm*, 'teaching,' تَعَلُّم *ta'allum*, 'becoming learned.' The idea of *intensiveness* (which is often found in the *second* form) exists in the *fifth* also: *e.g.* تَفَرُّق *tafarruḳ*, 'separation into many groups, or in various directions.' In English this form must often be rendered by the *passive*.

The *seventh* form (إِنْفِعَال) is *reflexive* or *effective* in signification, and approaches nearly to the *passive*, by which it must often be rendered into English.

The *eighth* form (إِفْتِعَال) is the *reflexive* of the *first*. The reflex object is either the accusative or the dative: *e.g.* إِعْتِرَاض *i'tirāẓ*, 'putting oneself in the way,' 'opposing' (from عَرْض 'placing something before one'); إِضْطِرَاب *iẓṭirāb*, 'moving oneself to and fro,' 'being agitated' (from ضَرْب 'beating'); إِقْتِدَار *iḳtidār*, 'seeking power for oneself,' 'becoming powerful' (from قُدْرَت 'being powerful,' 'power'). The reflexive signification often gives rise to the *reciprocal* (which this form has in common with the *sixth*), and occasionally passes into the *passive*. In many cases too the eighth form has the same signification as the first.

The *tenth* form (إِسْتِفْعَال) is commonly used in the sense of *taking*, *seeking*, *asking for* or *demanding* what is signified by the *first*: *e.g.* إِسْتِغْفَار *istigfār*, 'asking forgiveness' (from غفر 'to forgive'). It also often converts the *factitive* signification of the *fourth* form into the *reflexive*: *e.g.* إِسْتِعْدَاد *isti'dād*, 'getting oneself ready,' 'being prepared' (from إِعْدَاد *i'dād*, 'making ready,' 'preparing').

Rem. c. The verbal nouns of the first and derived forms are commonly used as abstract substantives: *e.g.* عِلْم *'ilm*, 'knowledge,' تَذْكِرَة *taẕkira*, 'mention.'

b) Verbal Adjectives of the Derived Forms.

The *measures* of these, with examples, are tabulated below. The difference between the form for the Active and that for the Passive Participle, consists simply in the vowel of the final syllable, the former taking *kasra*, and the latter *fatḥa*.

	MEASURE OF ACT. PART.	EXAMPLE.	MEASURE OF PASS. PART.	EXAMPLE.
II.	مُفَعِّل	مُعَلِّم *mŏ'allim*, 'a teacher' (from عِلْم).	مُفَعَّل	مُعلّم *mŏ'allam*, 'taught.'
III.	مُفَاعِل	مُحافِظ *muḥāfiẓ*, 'guarding,' 'custodian' (from حِفْظ).	مُفَاعَل	مُحافظ *muḥāfaẓ*, 'guarded.'
IV.	مُفْعِل	مُصْرِف *muṣrif*, 'squandering' (from صَرْف).	مُفْعَل	مُصْرَف *muṣraf*, 'squandered.'
V.	مُتَفَعِّل	مُتبدِّل *mutabaddil*, 'changing' (from بدل).	مُتَفَعَّل	مُتبدّل *mutabaddal*, 'changed.'
VI.	مُتَفَاعِل	مُتعارِف *muta'ārif*, 'knowing' (from عِرْف).	مُتَفَاعَل	مُتعارف *muta'āraf*, 'known.'
VII.	مُنْفَعِل	مُنْكَشِف *munkashif*, 'revealing' (from كَشْف).	مُنْفَعَل	مُنْكَشَف *munkashaf*, 'revealed.'
VIII.	مُفْتَعِل	مُعْتَمِد *mŏ'tamid*, 'trusting' (from عمْد).	مُفْتَعَل	مُعْتَمَد *mŏ'tamad*, 'trusted.'
X.	مُسْتَفْعِل	مُسْتَخْرِج *mustakhrij*, 'extracting' (from خرج).	مُسْتَفْعَل	مُسْتَخْرَج *mustakhraj*, 'extracted.'

108. Verbs consisting of four radicals also occur in Arabic, having a ground form and three derived forms; but the first and second forms alone occur in Urdū. Employing an additional ل to denote the fourth radical, the measures of the *verbal nouns* of these forms are:

I. فَعْلَلَة—*e.g.* ترْجمه *tarjama*, 'interpreting,' 'translation' (from ترْجم 'to interpret'); زلْزله *zalzala*, 'shaking' (from زلْزل 'to shake').

II. تَفَعْلُل—*e.g.* تَزَلْزُل *tazalzul*, 'becoming in a state of motion,' 'being shaken' (from زلْزل 'to shake').

109. The measures of the *verbal adjectives* corresponding to these nouns are:

I. { مُفَعِّل (Act.)—*e.g.* مُتَرْجِم *mutarjim*, 'an interpreter.'
  مُفَعَّل (Pass.) مُتَرْجَم *mutarjam*, 'interpreted.'

II. { مُتَفَعْلِل (Act.)—*e.g.* مُتَزَلْزِل *mutazalzil*, 'shaking.'
  مُتَفَعْلَل (Pass.) مُتَزَلْزَل *mutazalzal*, 'shaken.'

Possessive Adjectives.

110. These, as used in Urdū, are properly determinative compounds, in which the first noun governs the second in the genitive. The governing noun is generally one which conveys the idea of *possession*, *origin*, etc. The following are examples of those which occur in Urdū:

1) ابو *abū*, or بو *bū*, 'father,' 'originator,' etc.: *e.g.* ابو تُراب *abū-turāb* (or بُو تُراب), 'dusty,' from تُراب *turāb*, 'dust,' (*bū turāb* was the nickname given by Moḥammad to his son-in-law 'Alī); بُوالعجب *bu'l 'ajab*, 'cause of wonder,' 'wonderful;' بُو الهوَس *bu'l hawas*, 'causing desire,' 'desirous,' 'capricious.'

2) ذو *zū*, 'owner,' possessor' (nom. sing. ذُو *zū*, gen. ذِي *zī*, nom. plur. أولو *ulū*, gen. and acc. ذوي *zawī* or أولِي *ulī*): *e.g.* ذُوالجلال *zu'l-jalāl*, 'possessor of glory,' 'glorious;' ذُو القرنَين *zu'l ḳarnain*, 'possessor of two horns,' 'two-horned;' ذِي رُوح *zī-rūḥ*, 'animate,' ذِي اِستِعْداد *zī-istĕ'dād*, 'capable,' 'qualified;' أولو الالباب *ulu'l albāb*, 'intelligent persons;' أولُو العزم *ulu'l azm*, 'firm,' 'resolute;' ذوي الاقتِدار *zawi'l iḳtidār*, 'powerful;' أولِي الابصار *uli'l abṣār*, 'discerning,' 'wise.'

Rem. The form ذِي *zī* occurs most frequently in Urdū, being used even in ordinary conversation. It is combined with Persian words also: *e.g.* ذِي هوش *zī-hosh*, 'sensible,' 'intelligent.'

3) صاحِب *ṣāḥib*, 'companion,' 'possessor:' *e.g.* صاحِب جمال *ṣāḥib-jamāl*, 'beautiful;' صاحِب نصِيب *ṣāḥib-naṣīb*, 'fortunate;' صاحِب دل *ṣāḥib-dil*, 'pious,' صاحِب تخْت *ṣāḥib-takht*, 'a king.' In the last two examples the words *dil* and *takht* are Persian.

Rem. The genitive construction is occasionally indicated by the use of the *iẓāfat*: *e.g.* صاحِبِ تخْت *ṣāḥibĕ takht*, 'possessor of the throne,' 'a king.' Such is always the case when the governing nouns are اَرْباب *arbāb* (pl. of رب *rabb*), 'lords,' 'possessors,' and اَهْل *ahl*, 'possessor;' اَرْبابِ خِرد *arbābĕ khirad*, 'intelligent or wise persons;' اَهْلِ عقْل *ahlĕ 'akl*, 'wise.'

Relative Adjectives.

111. Relative adjectives are formed in the following ways: *a*) by adding to nouns (substantives, adjectives, or pronouns) and particles the suffix ـيّ (which, in Urdū, is changed to ـي *ī*, the *tashdīd* being dropped; but it is restored in the derivatives from the relative adjective). The suffix may often be added without any change taking place in the primitive noun: *e.g.* شمْسِي *shamsī*, 'solar,' from شمْس 'the sun;' اِنْسانِي *insānī*, 'human,' from اَنْسان 'a human being;' حُسَينِي *ḥŏsainī*, 'of, or relating to Hosain;' عِلْمِي *'ilmī*, 'scientific,' from عِلْم 'science;' نحْوِي *naḥwī*, 'pertaining to grammar,' from نحْو 'grammar.' In many cases however the noun undergoes some change in the auxiliary consonants, or in the vocalization, etc., before the suffix is added. In respect of these changes, so far as Urdū is concerned, the following rules may be laid down:

1) If the primitive noun be of the measure فَعِل, the *kasra* of the middle radical is changed into *fatḥa*: *e.g.* ملكي *malakī*, from ملِك 'a king.'

2) The feminine termination ت or ة is rejected: *e.g.* حقيقي *ḥaḳīḳī*, from حقيقت 'truth,' 'reality;' طبيعي *ṭabī'ī*, from طبيعت 'nature.'

3) Final ا, ى and ي are changed into و before adding the termination ـِي, and *kasra* of the preceding letter is changed into *fatḥa*: *e.g.* عصوي *aṣawī*, from عصا 'a staff;' معنوي *ma'nawī*, from معنى or معني 'meaning,' دِهْلوي *dĕhlawī*, from دِهْلي 'Dehlī.'

Rem. If, however, the primitive noun consist of more than four letters, final ا, ى or ي are rejected: *e.g.* مُصْطفِي *muṣṭafī*, from مُصْطفى 'chosen.'

b) by adding to nouns the termination ـَانِي; as

جِسْمانِي *jismānī*, 'corporeal,' from جِسْم 'body.'
رُوحانِي *rūḥānī*, 'spiritual,' from رُوح 'spirit.'
نفْسانِي *nafsānī*, 'pertaining to the soul,' 'lustful,' from نفْس 'soul.'
نُورانِي *nūrānī*, 'luminous,' 'bright,' from نُور 'light.'

Abstract Nouns of Quality.

112. Abstract nouns of quality are formed by adding the feminine termination ـَت *at* to relative adjectives, or, which amounts to the same thing, by adding the termination ـِيّت *īyat* to nouns and particles: *e.g.*

إِنسانِيّت *insānīyat*, 'humanity,' from إِنساني 'human.'
إِلٰهِيّت *ilāhīyat*, 'divinity,' 'Godhead,' from إِلٰهي 'divine.'

كَيْفِيّت *kaifīyat,* 'quality,' from كَيْفِي (from كيف 'how?').

ماهِيّت *māhīyat,* 'the what,' 'substance,' from ما 'what?'[1]

Rem. In a few words the Aramaic termination ـُوت *ūt* is used to form Abstract substantives; *e.g.* ملكُوت *malakūt,* 'royalty,' 'the world of angels,' from مَلِك *malik,* 'a king,' and مَلَك *malak,* 'an angel;' جبرُوت *jabarūt,* 'omnipotence,' from جبّار *jabbār,* 'magnifying oneself.'

NOUNS OF PLACE AND TIME.

113. Nouns of place and time (اسمائے مکان و زمان *asmā'ĕ makān o zamān*) generally take the form مَفْعَل or مَفْعِل, the initial syllable مَ *ma* being characteristic: *e.g.* مكتب *maktab,* 'a place where writing is taught,' 'a school' (from كتب 'to write'); مخرج *makhraj,* and مدخل *madkhal,* 'a place of egress, and ingress' (from خرج 'to go out,' and دخل 'to go in'); مجلِس *majlis,* 'the place where, or time when, several persons sit,' 'room,' 'assembly,' 'party' (from جلس 'to sit'); مسجِد *masjid,* 'a place of worship,' 'a mosque' (from سجد 'to worship').

114. Nouns that indicate the Instrument that one uses in performing the act expressed by a verb are called اسمائے آلات *asmā'e ālāt.* They generally have the form مِفْعَال or مِفْعَلہ, and are distinguished from the nouns of place by the *kasra* with which the prefixed م *m* is pronounced: *e.g.* مِفتاح *miftāḥ,* 'a key' (from فتح 'to open'); مِصقلہ *miṣḳala,* 'an instrument used in polishing' (from صقل 'to polish');

[1] Forbes, and other grammarians after him, say that "the Abstract noun is formed by means of the feminine termination *at* or *iyat,*" and give as examples the words *ḥukūmat, ḳismat, ḳudrat,* etc. These however are *infinitive nouns,* or *nouns of action,* and though, like all verbal nouns (*e.g.* *'ilm,* 'knowledge'), *they may be used as abstract nouns,* they are not "abstract nouns formed by means of the termination *at*;" this suffix can only form abstract substantives when added to *relative adjectives.* The other termination should be *īyat,* not *iyat.*

میزان *mīzān* (for موزان), 'a balance or pair of scales' (from وزن 'to weigh').

The Diminutive.

115. The Arabic Diminutive (اِسْم تَصْغِیر *ismĕ taṣġīr*) is not of common occurrence in Urdū. It generally takes the form فُعَیْل, though one or two words take the form فُعَیْلَه: *e.g.* حُسَین *Hŏsain* from حسن 'Hasan;' بُحَیْرَه *buḥaira*, 'a small sea,' 'a lake,' from بَحْر *baḥr*, 'a sea.'

Gender.

116. The most usual termination by the mere addition of which to masculines (chiefly adjectives) feminines are formed, is ـَة *at*, which in Urdū is changed into ـَه *a*: *e.g.* والِده *wālida*, 'mother,' from والِد *wālid*, 'father,' مَلِکَه *malika*, 'queen,' from مَلِك *malik*, 'king;' قادِره *ḳādira*, from قادِر *ḳādir*, 'powerful,' عظِیمه *'aẓīma*, from عظِیم *'aẓīm*, 'great;' مُعلِّمه *mŏ'allima*, 'a schoolmistress,' from مُعلِّم *mŏ'allim*, 'a teacher or schoolmaster.'

117. Adjectives of the measure اَفْعَل, when they have the *superlative* signification, form the feminine after the measure فُعْلیٰ: *e.g.* کُبْریٰ *kubrā*, from اکْبر *akbar*, 'greatest,' اُولیٰ *ūlā*, from اوّل *awwal*, 'first.' But when they denote *colour* or *deformity*, the measure of the feminine is فَعْلا: *e.g.* صفْرا *ṣafrā*, from اصْفر *aṣfar*, 'yellow;' عرْجا *'arjā*, from اعْرج *a'raj*, 'lame.'

Number.

118. Arabic nouns have three numbers, the singular, dual, and plural.

119. The dual is formed by adding the termination

ـَانِ *āni* to the singular; as كِتابانِ *kitābāni*, 'two books,' from كتاب 'a book.'

120. The plurals are of two kinds. The one, which has only a single form, is called جمعِ سالِم *jam'ĕ sālim*, 'the complete or entire plural,' because all the vowels and consonants of the singular are retained in it. The other, which has various forms, is called جمعِ تكسِير *jam'ĕ taksīr*, 'the broken plural,' because it is more or less altered from the singular by the addition or elision of consonants, or the change of vowels.

121. The *complete*, or *regular* plural of masculine nouns is formed by adding to the singular the termination ـُونَ *ūna*; *e.g.* حاضِرُونَ *ḥāẓirūna*, from حاضِر 'present.' That of feminine nouns by adding ـَاتٌ *ātun* to the singular, or, if the singular end in ة (ت or ه), by changing that letter into ـَاتٌ: *e.g.* ملكاتٌ *malakātun*, 'possessions,' from ملكة *malakat*.

122. The following is an example of the declension of a masculine noun.

	SINGULAR.	DUAL.	PLURAL.
Nom.	حاضِرٌ *ḥāẓirun*, 'present.'	حاضِرانِ *ḥāẓirāni*.	حاضِرُونَ *ḥāẓirūna*.
Gen.	حاضِرٍ *ḥāẓirin*.	حاضِرَينِ *ḥāẓiraini*.	حاضِرِينَ *ḥāẓirīna*.
Acc.	حاضِرًا *ḥāẓiran*.		

Rem. The genitive singular does not occur in Urdū. The accusative, with the *tanwīn*, frequently occurs, but always as an adverb. The final vowel of the nominative is always dropped.

123. The Urdū borrows from the Arabic, not only the various plural forms, but also its *dual*. But the terminations of the dual and the regular masculine plural are

always those of the Arabic accusative case, with the final vowels dropped: *e.g.* جانِبَین *jānibain*, 'two or both sides,' from جانِب 'side;' والِدَین *wālidain*, 'father and mother,' 'parents,' from والِد, 'father;' ناظِرین *nāzirīn*, 'beholders,' from ناظِر 'beholding;' آخِرین *ākhirīn*, 'those that come after,' 'posterity,' from آخِر 'the last.'

124. The termination ـَات *āt*, of the regular plural of feminine nouns in Arabic, with the final vowel dropped, is also used in Urdū. It may be added: 1) to verbal nouns of any measure, and either gender: *e.g.*

کمالات *kamālāt*,	'perfections,'	from the	masc.	کمال *kamāl*.
تسْلیمات *taslīmāt*,	'salutations,'	,,	fem.	تسْلیم *taslīm*.
إخْراجات *ikhrājāt*,	'disbursements,'	,,	masc.	إخْراج *ikhrāj*.
إصْطِلاحات *iṣṭilāḥāt*,	'technicalities,'	,,	fem.	إصْطِلاح *iṣṭilāḥ*.

2) To verbal adjectives which are used in the plural as substantives: *e.g.*

کائِنات *kā'ināt*,	'entities,'	from	کائِن 'being.'
مخْلوقات *makhlūḳāt*,	'creatures,'	,,	مخْلوق 'created.'
مَوْجُودات *maujūdāt*,	'beings,'	,,	مَوْجُود 'found,' 'existing.'

Rem. Plural nouns ending in *āt* are not necessarily feminine. Their gender is generally that of the singular from which they are formed: *e.g.* حَیْوانات *ḥaiwānāt*, خیالات *khayālāt*, کمالات *kamālāt*, مکانات *makānāt*, etc., are masculine because their singulars are masculine, and آیات *āyāt*, إصْطِلاحات *iṣṭilāḥāt*, حرکات *ḥarakāt*, etc., are feminine for a similar reason. One or two of these plurals are commonly used in the singular also; as ایک وارِدات هَوئِي هَي *ek wāridāt hū'ī hai*, 'a casualty has occurred;' تحْقِیقات هو رهِي هَي *taḥḳīḳāt ho rahī hai*, 'investigation is taking place.' And to some of those which are feminine the plural termination of the Hindī is occasionally added; *e.g.* صِفاتين *ṣifāten*, from صِفت *ṣifat*, 'an attribute or quality.'

125. The *broken plurals* of the Arabic are of frequent occurrence, and are found in a variety of forms. The most important of these forms are:

1) أَفْعَال—Singular triliterals of all forms may take this plural: *e.g.*

SINGULAR.	PLURAL.
جِسْم *jism*, 'body,'	اجْسام *ajsām*.
حُكْم *ḥukm*, 'an order,'	احْكام *aḥkām*.
وَقْت *wakt*, 'time.'	اَوقات *aukāt*.
شَي *shai* (from شيأ), 'a thing,'	اشْيا *ashyā*.
خبر *khabar*, 'information,' 'news,'	اخْبار *akhbār*.

Triliterals in which the second radical (originally و or ي) appears under the form ا, restore the original radical in the plural: *e.g.*

حال *ḥāl* (for حول), 'state.'	احْوال *aḥwāl*.
ناب *nāb* (for نيب), 'an eye-tooth,'	انْياب *anyāb*.

A few verbal adjectives of the measures فَاعِل and فَعِيل also take this form in the plural: *e.g.*

صاحِب *ṣāḥib*, 'companion,'	اصْحاب *aṣḥāb*.
شرِيف *sharīf*, 'noble,'	اشْراف *ashrāf*.

2) فُعُول—The singular is generally a triliteral of one of the measures فَعِل - فَعَل - فُعْل - فِعْل - فَعْل : *e.g.*

امْر *amr*, 'an affair,'	أُمُور *umūr*.
عِلْم *'ilm*, 'science,'	عُلُوم *'ulūm*.
بُرْج *burj*, 'a tower,'	بُرُوج *burūj*.
اسد *asad*, 'a lion,'	أُسُود *usūd*.
مَلِك *malik*, 'a king,'	مُلُوك *mulūk*.

A few verbal adjectives of the measure فَاعِل may take this form of plural: *e.g.*

SINGULAR.	PLURAL.
شاهِد *shāhid*, 'a witness,'	شُهُود *shuhūd*.

3). فُعَلا—This form is commonly used for the plural of verbal adjectives of the measure فَعِيل when they apply to rational beings, and have not a *passive* signification, nor are derived from verbs of which the second and third radicals are identical. Some masculine adjectives of the measure فَاعِل (with the same restrictions as above) also take this form for the plural: *e.g.*

امِير *amīr*, 'a noble,'	أُمرا *umarā*.
فقِير *faķīr*, 'poor,'	فُقرا *fuķarā*.
غرِيب *garīb*, 'strange,' 'poor,'	غُربا *gurabā*.
شاعِر *shā'ir*, 'a poet,'	شُعرا *shu'arā*.
عاقِل *'āķil*, 'wise,'	عُقلا *ukalā*.

4) أَفْعِلا—This form is commonly used for the plural of masculine adjectives of the measure فَعِيل, applicable to rational beings, and derived mostly from verbs of which the second and third radicals are identical, or the third radical is و or ي: *e.g.*

قرِيب *ķarīb*, 'near,' 'a relation,'	اقْرِبا *akribā*.
طبِيب *ṭabīb*, 'a physician,'	اطِبّا (for اطْبِبا) *aṭibbā*.
حبِيب *ḥabīb*, 'a friend,'	احِبّا (for احْبِبا) *aḥibbā*.
نبِي *nabī* (from نبو), 'a prophet,'	انْبِيا *ambiyā*.
ولِي *walī* (from ولي), 'a saint,'	أوْلِيا *auliyā*.

5) فِعَال—Triliterals of the measures فَعْلَة - فَعْل - فَعَل - فَعْل and فُعْلَة may take this form of plural: *e.g.*

SINGULAR.	PLURAL.
ثَوب *saub*, 'a robe,'	ثِياب *siyāb*.
بَحْر *baḥr*, 'the sea,'	بِحار *biḥār*.
جبل *jabal*, 'a hill,'	جِبال *jibāl*.
رجُل *rajul*, 'a man,'	رِجال *rijāl*.
خصْلت *khaṣlat*, 'a habit,'	خِصال *khiṣāl*.
رُقْعه *ruḳʻa*, 'a scrap of paper,' 'a letter,'	رِقاع *riḳāʻ*.

6) فُعَّال—This form is used for the plural of verbal adjectives of the measure فَاعِل not derived from verbs of which the third radical is و or ي; as

حاكِم *ḥākim*, 'a judge,' 'a magistrate,'	حُكّام *ḥukkām*.
جاهِل *jāhil*, 'ignorant,'	جُهّال *juhhāl*.
عاشِق *ʻāshiḳ*, 'a lover,'	عُشّاق *ʻushshāḳ*.
كافِر *kāfir*, 'an infidel,'	كُفّار *kuffār*.

7) أَفْعِلَة—A form used for the plural of quadriliterals of which the antepenult letter is quiescent (a long vowel), especially nouns of the measures فَعَال and فِعَال; and verbal adjectives of the measure فَعِيل derived from verbs of which the second and third radicals are identical, or the third radical is و or ي: *e.g.*

زمان *zamān*, 'time,'	أزْمِنه *azmina*.
دوا *dawā*, 'medicine,'	ادْوِيَه *adwiya*.
مِثال *miṣāl*, 'example,'	امْثِله *amṣila*.
عمُود *ʻamūd*, 'a pillar,'	اعْمِده *aʻmida*.
حبيب *ḥabīb*, 'dear,'	احِبّه *aḥibba* (for احْبِبه).
دليل *dalīl*, 'proof,'	ادِلّه *adilla* (for ادْلِله).

Rem. Form أَفْعِلَا (No. 4) is perhaps more commonly employed for the plural of adjectives of the measure فَعِيل.

8) فَعَائِل—This form is used for the plural of quadriliterals (all *originally* feminine) of which the third letter

is servile or quiescent (a long vowel), whether they have the feminine termination (ت) or not: *e.g.*

SINGULAR.	PLURAL.
جزيره *jazīra*, 'an island,'	جزائر *jazā'ir*.
حقيقت *ḥaḳīḳat*, 'reality,'	حقائق *ḥaḳā'iḳ*.
خصال *khiṣāl*, 'habits,'	خصائل *khaṣā'il*.
رساله *risāla*, 'a short treatise,'	رسائل *rasā'il*.
شمال *shamāl*, 'the north wind,' 'disposition,'	شمائل *shamā'il*.
دليل *dalīl*, 'proof,'	دلائل *dalā'il*.

Rem. The form دلائل is said by some grammarians to be the plural not of دليل, but of دليله; but as *dalīl* is feminine, its plural is very properly *dalā'il*. The lexicons also give عجائب *'ajā'ib*, and غرائب *garā'ib* as the plurals of عجيب *'ajīb*, غريب *garīb*; but these are, properly speaking, the plurals of the feminine forms عجيبه *'ajība* and غريبه *garība*.

9) فَوَاعِل—This is a common form of plural for substantives and adjectives of the measures فَاعِل and فَاعِلَه: *e.g.*

خاتم *khātim*, 'a signet ring.'	خواتم *khawātim*.
قالب *ḳālib*, 'a mould,'	قوالب *ḳawālib*.
تابع *tābi'*, 'a follower,' 'an appositive,'	توابع *tawābi'*.
خاص *khāṣṣ*, 'a noble,' etc.,	خواص *khawāṣṣ*.
نادره *nādira*, 'a rarity,'	نوادر *nawādir*.
فائده *fā'ida*, 'advantage,'	فوائد *fawā'id*.
قاعده *ḳā'ida*, 'a rule,'	قواعد *ḳawā'id*.

Rem. The plural of Persian nouns also sometimes takes this form; *e.g.* كواغذ *kawāgiz*, from كاغذ *kāgaz*, 'paper.'

10) فَعَالِل—This form is used for the plural of quadriliteral substantives and adjectives (final ه or ت not being counted as a letter), the consonants of which are all

radical, or which are formed from triliteral roots by prefixing ا, ت, or م, which are treated as radical letters: *e.g.*

SINGULAR.	PLURAL.
جَوْهر *jauhar*, 'a gem,'	جواہِر *jawāhir*.
اقْرب *aḳrab*, 'a near relative,'	اقارِب *aḳārib*.
اکْبر *akbar*, 'greatest,'	اکابِر *akābir*.
تجْرِبہ *tajriba*, 'experience,'	تجارِب *tajārib*.
مدْرسہ *madrasa*, 'a college, or school,'	مدارِس *madāris*.
مُصِیبت *muṣībat*, 'misfortune,'	مصایِب *maṣāyib*, or مصائِب *maṣā'ib*.

11) فَعَالِیل—The singulars are quinquiliteral substantives or adjectives (final ه or ت not included), of which the penultimate letter is a long vowel (*ā*, *ū*, or *ī*): *e.g.*

سُلْطان *sulṭān*, 'a Sultan,'	سلاطِین *salāṭīn*.
شَیْطان *shaiṭān*, 'Satan,'	شیَاطِین *shayāṭīn*.
صنْدُوق *ṣandūḳ*, 'a box,'	صنادِیق *ṣanādīḳ*.
تارِیخ *tārīkh*, 'a chronicle,'	توارِیخ *tawārīkh*.[1]
تصْنِیف *taṣnīf*, 'a composition,'	تصانِیف *taṣānīf*.
اِقْلِیم *iḳlīm*, 'a clime,'	اقالِیم *aḳālīm*.
مِفْتاح *miftāḥ*, 'a key,'	مفاتِیح *mafātīḥ*.

Rem. The above forms are such as commonly occur in Urdū. Others of less frequent occurrence are:

a). فُعُل—This is used for singulars of the measures فَعِيلَه - فَعِيل - فِعَال and فَعُول, not derived from verbs which have و or ي for the third radical: as, کُتُب *kutub*, 'books,' from کِتاب *kitāb*; رُسُل *rusul*, 'messengers,' 'prophets,' from رسُول *rasūl*; مُدُن *mudun*, 'cities,' from مدِینہ *madīna*.

[1] The first radical of the word *tārīkh* is *alif* with *hamza*, and when this is preceded by *fatḥa* and followed by an *alif* of prolongation, it passes into *wā'o*; hence the plural form *tawārīkh* in lieu of *ta'ārīkh*.

b). فِعَل—The form of the singular is generally فِعْلَة : *e.g.* حِكم *ḥikam*, 'maxims,' from حِكْمت *ḥikmat*; سِيَر *siyar*, 'morals,' etc., from سِيرت *sīrat*.

c). فَعَلَة—This is used to form the plural of verbal adjectives of the measure فَاعِل denoting rational beings, and not derived from verbs having و or ي for the third radical: *e.g.* طلبة *ṭalaba*, 'students,' 'pupils,' from طَالِب *ṭālib*; جهلة *jahala*, 'ignorant persons,' from جاهِل *jāhil*.

d). فُعَلَة—The singulars are verbal adjectives of the form فَاعِل denoting rational beings, and derived from verbs having و or ي for the third radical: *e.g.* قُضات *ḳuẓāt* (for قُضَيَت), 'judges,' from قاضِي *ḳāẓī*; وُلات *wulāt* (for وُلَيَت), 'governors,' from والِي *wālī*.

e). فِعْلَة—The singulars usually have the forms فَعَال - فُعَال - فَعِيل: *e.g.* غِزْلة *gizla*, 'gazelles,' from غزال *gazāl*; غِلْمة *gilma*, 'boys,' from غُلام *gulām*; رِفْقة *rifḳa*, 'companions,' from رفِيق *rafīḳ*.

f). أَفْعُل—The singular is generally a noun of one of the measures فَعْل - فِعْل or فُعْل : *e.g.* افْلس *aflas*, 'small copper coins,' from فلْس *fals*; احْرف *aḥraf*, 'letters,' from حرْف *ḥarf*.

g). فِعْلان—Used to form the plural of nouns of the measures فَعَل - فَعَال, and فَعِيل; the first and the last from verbs of which the second and the third radical respectively is و: *e.g.* جِيران *jīrān*, 'neighbours,' from جار *jār*; غِلْمان *gilmān*, 'slave boys,' from غُلام *gulām*; صِبْيان *ṣibyān*, 'boys,' from صبِي *ṣabī*; إِخْوان *ikhwān*, 'brethren,' from اخ *akh* (for اخو).

h). فَعَالِي—The singular is generally of the measure فَعْلى - فِعْلى, or فُعْلى : *e.g.* فتاوِي *fatāwī*, 'judicial replies,' from فتْوى *fatwā*; اعالِي *a'ālī*, 'the upper or highest parts,' from اعْلى *a'lā*. Similarly اهالِي *ahālī*, from اهْل *ahl*, 'people.'

i). فَعَالِلَة—Used to form the plural of substantives and adjectives of four, five, or more letters (principally words foreign to the Arabic), of which the penultimate letter is a long vowel: *e.g.* ملائِكه *malā'ika*, 'angels,' from ملک *malak* (for مَلأَك), 'an angel;' فلاسِفه *falāsifa*, 'philosophers,' from فَيْلَسُوف *failasūf*.

126. From the preceding examples it is evident that one singular may have several forms of the broken plural, and even a sound or regular plural besides. In such cases, if the singular has several meanings, each of them often has a plural form peculiar to it. For example, بَيْت *bait* means 1) *a house*, 2) *a verse of poetry*; in the former sense the broken plural is usually بُيُوت *buyūt*, in the latter أَبْيات *abyāt*.

127. The broken plurals, being properly *collective* nouns, or singulars with a *collective* signification, often have regular plurals formed from them by the addition of the Arabic termination ـَات *āt*, or the plural terminations of the Hindī: *e.g.* بُيُوتات *buyūtāt*, 'families,' 'household expenses;' جواہِرات *jawāhirāt*, 'jewels:' امراؤں کو *umarā'oṅ-ko*, 'to nobles;' حُکّاموں سے *ḥukkāmoṅ-se*, 'from those in authority.' For the same reason broken plurals are not necessarily of the same gender as the singulars from which they are formed; thus, of the feminine word طرف *ṭaraf*, 'a side,' the plural اطراف *aṭrāf* is masculine, and of the masculine word وقت *waḳt*, 'time,' the plural اَوْقات *auḳāt* is feminine. Moreover, in one or two instances these plurals are treated as singular in Urdū: *e.g.* میرا احوال *merā aḥwāl*, 'my circumstances, or case;' تجارت کا اسباب *tijārat-kā asbāb*, 'trading commodities;' آپ کا الطاف ایساهي *āp-kā alṭāf aisā*, 'Your majesty's kindness is (favours are) such.' The words *asbāb* and *alṭāf*, however, are also treated as plurals.

Rem. The usage of the two great centres of Urdū—Dehlī and Lucknow—differs somewhat in respect of these broken plurals; some words being treated as singular in Dehlī, and plural in Lucknow. For example, the word جواهِر *jawāhir*, is frequently used as a singular in the *Bāg-o-bahār*, but Lucknow authors always use it as a plural.

The Numerals.

128. The Arabic numerals are occasionally used in Urdū, but rarely beyond *ten* or *twelve*.

The Cardinal Numbers.

129. The cardinals from *one* to ten are:

	MASC.	FEM.		MASC.	FEM.
1.	احد *aḥad*,	اِحْدى *iḥdā*.	5.	خمْسه *khamsa*,	خمْس *khams*.
	واحِد *wāḥid*,	واحِده *wāḥida*.	6.	سِتّه *sitta*,	سِت *sitt*.
2.	اِثْنان *is̤nān*,	اِثْنان *is̤nān*.	7.	سبْعه *sab'a*.	سبْع *sab'*.
		ثِنان *s̤inān*.	8.	ثمانِيَه *s̤amāniya*,	ثمانِي *s̤amānī*.
3.	ثلاثه *s̤alās̤a*,	ثلاث *s̤alās̤*.	9.	تِسْعه *tis'a*,	تِسْع *tis'*.
4.	اَرْبعه *arba'a*,	اَرْبع *arba'*.	10.	عشره *'ashara*,	عشْر *'ashr*.

The numbers from eleven to nineteen are formed by prefixing the units to the *ten*; as احد عشر *aḥad 'ashar*, 'eleven,' etc.

The Ordinal Numbers.

130. The ordinals from the *second* to the *tenth* take the form فَاعِل, the radical letters being the same as in the cardinals: *e.g.* اوّل *awwal*, 'first,' ثانِي *s̤ānī*, 'second,' ثالِث *s̤ālis̤*, 'third,' and so on. The feminines are formed by adding the termination ـَه to the masculine; as ثالِثا *s̤ālis̤ā*, 'third;' the word اوّل *awwal* however, being of the measure اَفْعَل, and having the superlative signification, takes for its feminine أولى *ulā* (§ 117).

131. The ordinals from the *twelfth* to the *nineteenth* inclusive are formed by adding the cardinal number عشر 'ten' to the preceding ordinals; the *eleventh* is formed by prefixing the word حادِي to the cardinal عشر: *e.g.* حادِي عشر *ḥādī 'ashar*, 'eleventh,' ثانِي عشر *ṣānī 'ashar*, 'twelfth,' etc.

Distributive Numerals.

132. Arabic Distributives are not common in Urdū, and of the three measures used in Arabic, one alone is to be found; viz. فُعَال: *e.g.* ثُلاث *ṣulāṣ*, 'by threes.'

Multiplicatives.

133. The Multiplicatives (with the exception of *single*) are expressed by the Passive Participle of the *second form*, derived from the cardinal numbers: *e.g.* مُثنّى *muṣannā*, 'double,' 'a duplicate;' مُثلّث *muṣallaṣ*, 'threefold,' 'triple,' 'three-sided;' مُربّع *murabba'*, 'fourfold,' 'square.' *Single* or *simple* is expressed by مُفرد *mufrad*, the pass. part. of the *fourth* form.

Fractional Numbers.

134. The fractions from *a third* up to *a tenth* are expressed by words of the measures فُعْل or فُعُل derived from the cardinals: *e.g.* ثُلث *ṣuls*, 'a third,' رُبع *rub'*, 'a fourth,' خُمس *khums*, 'a fifth,' etc. *A half* is نِصْف *niṣf*.

V. THE PERSONAL PRONOUNS (ضمِير *ẓamīr*).

135. The Personal Pronouns are *two* in number; namely مَیں *main*, 'I,' and تُو *tū*, or تَیں *tain*, 'thou;' the form تَیں however, though still current in Hindī, has become obsolete in Urdū. The place of the pronoun of the *third* person is supplied by the Demonstrative pronouns, chiefly by the *Remote* Demonstrative وُہ *wŏh*.

136. The personal pronouns present certain peculiarities of declension. The Formative singular of the *first* person is مجھ *mujh*; that of the *second* تجھ *tujh*; the Agent and Genitive cases are generally formed from the *Nominative;* and the adjective affix کا *kā*, which is used to form the genitive of nouns, is changed to را *rā*, which in the plural has the connecting vowel *ā* prefixed to it. The plural Formatives are derived from the plural nominatives, by the addition of ـوں *oṅ*, or, in the second person, هوں *hoṅ*: *e.g.* nom. pl. هم *ham*, 'we,' Form. pl. هموں *hamoṅ*; nom. pl. تم *tum*, 'you,' Form. pl. تمهوں *tumhoṅ*; *but the termination* ـوں *oṅ is now always dropped*, and the *h* of the termination *hoṅ* is seldom used, except in the genitive, and the *additional* form of the dative case. This additional form ends in the singular in ـي *e*, and in the plural in يں *eṅ*, which last termination is always added to the contracted Formative تمهہ *tumh*.

Rem. The pronominal forms are clearly traceable to the Prākrit: *e.g.*

	HINDĪ.		PRĀKRIT.
Nom. sing. . . .	مَیں	=	मं *maṅ* (acc. sing.).
Gen. ,, ...	میرا	=	मे *me* (gen. sing. + affix *rā*).
Form. ,, ...	مجھ	=	मज्झ *majjha* (gen. sing. *cf.* § 39, 2, *Rem.*).
Nom. plur. . . .	هم	=	अम्हे *amhe* (acc. plur.).
Gen. ,, . . .	همارا	=	अम्हाणं *amhāṇaṅ* (gen. plur. + affix *rā*).
Form. ,, . .	هموں	=	अम्हाणं *amhāṇaṅ* (gen. plur.).
Nom. sing. . . .	تو	=	तुं *tuṅ* (acc. sing).
Gen. ,, ...	تیرا	=	ते *te* (gen. sing. + *rā*).
Form. ,, ...	تجھ	=	तुज्झ *tujjha* (gen. sing.).
Nom. plur. . . .	تم	=	तुम्हे *tumhe* (acc. plur.).
Gen. ,, . . .	تمہارا	=	तुम्हाणं *tumhānaṅ*, (gen. plur. + *rā*).
Form. ,,	تمهہ - تمهوں	=	तुम्हाणं *tumhānaṅ* (gen. plur.).

The forms هم *ham* and تم *tum* in the plural Formative are, as we have observed above, contractions of ہموں *hamoṅ* and تُمھوں *tumhoṅ*. So in Prākrit we find अम्ह *amha*, as well as अम्हाणं *amhānaṅ*, for the genitive. The dative forms مُجھے *mujhe*, ہمیں *hameṅ*, etc., would appear to be but varieties of the Formative.

137. The personal pronouns are thus declined:

FIRST PERSON.

مَیں *maiṅ*, 'I.'

	SINGULAR.	PLURAL.
Nom.	مَیں *maiṅ*, 'I.'	ہم *ham*, 'we.'
Agent	مَیں نے *maiṅ-ne*, 'by me.'	ہم نے *ham-ne*, 'by us.'
Gen.	میرا *me-rā*, 'my,' 'of me.'	ہمارا *ham-ārā*, 'our,' 'of us.'
Form.	مُجھ *mujh*.	ہم *ham* (for ہموں *hamoṅ*).
Dat. and Act.	مُجھکو *mujh-ko*, or مُجھے *mujhe*, 'to me,' 'me.'	ہمکو *ham-ko*, or ہمیں *hameṅ*, 'to us,' 'us.'
Abl.	مُجھ سے *mujh-se*, 'from, by, me.'	ہم سے *ham-se*, 'from, by, us.'
Loc.	مُجھ میں - پر *mujh-meṅ*, *-par*, 'in, on, me.'	ہم میں - پر *ham-meṅ*, *-par*, 'in, on, us.'

SECOND PERSON.

تُو *tū*, 'thou.'

Nom.	تُو *tū*, 'thou.'	تُم *tum*, 'you.'
Agent	تُونے *tū-ne*, 'by thee.'	تُم نے *tum-ne*, 'by you.'
Gen.	تیرا *te-rā* 'thy,' 'of thee.'	تُمھارا *tumh-ārā*, 'your,' 'of you.'
Form.	تُجھ *tujh*.	تُم or تُمھ *tum* or *tumh* (from تُمھوں).
Dat. and Act.	تُجھکو *tujh-ko*, or تُجھے *tujhe*, 'to thee.' 'thee.'	تُمکو *tum-ko*, or تُمھیں *tumheṅ*, 'to you,' 'you.'
Abl.	تُجھ سے *tujh-se*, 'from, by, thee.'	تُم سے *tum-se*, 'from, by, you.'
Loc.	تُجھ میں - پر *tujh-meṅ*, *-par*, 'in, on, me.'	تُم میں - پر *tum-meṅ*, *-par* 'in, on, you.'

Rem. a. The pronoun of the second person has no vocative case. The expression أي تو *ai tū* is only heard from the lips of Englishmen, or native Christians, who have learned it from the missionaries.

Rem. b. The forms ميرا *merā*, تيرا *terā*, همارا *hamārā*, تمهارا *tumhārā*, are properly possessive adjectives. The true genitive, which occurs occasionally (always in connection with an adjective), is identical with the *Formative*: *e.g.* مجھ کم بخت کي کتاب *mujh kam-ba<u>kh</u>t-kī kitāb*, 'the book of luckless me.' Similarly, if an adjective qualify a pronoun in the Agent case, the Formative is employed as the base; as تجھ بد بخت نے ايسا کيا *tujh bad-ba<u>kh</u>t-ne aisā kiyā*, 'thou, wretched one, actedst thus,' or *lit.* 'by thee, wretched one, it was done thus.' So also if the 'adjective of similitude' سا *sā*, follow the pronouns, the Formative is used as the base: *e.g.* تجھ سا عقلمند *tujh-sā 'aḳlmand*, 'a wise man like thee,' or, ironically, 'a wiseacre like thee.' In poetry the forms ميرا and تيرا are often contracted to مرا *mirā* and ترا *tirā*.

Rem. c. The Formatives مجھ *mujh*, تجھ *tujh*, are frequently contracted to مج *muj*, تج *tuj*; as مجکو *muj-ko*, تجکو *tuj-ko*; and the dative and accusative occasionally take the form ميري تئيں *mere ta'īn*, تيري تئيں *tere ta'īn* in the older literature, but these forms are now nearly obsolete.

138. The addition of the particle هي *hī* (pl. هيں *hīn*) to the pronouns gives them greater force, or, in some way, emphasizes them: *e.g.* ميں هي *main-hī*, '*I*,' ميرا هي *merā-hī*, 'mine,' 'mine alone.'

VI. THE DEMONSTRATIVE PRONOUN (اِسمِ اِشاره).

139. The *Proximate* Demonstrative (اِشارهٔ قريب *ishāra'ĕ ḳarīb*) is يه *yĕh*, 'this,' nom. pl. يه *yĕh*, or يے *ye*; the

Remote Demonstrative (اِشارۂ بعِيد *ishāra'ĕ ba'īd*) is وُہ *wŏh*, nom. pl. وُہ *wŏh*, وو *wo*, or وي *we*. Both are used for the pronoun of the third person, but the remote demonstrative is the one more commonly employed.

Rem. The pronoun يِہ *yĕh* (Hindī *yah*) is derived from the Sanskrit ई ī; وُہ *wŏh* (Hindī *wah*, Panjabī *uh*, Sindhī *hū*), probably from the Sanskrit स्व *sva* (see Bopp's Comp. Grammar, § 341). The Formatives are the contracted genitives (singular) of the Prākrit, with the initial vowel *a* of the genitive affix changed to *i*: *e.g.* اِس = अस्स *assa* = Sanskrit अस्य *asya*. In the old Formative وِس *wis*, a similar change of vowel occurs.

140. The demonstratives are declined as follows:

يِہ *yĕh*, 'this,' 'he,' 'she,' 'it.'

SINGULAR.	PLURAL.
Nom. يِہ *yĕh*, 'this,' 'he,' 'she,' 'it.'	يِہ - يے *yĕh*, or *ye*, 'these,' 'they.'
Form. اِس *is*.	اِنہوں - *اِنہ - *اِن *inhoṅ*, *inh*, or *in*.
Agent اِس نے - *اِن نے *is-ne*, or *in-ne*, 'by him,' etc.	اِنہوں نے - اِن نے *inhoṅ-ne*, or *in-ne*, 'by thee,' etc.
Gen. اِسکا *is-kā*, 'of this,' 'his,' etc.	اِنکا *in-kā*, 'of these,' 'their,' etc.
Dat. and Acc. اِسکو - *اِسے *is-ko*, or *ise*, 'to this, or him,' etc., 'this,' 'him,' etc.	اِنکوا - *اِنہیں *in-ko*, or *inh-eṅ*, 'to them,' etc. 'them,' etc.
Abl. اِس سے *is-se*, 'from, with, by, this,' etc.	اِن سے *in-se*, 'from these,' etc.
Loc. اِس میں - پر *is-meṅ*, *-par*, 'in, on, this,' etc.	اِن میں - پر *in-meṅ*, *-par*, 'in, on, these,' etc.

وه *wŏh*, 'that,' 'he,' 'she,' 'it.'

	SINGULAR.	PLURAL.
Nom.	وه *wŏh*, 'that, he,' etc.	وه - وو - وي *wŏh*, *wo*, or *we*, {'those,' 'they.'}
Form.	اُس *us*.	اُنهوں* - اُنهه* - اُن *unhoṅ*, *unh*, *un*.
Agent	اُس نے - اُن نے* *us-ne*, or *un-ne*, 'by him,' etc.	اُنهوں نے - اُن نے *unhoṅ-ne*, or *un-ne*, 'by them.'
Gen.	اُسکا *us-kā*, 'his,' etc.	اُنکا *un-kā*, 'their,' 'of them.'
Dat. and Act.	اُسکو - اُسے* *us-ko*, or *use*, {'to him,' etc., 'him,' etc.}	اُنکو - اُنهیں* *un-ko* or *unh-eṅ*, {'to them.' 'them.'}
Abl.	اُس سے *us-se*, 'from him,' etc.	اُن سے *un-se*, 'from them.'
Loc.	اُس میں - پر *us-meṅ*, *-par*, 'in, on, him,' etc.	اُن میں - پر *un-meṅ*, *-par*, 'in, on, them.'

141. The forms marked with an asterisk can only be used when the demonstratives are employed as *personal* pronouns. As adjectives the demonstratives cannot be said to take any postpositions after them beyond those which are added to the substantives they define; in other words, they have but two forms, the *Nominative* and the *Formative*: *e.g.* اُس آدمي کو *us admī-ko*, 'to that man,' اِس کِتاب میں *is kitāb meṅ*, 'in this book.' As adjectives moreover the demonstratives may also take the various nominative forms in the accusative: *e.g.* يِهه بات سُنکر *yĕh bāt sunkar*, 'having heard this matter.' As regards the Formatives اِنهه *inh* اُنهه *unh*, اِنهوں *inhoṅ* and *unhoṅ*, it may be observed that modern usage restricts the shorter forms to the Dative ending in ـيں *eṅ* and the longer to the Agent case. The forms اُن *in* and *un* of the *singular* Agent are obtained by assimilating the *s* of اِس *is* and *us* to the *n* of the postposition نے *ne*, and must not be confounded with the plural Formatives *in* and *un*, which may be used

in polite speech in any case of the singular in place of *is* and *us*; but where marked respect is to be indicated, the forms اُنہوں نے *inhoṅ* and *unhoṅ-ne* are employed for the third person singular in the Agent case.

Rem. a. Forms now obsolete or rare are: *a*) وِس *wis* and وِن *win*, as the Formatives of وُہ, in place of اُس *us* and اُن; *b*) اِسکے تئِیں *iske ta'īṅ* and *uske ta'īṅ*, etc., for the dative and accusative of both pronouns.

Rem. b. The Formatives of وُہ *wŏh* are commonly written اوس, اون (pronounced however *us*, *un*), in order to distinguish them from the Formatives of یِہہ *yĕh*, as, in the absence of vowel points, the two are likely to be confounded.

Rem. c. The plural forms یِہہ, وُہ, وو, are of frequent occurrence, both in old and modern writings, and are preferred by the Musalmāns of Northern India, and Urdū scholars generally, to the Hindī forms یے *ye* and وي *we*.

142. The emphatic particle ـي *ī* (plural ـين *īṅ*) is frequently added to the demonstratives, in order to point out the object with greater distinctness: *e.g.* یِہي *yĕhī*, 'this very,' 'the very same,' وُہي *wŏhī*, 'that very,' اِسي ميں *isī meṅ*, 'in this same,' or اِنهيں ميں *inhīṅ meṅ*, 'in these very.'

143. Like the demonstrative یِہہ *yĕh* are declined:

VII. THE RELATIVE PRONOUN (اِسْمِ مَوْصُول).

جو *jo* or جَوْن *jaun*, 'who,' 'which,' 'what,' 'he who,' etc.

	SINGULAR.	PLURAL.
Nom.	جَوْن or جو *jo* or *jaun*.	جَوْن or جو *jo* or *jaun*.
Form.	جِس *jis* (and, for the Agent, جِن* *jin*).	جِن, جِنهہ*, or جِنهوں* *jin*, *jinh*, or *jinhoṅ*.

Rem. The repetition of the relative pronoun gives it an indefinite, or a distributive signification: *e.g.* جو جو *jo jo*, 'whatever,' Formative جِس جِس *jis jis*.

VIII. THE CORRELATIVE (جوابِ اِسْمِ مَوْصُول).

سو *so*, or تَوْن *taun*, 'he,' 'she,' 'it,' 'that.'

	SINGULAR.	PLURAL.
Nom.	تَوْن or سو *so* or *taun*.	تَوْن or سو *so* or *taun*.
Form.	تِس *tis* (and, for the Agent, تِن* *tin*).	تِن, تِنھ*, or تِنھوں* *tin, tinh, tinhoṅ*.

Rem. The correlative generally accompanies the relative as its complement; as جو چڑھیگا سو گِریگا *jo chaṛhegā so giregā*, 'he who climbs will fall' (*lit.* 'whoever climbs, he will fall'). Modern usage prefers the pronoun وُہ *wŏh* to سو *so* in the place of the correlative. When the relative is repeated, so also is the correlative.

IX. THE INTERROGATIVE (اِسْمِ اِسْتِفْهام).

کَون *kaun* 'who?' 'what?' 'which?'

	SINGULAR.	PLURAL.
Nom.	کَون *kaun*.	کَون *kaun*.
Form.	کِس *kis* (and, for the Agent, کِن* *kin*).	کِن, کِنھ*, or کِنھوں*, *kin, kinh,* or *kinhoṅ*.

Rem. a. The forms marked with an asterisk cannot be employed when these pronouns are used as adjectives. In poetry, the interrogative, when used adjectively, occasionally employs the nominative (کَون) for the Formative.

Rem. b. The pronoun جو = the Prākrit जो *jo*, = Sanskrit यः *yah*; جَون *jaun* = P. जं *jam* (the acc. of *jo*); سو *so* = P. सो *so*; تَون *taun* = P. तं *tam* (the acc. of *so*). Similarly کَون *kaun* = कं *kam*, the acc. of the Sanskrit किम *kim*. The Formatives are the Prākrit genitives with the feminine bases, *i.e.* with the vowel *a* changed to *i*: *e.g.* جِس *jis* = P. gen. sing. जस्स *jassa* = S. यस्य *yasya*; جِن *jin* = P. gen. pl. जाणं *jāṇam*.

144. The interrogative کَون *kaun* is applicable to both persons and things. A second interrogative pronoun کیا *kyā*, 'what?' is applicable to things only. It has no plural: in the singular it is declined as follows:

کیا *kyā*, 'what?'

Nom. کیا *kyā*.	Formative کاهے *kāhe*.

The Formative کاهے *kāhe* however is now rarely used, except in the genitive and dative cases, the Formative کِس *kis* of the interrogative کَون *kaun* being generally used instead. The genitive کاهے کا *kāhe-kā* has the signification of 'of what (thing, or material?),' which however is more generally expressed by کِس چیزکا *kis chīz-kā*. The dative کاهے کو *kāhe-ko* always signifies, 'for what?' 'why?' and even this is more commonly expressed in Urdū by the interrogative adverbs کِس واسطے *kis-wāsṭe*, and کیوں *kyoṅ*.

Rem. a. Like the English 'what,' کیا *kyā* may be used to express *indignation, surprise,* etc.; *e.g.* کیا کرتا هَي *kyā kartā hai*, 'what art thou doing!' کیا جوانمردي *kyā jawān-mardī*, 'what valour or generosity!' In some instances it has the signification of 'how;' as کیا خُوب *kyā khūb*, 'how excellent!' It may also be repeated, as is the English 'what,' to connect sentences, or to convey a partitive signification. (See Syntax.)

Rem. b. The interrogative کیا *kyā* (for *kiā*) is derived from the Sanskrit किम *kim*: the form کاهے *kāhe* is properly the Formative of the Hindī interrogative काहा *kahā*, 'what?' which would appear to be derived from the Sanskrit कः *kaḥ*.

X. THE INDEFINITE PRONOUNS (اسمائے تنکیر).

145. The Indefinite pronouns are of two kinds, simple and compound. The simple indefinite pronouns are کوئي *kōī*, 'some one,' 'some,' 'any,' 'a certain,' and کچھ *kuchh*, 'some,' 'something,' 'any,' 'a few,' etc.

146. The pronoun کوئي *ko'ī*, is declined in the singular only; thus—

Sing. Nom. کوئي *ko'ī*, 'some,' etc. Formative کِسي *kisī*, or کِسُو *kisū*.

The Formative کِسُو *kisū*, however, is not so generally used at the present time as کِسي *kisī*, which is applied to things as well as persons: *e.g.* کِسي کِتاب میں *kisī kitāb-men*, 'in some book.'

The pronoun کچھ *kuchh* is indeclinable.

Rem. a. The indefinite pronouns are both derived from the same source as the interrogatives: *e.g.* کوئي *kō'ī* = Sanskrit कोऽपि *ko'pi* (*kas* + *api*); کچھ = S. कच्चित् *kachchit* (किंचित् *kiṁchit*).

Rem. b. In poetry the Formative of کوئي *ko'ī* as an adjective is occasionally identical with the nominative: *e.g.* مُجھ سے مت جي کو لگاؤ کِہ نہیں رہنے کا ـ مَیں مُسافِر ہُوں کوئي دِن کو چلا جاؤنگا *mujh-se mat jī-ko lagā'o ki nahīn rahne-kā; main musāfir hūn, ko'ī din-ko chalā-jā'ūngā*, 'Set not your heart on me' (*lit.* 'unite not your soul with me'); 'I shall not stay; I am a traveller, some day I shall depart.'

147. Emphatic forms of these pronouns are obtained: 1) by repeating them: *e.g.* کوئي کوئي *ko'ī ko'ī*, 'a very few,' 'some few;' کچھ کچھ *kuchh kuchh*, 'somewhat,' 'a very little:' 2) by combining them with the pronominal adjective ایک *ek*: *e.g.* کوئي ایک *ko'ī ek*, or ایک کوئي *ek ko'ī*, 'some one,' 'a few;' کچھ ایک *kuchh ek*, 'some little,'

'somewhat:' 3) by repetition and insertion of the negative نہ *na*: *e.g.* كوئي نہ كوئي *ko'ī na ko'ī*, '*some* one,' 'some one or other;' كُچھ نہ كُچھ *kuchh na kuchh*, 'something or other.'

Rem. The phrase كُچھ كا كُچھ *kuchh-kā kuchh* is used to signify 'something very or quite different.'

148. By placing the negative substantive verb نہِیں *nahīn* after the simple indefinite pronouns we have كوئي نہِیں *ko'ī nahīn*, 'it is, or there is, no one or nobody,' كُچھ نہِیں *kuchh nahīn*, 'it is nothing.'

Rem. The word نہِیں is both a negative *particle* and a negative *substantive verb* = نہ هَي *na hai*, and as a verb it occurs at the end of a sentence: *e.g.* كوئي نہِیں *ko'ī nahīn*, 'there is nobody;' but كوئي نہِیں آيا *ko'ī nahīn āyā*, 'anyone did not come,' *i.e.* 'no one came.' The same distinction is found in the sister dialects: *e.g.* Sindhī كونهے *konhe* = كو نہ آهے *ko na āhe*, 'there is no one.'

149. Compound indefinite pronouns are commonly formed by combining the simple indefinites with the relative جو *jo*, or one of the pronominal adjectives آوّر *aur*, 'other,' دُوسّرا *dūsrā*, 'other,' سب *sab*, 'all,' هر *har*, 'every.'

The compounds with كوئي *ko'ī* are declinable: *e.g.*

SING. NOM.		SING. FORMATIVE.
جو كوئي *jo ko'ī*,	'whoever,' 'whosoever,'	جس كِسي *jis kisī*.
آوّر كوئي *aur ko'ī*,	'some other,'	آوّر كِسي *aur kisī*.
كوئي آوّر *ko'ī aur*,	'some one else,'	كِسي آوّر *kisī aur*.
دُوسّرا كوئي *dūsrā ko'ī*,	'some other,'	دُوسّري كِسي *dūsre kisī*.
كوئي دُوسّرا *ko'ī dūsrā*,	'some one else,'	كِسي دُوسّري *kisī dūsre*.
سب كوئي *sab ko'ī*,	'all persons,' 'every one,'	سب كِسي *sab kisī*.
هر كوئي *har-ko'ī*,	'every one,' 'everybody,'	هر كِسي *har kisī*.

The compounds with کچھ *kuchh* are indeclinable. Examples are:

جو کچھ *jo kuchh*, 'whatever,' سب کچھ *sab kuchh*, 'what all,' 'everything.'

اور کچھ *aur kuchh*, 'something else,' بہت کچھ *bahut kuchh*, 'a great deal.'

XI. THE REFLEXIVE PRONOUN.

150. The Reflexive pronoun is آپ *āp*, 'self,' 'myself,' 'himself,' 'I myself,' etc. It has but one form for the singular and plural, and is declined as follows:

Nom. آپ *āp*.

Gen. (adj.) اپنا *ap-nā* (fem. اپنی *ap-nī*).

Dat. and Act. اپنے تئیں - اپنے کو - آپکو *apne ta'īṅ*, *apne-ko* or *āp-ko*.

Abl. آپ سے *āp-se*.

Loc. آپ میں - پر *āp-meṅ,-par*.

Rem. a. The reflexive is combined emphatically with the other pronouns: *e.g.* میں آپ *maiṅ āp*, 'I myself;' وہ آپ *wŏh āp*, 'he himself;' تم آپ سے *tum āp-se*, 'you of yourselves' (*lit.* 'from or by yourselves').

Rem. b. آپ *āp* = Prākrit अप्पा *appā* = Sanskrit आत्मा *ātmā*, 'soul,' 'self.'

151. Besides the Formative آپ *āp*, the form آپس *āpas* also occurs, but only in the genitive and locative plural: *e.g.* آپس کا *āpas-kā*, 'of, or pertaining to, ourselves, yourselves, or themselves;' آپس میں *āpas-meṅ*, 'among ourselves,' etc. The use of one or other of the personal pronouns depends on the context.

Rem. The Persian reflexive pronoun خود *khwud*, is also commonly used in Urdū. Unlike آپ *āp*, however, it is generally used with the personal and demonstrative pronouns alone: *e.g.* میں خود *maiṅ khwud*, 'I myself;' وے خود *we khwud*, 'they themselves.' To express the signification of the ablative آپ سے *āp-se* (or the phrase آپ سے آپ *āp-se āp*), the Persian preposition از *az* = سے *se*, is prefixed to خود : *e.g.* از خود *az khwud*, 'from, or of, itself,' ('myself,' 'himself,' etc.), 'voluntarily,' 'spontaneously.' In Persian phrases it is also employed adjectively in the sense of 'own:' *e.g.* بچشمِ خود *ba-chashmĕ khwud*, 'with my own eyes.'

152. آپ *āp* is also very commonly used as the *pronomen reverentiæ*, in both the second and the third person. When so used it is declined as follows:

NOM. SING.	FORM. SING.
آپ *āp*, 'your honour,' 'his honour.'	آپ *āp*.

Thus it differs from the reflexive by taking for its genitive the form آپکا *āp-kā*, and for its dative the form آپکو *āp-ko* alone. Like the English 'you,' though used in the singular, it is treated as a plural: *e.g.* آپ امیر ہیں *āp amīr hain*, 'your honour is (*lit.* are) a great man,' or 'you are a great man;' آپ فرماتے ہیں *āp farmāte hain*, 'his honour says' (*lit.* 'say').

Rem. Other words which, like آپ *āp*, are commonly used for the sake of politeness, respect, or euphemy, and require the verb to be in the plural, are حضرت *hazrat*, حضور *huzūr*, خداوند *khudā-wand*, خداوندِ نعمت *khudā-wandĕ nĕʻmat*, جناب *janāb*, جنابِ عالي *janābĕ ʻālī*, عالي جاه *ʻālī jāh*, غريب پرور *garīb-parwar*, بنده نواز *banda-nawāz*, صاحب *sāhib*, مخدوم *makhdūm*, etc.—all synonymous words or phrases used as the corresponding English words 'you,' 'Sir,' 'Master,' etc. Similarly when speaking of himself, instead of using the pronoun میں *main*, 'I,' a native frequently uses such words as بنده *banda*, 'slave, or humble servant,' کمترین *kamtarīn*, 'least of slaves,' احقر *ahkar*, 'meanest servant,' خاکسار *khāk-sār*, 'humble slave,' غلام *gulām*, 'slave,' 'servant,' فدوي *fidwī*, 'devoted servant,' etc. On the same principle too 'my son' is expressed by بنده زاده *banda-zāda*, 'the son of this slave,' and a wife is spoken of as قبيله *ḳabīla*, 'family,' گهرکے آدمي *ghar-ke ādmī*, 'the household or family,' etc.

XII. RECIPROCAL PRONOUNS.

153. Reciprocal pronouns have no special form in Urdū. Reciprocity of feeling or action is expressed, as in English, by combining the pronominal adjectives ايک *ek*, 'one,' and دُوسرا *dūsrā*, 'another:' *e.g.* Nom. ايک دُوسرا *ek dūsrā*, 'each other,' 'one another,' Formative ايک دُوسري *ek dūsre.*

XIII. POSSESSIVE PRONOUNS (ضمِيرِ مُضاف اِلَيه).

154. The Possessive pronouns are the genitive cases of the personal, demonstrative, relative, interrogative, and reflexive pronouns: *e.g.*

SINGULAR.	PLURAL.
ميرا *merā*, 'my,' 'thine.'	همارا *hamārā*, 'our,' 'ours.'
تيرا *terā*, 'thy,' 'thine.'	تُمهارا *tumhārā*, 'your,' 'yours.'
اِسکا *iskā*, } 'his,' 'hers,' 'its.'	اِنکا *inkā*, } 'their,' 'theirs.'
اُسکا *uskā*, }	اُنکا *unkā*, }
جِسکا *jiskā*, 'whose,' etc.	جِنکا *jinkā*, 'whose,' etc.
تِسکا *tiskā*, 'his,' etc.	تِنکا *tinkā*, 'their,' 'theirs.'
کِسکا *kiskā*, 'whose?'	کِنکا *kinkā*, 'whose?'
اپنا *apnā*, 'own.'	

These are all declined like other adjectives ending in *ā*; *e.g.* masc. ميرا *merā*, fem. مري *merī*; Form. sing. masc. ميري *mere*, Nom. and Form. pl. masc. ميري *mere.* The pronoun اپنا *apnā* however is more commonly used as a substitute for the possessive pronouns *merā*, *terā*, and *uskā* than as a distinct reflexive adjective, and when so used it always refers to the principal subject, whether this be expressed or understood: *e.g.* اپنا سبق سُنا *apnā sabaḳ sunā*, 'repeat thy lesson,' (*lit.* 'cause me to, or let me, hear thy lesson');

مَیں نے اپنا گہوڑا بیچا *main-ne apnā ghoṛā benchā*, 'I have sold my horse' (*lit.* 'my horse has been sold by me').

Rem. The genitive of the adjective نِج *nij*, 'own,' is also used in Urdū as a reflexive adjective: *e.g.* میرا نِجکا ہاتھي *merā nij-kā hāthī*, 'my own elephant.'

XIV. PRONOMINAL ADJECTIVES.

155. Under this head may be classed such adjectives as partake more or less of the nature of pronouns. They are of two kinds; *primitive* and *derivative*. The primitive are:

ایک *ek*, 'one.'
دُوسرا *dūsrā*, 'another,' 'other.'
دونوں *donoṅ*, 'both.'
اَور *aur*, 'other,' 'more.'
بہُت *bahut*, 'much,' 'many.'
بعض *ba'z*, }
بعضے *ba'ze*, } 'some,' 'certain.'
غَیر *gair*, 'other' ('different').

سب *sab*, 'all,' 'every one.'
ہر *har*, 'each,' 'every.'
فُلاں *fulāṅ*, }
فُلانہ *fulāna*, } 'such-and-such.'
فُلانا *fulānā*, }
کئِي *ka'ī*, }
چند *chand*, } 'several,' 'many.'
کُل *kull*, 'all,' 'the whole.'
کَي *kai*, 'how many?'

As adjectives they are all (with the exception of دُوسرا *dūsrā* and فُلانا *fulānā*) *indeclinable*; but as nouns they are (with the exception of ایک *ek*, دونوں *donoṅ*, کئِي *ka'ī*, and کَي *kai*) declined in the plural: *e.g.* Nom. pl. اَور *aur*, Formative اَوروں *auroṅ*. The word سب *sab* generally aspirates the *b* in the Formative: *e.g.* سبہوں *sabhoṅ*.

Rem. The origin of the words ایک *ek*, دُوسرا *dūsrā*, and دونوں *donoṅ* has been given in treating of the numeral adjectives; بہُت *bahut* = Sanskrit बहु *bahu*(?); سب *sab* = S. सर्व *sarva*; کئِي *ka'ī* and کَي *kai* = S. कति *kati*; بعض *ba'z*, غَیر *gair*, فُلاں *fulāṅ*, فُلانہ *fulāna*, and کُل *kull* are borrowed from the Arabic; ہر *har* and چند *chand* from the Persian.

156. The *derivatives* are such adjectives as are formed from the original pronominal bases by means of the terminations تّا *ttā*, تنا *tnā*, and سا *sā*, the first two being used to form pronominal adjectives denoting *measure* or *quantity*, and the last such as denote *kind* or *similitude*. A long vowel in the base is shortened before the terminations *ttā* and *tnā* are added, and a short vowel in the base is lengthened to *e* or *ai* (in Urdū generally to *ai*) before the termination *sā* is added : *e.g.*

PRONOMINAL BASES.	ADJECTIVES OF QUANTITY.	ADJECTIVES OF KIND, ETC.
ī, *i* or *ĕ*.	اِتّا *ittā* (*ĕttā*), اِتنا *itnā* (*ĕtnā*), } 'this much.'	اَیسا *aisā*, 'of this kind,' 'like this,' 'such.'
ū or *wa*.	اُتّا *uttā*, اُتنا *utnā*, } 'that much.'	وَیسا *waisā*, 'of that kind,' 'like that.'
ji (fem. of *ja*, the base of *jo*).	جِتّا *jittā* (*jĕttā*), جِتنا *jitnā* (*jĕtnā*), } 'as much.'	جَیسا *jaisā*, 'of which kind,' 'like which.'
ti (fem. of the base of *so*).	تِتّا *tittā* (*tĕttā*), تِتنا *titnā* (*tĕtnā*), } 'so much.'	تَیسا *taisā*, 'of what kind,' 'like that.'
ki (fem. of base of *ka*).	کِتّا *kittā* (*kĕttā*), کِتنا *kitnā* (*kĕtnā*), } 'how much.'	کَیسا *kaisā*, 'of what kind?' 'like what?'

Rem. Although these pronominal adjectives may be conveniently described as formed in the manner mentioned above, there can be little doubt of their being really modifications of Prākrit forms: *e.g.* کِتّا *kittā*, = Prākrit केत्तिअ *kĕttia* = Sanskrit कियत् *kiyat*: in کِتنا *kitnā* the second *t* is, perhaps for the sake of euphony, changed into *n*. Similarly اَیسا *aisā* = P. एरिसो *ĕriso* = S. ईदृश *īdṛiśa*; کَیسا *kaisā* = केरिसो *kĕriso* = S. कीदृश *kīdriśa*. By the elision of the syllable *ri* in the Prākrit forms, are obtained the common Hindī forms *esā* and *kesā*, the short vowel *ĕ* of the Prākrit being lengthened.

CHAPTER III.

THE VERB (فِعّل).

157. The Urdū verbs may be conveniently divided into the two classes of *Transitive* (فِعّل مُتعدّي *fĕʻlĕ mutaʻaddī*, 'the verb that passes on' to an object), and *Intransitive* (فِعّل لازِمي *fĕʻlĕ lāzimī*, 'the verb that is confined to the subject'), the last including both *active* and *neuter* verbs, as *to run*, *to sleep*. For although *there is but one conjugation*, and *the inflectional terminations are the same in all verbs*, there is a marked difference in the formation of some of the tenses of the transitive verbs.

158. Transitive verbs have two Voices, viz. the *Active* and the *Passive*. The other verbal forms, such as Mood, etc., it will be more convenient to notice after we have spoken of the nouns and adjectives which are derived from the verbal root.

159. The root or crude form of a verb is found in the second person singular of the Imperative. It is in many cases used as an abstract verbal noun.

160. The verbal nouns are *two* in number:—

1). THE INFINITIVE OR GERUND (مصّدر),

which is formed by adding to the verbal root the termination نا *nā*: *e.g.* Root چل *chal*, 'to move,' etc., Infinitive چلّنا *chal-nā*, 'to move or go,' 'moving or going.' The infinitive is the form in which verbs are usually given in

Dictionaries, so that the verbal root may always be known by dropping the termination نا *nā*.

Rem. In most instances the infinitive is, no doubt, the Sanskrit verbal noun ending in *ana*, modified, it may be, by the laws of transformation obtaining in the Prākrits. At the same time it is evident that the Sanskrit affix *ana* alone has been borrowed, and changed to *nā*; for we find it joined to Persian and Arabic verbal nouns, and occasionally to other nouns and adjectives: *e.g.* خريدنا *kharīd-nā*, 'to purchase' (from the Persian خريد); بدلنا *badal-nā*, 'to change or exchange' (from the Arabic بدل); گرمانا *garmā-nā*, 'to get warm or heated' (from گرم *garm*, 'hot'); پنيانا *paniyā-nā*, 'to water,' 'to irrigate' (from پاني *pānī*, 'water'). It may be observed also that the Sanskrit verbal noun, with the final vowel dropped, is occasionally employed in Urdū (in Hindī frequently) as an abstract noun: *e.g.* چلن *chalan*, 'going,' 'gait,' 'conduct,' etc.

2). The Noun of Agency (إسم فاعل),

which is also a Future Active Participle. It is formed by adding to the *inflected* infinitive, the termination والا, *wālā*: *e.g.* چلنے والا *chal-ne-wālā*, 'mover,' 'goer,' and, 'about to move or go.'

Rem. Instead of والا, *wālā*, the affix هار *hār* or هارا *hārā* is occasionally used, but more commonly in Hindī than in Urdū. In the former of these dialects it is also frequently added to the Sanskrit form of the verbal noun; as مرن هار *maran-hār*, 'about to die,' or 'one who is about to die.' The affix *wālā* corresponds to the Sanskrit वल *vala*; هارا *hārā*, to the Sanskrit कार *kāra*, which, according to Dr. Trumpp, is first changed to *khārā*, and thence, by elision of *k*, to *hārā*.

The noun of agency is declined like other adjectives ending in *ā* (§ 45).

161. The infinitive as a gerund is used in the singular only, and is declined like masculine nouns ending in اَ *ā* (§ 42). But it is also frequently used as a *gerundive*, and then agrees with its substantive in gender and number.

162. The Participles are *three* in number; namely the Imperfect, Perfect, and Past Conjunctive. They are all derived from the verbal root.

163. The Imperfect Participle (اِسْم حالِيَه),

is formed by adding to the root the termination تا *tā*; as چلتا *chal-tā*, 'moving,' 'going.'

164. The addition to the participle of the word هُوا *hūā* (the perfect participle of the verb هونا *ho-nā*, 'to be or become'), gives it an *active* or *progressive* form, and more of the character of an adjective; as چلتا هُوا *chal-tā hūā*, 'moving or going,' *lit.* 'become moving,' *i.e.* 'in a state of motion.' But, by ellipsis, the shorter form of the participle is frequently used instead: *e.g.* چلتي چکّي ديکھ *chal-tī chakkī dekh* = چلتي هُوئي چکّي ديکھ *chaltī hūī chakkī dekh*, 'having seen a moving millstone' (*i.e.* a millstone when it was moving).

Rem. The affix تا *tā* corresponds to the affix अत् *at* of the Sanskrit present participle. In Hindī the termination is *at* (strictly speaking, perhaps, *atu*, but the final vowel is never heard in pronunciation): *e.g.* चलत् *chalat* = چلتا *chal-tā*.

165. The Perfect Participle

is formed by adding to the verbal root the termination اَ *ā*: in its formation the following rules are to be observed:

1) If the root ends in a consonant, the termination is in most cases added without any change being made; as

چلا *chal-ā*, 'moved or gone.' But if the root consist of two short syllables, the vowel of the last being *fatḥa*, this vowel is generally elided in the participle: *e.g.* بدْلا *badl-ā*, 'exchanged,' from بدل *badal*; نِكْلا *nikl-ā*, 'come out,' from نِكل *nikal* (see § 34, *Rem. c.*).

2) If the root end in one of the vowels ـَا *ā* or ـو *o*, a euphonic ي *y* is inserted between it and the termination; as كهايا *khāy-ā*, 'eaten' (root كها *khā*); بويا *boy-ā*, 'sown' (root بو *bo*).

3) If the final letter of the root be the vowel ـِي *ī*, the *fatḥa* of the termination (ـَا) changes the letter of prolongation ي into the consonant *y*: *e.g.* پِيا *piyā*, 'drunk' (root پِي *pī*).

166. The following participles are irregular:

PERF. PART.		INFINITIVE.	
كِيا *kiyā*,	'done.'	كرْنا *kar-nā*,	'to do.'
دِيا *diyā*,	'given.'	دينا *de-nā*,	'to give.'
لِيا *liyā*,	'taken.'	لينا *le-nā*,	'to take.'
مُوا *mū'ā*,	'dead.'	مِرْنا *mar-nā*,	'to die.'
گيا *gayā*,	'gone.'	جانا *jā-nā*,	'to go.'
هُوا *hū'ā*,	'been or become.'	هونا *ho-nā*,	'to be,' etc.

But the forms كرا *karā*, 'done,' and مرا *marā*, 'dead,' are also occasionally used; and the form جايا *jāyā* is that invariably used in compounds, such as جايا كرْنا *jāyā karnā*, 'to go habitually or constantly,' جايا چاهْنا *jāyā chāhnā*, 'to wish to go,' or 'to be about to go.'

Rem. It is incorrect to say that "the words *karnā* and *kiyā* are derived from *kar* and *kī*, two different forms of the Sanskrit root *kṛi*, and the words *marnā* and *mū'ā*, from *mar* and *mū*, two different forms of the Sanskrit root *mṛi*," etc.; for there can be little doubt that though the affix *ā* (which corresponds to the Sanskrit affix *ta*) is used in forming perfect participles—*e.g.* خريدا *kharīd-ā*, 'purchased,' بدلا *badl-ā*, 'exchanged'—yet the Hindī participles are for the most part derived bodily from those of the Sanskrit (just as the infinitives are from the Sanskrit verbal noun in *ana*), through the medium of the Prākrit, and the change of form is due to the laws which obtain in the latter language: *e.g.* کيا *kiyā* (for *kiā*) = P. किओ *kio* = S. कृत *krita*; موا *mū'ā* = P. मुओ *mu'o* = S. मृत *mṛita*; گيا *gayā* (for *gaā*) = P. गओ *gaö* = S. गत *gata*. The verb جانا *jānā*, from the Sanskrit root या *yā*, 'to go,' is *defective*, its perf. part. having been formed in Prākrit from a distinct root गम् *gam*, 'to go,'

167. The addition of the participle هوا *hū'ā* to another perf. part. adds to the completeness of the act or state, if the verb be intransitive, and converts it into a *passive* participle (إسم مفعول *ism maf'ūl*), if the verb be transitive, imparting to it also in each case more of the character of an adjective.

Rem. The imperfect and perfect participles, when compounded with هوا *hū'ā*, may also be used as nouns: *e.g.* ميرا ديا هوا *merā diyā hū'ā* (and, elliptically, ميرا ديا *merā diyā*), 'what has been given by (*lit.* of) me,' 'my giving or gift.'

168. The imperfect and perfect participles are declined like other adjectives ending in ـا *ā*, with a slight difference in the feminine plural, which takes a contracted form of the nom. pl. of feminine nouns ending in *ī*: *e.g.*

	MASCULINE. Singular.	Plural.	FEMININE. Singular.	Plural.
Nominative	چلا *chalā*,	چلے *chale*.	چلي *chalī*,	چليں *chalīn*.
Formative	چلے *chale*,	چلے *chale*.	چلي *chalī*,	چليں *chalīn*.

But the euphonic *y* of such perfect participles as لايا *lāyā*, سويا *soyā*, is generally dropped in all the inflected forms:

e.g. لائے *lā'e*, لائي *lā'ī*, سوئيں *so'īṅ*. The same change takes place in the inflected masc. forms of such participles as پِيَا *piyā*, دِيا *diyā*: *e.g.* پِيئے *pī'e*; but in the feminine the two long vowels ī, ī, are generally contracted into one; as پِي *pī* for پِيئي *pī'ī*; کِي *kī* for کِيئي *kī'ī*.

169. In the compound participles formed with هُوا *hū'ā*, both parts of the compound are inflected in the same way, but the plural termination of the feminine is usually added to the last, هُوا, alone: *e.g.* چلي هُوئيں *chalī hū'īṅ*.

Rem. As the plural is obvious from the termination of the last part of the compound, the addition of the same termination to the first part also is unnecessary, and is now rarely made. We occasionally meet with the full plural termination *āṅ*, as چلِيَاں *chaliyāṅ*, but current usage is averse to the form.

170. The addition of the emphatic particle هِي *hī* to the locative of the imperfect participle (with the postposition suppressed), gives it the force of an adverb: *e.g.* چلتے هِي *chalte-hī*, 'in the very act, or on the instant, of moving.'

THE PAST CONJUNCTIVE PARTICIPLE (ماضِي معطُوف).

171. This participle, which is indeclinable, may take the form: 1) Of the simple root; as چل *chal*, 'having moved or gone; 2) of the root with the addition of one of the affixes ـــي *e*, or کے *ke*; as چلے *chal-e*, or چلکے *chal-ke*; 3) of the root with the addition of کر *kar*, or کرکے *kar-ke* (which are themselves past conj. part. of the verb کرّنا *kar-nā*); as چلکر *chal-kar*, or چلکرکے *chal-kar-ke*. The affix *e* is seldom or never employed; *ke* and *kar* are those most frequently used.

Rem. a. We occasionally meet with the form کرکر *kar-kar*, as چلکرکر *chal-kar-kar*; this, however. is now generally condemned as barbarous.

Rem. b. The conjunctive participle of the verb آنا *ānā*, 'to come,' takes the forms آن *ān*, آنکر *ānkar*, etc., besides the regular forms آ *ā*, آکر *ākar*, etc.

Rem. c. The affixes *e* and *ke* both spring from the Prākrit form *ia* of the Sanskrit affix *ya*, which is used to form indeclinable past participles: *ia* transposed = *ai* = *e*; in the case of *ke*, however, *ia* is first changed to *ja*, *je* (the form current in Sindhī), and *j* is then changed to *k*. In the first or root form of the participle the affix *e* is dropped.

Gender, Number, Person.

172. The Urdū verb has *two* genders, the masculine and feminine; *two* numbers, the singular and plural; and three persons in each number.

Moods (صُورتیں *ṣūraten*).

173. There are *three* moods; namely the Indicative, Imperative, and Subjunctive or Conditional, which is also the Optative. The Indicative and Subjunctive will be noticed in connection with the tenses.

The Imperative (امر *amr*).

174. The second person singular of the Imperative is, as has already been observed, the root or crude form of the verb. The second person plural is formed by adding to the singular the termination و— *o*; as چل *chal*, 'go thou,' چلو *chalo*, 'go you.' It is identical with the second person plural of the Aorist, from which tense the other persons of the Imperative are taken.

175. If the root end in ي— *e*, or و— *o*, the plural imperative may be formed as described above; but the more usual course is to elide the radical *e* or *o* before adding the *o*: *e.g.* sing. دي *de*, 'give thou,' pl. *do*, 'give you;' sing.

هو *ho*, 'be thou,' plural هو *ho*, 'be ye.' The forms ديو *de'o* and هوو *ho'o* are now regarded as provincial and barbarous.

Rem. The terminations of the Prākrit imperative are—Sing. *u* or *a*, *āhi*, etc.; pl. *dha* or *ha*: the first of these is dropped in Hindī, and the plural termination *ha* is changed to *o* by elision of *h* and compensatory lengthening of the final vowel.

The Precative.

176. There is another form of the Imperative which is properly a Precative, but which is also commonly used in polite speech for the Imperative. It is formed by adding to the verbal root the termination ـِيے *iye* for the singular, and ـِيو *iyo* for the plural;[1] as چلِيے *chaliye*, 'please go,' or simply 'go;' چلِيو *chaliyo*, 'go you.' But at the present time the two forms are both commonly employed in both the singular and the plural, the only difference between them being, that the form ending in *iye* is always used with the *pronomen reverentiæ* آپ *āp*, and usually refers to *present* time; whereas that ending in *iyo* is used with the pronouns تُو *tū* and تُم *tum*, and is generally a *future* imperative: *e.g.* آپ چلِيے *āp chaliye*, 'please come, or come, Sir, or Sirs;' اِس دِرخت کے پاس نجائِيو *is dirakht-ke pās na jā'iyo*, 'near this tree thou shalt not go;' هرگز اِنکے بيچنے اور آزاد کرنے کا اِرادہ نہ کِيجِيو *hargiz inke bechne aur āzād karne-kā irāda na kījiyo*, 'never form the design of selling or setting free these (animals).' The form ending in *iyo* is also frequently

[1] Mr. Etherington (*Hindī Grammar*, p. 78) observes that it is incorrect to term the precative ending in *iyo* the plural of that ending in *iye*, and in this opinion he is supported by native scholars; but though the opinion of these is invaluable in respect of the usage and signification of words, it is utterly untrustworthy where their origin or derivation is concerned, especially in Hindī forms. By comparison with the same form in the sister dialects—Panjābī, Sindhī, etc.—we obtain conclusive evidence of the form ending in *iyo* being originally the plural of that ending in *iye*.

employed in benedictions and imprecations: *e.g.* جُدا تُمکو زِنْدہ رکھیو *khudā tum-ko zinda rakhiyo*, 'may God preserve you alive;' خُدا کِي لَعْنت کافِروں اَور مُشْرِکوں پر هُوجِيو *khudā kī la'nat kāfiroṅ aur mushrikoṅ par hūjiyo*, 'God's curse on infidels and believers in a plurality of gods!'

Rem. a. The termination *iye* is derived from the increment *ija* or *ijja*, which is inserted between the root and the terminations in the present, imperative, and definite future of Prākrit verbs (*Prākṛit-Prakāśa*, ed. Cowell, p. 30 of Introduction). This increment is traced by Lassen to the Sanskrit precative. In Hindī and Urdū also the Aorist frequently takes the form of the Precative for the three persons of the singular, and adds nasal *n* thereto for the plural: *e.g.* حُکْم قتْل کا فرمائِيين *ḥukm ḳatl-kā farmā'iyeṅ*, '(your Majesty) is pleased to give the order to put to death.' (See Syntax.)

177. If the root end in ـِي *ī* or *e*, the letter *j* is inserted between it and the affixes of the Precative, and *majhūl e* of the root is changed to the *ma'ruf ī* before the affixes are added: *e.g.* پِيجِيے *pījiye*, from the root پِي *pī*, 'to drink;' دِيجِيے *dījiye*, from the root دي *de*, 'to give.' Instead of inserting *j* however, the initial *i* of the affixes may be dropped, and *y* changed to *j*; as پِيجے *pīje*, پِيجو *pījo*, دِيجے *dīje*, دِيجو *dījo*.

178. The precatives of the verbs هونا *honā*,[1] 'to be or become,' and مرنا *marnā*, 'to die,' also insert *j*: *e.g.* هُوجِيے

[1] Forbes and others after him state that "when the root ends in *ī* or *ū*, *j* is inserted for euphony," etc. But they give no example of a verbal root ending in *ū*, which forms its precative thus, and we doubt much whether a single example could be given, unless it be the verb *mūnā*, which is rarely if ever used. Indeed, *mūjiye* and *mū'ā* are generally regarded as the precative and perfect participle, not of *mūnā*, but of *marnā*. Examples of verbal roots ending in *ū* are *chhūnā*, 'to touch,' and *chūnā*, 'to drip,' but these would certainly not take *j* in the precative: *e.g. chhū'iye*, not *chhūjiye*. The rule would be equally incorrect if *o* were substituted for *ū*, for *honā* is the only verb of this class that forms its precative with *jiye*.

hūjiye, هوجيو *hūjiyo,* مُوجِيے *mūjiye.* This last, however, also takes the regular forms مرِيے *mariye,* مرِيو *mariyo.*

Rem. a. The form of the root employed in the precative, it may be observed, is generally that which occurs in the perfect participle, and hence we find کِيجِيے *kījiye,* کِيجے *kīje,* کِيجِيو *kījiyo,* کِيجو *kījo,* as the precatives of کَرنا *karnā,* 'to do,' the forms کرِيے *kariye* and کرِيو *kariyo,* though occasionally used, being regarded as unchaste. A remarkable exception to this rule, however, is the precative جائِيے *jā'iye,* of the verb جانا *jānā,* 'to go.'

Rem. b. The affixes ـِيے *iye* and ـِيو *iyo,* are frequently written ـِيئے *ī'e* and ـِيئو *ī'o,* or ـئے *i'e,* ـئو *i'o*: *e.g.* چلِيئے *chalī'e,* or چلِئے *chali'e*; and when the root ends in *ā,* the initial vowel (*i*) of the affixes may be elided; as فرمائِيے *farmā'iye,* or فرمايے *farmāye.*

179. The addition of the termination گا *gā* to the precative ending in *iye* gives it a *future* signification: *e.g.* أن کے حوالے کِيجِيگا *un-ke ḥawāle kījiyegā,* 'you will be pleased to make (them) over to them.'

THE TENSES.

180. The tenses in common use, and which are those allowed by native grammarians, are *nine* in number, exclusive of the Imperative. Of these tenses four relate to an *imperfect* act; viz. 1) the Aorist (مُضارِع *muẓāri'*), which has both a present and a future signification: 2) the Present Imperfect (حال *ḥāl*): 3) the Past Continuous or Imperfect (ماضِي اِستِمراري يا ناتمام *māẓī istimrārī yā nā-tamām*): 4) the Simple Future مُستَقبِل *mustaḳbil*): Four relate to a *perfect* or *complete* action, namely: 1) the Past Absolute or Indefinite (ماضِي مُطلق *māẓī mutlaḳ*): 2) the Proximate or Present Perfect (ماضِي قرِيب *māẓī ḳarīb*): 3) the Remote or Past Perfect ماضِي بعِيد *māẓī ba'īd*): 4) the

Future Perfect or Past Potential ماضي شكّي *māẓī shakkī*). Two of these tenses, viz. the Aorist[1] and the Future Perfect, are common to the Indicative and Subjunctive Moods (though the latter is rarely used in the Indicative); the rest pertain to the Indicative Mood. One tense, namely the Past Conditional or Optative, is peculiar to the Subjunctive Mood.

181. The tenses rarely used, and which the native grammarians do not even notice, need not detain the student here: they will be explained hereafter.

FORMATION OF THE TENSES.

a) The Simple Tenses.

182. The simple tenses of the Active Voice are *three;* namely, the Aorist, the Past Absolute or Indefinite, and the Past Conditional or Optative.

1) The Aorist.

183. The Aorist is the only tense that is formed by means of inflectional terminations.[2] These are:

[1] It is inexplicable to us how Mr. Etherington can say (*Hindī Grammar*, p. 76), "The so-called aorist of the Hindī is not indicative at all; for it never simply asserts, except in ungrammatical *patois*." He must surely have repeatedly heard the expressions *kyā karūṅ*, 'What am I to do?' *kahān jā'ūṅ*, 'Where shall I go?' *khudā jāne*, 'God knows?' And he should have known that the aorist is commonly employed in the indicative mood in proverbs: *e.g.* *ūṅṭ-chaṛe kuttā kāṭe*, 'the dog bites (or will bite) one mounted on a camel.' To call the tense the *prospective conditional* is to give it a new name, which, so far from being an improvement on the old one, is calculated to mislead. The fact is, this tense is the equivalent of the Prākrit *present* indefinite, which (since the Sanskrit potential has disappeared from the Prākrits) also expresses some of the significations of the potential, and hence is used in both the indicative and subjunctive moods.

[2] The aorist corresponds to the present of the Prākrit, the personal terminations of which tense are:

	SINGULAR.	PLURAL.
1st person	*āmi* (S. *āmi*).	{ *āmo, āmu, āma* / *amo, amu, ama* } S. *āmah*.
2nd "	*asi* (S. *asi*).	*aha* (S. *a-tha*).
3rd "	*a-di, aï* (S. *a-ti*).	*a-nti* (S. *a-nti*).

Comparing these terminations with those of the Hindī, we perceive that, in the

SINGULAR.		PLURAL.
1st person	ـُوں *ūn.*	ـیں *eṅ.*
2nd "	ـي *e.*	ـو *o.*
3rd "	ـي *e.*	ـیں *eṅ.*

They are added to the verbal root, and are the same for both genders.

184. If the root end in a vowel, certain euphonic changes may be necessary before the terminations are added to it: *e.g.*

1) If the vowel be ـَا *ā*, ـو *o*, or ـِي *ī*, the letter و *w* may be inserted between it and the terminations ـي *e* and ـیں *eṅ*; as جاوي *jā-w-e*, (thou or he) 'will go;' سووي *so-w-e*, (thou or he) 'will sleep;' جِیویں *jī-w-eṅ*, (we or they) 'will live.' In the case of the verb هونا *honā*, 'to be,' we find, moreover, that the vowels of the terminations are frequently elided, so that we have the forms: 1st person sing. هوُوں *ho-ūṅ*, or هوں *hoṅ*; 2nd pers. هوئي *ho'e*, or هووي *ho-w-e*, or هو *ho*, etc.

Rem. In Urdū, however, *w* is not very generally inserted, *hamza* between the vowels being preferred; *e.g.* جاؤں *jā'ūṅ*, سوئي *so'e*, جِيئے *jī'e*; and the form هوُوں *ho'ūṅ* is obsolete.

2) If the root end in ـي *e*, a euphonic *w* may be inserted, as in the case of the other vowels, but the usual practice is, as has been shown in the case of the imperative (§ 175) to drop the root vowel in all the persons: *e.g.* the aorist of دينا *denā*, 'to give,' is دُوں *dūṅ*, 'I give or shall give;' دي *de*, (thou or he) 'will give' ... دیں *deṅ*, (we or they) 'will give.'

latter, the consonants have all been elided (but the letters *m* and *n* have left their mark in the form of the *anusvāra* or nasal), and the vowels *a*, *i* of the second and third persons sing. and the 3rd pers. pl. have coalesced into *e*. In the first person the vowel *ā* has been changed to *ū*, and final *i* has been elided. In the second person *h* has been elided, and *a* lengthened to *ā*.

Rem. a. The personal pronouns may either precede or follow the verb, or they may be omitted. But if any stress is to be laid on the person, the proper pronoun must be expressed, and be placed *before* the verb.

Rem. b. The aorist frequently takes the form of the precative: *e.g.* کیا کِیجِیے کُچھ بن نہیں پڑتی *kyā kī-jiye, kuchh ban nahīṅ paṛtī*, 'what shall I do? nothing is of any avail;' where *kījiye = karūṅ*. The subject will be noticed in the Syntax.

2) The Past Indefinite.

185. The Past Indefinite or Absolute is formed from the perfect participle, which, in the case of an intransitive verb, is inflected to agree in gender and number with its subject or nominative; but if the verb be transitive, a passive construction is employed, the *actor* is put in the Agent case and the *object* of the action becomes the subject or nominative, with which the participle agrees in gender, etc. For example, instead of saying directly, 'the king killed a tigress,' the Urdū uses the form, 'by the king a tigress was killed' (راجانے شیرنی ماری *rājā-ne shernī mārī*). The same construction is employed in all such tenses of the active voice of a transitive verb as are composed of the passive participle, provided the *object* of the act have the *nominative* form; but the object may take the *dative* form, in which case the participle is never inflected.

Rem. This construction is derived from the Sanskrit through the Prākrit, and would appear to be preferred in Sanskrit to the active construction. In Prākrit it is very commonly employed, few traces of the Sanskrit preterite tenses remaining in the dialects thereof. The Hindī departs from the Prākrit, however, in discarding all inflectional terminations, which in the Prākrit were optionally used.

3) The Past Conditional.

186. The Past Conditional or Optative is formed from the imperfect participle, which is inflected to agree in gender and number with the subject or nominative.

Rem. This tense appears to perplex English writers on Urdū grammar greatly. It is called 'The Indefinite,' 'The Present Indefinite,' 'The Retrospective Conditional,' etc., and rendered mostly by the English present. Now the fact is, it is not a *present* tense at all, but a *past subjunctive*. The error is probably due to the fact that the present tense is sometimes used elliptically without the auxiliary, and so has the appearance of the conditional; but the two should not be confounded. The conditional was, in all probability, a compound tense originally.

b) The Compound Tenses.

1) The Future.

187. The Future is formed by adding to the Aorist the participle گا *gā* (a contraction of *gaā*, whence *gayā*, 'gone'), which is inflected to agree with the nominative in gender and number. The Future is therefore properly a Desiderative, or Intentional: *e.g.* مَیں چلونگا *main chalūngā*, 'I shall go or move,' is literally, 'I am gone (that) I move,' *i.e.* 'I wish to move,' or 'I am going to move;' and hence we occasionally find it so used: *e.g.* مَیں دیکھونگا *main dekhūngā*, 'I wish to see,' 'I would see' = مَیں دیکھنے چاھتا هوں *main dekhne chāhtā hūn*.

188. The remaining compound tenses (with the exception of the Future Perfect) are composed of the imperfect or perfect participle and the following auxiliaries, which are also used alone to express simple existence.

PRESENT.

Singular.	Plural.
مَیں هُوں *main hūn*, 'I am.'	هم هَیں *ham hain*, 'we are.'
تُو هَي *tū hai*, 'thou art.'	تُم هو *tum ho*, 'you are.'
وُہ هَي *wŏh hai*, 'he is.'	وي هَیں *we hain*, 'they are.'

PAST.

Singular.	Plural.
مَیں تها *main thā*, 'I was.'	هم تهے *ham the*, 'we were.'
تُو تها *tū thā*, 'thou wast.'	تُم تهے *tum the*, 'you were.'
وُہ تها *wŏh thā*, 'he was.'	وي تهے *we the*, 'they were.'

If the subject or nominative be feminine, تها *thā* takes the feminine termination: *e.g.* sing. تهِي *thī*, pl. تهِیں *thīn*.

Rem. These are not "anomalous formations derived from *hona*," as Professor Williams calls them, for *honā* springs from the Sanskrit *bhū*, 'to be or become,' the Prākrit form of which is *ho* or *huva*; whereas the forms هُوں *hūn*, etc., are derived from the present tense of the Sanskrit *as*, 'to be:' *e.g.* *hūn* = P. *amhi* = S. *asmi*; *hai* = P. *asi* = S. *asi*, and so on, the process of transformation in Hindī being analogous to that of the terminations of the aorist; *h*, however (into which the *s* also of *asi*, etc., is changed), being in no instance elided, but transposed. The form تها *thā* is traceable to the Sanskrit root *sthā*, 'to stand,' which is used even in Sanskrit as a substantive verb with the sense of 'to be.'

2) The Present Imperfect.

189. The Present Imperfect is formed by adding the first of the above auxiliary tenses to the imperfect participle of a verb: *e.g.* masc. چلتا هُوں *chaltā hūn*, fem. چلتِي هُوں *chaltī hūn*, 'I am going.'

Rem. a. The present tense is sometimes formed by adding the same auxiliary to the *aorist* of a verb; as چلوں هُوں *chalūn hūn*, 'I go or am going.' This form, which is properly an *indefinite* present, was at one period general; numerous instances of its use occur in the poets, and it is still very common in the tract of country extending from Agra to Sindh; but in other parts of Northern India it is now seldom used, except by the uneducated.

Rem. b. The termination گا *gā* is occasionally added to the auxiliary in the present and present perfect tenses, and even when it is used independently, sometimes intensifying, but often without affecting the sense; for example, هَيگا *haigā* = هَي *hai*; چلْتا هَيگا *chaltā haigā* = چلْتا هَي *chaltā hai*. Such forms, it may be observed, are regarded as unchaste (*gair faṣīḥ*) by native scholars.

3) The Past Imperfect or Continuous.

190. This tense is formed by adding the auxiliary تها *thā* to the imperfect participle of a verb: *e.g.* masc. مَيں چلْتا تها *main chaltā thā*, fem. مَيں چلْتي تهي *main chaltī thī*, 'I was going.' It frequently denotes a *habitual* or *repeated act in past time*, as 'I used (to go),' etc., and when used in this sense the auxiliary, *thā*, is often omitted, so that the tense then assumes the form of the Past Conditional.

4) The Proximate or Present Perfect.

191. The Present Perfect is formed by adding the first of the auxiliary tenses to the *perfect* participle of a verb: *e.g.* چلا (fem. چلِي) هُوں *chalā* (fem. *chalī*) *hūn*, 'I have gone or set out.' If the verb be *transitive*, the construction is the same as in the Past Absolute (§ 185), the auxiliary always taking the form of the 3rd person sing. or plural: *e.g.* راجانے شير مارا هَي *rājā-ne sher mārā hai*, 'the king has killed a tiger,' or *lit.* 'by the king a tiger has been killed;' راجانے تِين شير مارے هَيں *rājā-ne tīn sher māre hain*, 'the king has killed three tigers;' راجانے تِين شيرْنِي (or شيرْنِياں) مارِي هَيں *rājā-ne tīn shernī* (or *sherniyān*) *mārī hain*, 'the

king has killed three tigresses;' (مجهے or) اُس لڑکے نے مجهکو مارا هے *us larke-ne mujhko* (or *mujhe*) *mārā hai*, 'that boy has beaten me.' When the object of the act is represented by a personal pronoun, the participle will always remain uninflected, since such pronouns admit of the *dative* form of the accusative alone.

5) The Remote or Past Perfect.

192. The Past Perfect is formed by adding the auxiliary تها *thā* to the perfect participle of a verb: *e.g.* مَیں چلا تها *main chalā thā*, 'I had gone;' هم چلے تهے *ham chale the*, 'we had gone,' feminine هم چلی تهیں *ham chalī thīn*, it being sufficient to add the plural termination to the auxiliary. If the verb be *transitive*, the same construction is employed as in the Past Absolute and Present Perfect: *e.g.* مَیں نے تین گهوڑیاں (یا گهوڑی) خریدی تهیں *main ne tīn ghoṛiyān* (*yā ghoṛī*) *kharīdī thīn*, 'I had purchased three mares,' *lit.* 'by me three mares had been purchased.'

6) The Future Perfect, or Past Potential.

193. This tense is formed by adding the Future of the verb هونا *honā*, 'to be or become,' to the perfect participle of a verb: *e.g.* مَیں چلا هُونگا *main chalā hūngā*, 'I shall have gone,' or, more commonly, 'I may have gone.' The termination گا *gā* of the Future is occasionally dropped, or, in other words, the Aorist of the verb *honā* is added to the perfect participle, and then the signification is invariably that of the Past Potential: *e.g.* مَیں چلا هوں *main chalā hon*, 'I may have

gone.' If the verb be *transitive*, the construction is the same as in the case of other tenses composed of passive participles.

Rem. It is a mistake to say that this tense "is not of very frequent occurrence," as all English writers on Hindī and Urdū grammar do. It is commonly employed, both colloquially and in writing; not however as a *Future Perfect*, but as a *Past Potential*, *expressing the possibility*, or *uncertainty*, of an act.

CONJUGATION.

194. We now proceed to conjugate three verbs: viz. the *transitive-active* verb لِکھنا *likhnā*, 'to write;' the *intransitive-active* verb چلنا *chalnā*, 'to move or go,' and the *substantive* verb هونا *honā*, 'to be.' The masculine forms alone will be given; it will therefore be borne in mind that, in the Future and all tenses composed of the imperfect and perfect participles, the final vowel *ā* of the sing. is changed to *ī* for the feminine, and the final vowel *e* of the plural to *īṅ*. The verbal nouns and adjectives are declined like other nouns and adjectives ending in *ā*. The arrangement of the moods and tenses differs but slightly from that found in existing grammars; it is necessary therefore to again direct attention to the fact that the Conditional, though classed with the tenses derived from the imperfect participle, is a *past* tense of the *subjunctive* mood. The Imperative, properly speaking, consists of the second person alone, and this is all that is given; the remaining persons are

identical with those of the Aorist, from which indeed they are borrowed.

I. ROOT لِکھ *likh*, 'to write.'

Infinitive or Gerund, لِکھنا *likhnā*, 'to write,' 'writing.'

Noun of Agency, and Future Act. Participle, } لِکھنے والا *likhne-wālā*, 'writer,' 'about to write.'

Participle.

- Imperfect, لِکھتا *likhtā*, 'writing.'
- Perfect, لِکھا *likhā*, 'written.'
- Progressive, لِکھتا هُوا *likhtā hū'ā*, 'in the act of writing,' 'one who is in the act of writing.'
- Passive, لِکھا هُوا *likhā hū'ā*, 'been written,' 'what has been written.'
- Past Conjunctive { لِکھ - لِکھکر - لِکھکرکے *likh*, *likh-kar*, or *likh-kar-ke*, } 'having written.'
- Adverbial, لِکھتے هِي *likhte-hī*, 'in the very act, or on the instant, of writing.'

TENSES FORMED FROM THE ROOT.

1). The Imperative.

SINGULAR.	PLURAL.
تُو لِکھ *tū likh*,[1] 'write thou.'	تُم لِکھو *tum likho*, 'write you,'
Precative, لِکھیے *likhiye*, 'write, or be pleased to write.'	لِکھیو *likhiyo*, 'you shall or will write.'

Future لِکھیٔیگا *likhi'egā*, 'you will be pleased to write.'

[1] It should be observed that there is no necessity to express the personal pronoun in the Imperative, the Aorist, and the Present Perfect (and, in the case of intransitive verbs, in the Past Perfect, and Past Potential), unless any stress is to be laid on the person; and that, in all the tenses, the pronouns, if expressed, as commonly *follow* as precede the verb.

2). The Aorist.

'I write, or shall write, or should write,' etc.

SINGULAR.	PLURAL.
مَیں لِکھُوں *maiṅ likhūṅ.*	ہم لِکھیں *ham likheṅ.*
تُو لِکھے *tū likhe.*	تُم لِکھو *tum likho.*
وُہ لِکھے *wŏh likhe.*	وي لِکھیں *we likheṅ.*

3). The Future.

'I shall write,' etc.

مَیں لِکھُونگا *maiṅ likhūṅgā.*	ہم لِکھینگے *ham likheṅge.*
تُو لِکھیگا *tū likhegā.*	تُم لِکھوگے *tum likhoge.*
وُہ لِکھیگا *wŏh likhegā.*	وي لِکھینگے *we likheṅge.*

TENSES FORMED FROM THE IMPERFECT PARTICIPLE.

1). The Past Conditional or Optative.

'Had I written,' or 'Did I write,' or (Would that) 'I had written,' etc.

مَیں لِکھْتا *maiṅ likhtā.*	ہم لِکھْتے *ham likhte.*
تُو لِکھْتا *tū likhtā.*	تُم لِکھْتے *tum likhte.*
وُہ لِکھْتا *wŏh likhtā.*	وي لِکھْتے *we likhte.*

2). The Present Imperfect.

'I am writing,' etc.

مَیں لِکھْتا ہُوں *maiṅ likhtā hūṅ.*	ہم لِکھْتے ہَیں *ham likhte haiṅ.*
تُو لِکھْتا ہَي *tū likhtā hai.*	تُم لِکھْتے ہو *tum likhte ho.*
وُہ لِکھْتا ہَي *wŏh likhtā hai.*	وي لِکھْتے ہَیں *we likhte haiṅ.*

3). The Past Continuous or Imperfect.

'I was writing,' and 'I used to write.'

مَیں لِکھْتا تھا *maiṅ likhtā thā.*	ہم لِکھْتے تھے *ham likhte the.*
تُو لِکھْتا تھا *tū likhtā thā.*	تُم لِکھْتے تھے *tum likhte the.*
وُہ لِکھْتا تھا *wŏh likhtā thā.*	وي لِکھْتے تھے *we likhte the.*

TENSES FORMED FROM THE PASSIVE PARTICIPLE.

1). The Past Absolute or Indefinite.

'I wrote,' or *lit.* 'By me (it) was written,' etc.

SINGULAR.	PLURAL.
مَیں نے لِکھا *main-ne likhā.*[1]	هم نے لِکھا *ham-ne likhā.*
تُونے لِکھا *tū-ne likhā.*	تُم نے لِکھا *tum-ne likhā.*
اُن نے لِکھا or اُسنے *us-ne* or *un-ne likhā.*	اُنہوں نے لِکھا *unhon-ne likhā.*[2]

2). The Proximate or Present Perfect.

'I have written,' *lit.* 'By me (it) has been written,' etc.

مَیں نے لِکھا هَي *main-ne likhā hai.*	هم نے لِکھا هَي *ham-ne likhā hai.*
تُونے لِکھا هَي *tū-ne likhā hai.*	تُم نے لِکھا هَي *tum-ne likhā hai.*
اُن نے لِکھا هَي or اُسنے *us-ne* or *un-ne likhā hai.*	اُنہوں نے لِکھا هَي *unhon-ne likhā hai.*

3). The Remote or Past Perfect.

'I had written,' *lit.* 'By me (it) had been written.'

مَیں نے لِکھا تها *main-ne likhā thā.*	هم نے لِکھا تها *ham-ne likhā thā.*
تُونے لِکھا تها *tū-ne likhā thā.*	تُم نے لِکھا تها *tum-ne likhā thā.*
اُن نے لِکھا تها or اُسنے *us-ne* or *un-ne likhā thā.*	اُنہوں نے لِکھا تها *unhon-ne likhā thā.*

4). The Future Perfect, or Past Potential.

'I shall have written,' (more commonly) 'I may have written,' etc.

مَیں نے لِکھا هوگا *main-ne likhā hogā.*	هم نے لِکھا هوگا *ham-ne likhā hogā.*
تُونے لِکھا هوگا *tū-ne likhā hogā.*	تُم نے لِکھا هوگا *tum-ne likhā hogā.*
اُن نے لِکھا هوگا or اُسنے *us-ne* or *un-ne likhā hogā.*	اُنہوں نے لِکھا هوگا *unhon-ne likhā hogā.*

[1] It will be understood that the participle takes this form only when the *object* of the act is in the sing. masc., or in the form of the *dative*; in every other case it will be inflected to agree with the object in gender and number: *e.g.* مَیں نے چِٹّهي لِکهي *main-ne chiṭṭhī likhī*, 'I wrote a letter.'

[2] The form اُن نے *un-ne* of the Agent case may also be used; but as this form is generally used for the sing. (not "to indicate respect," as is generally supposed, see § 141), the form اُنہوں نے *unhon-ne* is commonly employed for the plural.

Rem. a.—The termination گا *gā* of *hogā* may even be dropped, in which case the signification is invariably that of the Past Potential: *e.g.* اُسنے لِکھا هو *us-ne likhā ho,* 'he may have written.'

Rem. b.—If the root ends in a vowel, the conjugation is effected in the same way: the perfect participle is formed by inserting a euphonic *y* between the root and the termination *ā* (this *y,* however, being generally dropped again in the masc. pl. and in the fem.), and certain optional forms of the Aorist occur (§ 184): *e.g.*

Root کها *khā,* 'to eat.' Perf. part. کهايا *khāyā,* 'eaten.'

AORIST.

SINGULAR.	PLURAL.
مَیں کهاؤں *main khā'ūn.*	هم کهائیں or کهاویں *ham khā'en* or *khāwen.*
تُوکهائے or کهاوي *tū khā'e* or *khāwe.*	تُم کهاؤ *tum khā'o.*
وُہ کهائے or کهاوي *wŏh khā'e* or *khāwe.*	وي کهائیں or کهاویں *we khā'en* or *khāwen.*

PAST ABSOLUTE.

مَیں نے کهايا *main ne khāyā.*	همنے کهايا *ham-ne khāyā.*
تُونے کهايا *tū-ne khāyā.*	تُمنے کهايا *tum-ne khāyā.*
اُن نے کهايا *un-ne khāyā.*	اُنهوں نے کهايا *un-hon-ne khāyā.*

II. ROOT چل *chal,* 'to move, or go.'

Infinitive or Gerund, چلنا *chal-nā,* 'to go,' 'going.'

Noun of Agency, and Future Active Participle, } چلنے والا *chalne-wālā,* 'goer,' 'about to go.'

Participle.
- Imperfect چلتا *chal-tā,* 'moving or going.'
- Perfect چلا *chal-ā,* 'moved or gone.'
- Progressive چلتا هُوا *chaltā hū'ā,* 'in the act of moving,' etc.
- Past Perfect چلا هُوا *chalā hū'ā,* 'become moved,' 'gone.'
- Past Conjunctive { چل - چلکر - چلکرکے *chal, chal-kar, chal-kar-ke,* } 'having moved,' etc.
- Adverbial چلتے هِي *chalte-hī,* 'in the very act, or on the instant of moving,' etc.

The Imperative.

SINGULAR.	PLURAL.
تُو چل *tū chal,* 'go thou.'	تُم چلو *tum chalo,* 'go you.'
Precative, چلِيے *chaliye,* 'go, or be pleased to go.'	چلِيو *chaliyo,* 'you shall or will go.'

Future چلِئيگا *chali'egā,* 'you will be pleased to go.'

The Aorist.

'I go, or shall go, or should go,' etc.

مَيں چلوں *main chalūn.*	هم چليں *ham chalen.*
تُو چلے *tū chale.*	تُم چلو *tum chalo.*
وُه چلے *wŏh chale.*	وي چليں *we chalen.*

The Future.

'I shall go,' etc.

مَيں چلونگا *main chalūngā.*	هم چلينگے *ham chalenge.*
تُو چليگا *tū chalegā.*	تُم چلوگے *tum chaloge.*
وُه چليگا *wŏh chalegā.*	وي چلينگے *we chalenge.*

The Past Conditional or Optative.

'Had I gone,' 'Did I go,' (Would that) 'I had gone,' etc.

مَيں چلتا *main chaltā.*	هم چلتے *ham chalte.*
تُو چلتا *tū chaltā.*	تُم چلتے *tum chalte.*
وُه چلتا *wŏh chaltā.*	وي چلتے *we chalte.*

The Present Imperfect.

'I am going,' etc.

مَيں چلتا هُوں *main chaltā hūn.*	هم چلتے هَيں *ham chalte hain.*
تُو چلتا هَي *tū chaltā hai.*	تُم چلتے هو *tum chalte ho.*
وُه چلتا هَي *wŏh chaltā hai.*	وي چلتے هيں *we chalte hain.*

The Past Continuous or Imperfect.

'I was going,' etc.

SINGULAR.	PLURAL.
مَیں چلتا تھا *maiṅ chaltā thā.*	ہم چلتے تھے *ham chalte the.*
تُو چلتا تھا *tū chaltā thā.*	تُم چلتے تھے *tum chalte the.*
وُہ چلتا تھا *wŏh chaltā thā.*	وي چلتے تھے *we chalte the.*

The Past Absolute or Indefinite.

'I went,' etc.

مَیں چلا *maiṅ chalā.*	ہم چلے *ham chale.*
تُو چلا *tū chalā.*	تُم چلے *tum chale.*
وہ چلا *wŏh chalā.*	وي چلے *we chale.*

The Proximate, or Present Perfect.

'I have set out, or gone,' etc.

مَیں چلا ہُوں *maiṅ chalā huṅ.*	ہم چلے ہَیں *ham chale haiṅ.*
تُو چلا ہَي *tū chalā hai.*	تُم چلے ہو *tum chale ho.*
وُہ چلا ہَي *wŏh chalā hai.*	وي چلے ہَیں *we chale haiṅ.*

The Remote, or Past Perfect.

'I had started or gone,' etc.

مَیں چلا تھا *maiṅ chalā thā.*	ہم چلے تھے *ham chale the.*
تُو چلا تھا *tū chalā thā.*	تُم چلے تھے *tum chale the.*
وُہ چلا تھا *wŏh chalā thā.*	وي چلے تھے *we chale the.*

The Future Perfect, or Past Potential.

'I shall have gone,' or (more commonly) 'I may have gone,' etc.

مَیں چلا ہُونگا or ہوں *maiṅ chalā hūṅgā* or *hoṅ.*	ہم چلے ہونگے or ہوں *ham chale hoṅge* or *hoṅ.*
تُو چلا ہوگا or ہو *tū chalā hogā* or *ho.*	تُم چلے ہوگے or ہو *tum chale hoge* or *ho.*
وُہ چلا ہوگا or ہو *wŏh chalā hogā* or *ho.*	وي چلے ہونگے or ہوں *we chale hoṅge* or *hoṅ.*

Rem. The above is the conjugation of an intransitive-active verb, the root of which ends in a consonant. If the root ends in a vowel, the aorist

admits of certain optional forms, and the masculine singular of the perfect participle takes an euphonic *y* between the root and the termination. The following tenses will therefore suffice to show the process of conjugation :

Root آ *ā*, 'to come.' Pref. Part. آيا *āyā*, 'come.'

The Aorist.

'I come, or shall come, or should come,' etc.

SINGULAR.	PLURAL.
مَيں آؤں *maiṅ ā'ūṅ*.	هم آئيں or آويں *ham ā'eṅ* or *āweṅ*.
تُو آئے or آوے *tū ā'e* or *āwe*.	تُم آؤ *tum ā'o*.
وُہ آئے or آوے *wŏh ā'e* or *āwe*.	وے آئيں or آويں *we ā'eṅ* or *āweṅ*.

The Past Absolute, or Indefinite.

'I came,' etc.

مَيں آيا *maiṅ āyā*.	هم آئے *ham ā'e*.
تُو آيا *tū āyā*.	تُم آئے *tum ā'e*.
وُہ آيا *wŏh āyā*.	وے آئے *we ā'e*.
Fem. مَيں آئِي *maiṅ ā'ī*, etc.	Fem. هم آئِيں *ham ā'īṅ*, etc.

III. Root هو *ho*,[1] 'to be, or become.'

Infinitive or Gerund هونا *honā*, 'to be, or become,' 'being,' etc.

Fut. Act. Part. هونے والا *hone-wālā*,[2] 'about to be, or become,' 'one who, or what, is, or is about, to be or become.'

Participle.
- Imperfect هوتا *hotā*, 'being, or becoming.'
- Perfect هُوا *hū'ā*, 'been, or become.'
- Progressive هوتا هُوا *hotā hū'ā*, 'in the act of being or becoming.'
- Conjunctive { هو۔ هوکر۔ هوکرکے *ho, hokar, hokar-ke*, } 'having been or become.'
- Adverbial هوتے هِي *hote-hī*, 'in the very act, or in the instant of being,' etc.

[1] Urdū grammarians, after the example of the Arabic, have two names for the verb *honā*, and the other auxiliary verbs with the same signification. When the substantive verb is used to denote simple *being* or *existence*, they term it *fĕ'lĕ nāķis*, 'the incomplete or defective verb,' because an attribute is required to complete the sense; but when it contains the attribute in itself, and requires no other, they term it *fĕ'lĕ tāmm*, 'the complete or absolute verb.'

[2] Urdū also occasionally employs the common Hindī form *honhār*, 'what is to be,' etc., where the affix *hār* is added to the verbal noun *hoṅ*.

The Imperative.

SINGULAR.	PLURAL.
تُو هو *tū ho*, 'be or become thou.'	تُم هو *tum ho*, 'be or become you.'
Precative هُوجِيے *hūjiye*, 'be pleased to become,' etc.	هُوجيو *hūjiyo*, 'you shall be or become.'

Fut. هُوجِئيگا *hūji'egā*, 'will you be pleased to become.'

The Aorist.

'I am, I shall be, I should be, or become,' etc.

مَیں *هووں - هوں *main ho'ūn* or *hon*.[1]	هم هووين - *هوئيں - هوں *ham howen, ho'en*, or *hon*.
تُو هووي - *هوئي - هو *tu howe, ho'e*, or *ho*.	تُم هو *tum ho*.
وُه هووي - *هوئي - هو *wŏh howe, ho'e*, or *ho*.	وي هووين - *هوئيں - هوں *we howen, ho'en*, or *hon*.

The Future.

'I shall be, or become,' etc.

مَیں *هوونگا - هُونگا *main ho'ūngā*, or *hūngā*.[3]	هم *هووينگے - هونگے *ham howenge* or *honge*.
تُو *هوويگا - هوگا *tū howegā*, or *hogā*.	تُم هوگے *tum hoge*.
وُه *هوويگا - هوگا *wŏh howegā*, or *hogā*.	وي *هووينگے - هونگے *we howenge, honge*.

The Past Conditional or Optative.

'Were I,' 'Did I become,' (Would that) 'I were,' etc.

مَیں هوتا *main hotā*.	هم هوتے *ham hote*.
تُو هوتا *tū hotā*.	تُم هوتے *tum hote*.
وُه هوتا *wŏh hotā*.	وي هوتے *we hote*.

[1] The forms marked with an asterisk are now seldom or never used. The forms *ho'egā* and *ho'enge* in the 2nd and 3rd pers. sing. and the 1st and 3rd pers. plural of the Future, which are given in Forbes' and other grammars, rarely if ever occur in the Urdū of the present period.

The Present Imperfect.

'I am becoming,' etc.

SINGULAR.	PLURAL.
مَیں هوتا هُوں *maiṅ hotā hūṅ.*	هم هوتے هَیں *ham hote haiṅ.*
تُو هوتا هَي *tū hotā hai.*	تُم هوتے هو *tum hote ho.*
وُہ هوتا هَي *wŏh hotā hai.*	وي هوتے هَیں *we hote haiṅ.*

The Past Continuous or Imperfect.

'I was becoming,' etc.

مَیں هوتا تها *maiṅ hotā thā.*	هم هوتے تهے *ham hote the.*
تُو هوتا تها *tū hotā thā.*	تُم هوتے تهے *tum hote the.*
وُہ هوتا تها *wŏh hotā thā.*	وي هوتے تهے *we hote the.*

The Past Absolute or Indefinite.

'I became,' etc.

مَیں هُوا *maiṅ hū'ā.*	هم هُوئے *ham hū'e.*
تو هُوا *tū hū'ā.*	تُم هُوئے *tum hū'e.*
وُہ هُوا *wŏh hū'ā.*	وي هُوئے *we hū'e.*

The Proximate or Present Perfect.

'I have become,' etc.

مَیں هُوا هُوں *maiṅ hū'ā hūṅ.*	هم هُوئے هَیں *ham hū'e haiṅ.*
تُو هُوا هَي *tū hū'ā hai.*	تُم هُوئے هو *tum hū'e ho.*
وُہ هُوا هَي *wŏh hū'ā hai.*	وي هُوئے هَیں *we hū'e haiṅ.*

The Remote or Past Perfect.

'I had become,' etc.

مَیں هُوا تها *maiṅ hū'ā thā.*	هم هُوئے تهے *ham hū'e the.*
تُو.هُوا تها *tū hū'ā thā.*	تُم هُوئے تهے *tum hū'e the.*
وہ هُوا تها *wŏh hū'ā thā.*	وي هُوئے تهے *we hū'e the.*

The Future Perfect and Past Potential.

'I shall have become,' or 'I may have become,' etc.

SINGULAR.	PLURAL.
مَیں ہُوا ہُونگا - ہوں *maiṅ hū'ā hūṅgā*, or *hoṅ*.	ہم ہُوئے ہونگے - ہوں *ham hū'e hoṅge*, or *hoṅ*.
تو ہُوا ہوگا - ہو *tū hū'ā hogā*, or *ho*.	تم ہُوئے ہوگے - ہو *tum hū'e hoge*, or *ho*.
وُہ ہُوا ہوگا - ہو *wŏh hū'ā hogā*, or *ho*.	وے ہُوئے ہونگے - ہوں *we hū'e hoṅge*, or *hoṅ*.

ADDITIONAL TENSES.

195. We may here notice the tenses not in common use, spoken of in § 181. These are: 1). The *Future Imperfect*, which is formed by adding the *Future* of the verb ہونا *honā* to the imperfect participle of a verb: 2). The *Present Potential*, formed by adding the *Aorist* of the verb ہونا *honā* to the imperfect part. of a verb: 3). The *Past Perfect Continuous* of the *Subjunctive* mood, formed by adding the imperfect participle of the verb ہونا *honā* to the imperfect participle of another verb: 4) the *Past Perfect Subjunctive*, formed by adding the imperfect participle of the verb ہونا *honā*, to the perfect part. of another verb. The first and second of these tenses are both called حالِ مُتشکّي *ḥālĕ mutashakkī*, 'the present potential,' by native grammarians, because the first is frequently used, the second always, to express *uncertainty* or *possibility*. The third and fourth are both termed ماضِي شرطِي *māẓī sharṭī*, 'the past conditional.' They are very seldom used; the shorter form of the *māẓī sharṭī*, given among the tenses in common use, being preferred. The four tenses are subjoined:

1). The Future Imperfect.

'I shall be going,' or 'I may be going,' etc.

SINGULAR.	PLURAL.
مَیں چلتا هُونگا *maiṅ chaltā hūṅgā.*	هم چلتے هونگے *ham chalte hoṅge.*
تُو چلتا هوگا *tū chaltā hogā.*	تُم چلتے هوگے *tum chalte hoge.*
وُہ چلتا هوگا *wŏh chaltā hogā.*	وي چلتے هونگے *we chalte hoṅge.*

2). The Present Potential.

'I may be going,' etc.

مَیں چلتا هوں *maiṅ chaltā hoṅ.*	هم چلتے هوں *ham chalte hoṅ.*
تُو چلتا هو *tū chaltā ho.*	تُم چلتے هو *tum chalte ho.*
وُہ چلتا هو *wŏh chaltā ho.*	وي چلتے هوں *we chalte hoṅ.*

3). The Past Perfect Continuous (Subjunctive).

'Had I been going,' or 'I might have been going,' etc.

مَیں چلتا هوتا *maiṅ chaltā hotā.*	هم چلتے هوتے *ham chalte hote.*
تُو چلتا هوتا *tū chaltā hotā.*	تُم چلتے هوتے *tum chalte hote.*
وُہ چلتا هوتا *wŏh chaltā hotā.*	وي چلتے هوتے *we chalte hote.*

4). The Past Perfect (Subjunctive).

'Had I gone,' etc.

مَیں چلا هوتا *maiṅ chalā hotā.*	هم چلے هوتے *ham chale hote.*
تُو چلا هوتا *tū chalā hotā.*	تُم چلے هوتے *tum chale hote.*
وُہ چلا هوتا *wŏh chalā hotā.*	وي چلے هوتے *we chale hote.*

THE PASSIVE VOICE.

196. Only *transitive* verbs have a passive voice. The tenses of this are regularly formed in all verbs by means of the tenses of the verb جانا *jānā*, 'to go' (the perfect participle of which is گیا *gayā*); though every form in which the verb جانا *jānā* is found is not passive: *e.g.* چلا جانا *chalā jānā*, 'to go away,' اُٹھا جانا *uṭhā jānā*, 'to rise up,' 'to be able to rise,' are active forms of intransitive

verbs. Whether the verb is passive or intransitive is decided not by the presence of the auxiliary *jānā*, but by the nature of the participle prefixed to it. If this be *passive*, so also, generally, is the verb: if it is not passive, but only a perfect participle of an intransitive verb, neither is the verb passive.

197. In the following conjugation of the passive voice of the verb دیکھنا *dekhnā*, 'to see,' the masculine forms alone are given. If the nominative to the verb be feminine, the termination of the passive participle must be changed to ـی *ī* in both the singular and the plural; and that of all the participial forms, and of the Future, of the auxiliary must be changed to ـی *ī* in the singular, and ـیں *īṅ* in the plural.

Passive Verb, دیکھا جانا *dekhā jānā*, 'to be seen.'

Infinitive or Verbal Noun, دیکھا جانا *dekhā jānā*, {'to be seen,' 'being seen.'
Imperfect Participle, دیکھا جاتا *dekhā jātā*, 'being seen.'
Passive Participle, دیکھا گیا *dekhā gayā*, 'been seen.'[1]

The Imperative.

SINGULAR.	PLURAL.
تو دیکھا جا *tū dekhā jā*, 'be thou seen.'	تم دیکھے جاؤ *tum dekhe jā'o*, 'be you seen.'

The Aorist.

'I am, or shall be, or should be, seen,' etc.

مَیں دیکھا جاؤں *main dekhā jā'ūṅ.*	ہم دیکھے جاویں - جائیں *ham dekhe jāweṅ* or *jā'eṅ.*
تو دیکھا جاوے - جائے *tū dekhā jāwe* or *jā'e.*	تم دیکھے جاؤ *tum dekhe jā'o.*
وہ دیکھا جاوے - جائے *woh dekhā jāwe* or *jā'e.*	وے دیکھے جاویں - جائیں *we dekhe jāweṅ* or *jā'eṅ.*

[1] It is needless to give the remaining participles, as none of them, except perhaps the adverbial (دیکھے جاتے ہی) *dekhe jāte-hī*, 'on the instant of being seen,' are ever used.

The Future.

'I shall be seen,' etc.

SINGULAR.	PLURAL.
مَیں دیکھا جاؤنگا *maiṅ dekhā jā'ūṅgā.*	ہم دیکھے جائینگے *ham dekhe jā'eṅge.*
تُو دیکھا جاویگا - جائیگا *tū dekhā jāwegā,* or *jā'egā.*	تُم دیکھے جاؤگے *tum dekhe jā'oge.*
وُہ دیکھا جاویگا - جائیگا *wŏh dekhā jāwegā,* or *jā'egā.*	وي دیکھے جاوینگے *we dekhe jāweṅge.*

The Past Conditional or Optative.

'Had I been seen,' 'Were I seen,' etc.

مَیں دیکھا جاتا *maiṅ dekhā jātā.*	ہم دیکھے جاتے *ham dekhe jāte.*
تُو دیکھا جاتا *tū dekhā jātā.*	تُم دیکھے جاتے *tum dekhe jāte.*
وُہ دیکھا جاتا *wŏh dekhā jātā.*	وي دیکھے جاتے *we dekhe jāte.*

The Present Imperfect.

'I am being seen,' etc.

مَیں دیکھا جاتا ھُوں *maiṅ dekhā jātā hūṅ.*	ہم دیکھے جاتے ھَیں *ham dekhe jāte haiṅ.*
تُو دیکھا جاتا ھَي *tū dekhā jātā hai.*	تُم دیکھے جاتے ھو *tum dekhe jāte ho.*
وُہ دیکھا جاتا ھَي *wŏh dekhā jātā hai.*	وي دیکھے جاتے ھَیں *we dekhe jāte haiṅ.*

The Past Continuous or Imperfect.

'I was being seen,' etc.

مَیں دیکھا جاتا تھا *maiṅ dekhā jātā thā.*	ہم دیکھے جاتے تھے *ham dekhe jāte the.*
تُو دیکھا جاتا تھا *tū dekhā jata thā.*	تُم دیکھے جاتے تھے *tum dekhe jāte the.*
وُہ دیکھا جاتا تھا *wŏh dekhā jātā thā.*	وي دیکھے جاتے تھے *we dekhe jāte the.*

The Past Absolute or Indefinite.

'I was seen,' etc.

SINGULAR.	PLURAL.
مَیں دیکھا گیا *main dekhā gayā.*	هم دیکھے گئے *ham dekhe ga'e.*
تُو دیکھا گیا *tū dekhā gayā.*	تُم دیکھے گئے *tum dekhe ga'e.*
وُہ دیکھا گیا *wŏh dekhā gayā.*	وي دیکھے گئے *we dekhe ga'e.*

The Proximate or Present Perfect

'I have been seen,' etc.

مَیں دیکھا گیا هُوں *main dekhā gayā hūn.*	هم دیکھے گئے هَیں *ham dekhe ga'e hain.*
تُو دیکھا گیا هَي *tū dekhā gayā hai.*	تُم دیکھے گئے هو *tum dekhe ga'e ho.*
وُہ دیکھا گیا هَي *wŏh dekhā gayā hai.*	وي دیکھے گئے هَیں *we dekhe ga'e hain.*

The Remote or Past Perfect.

'I had been seen,' etc.

مَیں دیکھا گیا تها *main dekhā gayā thā.*	هم دیکھے گئے تهے *ham dekhe ga'e the.*
تُو دیکھا گیا تها *tū dekhā gayā thā.*	تُم دیکھے گئے تهے *tum dekhe ga'e the.*
وُہ دیکھا گیا تها *wŏh dekhā gayā thā.*	وي دیکھے گئے تهے *we dekhe ga'e the.*

The Future Perfect, or Past Potential.

'I shall have been seen,' or more commonly, 'I may have been seen,' etc.

مَیں دیکھا گیا هُونگا ـ هوں *main dekhā gayā hūngā*, or *hon.*	هم دیکھے گئے هونگے ـ هوں *ham dekhe ga'e honge*, or *hon.*
تُو دیکھا گیا هوگا ـ هو *tū dekhā gayā hogā*, or *ho.*	تُم دیکھے گئے هوگے ـ هو *tum dekhe ga'e hoge*, or *ho.*
وُہ دیکھا گیا هوگا ـ هو *wŏh dekkā gayā hogā*, or *ho.*	وي دیکھے گئے هونگے ـ هوں *we dekhe ga'e honge*, or *hon.*

DERIVATIVE VERBS.

198. Derivative verbs may be classed under the three heads of *Causals*, *Denominatives*, and *Compound Verbs*.

I. CAUSAL VERBS.[1]

199. From nearly every verb in the language a causal may be derived. This causal will be *transitive* if formed from an *intransitive* verb, *doubly transitive* or *causative* if formed from a *transitive* verb. From most causals again a second or *double* causal may be formed.

200. Simple verbal roots are generally changed into causal bases by the addition of the increment ـَا *ā*, and into those which are doubly causal by means of the increment وَا *wā*,[2] and the root is then treated as a primitive root ending in *ā*. But in some verbs the causal characteristic *ā* becomes لا *lā*; and in others it is inserted in the root itself: hence three cases arise:

a) The causal may, generally speaking, be formed by adding ـَا *ā* to the root of a primitive verb, whether it be transitive or intransitive, and the double causal by inserting *w* before the increment *ā* of the causal: *e.g.*

PRIMITIVE VERB.	CAUSAL.	DOUBLE CAUSAL.
پڑھنا *paṛh-nā*, 'to read.'	پڑھانا *paṛhā-nā*, 'to cause to read,' 'to teach.'	پڑھوانا *paṛhwā-nā*, 'to have or get (one) taught (something by some one).'
گِرنا *girnā*, 'to fall.'	گِرانا *girā-nā*, 'to cause to fall,' 'to fell,' etc.	گِروانا *girwā-nā*, 'to get or have (a thing) thrown down (by some one).'
اُٹھنا *uṭhnā*, 'to rise.'	اُٹھانا *uṭhā-nā*, 'to raise.'	اُٹھوانا *uṭhwā-nā*, 'to have (a thing) raised (by some one).'

[1] A causal verb is termed by the native grammarians *fe'lĕ muta'addī bi'l wāsiṭa*, 'a verb which passes on (to an object) by means of (an increment),' in contradistinction to 'a verb which is transitive *per se*,' or *fe'lĕ muta'addī bi nafsihi*.

[2] In a few verbs *w* would appear to be inserted before the causal increment *ā* for the sake of euphony alone.

Subordinate to this rule are the two following:

1) If the root of the primitive verb be dissyllabic, the vowels of both syllables being short and that of the second *fatḥa* (*a*), this *fatḥa* is dropped in the first causal (*cf.* § 34, 4, *Rem. c.*): *e.g.*

PRIMITIVE VERB.	CAUSAL.	DOUBLE CAUSAL.
سمجهنا *samajh-nā*, 'to understand.'	سمجهانا *samjhā-nā*, 'to explain.'	سمجهوانا *samajhwā-nā*, 'to have (a thing) explained (to one person by another).'
پگهلنا *pighal-nā*, 'to melt' (intrans.).	پگهلانا *pighlā-nā*, 'to melt' (trans.).	پگهلوانا *pighalwā-nā*, 'to have (a thing) melted (by some one).'

2) If the root of the primitive verb be monosyllabic and enclose a long vowel or diphthong, the vowel or diphthong is changed in both causals into the corresponding short vowels, or, in other words, the letters of prolongation ا, و, ي, are dropped: *e.g.*

جاگنا *jāg-nā*, 'to be awake.'	جگانا *jagā-nā*, 'to wake.'	جگوانا *jagwā-na*, 'to cause (one) to be wakened.'
بهيگنا *bhīg-nā*, 'to become wet.'	بهگانا *bhigā-nā*,[1] 'to wet.'	بهگوانا *bhigwā-nā*, 'to have (a thing) wetted.'
ڈوبنا *ḍūbnā*, 'to sink' (intrans.).	ڈبانا *ḍubā-nā*, 'to sink,' 'to immerse.'	ڈبوانا *ḍubwā-nā*, 'to have (a thing) sunk.'
بولنا *bol-nā*, 'to speak.'	بلانا *bulā-nā*, 'to call (one) to (come and) speak.'	بلوانا *bulwā-nā*, 'to have (one) called.'
بيٹهنا *baiṭh-nā*, 'to sit down.'	بٹهانا *biṭhānā*,[1] 'to seat.'	بٹهوانا *biṭhwā-nā*, 'to cause (one) to be seated.'

b) If the root of the primitive verb end in a long vowel (*ā*, *ī*, *e*, *ū*, *o*), the increment generally takes the form لا *lā* in the causal, and لوا *lwā* in the double causal; and the long vowel of the root is shortened as in the preceding rule: *e.g.*

[1] The causals of *bhīgnā* and *ḍūbnā* may also take the forms *bhigonā* and *ḍubonā* (See *Rem.* § 202), and that of *baiṭhnā* other forms, which are given under Rule c.

PRIMITIVE VERB.	CAUSAL.	DOUBLE CAUSAL.
کهانا *khā-nā*, 'to eat.'	کِهلانا *khilā-nā*,[1] 'to give to eat,' 'to feed.'	کِهلْوانا *khilwā-nā.*
پِینا *pī-nā*, 'to drink.'	پِلانا *pilā-nā*, 'to give to drink.'	پِلْوانا *pilwā-nā.*
دینا *de-nā*, 'to give.'	دِلانا *dilā-nā*, 'to cause to give.'	دِلْوانا *dilwā-nā.*
چهُونا *chhū-nā*, 'to touch.'	چهُلانا *chhulā-nā*, 'to cause to touch.'	چهُلْوانا *chhulwā-nā.*
سونا *so-nā*, 'to sleep.'	سُلانا *sulā-nā*, 'to put to sleep.'	سُلْوانا *sulwā-nā.*

A few verbs take the form of the double causal alone: *e.g.* کهونا *khonā*, 'to lose,' causal کهُوَانا *khuwā-nā*; گانا *gānā*, 'to sing,' causal گوَانا *gawānā*; لینا *lenā*, 'to take,' causal لِوانا *liwā-nā.*

Some verbs, the roots of which end in consonants (chiefly *h*, *kh* *ṭh*), may take the increment *lā* in the causal, as well as *ā*; but in the double causal the increment is always *wā*: *e.g.*

کہْنا *kah-nā*, 'to say,'	causal	کہْلانا *kahlā-nā*, or کہانا *kahā-nā.*
دیکهْنا *dekh-nā*, 'to see,'	,,	دِکهْلانا *dikhlā-nā*, or دِکهانا *dikhā-nā.*
سِیکهْنا *sīkh-nā*, 'to learn,'	,,	سِکهْلانا *sikhlā-nā*, or سِکهانا *sikhā-nā.*
سُوکهْنا *sūkh-nā*, 'to dry,'	,,	سُکهْلانا *sukhlā-nā*, or سُکهانا *sukhā-nā.*
بَیٹهْنا *baiṭh-nā*, 'to sit,'	,,	بِٹهْلانا *biṭhlānā*, or بِٹهالنا *biṭhāl-nā*, بِٹهانا *biṭhānā*, and بَیٹهانا *baiṭhānā.*
پهانْدْنا *phānd-nā*, 'to ensnare,'	,,	پهنْدْلانا *phandlā-nā.*

Rem. The same causal forms are also found in cases where the roots of the primitive verbs (which have become obsolete) end in *t* (*d*), and *s*: as بتْلانا *batlā-nā*, 'to tell,' to point out;' پهُسْلانا *phuslā-nā*, 'to wheedle,' 'to coax.'

[1] The instances of radical *ā* changing to *i* in the causal are not numerous; and even the example given above takes the form *khalānā* in Southern India.

c) Intransitive roots enclosing short vowels are frequently made transitive by the insertion of *ā* in the root itself, this *ā* coalescing with radical *a* into *ā*, with radical *i* into *e*, and with radical *u* into *o*: (final *ṭ* of the root, it may be observed, is frequently changed into *ṛ* in the transitive verb):[1] *e.g.*

دبنا	*dabnā*,	'to be pressed,'	transitive	دابنا	*dābnā*,	'to press.'
کتنا	*katnā*,	'to be spun,'	,,	کاتنا	*kātnā*,	'to spin.'
کٹنا	*kaṭnā*,	'to be cut,'	,,	کاٹنا	*kāṭnā*,	'to cut.'
پھٹنا	*phaṭnā*,	'to be torn,'	,,	پھاڑنا	*phāṛnā*,	'to tear.'
لدنا	*ladnā*,	'to be laden,'	,,	لادنا	*lādnā*,	'to load.'
بندھنا	*bandhnā*,	'to be bound,'	,,	باندھنا	*bāndhnā*,	'to bind.'
مرنا	*marnā*,	'to die,'	,,	مارنا	*mārnā*,	'to kill.'
گڑنا	*gaṛnā*,	'to be buried,'	,,	گاڑنا	*gāṛnā*,	'to bury.'
پلنا	*palnā*,	'to be protected,'	,,	پالنا	*pālnā*,	'to protect.'
نکلنا	*nikalnā*,	'to come out,'	,,	نکالنا	*nikālnā*,	'to take out.'
تھمنا	*thamnā*,	'to be held,		تھامنا	*thāmnā*,	'to hold,
تھمبھنا	*thambhnā*,	or supported,'	,,	بھانبھنا	*thāṅbhnā*,	or support.'
رتنا	*ritnā*,	'to be filed,'	,,	ریتنا	*retnā*,	'to file.'
چھدنا	*chhidnā*,	'to be perforated,'	,,	چھیدنا	*chhednā*,	'to perforate.'
بکنا	*biknā*,	'to be sold,'	,,	بیچنا	*bechnā*,[2]	'to sell.'
پھٹنا	*phuṭnā*,	'to burst,				
پھوٹنا	*phūṭnā*,	or split asunder,'	,,	پھوڑنا	*phoṛnā*,	'to break.'
کھلنا	*khulnā*,	'to become open,'	,,	کھولنا	*kholnā*,	'to open.'

[1] The softening of the tenuis *ṭ* into the media *ḍ* (*ṛ*), and of *ṭh* into *ṛh*, occurs most commonly after the letters *p*, *ph*, *ch*, *chh*, and *gh*: *e.g. paṛhnā*, 'to read' = Sanskrit *paṭhanam*; *pīṛhā*, 'a stool' = S. *pīṭha*; *phoṛā*, 'a boil' = S. *sphoṭaka*; *chiṛiyā*, 'a bird' = S. *chaṭaka*; *chhakṛā*, 'a cart' = S. *śakaṭa*; *ghaṛa*, 'an earthen pot' = S. *ghaṭa*; *ghoṛā*, 'a horse' = S. *ghoṭaka*. If *ph* and a long vowel precede *ṭ*, it generally passes into *ṛ*.

[2] This change of *k* into *ch* is almost inexplicable. I can find no mention of such a change in the *Prākṛita-Prakāśa*. But there would appear to be in Sanskrit some connection between the guttural class of letters and the palatal; for when a verb beginning with a guttural is reduplicated, the corresponding palatal is used; and, reversely, final *ch* of nominal bases is changed into *k* before certain case-endings.

Rem. a. In a few transitive verbs the root vowels of the corresponding intransitives are simply lengthened: *e.g.* پیسنا *pīsnā*, 'to grind,' from پسنا *pisnā*; پیٹنا *pīṭnā*, 'to beat,' from پٹنا *piṭnā*; چھیلنا *chhīlnā*, 'to peel,' from چھلنا *chhilnā*; گوتھنا *gūthnā*, 'to plait,' from گتھنا *guthnā*.

Rem. b. Under this class of verbs (which are strangely termed "anomalous") existing grammars place the verb رکھنا *rakhnā*, 'to keep,' as the causal of رہنا *rahnā*, 'to remain;' but this is a mistake: the two verbs are derived from distinct Sanskrit forms.

201. These verbs, though derived (as we shall presently see) from Sanskrit causals, have in many, if not most, cases lost the causal signification, and become simply transitive. Hence we find that some of the intransitive verbs of this class, as well as their transitive derivatives, have also regular causals (and double causals) formed from them; but these, as a rule, retain the true causal character; and where the primitive intransitive verb has various significations, it will often be found that some of them are peculiar to the transitive and some to the causal derivative: *e.g.* from the verb پھوٹنا *phūṭnā* is formed the transitive پھوڑنا *phoṛnā*, and the causal پھٹانا *phuṭānā*;[1] but the former signifies 'to break,' and the latter 'to make (water, etc.) boil,' a sense which *phoṛnā* never has.

[1] This common word, strange to say, is not found in Shakespear's Dictionary, and, though given in Forbes', is said to mean 'to increase,' etc. But the dictionaries make sad confusion among the causal verbs. گڑانا *gaṛānā*, for example, is given as the causal of گڑنا *gaṛnā* alone; but there can be no doubt of its being the causal of گاڑنا *gāṛnā* also: in the first case it signifies 'to prick,' 'to thrust in,' etc.; in the second, 'to have or get (a thing or person) buried.' Similarly *kaṭānā* is the causal of both کٹنا *kaṭnā* and کاٹنا *kāṭnā*, but more commonly that of the latter. We may here observe that in some verbs the *first* causal derived from a transitive verb is sometimes identical in meaning with the *second*: *e.g.* *kaṭāna* = *kaṭwāna*; *rakhānā* = *rakhwānā*.

202. The following sentences will exemplify the use of the primitive and causal forms of a verb:

مکان گِرتا هَي *makān girtā hai*, 'the house is falling:'

وُه آدمِي مکان کو گِراتا هَي *woh ādmī makān-ko girātā hai*, 'that (or the) man is throwing (or pulling) down the house:'

مالِک اُس آدمِي سے اپنے مکان کو گِرواتا هَي *mālik us ādmī se apne makān-ko girwātā hai*, 'the owner is having his house pulled down by that man.'

مَيں عربِي پڙهتا هُوں *main 'arabī paṛhtā hūn*, 'I am reading Arabic:'

اپنے لڙکے کو عربِي پڙهاتا هُوں *apne laṛke-ko 'arabī paṛhātā hūn*, 'I am teaching my boy Arabic:'

مَولوِي صاحِب سے اپنے لڙکے کو عربِي پڙهواتا هُوں *maulavī ṣāḥib-se apne laṛke-ko 'arabī paṛhwāta hūn*, 'I am having my boy taught Arabic by the Maulavī-ṣāḥib.

Rem. The causal affix of the Sanskrit is *ay*, which in many verbs (chiefly when the verbal root ends in a long vowel) takes the form *āpay*. The Prākrit changes *ay* into *e*, and *āpay* into (*ābe*, and then) *āve*, and uses both forms without any apparent distinction. In Hindī and its sister dialects the first affix is not used, and the second is changed to *āü*, by elision of final *e*, and weakening of *v* to *u*; and from *āü*, by elision of *u*, is derived the causal characteristic *ā* of the modern Hindī. But in a few verbs the vowels *ā*, *u*, would appear to have coalesced into *o*: *e.g. bhīgonā*, *ḍubonā*, *gaṛonā*, etc., the causals of *bhīgnā*, *ḍūbnā*, and *gaṛnā*.

The modern dialects also use *lā* as a causal characteristic, and in this form the *l* is generally supposed to be inserted for the sake of euphony. But in this opinion we cannot concur; for when these languages desire to avoid a hiatus (and we may observe in passing that they are by no means averse to a hiatus), they generally insert *y*, or *h*, and not *l*. Besides, we find *lā* used as the causal affix even in cases where the verbal root ends in a consonant, and no insertion of euphonic *l* is called for. It seems more probable that *lā* is derived from the Sanskrit causal affix *ay*, which was first changed to *āl*, or *ār* (the two letters *l* and *r* being commonly interchangeable), and then to *lā*, or *rā*. Hindī and Panjābī show a preference for *lā*, while Sindhī and Gujarātī prefer *rā*. We can only call to mind one example of the form *āl* of the increment in Hindī, namely *biṭhālnā*; but numerous examples of the form *ār* are to be found in Sindhī. That *y* is occasionally changed into *l* is seen from the Prākrit *laṭṭhi* (the Hindī *lāṭhī*, 'a stick,' or *laṭh*, 'a column') = Sanskrit *yashṭi* (*Prākṛita-Prakāśa*, ed. Cowell, sect. ii. 32).

As regards the verbs given under Rule *c.*), it may be mentioned that their bases are not formed in Hindī in the manner described; but the rule is an attempt to explain the modification which a verbal root undergoes in Sanskrit before it receives the causal affix. These verbs are incorrectly called "anomalous:" they are simply derived from the verbal nouns of Sanskrit causals: *e.g.* the verbal noun *maraṇam* of the Sanskrit root *mṛi*, is the source of the Hindī intransitive verb *marnā*, 'to die;' in the causal the root *mṛi* takes the form *mār*, and the verbal noun is *māraṇam*, whence the Hindī transitive verb *mārnā*, 'to kill.' In not a few cases a process the reverse of that described in the rule takes place; namely, the *intransitive* verb is formed from the *transitive* in Hindī itself: *e.g.* the Sanskrit causal form *pālanam* = Hindī *pālnā*, 'to protect,' whence is formed *palnā*, 'to be protected;' the Sanskrit *māpanam* = Hindī *māpnā*, 'to measure,' whence *mapnā*, 'to be measured.' Some transitive verbs, it may be observed, have no corresponding intransitive, and retain no trace of their being causals; as *bhejnā*, 'to send' = S. *bhedanam*, 'dividing.'

II. DENOMINATIVE VERBS.

203. Denominatives may be conveniently noticed under the two following heads:—

1) Denominatives formed from Verbal Nouns.

These are formed by adding the infinitive increment نا *nā* to a Persian or Arabic verbal noun; *e.g.* بخشنا *ba<u>kh</u>shnā*, 'to forgive,' from the Persian بخش *ba<u>kh</u>sh*; خريدنا *<u>kh</u>arīd-nā*, 'to purchase,' from the Persian خريد *<u>kh</u>arīd*; بدلنا *badalnā*, 'to change,' from the Arabic بدل *badal*; قبولنا *ḳabūlnā*, 'to accept,' from the Arabic قبول *ḳabūl*. In some words ending in two quiescent consonants, the penultimate letter is made movent with *fatḥa* (*a*) before the termination *nā* is added: *e.g.* ترسنا *tarasnā*, 'to fear,' from ترس *tars*, 'fearing,' 'fear;' بحثنا *baḥas̤nā*, 'to dispute,' from بحث *baḥs̤*, 'controversy.'

2) Denominatives derived from other nouns.

These are formed by adding the termination انا *ānā* to a substantive or adjective, final ي *ī* being changed to يَ *iy* before the termination is added, and a long vowel in a dissyllabic noun shortened: *e.g.* شرمانا *sharmānā*, 'to be bashful,' from شرم *sharm*, 'shame;' گرمانا *garmānā*, 'to be heated,' 'to become warm or angry,' from گرم *garm*, 'hot;' پنيانا *paniyānā*, 'to water, or irrigate,' from پاني *pānī*, 'water;' مكيانا *mukiyānā*, 'to hit with the fist,' 'to knead dough,' from مكّي *mukkī*, 'the fist.' If the noun or adjective end in *ā*, the termination *nā* alone is added; as چوڑانا *chauṛānā*, 'to widen,' from چوڑا *chauṛā*, 'wide;' لنگڑانا *langṛānā*, 'to go lame,' 'to limp,' from لنگڑا *langṛā*, 'lame.' A few Persian nouns also, which are monosyllabic and enclose a long vowel, take the termination *nā* instead of *ānā*: *e.g.* داغنا *dāgnā*, 'to brand, or cauterize,' from داغ *dāg*, 'a spot or mark.'

Rem. Denominatives are not of very common occurrence in Urdū, compound forms being generally preferred: *e.g.* بخش دينا *ba<u>kh</u>sh denā*, 'to forgive,' قبول كرنا *kabūl karnā*, 'to accept,' مكي مارنا *mukkī mārnā*, 'to hit with the first,' پاني دينا *pānī denā*, 'to water,' چوڑا كرنا *chauṛā karnā*, 'to widen.'

III. COMPOUND VERBS.

204. Compound verbs, or what are commonly regarded as such, are very numerous in Hindūstānī. They are generally divided into Nominals, Intensives, Potentials, Completives, Continuatives, Staticals, Frequentatives, Desideratives, Inceptives, Permissives, Acquisitives, and Reiteratives; but not a few of these are, strictly speaking, not compound verbs, but phrases, as we shall show in noticing them.

Nominals.

205. These are formed by prefixing a noun (substantive or adjective) to a verb: *e.g.*

جمع هونا *jam' honā*, 'to be or become collected,' 'to collect.'
جمع كرنا *jam' karnā*, 'to make collected,' 'to collect.'
دم مارنا *dam mārnā*, 'to breathe a word,' 'to speak,' 'to boast.'
دم دينا *dam denā*, 'to wheedle or deceive.'
مول لينا *mol lenā*, 'to take by purchase,' 'to buy.'
پاني دينا *pānī denā*, 'to give water,' 'to irrigate.'
چوڑا كرنا *chauṛā karnā*, 'to make wide,' 'to widen.'

Such forms, it is clear, are not compound verbs; the noun in every instance simply serves to complete the notion of the verb, forming the *predicative noun* in the *Nominative* when the verb is *intransitive*, and in the *Accusative* when the verb is *transitive*. It is even (as we shall show in the Syntax) in not a few instances separated from the verb by other words.

206. Similar in character to the Nominal verbs are the

few compounds formed by prefixing a Persian preposition or adverb to a Hindī verb: *e.g.*

برآنا *bar-ānā*, 'to come up or forth,' 'to succeed.'

برلانا *bar-lānā*, 'to bring up or forth,' 'to accomplish.'

بہم آنا *ba-ham-ānā*, 'to come together,' 'to be acquired.'

بہم پہنچنا *ba-ham-pahuṅchnā*, 'to arrive or come together,' 'to be procured.'

بازآنا *bāz-ānā*, 'to come back,' 'to decline,' 'to abstain.'

بازرکھنا *bāz-rakhnā*, 'to keep or hold back,' 'to restrain.'

پیش آنا *pesh-ānā*, 'to come before,' 'to present (itself),' 'to treat,' etc.

در آنا *dar-ānā*, 'to come in,' 'to enter.'

207. The remaining compound verbs may be arranged under four classes, according as they are formed with the *verbal root*, the *imperfect participle*, the *perfect participle*, or the *conjunctive participle*.

a) Compounds formed with the Root.

These are the Intensives, Potentials, and Completives.

1) Intensives.

208. Intensives are formed by prefixing the root of a verb to another verb, which is regularly conjugated, the root remaining unchanged. The signification of the compound is that of the root intensified by the second member. In many cases however the effect produced by the second member of the compound is not obvious. Examples are:—

پی جانا *pī-jānā*, 'to drink up or off.'

بول اٹھنا *bol-uṭhnā*, 'to speak or call out.'

کاٹ ڈالنا *kāṭ-ḍālnā*, 'to cut up or off.'

کھا جانا *khā-jānā*, 'to eat up.'

گر پڑنا *gir-paṛnā*, 'to tumble down.'

Rem. The appropriate verb for intensifying another, like the appropriate adverb in English, is determined by usage. Not a few verbs, which existing grammars call *intensives*, have nothing intensive in their signification; some of them are properly *completives*; others simply *transitives*, formed by prefixing the root form of the conjunctive participle of the verb لینا *lenā* to an intransitive verb (§ 215): *e.g.* هو جانا *ho-jānā* = هو چُکنا *ho-chuknā*; کاغذ هو گیا *kāgaz ho-gayā* = کاغذ هو چُکا *kāgaz ho-chukā*, 'the paper is finished'; مَیں نَوکر هو گیا *maiṅ naukar ho-gayā*, 'I have become an *employée*,' i.e. 'my becoming an *employée* is an accomplished fact;' لے آنا *le-ānā*[1] = لیکر آنا *lekar-ānā*, 'having taken, to come,' *i.e.* 'to come with,' or 'to bring.' Similarly سو جانا *so-jānā*, and سو رهْنا *so-rahnā*, are not intensives, any more than their English equivalents 'to go to sleep,' and 'to be asleep' are.[2]

2) Potentials.

209. These verbs express the ability to perform an action. They are formed by adding the verb سکْنا *saknā*, 'to be able,' to the root form of another verb: *e.g.*

جا سکْنا *jā-saknā*, 'to be able to go.'
دیکھ سکْنا *dekh-saknā*, 'to be able to see.'
کر سکْنا *kar-saknā*, 'to be able to do.'
مَیں کر سکْتا هُوں *maiṅ-kar-saktā huṅ*, 'I can do.'
وُہ دیکھ سکا *wŏh dekh-saka*, 'he could see.'

[1] A recent writer on Urdū Grammar observes: "The verbs *le-ānā*, *le-jānā*, *khā-jānā*, etc., are *neuter*, because the verbs *ānā* and *jānā* are neuter." This is simply incorrect. They are *transitive*, and are so called by native grammarians; but, like a few other transitive verbs, *do not take the passive construction in the tenses composed of the past participle* because a *passive* participle cannot be formed from them.

[2] The same grammarian tries to "discriminate" between the forms *ho-jānā* and *ho-rahnā*; *so-jānā* and *so-rahnā*; but his remarks show that he is not aware of the fact that the verbs *jānā* and *rahnā* are frequently synonymous, and are commonly used in the sense of *honā*, and are called by the native grammarians 'the sisters of *hona*.' Had he lived in India, he would have often heard the expression *so raho* used in the sense of 'go to sleep,' and *ṣāḥib so rahā hai*, in the sense of both 'the master is sleeping,' and 'the master has gone to sleep.' So, in the *Khirad Afroz*, p. 74, *nahā rahī hai* = *nahātī hai*.

Rem. It is very probable that the first part of these compounds is the *apocopated infinitive,* and not the root. Indeed we occasionally find the full form of the infinitive (always inflected however) expressed; as وہ دیکھنے سکتا ہے *wŏh dekhne saktā hai,* 'he can see.' It may be observed that the verb *saknā* occurs only in compounds.

3) Completives.

210. These are obtained by adding the verb چکنا *chuknā,* 'to come to an end,' 'to be finished,' to the root of a verb; as

بول چکنا *bol-chuknā,* 'to have done speaking.'
پڑھ چکنا *paṛh-chuknā,* 'to have done reading.'

In the past tenses the compound may also imply that the act is really finished in agreement or disagreement with what preceded it, or just a little before the time of speaking; as مَیں کر چکا *main kar-chukā,* 'I have already done' (it or so). The Past Indefinite tense is often used most idiomatically to express the utter improbability of the speaker's performing an act, or of his belief in the improbability of another's performing it; as مَیں کر چکا *main kar-chukā,* 'I am not at all likely to do' (in vulgar English 'catch me doing it!'); وہ جا چکا *wŏh jā-chukā,* 'he is gone (as much as he is ever likely to go),' *i.e.* 'he is not gone at all, and is not likely to go.' The Future of the compound may serve the purpose of a Future Perfect; مَیں جا چکونگا *main jā-chukūngā,* 'I shall have gone.'

Rem. The verb *chuknā,* like the verb *saknā,* occurs only in compounds.

b) Compounds formed with the Imperfect Participle.

211. These are the Continuatives and Staticals of existing grammars. They are not compound verbs, but phrases wherein the participle is used adjectively or adverbially to denote a حال *ḥāl,* or circumstance.

1) Continuatives.

212. Continuatives are formed by prefixing an imperfect participle to one of the verbs جانا *jānā* or رهنا *rahnā*, used as synonymous with هونا *honā*; the participle *which always takes the inflected masculine form* conveying the idea of a *continuous* or *habitual* act or state: *e.g.*

بکتے جانا *bakte jānā*, 'to be continually prating,' 'to go on prating.'
گهومتے رهنا *ghumte rahnā*, 'to be ever revolving,' 'to keep revolving.'
پڑهتے جانا *paṛhte jānā*, } 'to continue or go on reading.'
پڑهتے رهنا *paṛhte rahnā*, }

Rem. The participle in these forms is in the locative case, and is used adverbially.

2) Staticals.

213. In these the imperfect participle of a verb, or rather the elliptical form of the *active* or *progressive* participle, precedes another verb, and, as in English, agrees in gender and number with the subject or object of which it forms the attribute. There is nothing approaching to a compound verb in such forms: *e.g.* موهن هنستا (or هنستا هوا) جاتا هے *mohan hanstā* (or *hanstā hūā*) *jātā hai*, 'Mohan is going along laughing;' وه لڑکي جو گاتي (or گاتي هوئي) آتي هے *wŏh laṛkī jo gātī* (or *gātī hūī*) *ātī hai*, 'the girl who is coming along singing;' وه پڑهتي رهتي هے *wŏh paṛhtī rahtī hai*, 'she remains or continues reading' (in this example the idea of *duration* or *continuity* is implied in the verb); مَیں نے اُسکو سوتا دیکها *main-ne usko sotā dekhā*, 'I saw him sleeping' (here the concord of the participle is interrupted, because the object is in the *dative* form of the accusative;

but) مَیں نے اُسکو دَوڑتے پکڑا *main-ne usko daurte pakṛā*, 'I caught it (while I was) running.'

Rem. The so-called Staticals differ from Continuatives in denoting a *temporary* or *accidental* state. The two forms are clearly distinguished in most native grammars, but are strangely misunderstood by European grammarians, who teach that *the participle is inflected in Staticals, and not inflected in Continuatives!* Now, the fact is, that it is just to indicate *duration* or *continuity* (and, occasionally, a *habitual* state) that the particle or verbal adjective is changed into an adverb and inflected. This is evident from such forms as چلتے چلتے تھک گیا *chalte chalte thak gayā*, 'I wearied through much or continued walking;' چلتے چلتے ایک جزیرے میں پہنچے *chalte chalte ek jazīre meṅ pahuṅche*, 'Keeping on our way we reached an island;' ہم گاتے گاتے سیتے ہیں *ham gāte gāte sītī hain*, 'We stitch singing the while,' or 'We keep on singing whilst we stitch.'

c) Compounds formed with the Perfect Participle.

214. A perfect participle, used as *an abstract substantive in the Accusative* or *the Formative*, is prefixed to one of the verbs کرنا 'to make,' جانا 'to go,' and چاہنا 'to desire,' and the compound verb thus formed assumes an *intransitive* character.[1] Such compounds are of two kinds:

[1] Hence these verbs are never constructed *passively* with the Agent case in the tenses formed with the perfect participle (see § 185): e.g. *wŏh chupke but-kī ṭarah baiṭhe sunā kī*, 'she seated silent, like a statue, continued to listen;' *ek muddat talak us gam-meṅ royā kiye*, 'for a long period they continued to mourn in that affliction;' *main tamām din aur tamām rāt pānī-meṅ hāth pā'oṅ mārā kiyā*, 'I kept striking (out) my hands and legs in the water the whole day and the whole night.' Similarly if any verbal noun be combined with a transitive verb in the same way, the compound verb is intransitive: e.g. *do ādmī dekhā'ī diye*, 'two men appeared' (gave an appearance); *ādmī kī āwāz sunā'ī dī*, 'a man's voice was heard.' This, it may be observed, is directly opposed to the teaching of European grammarians. If however the grammarians simply confined themselves to laying down incorrect or unsound rules, the offence might be pardoned; but when they pronounce the composition of standard authors "ungrammatical" because it does not conform to those rules (as a recent writer does in more than one instance), the offence becomes unpardonable. We may here remark that if there is one point about which an educated native is not likely to be mistaken, it is the use of the Agent case.

1) FREQUENTATIVES OR CONTINUATIVES.

These denote the *frequent*, *continual*, or *habitual* performance of an act, and are formed: *a*) by adding the verb کرنا to a perfect participle, which (being the direct object of the verb) retains the nominative form of the masculine singular under all circumstances: *e.g.*

جایا کرنا *jāyā karnā*, 'to go frequently,' 'to keep going' (*lit.* 'to make the going').

بیچا کرنا *bechā karnā*, 'to sell habitually.'

رویا کرنا *royā karnā*, 'to weep perpetually,' 'to continue weeping.'

سُنا کرنا *sunā karnā*, 'to continue listening.'

وُہ سُنا کی *wŏh sunā kī*, 'she kept listening.'

b) By adding the verb جانا 'to go,' to a perfect participle used as an abstract substantive; but in this case the verb being *neuter*, the participle is put in the Formative: *e.g.*

چلے جانا *chale jānā*, 'to keep moving or walking on' (lit. 'to go on *with* or *in* walking').

کیے جانا *kiye jānā*, 'to continue or go on doing.'

Rem. The verb جانا added to an *uninflected* perfect participle has occasionally the signification of هو سکنا *ho saknā*, 'to be possible.' Such forms, however, are not compound verbs, nor is the construction a *passive* one, as some grammarians mistakenly suppose; but the participle is used as a verbal noun, and forms the *subject* or nominative of the verb: *e.g.* مُجھ سے آج کھانا کھایا گیا *mujh se āj khānā khāyā gayā* (= *khānā-kā khānā āj mujh se ho sakā*), 'I was able to eat my food to-day,' or *lit.* 'by me eating food to-day was possible;' تقدیر سے لڑا نہیں جاتا *taḳdīr-se laṛā nahīn jātā*, 'there is no fighting against what is predestined,' or *lit.* 'fighting against destiny is impossible.'

2) Desideratives.

These are formed by adding the verb چاهنا *chāhnā*, 'to wish or desire,' to a perfect participle used as a verbal noun in the Accusative, and hence uninflected. They express the desire to perform the act or enter the state signified by the participial noun: *e.g.*

جايا چاهنا *jāyā-chāhnā*, 'to wish to go.'
ديكها چاهنا *dekhā-chāhnā*, 'to wish to see.'
پڙها چاهنا *paṛhā-chāhnā*, 'to wish to read.'
مرا چاهنا *marā-chāhnā*, 'to wish to die.'

The same forms are also commonly employed to express the fact of an act or state being imminent: *e.g.* وه جايا چاهتا هَي *wŏh jāyā-chāhtā hai*, 'he is about to go;' وه مرا چاهتي هَي *wŏh marā chāhtī hai*, 'she is about to die;' وي بهاگا چاهتے تهے *we bhāgā-chāte the*, 'they were on the point of running away.'

Rem. a. In these compounds the participles of the verbs جانا *jānā*, 'to go,' and مرنا *marnā*, 'to die,' always take the regular forms جايا *jāyā* and مرا *marā*.

Rem. b. The perfect participle is said by some grammarians to be prefixed to another verb to form *intensives*; and some of the examples given are: وي چلے جاتے تهے *we chale jāte the*, 'they were going along;' لومڙي پڙي پهرتي تهي *lomṛī paṛī phirtī thī*, 'the fox was prowling about;' خجالت سے مؤا جاتا هَي *khijālat se mū'ā jātā hai*, 'he is dying with shame.' But in these and all similar cases, there is no intensive signification whatever, nor is there an approach to a compound verb: the perfect participle is simply used as an attributive (as we have shown that the imperfect participle is), *to denote a state*, and agrees in gender and number with the noun it qualifies. The literal translation of the first of the above sentences is, 'they were going walking' (the perfect part. may in most cases be conveniently rendered into English by the imperfect); that of the second, 'the fox, lying in wait, was moving about;' and in the third sentence *jānā* is used in the sense of *honā*, so that the translation is, 'I was becoming dead,' etc., *i.e.* 'I was dying,' etc. As in the case of the imperfect participle, the inflected form of the perf. part. denotes a *prolonged* or *continued* act or state: *e.g.* چلے جانا *chale-jānā*, 'keep walking on' (*vide* §. 213).

d) COMPOUNDS FORMED WITH CONJUNCTIVE PARTICIPLES.

215. These are formed by prefixing a conjunctive participle, commonly لے *le*, of the verb لینا *lenā*, 'to take,' to an intransitive verb of motion: *e.g.*

لے آنا *le-ānā* (by contraction, لانا *lānā*), 'to come with,' 'to bring' (*lit.* 'having taken, to come').

لے جانا *le-jānā*, 'to go away with,' 'to take away,' 'to remove.'

لے اُڑنا *le-uṛnā*, 'to fly away with'

لے بھاگنا *le-bhāgnā*, 'to run away with.'

لے پہنچنا *le-pahuṅchnā*, 'to arrive or come with,' 'to bring'

Rem. That the first member in these compounds is the conjunctive participle, and not the verbal *root*, as English writers on Urdū grammar call it, is evident enough from the examples given above. Another error of existing grammars in respect of these compounds is the calling them "neuter." We need only point out that the native grammarians do not countenance this view, but term them مُتعدّي بيک مفعول *muta'addī ba-yak maf'ūl*, 'transitives with one object;' and that in other languages—*e.g.* Latin and Arabic—such verbs are classed under the head of transitive verbs. That they cannot take the passive construction in the tenses formed with the perfect participle, is simply owing to the fact that the last member of the compound (which alone is conjugated), being intransitive, cannot form a *passive* participle:

this, however, is not the criterion of a transitive, but of a *directly* transitive verb.

216. Some verbs invariably take an inflected infinitive before them, the infinitive or verbal noun being either in the locative or dative case. These forms, which cannot be regarded as compound verbs, are termed by the grammarians Inceptives, Acquisitives, and Permissives. To these may also be added *Desideratives*.

1) Inceptives,

in which an inflected infinitive precedes the verb لگنا *lagnā*, 'to come in contact (with),' 'to take to,' and hence 'to begin:' *e.g.* بهاگنے لگا *bhāgne lagā* (= بهاگنے میں لگا *bhāgne-meṅ lagā*), 'he took to, or began running;' وُہ رونے لگتي هَي *wŏh rone lagtī hai*, 'she takes to, or begins, crying.'

2) Permissives.

An inflected infinitive is followed by the verb دینا *denā* 'to give or grant,' and (with the infinitive, as in Sanskrit), 'to allow or permit:' *e.g.* اُسے جانے دو *use jāne do* (= اُسے جانے کو دو *use jāne-ko do*), 'allow him to go,' 'let him go;' وُہ مُجهے آنے دِیا *wŏh mujhe āne diyā*, 'he allowed me to come.'

3) Acquisitives.

An inflected infinitive is followed by the verb پانا *pānā*, 'to get or obtain,' and (with the infinitive), 'to obtain permission,' 'to be allowed;' *e.g.* آنے پایا *āne pāyā* (= *āne-ko pāyā*), 'he was allowed, or got permission, to come;' جانے پاویگا *jāne pāwegā*, 'he will be allowed to go.'

4) Desideratives.

An inflected infinitive precedes one of the verbs چاهْنا *chāhnā*, 'to wish or desire,' مانْگْنا *māṅgnā*, 'to request permission,' 'to want or desire:' *e.g.* وُہ پِينے چاهْتا هَي *wŏh pīne chāhtā hai*, 'he wishes to drink,' جانے مانْگْتا هَي *jāne māṅgtā hai*, 'he wishes, or requests permission, to go.'

Reiteratives.

217. It remains to notice the compound forms termed *Reiteratives* by European grammarians. These consist in the asyndetic connection of two verbs, or participles (most commonly of two conjunctive participles, or two imperfect participles followed by the auxiliary verb), the second of which usually rhymes with the first, and is either synonymous with it, or without any signification: *e.g.* سوچ ساچ کر *soch sāch kar*, 'having reflected;' بول چال کر *bol chāl kar*, 'having conversed;' سَمْجها بُجها کر *samjhā bujhā kar*, 'having explained,' or 'having reasoned;' بغَير پُوچهے گچهے *ba-gair pūchhe gachhe*, 'without asking or enquiring;' اُن دونوں زَخْمِيوں کو گاڑنے دابْنے کِي فِکْر میں رها *un donoṅ zakhmiyoṅ ko gāṛne dābne kī fikr meṅ rahā*, 'he was busy with the thought of burying the two murdered persons;' کُچه پِيس پاس رهے تهے *kuchh pīs pās rahe the*, 'they were pulverizing something;' مَیں هارا تهکا تها *maiṅ hārā thakā thā*, 'I was worn out (and) tired;' اور وُہ اپْنا گهر دیکهے بهالے *aur wŏh apnā ghar dekhe bhāle*, 'and he shall look after his own house.' In such constructions the last verb may sometimes be one which, although possessing a signification of its own, is rarely used except in combination with another

verb or particle; *e.g.* بهالنا *bhālnā* (from the Sanskrit root *bhṛi*), in the last example, and in the word سنبهالنا *sambhālnā*, 'to support,' etc. Similarly دهو دها کر *dho dhā kar*, 'having washed,' where the form دها *dhā* (which sometimes occurs alone) has the same signification as دهو *dho*, and, like it, is derived from the Sanskrit root *dhāv*, 'to wash.' Under no circumstances, however, can Reiteratives be regarded as compound verbs.

218. It is evident then from the preceding remarks that the compound verbs are, strictly speaking, of seven kinds; namely, Intensives, Potentials, Completives, Continuatives, Frequentatives, and Desideratives formed with the perfect participle, and Transitives formed by prefixing a past conjunctive participle to a verb denoting motion. In these the second member alone is conjugated, the first undergoing no change.

CHAPTER IV.

PARTICLES OR INDECLINABLE WORDS (حرف *ḥarf*).

I. ADVERBS.

219. Adverbs are used to qualify any attribute. As in other languages, they may be classified according to their meaning and logical connection, or according to their origin. In the few adverbs which we purpose noticing we shall adopt both these principles of classification, giving the preference however to the latter. Persian and Arabic adverbs will, as far as possible, be kept distinct from those of the Hindī.

220. Original Hindī adverbs are not numerous. The following are some of the most common:

1. Time: آج *āj*, 'to-day' (Sanskrit *adya*).
   کل *kal*, 'yesterday, or to-morrow' (S. *kalya*).
   پرسوں *parsoṅ*, 'the day before yesterday,' or 'the day after to-morrow' (S. *paras* + *śvas*).
   ترسوں *tarsoṅ*, 'three days ago, or hence' (S. *tri* + *śvas*).
   نرسوں *narsoṅ*, 'four days ago, or hence' (Dravid. *nal*, 'four' + *soṅ* = *śvas*).
   جھٹ *jhaṭ*, 'instantly,' 'in a moment' (S. *jhaṭiti*).
2. Manner: ترت *turt*, ترنت *turant*, 'swiftly,' 'quickly' (S. *tvaritam*).

(Assent or negation). هاں *hāṅ*, 'yes' (S. *ām*).

نہ *na*, 'not' (S. *na*).

نہیں *nahīṅ*, 'no,' 'not' (S. *nahi*).

مت *mat* (used as a prohibitive with the imperative), 'do not' (S. *mā*).

(Emphasis). تو *to*, 'indeed' (S. *tu*).

بِهي *bhī*, 'also,' 'too,' 'even' (S. *api*).

221. Some adverbs are originally nouns or adjectives in the locative case: *e.g.*

آگے *āge*, 'in front,' 'before,' 'ahead' (S. *agre*).

پار *pār*, 'on the opposite side,' 'across' (S. *pāre*).

پاس *pās*, 'at the side,' 'near' (S. *pārśve*).

دهِيري *dhīre*, 'gently' (S. *dhīra*).

سامْهنے *sāmhne*, 'in front' (S. *sam* + *mukha*).

سويري *sawere*, 'early' (S. *sa* + *vela*).

نِيچے *nīche*, 'below' (S. *nīche*).

222. Nouns in the ablative case may also be used as adverbs (تمِيز *tamīz*, 'the specification'):

بهُولے سے *bhūle-se*, 'by mistake,' 'forgetfully.'

پهُرتي سے *phurtī-se*, 'with agility,' etc., 'actively,' 'nimbly.'

خُوشي سے *khwushī-se*, 'with pleasure,' etc., 'gladly,' 'willingly.'

زورسے *zor-se*, 'with or by force,' 'perforce,' 'forcibly,' 'strongly,' 'hard.'

223. Adjectives in the *uninflected* form (*i.e.* in the nom. sing. masc.) are also employed as adverbs, generally when it is intended to express rather the quality of the agent as seen in the act, or after the act, than the quality of the act itself: *e.g.*

وہ بڑا سیانا ہے *wŏh baṛā siyānā hai*, 'he is very knowing, or cunning.'
وہ بہت اچھا لکھتا ہے *wŏh bahut achchhā likhtā hai*, 'he writes very well.'

224. The following useful series of adverbs are formed from pronominal bases by means of certain affixes:[1]

PRONOMINAL BASES.

	PROXIMATE DEMONSTRATIVE. *a*, *i* or *y*, *ya*.	REMOTE DEMONSTRATIVE. *u* or *w*, *wa*.	INTERROGATIVE. *ka*, *ki* or *ky*.	RELATIVE. *j*, *ja* or *ji* or *jy*.	CORRELATIVE. *t*, *ta*, *ti* or *ty*.
1. Time...	اب *ab*, 'now.'	......	کب *kab*, 'when?'	جب *jab*, 'when.'	تب *tab*, 'then.'
2. Place...	یہاں *yahāṅ*, 'here.'	وہاں *wahāṅ*, 'there.'	کہاں *kahāṅ*, 'where?'	جہاں *jahāṅ*, 'where.'	تہاں *tahāṅ*, 'there.'
3. Direction	اِدھر *idhar*, 'hither.'	اُدھر *udhar*, 'thither.'	کِدھر *kidhar*, 'whither?'	جِدھر *jidhar*, 'whither.'	تِدھر *tidhar*, 'thither.'
4. Manner..	یوں *yūṅ*, *yoṅ*, 'thus,' etc.	ووں *wūṅ*, *woṅ*, 'thus,' 'so.'	کیوں *kyūṅ*, *kyoṅ*, 'how? why?'	جیوں *jyūṅ*, or *jyoṅ*, جوں or *joṅ*, 'as.'	تیوں *tyūṅ* or *tyoṅ*, توں *toṅ*. 'so.'

[1] The grammarians would have us believe that these series of adverbs are formed in Hindī or Urdū itself from the pronouns *yĕh*, *wŏh*, etc., by adding the affixes *b*, etc.: but there can be no doubt that they are all derived from the Sanskrit, or that, at least, one or two of a series are derived from the corresponding Sanskrit series, and the rest formed after the same model. In the first series, for example, *jab* and *tab* spring, most probably, from the Sanskrit *yāvat* and *tāvat*, through the Prākrit *jāva*, *tāva*; and *ab* and *kab* were similarly formed afterwards. That this series is derived from *jad*, *tad*, etc., as some suppose, by change of *d* into *b*, is highly improbable, for *d* does not pass into *b*.

The termination *hāṅ* of the second series corresponds to the Sanskrit *sthāne*, the loc. of *sthāna*, 'place:' *e.g.* *tahāṅ* = *tatsthāne*. *Hāṅ*, it may be observed, is in common use at the present day as a noun in the locative, signifying 'place,' 'house:' *e.g.* *mere hāṅ ānā*, 'come to my place or house;' *ṣāḥib ke hāṅ jānā*, 'go to the gentleman's house;' not *mere yahāṅ*, and *ṣāḥib ke yahāṅ*.

The termination of the third series is not easy to trace. It would appear to correspond to the Sanskrit *tas* (*idhar* = *itas*), or to the Sanskrit affix *ha* (*dha*); *e.g.* *idhar* = *iha*; most probably to the latter, for the Persian word corresponding to *idhar* is *īdar* = Zend *idha* = Sanskrit *iha*.

The termination of the fourth series is supposed to spring from the Sanskrit affix *thā* or *tham*: *e.g.* *ittham* = Prākrit *ia* = Hindī *yoṅ*; but we prefer to derive it from the Sanskrit *evam* (the Prākrit *ĕvvam*), and to suppose that the other adverbs of the series are formed after the model of it.

Rem. Instead of the forms *kab, jab, tab,* in the first series, the forms *kad, jad, tad,* are occasionally used (in Hindī commonly), and the first vowel of the series *idhar,* etc., is occasionally lengthened, *e.g. jīdhar.* etc.

225. The adjectives derived from the same pronouns (§ 156) are also employed (in the inflected form generally) as adverbs of *manner* and *degree* (measure, quantity): *e.g.*

ایسے *aise,* 'like this,' 'thus,' 'so.'	اِتّے or اِتنے *itne* or *itte,* 'as much as this,' 'so much.'
وَیسے *waise,* 'like that,' 'so.'	اُتّے or اُتنے *utne* or *utte,* 'as much as that,' 'so much.'
کَیسے *kaise,* 'in what way?' 'how?'	کِتّے or کِتنے *kitne* or *kitte,* 'how much or many?'
جَیسے *jaise,* 'in what way,' 'as.'	جِتّے or جِتنے *jitne* or *jitte,* 'as much as.'
تَیسے *taise,* 'in that way,' 'so.'	تِتّے or تِتنے *titne* or *titte,* 'so much.'

Occasionally however, like other adjectives (§ 223), they are used in the uninflected (masc.) form.

Rem. Of the double forms *itne* or *itte,* etc., the first are more generally used.

226. The pronominal adverbs, like most other adverbs, may be intensified by the addition to them of the emphatic particle هِي *hī* or هِيں *hīṅ,* the latter form being employed with those of the second and fourth series. *E.g.* 1) from the first series we get:

ابهي *abhī,* 'this very instant,' 'just now,' 'immediately.'
کبهي *kabhī,* 'ever' (کبهي نہيں *kabhī nahīn,* 'never').
جبهي *jabhī,* 'hence,' 'for such a reason' (frequently used for *tabhī*).
تبهي *tabhī,* 'at that very time,' 'thence,' 'for that reason.'

Rem. *Hū* would appear to be an old form of *hī*; but it is now only used, occasionally, with the derivatives from the interrogative pronoun: *e.g.* کبهو *kabhū* = کبهي *kabhī*.

2) In the second series, the termination *hāṅ* is elided before the emphatic particle هين *hīṅ* is added; in some cases though the nasal of *hāṅ* is retained: *e.g.*

يهين *yahīṅ* (or *yaṅhīṅ*), 'this very place,' 'just here.'

وهين *wahīṅ* (or *waṅhīṅ* or *wuṅhīṅ*), 'that very place,' 'just there.'

كهين *kahīṅ*, 'anywhere' (كهين نهين *kahīṅ nahīṅ*, 'nowhere').

جهين *jahīṅ*, 'wheresoever.'

تهين *tahīṅ*, 'that same or very place.'

Rem. These forms are all contractions, and the two nasals, though not usually *written*, may often be distinctly *heard* in the pronunciation of a native, especially in the words *yaṅhīṅ* and *wuṅhīṅ*; it is not correct therefore to say that they are formed "by changing *hāṅ* (or *āṅ*) into *hīṅ* (or *īṅ*)." It may be observed further, that, with the exception of كهين 'somewhere, somehow,' they are never used as adverbs of *manner*, as some grammarians say they are.

3) Examples of the fourth series are:

يونهين *yūṅhīṅ* or *yoṅhīṅ*, 'just this way,' 'without any ground or reason.'

وونهين *wūṅhīṅ* or *woṅhīṅ*, 'in that very way,' 'on that very instant.'

جونهين *joṅhīṅ*, 'as,' 'as soon as.'

Rem. These forms never convey a *local* signification, as the grammarians assert.

4) The remaining series take *hī* after them for emphasis; as إدهر هي *idhar-hī*, 'in this very direction,' 'to *this* place;' أيسے هي *aise-hī*, 'precisely like this;' كيسے هي *kaise-hī*, 'in whatever way,' 'however,' 'how—soever;' كتنے هي *kitne-hī*, 'how much soever.'

227. Adverbs of *time* and *place* may be used as nouns, and put in the genitive and ablative cases. With the

genitive postposition they become adjectives: *e.g.* اب کي دفعہ *ab-kī daf'a*, 'this time;' يہاں کے باشِندي *yahāṅ-ke bāshinde*, 'the people of this place.' An adverb of *time* in the ablative changes its signification from a *point* to *duration* of time; as کل سے *kal-se*, 'since yesterday;' کب سے *kab-se*, 'since when?' تب سے *tab-se*, 'since then:' and an adverb of place changes its signification from *rest in*, or *motion to*, to *motion from* a place: *e.g.* يہاں سے *yahāṅ-se*, 'from this place,' 'hence.'

Rem. Adverbs of *degree* are said by some writers on Urdū grammar to be used in the locative case, and to change their signification to that of *relative time, e.g.* اِتنے ميں *itne-meṅ*, 'meanwhile.' It is however more correct to regard *itne*, etc., in such cases as adjectives qualifying a noun of time understood: *e.g. itne 'arṣe meṅ.* Similarly, when *itne-men* signifies 'for so much' (*meṅ* being here used for *ko*, as it often is), *itne* is an adjective qualifying a noun of price or value understood.

228. Adverbs of time may also take the postposition تک *tak* ('till,' 'up to') after them, to signify the point up to which something lasts or continues: *e.g.* کل تک *kal-tak*, 'up to yesterday,' اب تک *ab tak*, 'till now,' 'as yet;' کب تک *kab tak*, 'till when?' 'how long?'

229. The same postposition after an adverb of place gives it the signification of *motion towards* the place, and also of *degree*: يہاں تک *yahāṅ tak*, 'up to, or as far as, this place,' 'to this degree,' 'so much so;' کہاں تک *kahāṅ-tak* 'up to where,' 'to what extent?' 'how far?'

230. The locative case of the demonstrative and relative pronouns may be used adverbially: *e.g.* اِس پر *is-par*, 'on this,' 'hereupon;' جِس پر *jis-par*, 'whereupon.'

231. The pronouns, followed by the postpositions لِیے *liye*, and واسطے, *wāsṭe*, may be used as *causal* adverbs: *e.g.* اِس لِیے *is liye*, or اِس واسطے *is wāsṭe*, 'on account of this,' 'therefore;' کِس لِیے *kis liye*, 'on account of what?' 'wherefore?'

232. The conjunctive participle is sometimes used adverbially: *e.g.* جان بُوجھ کر *jān-būjh-kar*, 'wittingly,' 'of set purpose.' This participle in many other cases also may be conveniently rendered by an English adverb.[1]

233. Compound adverbs are of frequent occurrence in Urdū. They generally consist of a repeated adverb or noun (the negative *na* being sometimes inserted between them to add indefiniteness, etc., to the idea), or of two similar nouns or adverbs, or of elliptical phrases.

The following are a few examples:

دھیری دھیری *dhīre dhīre*, 'gently.'

گھڑي گھڑي *gharī gharī*, 'every moment,' 'constantly.'

دِن دِن *din din* (= دِن به دِن *din ba din*), 'from day to day,' 'daily.'

جہاں جہاں *jahāṅ jahāṅ*, 'wherever.'

کبھِي کبھي *kabhī kabhī*, 'now and again,' 'sometimes.'

کبھِي نه کبھي *kabhī na kabhī*, 'sometime or other.'

کہیں نہ کہیں *kahīṅ na kahīṅ*, 'somewhere or other.'

آج کل *āj-kal*, 'now-a-days,' 'in a day or two.'

جہاں کہیں *jahāṅ kahīṅ*, 'wherever.'

جوں توں *joṅ-toṅ*, 'in any way,' 'somehow or other.'

[1] We may here point out that چُپکے *chupke* is not a *conjunctive participle*, as some of the grammarians term it, but the inflected form of the adjective *chupkā*, 'silent.' As there is no such verb as *chupnā*, there can be no conjunctive participle of the form *chupke*.

جھٹ پٹ *jhaṭ-paṭ*, 'instantly.'
رات و دِن *rāt-o-din*, } 'night and day,' 'incessantly.'
دِن رات *din-rāt*, }
ھاں تو *hāṅ to*, 'yes, indeed.'
نہیں تو *nahīṅ to*, 'no, indeed.'

For the adverbs formed from the numerals see § 62 *et seq.*

PERSIAN ADVERBS.

234. Persian adverbs are not to be distinguished from other parts of speech by termination or form; and only a few of them are genuine adverbs. They may be classed according to their origin, as—

a) Nouns in the Accusative Case:

1) Simple Substantives, in the singular or plural: *e.g.*

باز *bāz*, 'back,' 'again.'
پس *pas*, 'after,' 'then,' 'therefore,' 'hence.'
بار *bār*, 'time' (بار بار *bār bār*, 'repeatedly,' 'constantly').
باري *bāre* (*e* being the suffix of *unity*), 'once,' 'at length.'
بارّھا *bārhā* (*hā* being the plural suffix), 'many times,' 'often.'
تنّہا *tanhā*, 'alone.'
قضارا *ḳaẓā-rā* (= ازقضا *az ḳaẓā*), 'by the will of God,' 'providentially.'

2) Compound Substantives; as

قضاکار *ḳaẓā-kār* (= *az kārĕ ḳaẓā*), 'by the work of God,' 'providentially.'
ناگہاں *nāgahāṅ*, or ناگاه *nāgāh*, 'suddenly.'
شب و روز *shab-o-roz*, 'night and day,' 'always.'
هر روز *har roz*, 'daily,'
سراسر *sar-ā-sar*, 'altogether,' 'throughout.'
حاصلِ کلام *ḥāṣilĕ kalām*, 'the gist of the matter,' 'in brief.

b) Substantives with a Preposition.

The preposition most commonly met with in Urdū is *ba*, 'with or by;' but others also occur: *e.g.*

بزور *ba-zor* (Urdū *zor-se*), 'perforce,' 'forcibly.'

بجبر *ba-jabr*, 'violently.'

بخوبي *ba-khūbī*, 'well,' 'excellently.'

درحال *dar ḥāl*, 'just now,' 'immediately.'

c). Adjectives, Simple or Compound.

تيز *tez*, 'quickly,' 'swiftly.'

جلد *jald*, 'quickly,'

دير *der*, 'late.'

دور *dūr*, 'far.'

بلند *baland*, 'high.'

چنانچه *chunāṅchi* (= *chūṅ* + *āṅ* + *chi*), 'so,' 'accordingly.'

d). Genuine Adverbs.

جدا *judā*, 'separately.'

نيز *nīz*, 'even,' 'also.'

هرگز *hargiz*, 'ever' (with neg. 'never').

هم *ham*, 'even.'

هميشه *hamesha*, 'always.'

هنوز *hanoz*, 'hitherto,' 'as yet.'

e). Interrogative: *e.g.* آيا *āyā*, 'whether?' (Lat. *num*?).

Rem. The adverb of *probability* and *doubt* (which is most commonly used in Urdū) is شايد *shāyad*, 'may-be,' 'perhaps.' It is the third pers. sing. of the aorist of the verb *shāyistan*, 'to be suitable.' For the adverbs formed by means of the affix ـانه *āna*, and the numeral adverbs, see the section on Persian Constructions.

ARABIC ADVERBS.

235. The adverbs borrowed from the Arabic may be classed under five heads: 1) Particles; 2) Substantives in the nominative case; 3) Substantives (simple or compound) in the accusative case; 4) nouns in the genitive case governed by a preceding preposition; 5) Phrases.

1) Particles.

Extremely few of these occur in Urdū. Examples are: فقط *faḳaṯ*, 'only,' 'merely' (*lit.* 'and enough'); لا *lā* 'not' (used in composition alone).

2) Substantives in the Nominative.

These are not numerous in Urdū. Examples are: بعْد *baʻd*, and مِن بعْد *mim-baʻd*, 'afterwards;' قبْل *ḳabl*, 'before.'

3) Substantives in the Accusative.

The accusative is notably the adverbial case in Arabic, and hence such adverbs are of common occurrence in Urdū: *e.g.*

اِتِّفاقًا *ittifāḳan*, 'fortuitously,' 'by chance.'	دفْعةً *dafʻatan*, 'all at once.'
خُصُوصًا *khuṣūṣan*, 'particularly,' 'specially.'	مثلًا *masalan*, 'for example.'

Rem. Occasionally the *tanwīn* is changed to *fatḥa*, the accusative taking the *pausal* form of the Arabic: *e.g.* ظاهِرا *ẓāhirā*, 'apparently.'

If the noun is determined by having the article *al* prefixed, or by being put in the construct state, it loses the *tanwīn*, and (in Urdū and Persian) in the first case, the final vowel also: *e.g.*

البتّه *al-batta* (for البتّةَ *albattata*), 'decidedly.'
الحال *al-ḥāl*, 'at the present time,' 'just now.'
الغرض *al-garaẓ*, 'the gist or purport (of it),' 'in short.'
القِصّه *al-ḳiṣṣa*, 'the story,' 'in short.'
آخِرَ الْامْر *ākhira'l amr*, 'at last,' 'finally.'
حاصِلَ الْكلام *ḥāṣila'l kalām* (or, more commonly, after the Persian, حاصِلِ كلام *ḥāṣilĕ kalām*), 'the gist of the matter,' 'to sum up,' 'in brief.'

Rem. In some cases, even where the noun is not defined, the *tanwīn* is dropped in Urdū: *e.g.* آخِر *ā<u>kh</u>ir*, 'at last,' for آخِراً.

4) Noun Governed by a Preposition.

عنْقريب *'ankarīb*, 'nearly,' 'almost.'

فِي ٱلجُمْلہ *fi'l jumla*, 'on the whole,' 'altogether.'

فِي ٱلحال *fi'l ḥāl*, 'at present,' 'just now.'

فِي ٱلفَور *fi'l faur*, 'instantly.'

بِالفِعل *bi'l fe'l*, 'for the present,' 'at present,' 'just now.'

بِالكُل *bi'l kull*, 'in the totality,' 'totally,' 'altogether.'

5) Phrases:

Such as من و عن *min wa 'an*, 'circumstantially.'

فبِها *fabihā* (the conj. *fa* + prep. *bi* + pron. *hā*), 'well and good.'

يعْنے *ya'ne* (properly *ya'nī*; third pers. sing. masc. Imperf. of the verb *'and*), 'that is to say,' 'to wit,' 'namely' (*lit.* 'it signifies').

كمايَنْبغِي *ka-mā-yambagī* (prep. *ka* + pron. *mā* + vero *yambagī*), 'as is proper,' 'fittingly' (*lit.* 'like that which is proper').

II. PREPOSITIONS AND POSTPOSITIONS.

236. The Urdū prepositions are, for the most part, originally adverbs (that is to say, Hindī nouns in the locative or ablative case, determined by a following genitive), or Persian and Arabic nouns used adverbially in the construct accusative: hence the use of the form کے *ke* of the genitive affix when the preposition (or governing noun) is masculine.

237. The genuine *prepositions* are nearly all Persian or Arabic, and invariably precede the noun they govern.

The other prepositions as commonly follow as precede the governed noun.

238. The following are real *postpositions*, which invariably *follow* the noun they govern, and for the most part require that noun to be in the Formative:

بِنا *binā*, 'without' (Sanskrit *vinā*).

پر *par*, 'on,' 'upon' (S. *upari*).

تک *tak*, 'till,' 'up to,' 'as far as,' 'inclusive' (S. *daghna* ?).

تئِیں *ta'īn*, 'up to,' 'to' (S. *sthāne* :—*ta'īn* governs the genitive).

سُدّھاں *suddhān*, 'along with' (S. *sārddham*).

سمیت *samet*, 'together with,' 'having' (S. *sameta*).

سے *se*, 'from,' 'with,' 'by' (S. *sachā*, or perhaps the Prāk. gen. affix *he*).

کر *kar*, 'by means of,' 'on account of,' 'by the name of,' (S. *kṛite*).

کو *ko*, 'to,' 'for the sake of,' 'for,' etc. (S. *kṛite*).

کے *ke* (= کو *ko*), 'to' (S. *kṛite* ?).

لِیئے *lī'e*, 'for the sake of,' 'for' (from the S. root *rā*, 'to give:' it generally governs the genitive).

میں *meṅ*, 'in' (S. *madhye*).

Rem. The postposition بِنا *binā*, as also its contraction بِن *bin*, may either precede or follow the noun in the Formative: *e.g.* بِن دانے پانِي *bin dāne pānī*, 'without food.' The word کر *kar*, as a postposition (in which character it is not noticed by the grammarians), is distinct from the affix کر *kar* of the past conjunctive participle; examples of its use are: گھر ھمارا خانۂ الله کر مشہُور تھا *ghar hamārā khāna'ĕ allāh-kar mashhūr thā*, 'my (*lit.* our) house was famous on account of the house of God;' جِس نے اپنے تئِیں سَوداگر بچہ کر مشہُور کِیا تھا *jis-ne apne ta'īn saudāgar-bacha-kar mashhūr kiyā thā*, 'who had made himself known by (the title of) a merchant's son;' مُجھے کلُّو کر پُکارا کرتے هَیں

mujhe kallū-kar pukārā-karte hain, 'they are in the habit of calling me by (the name of) Kallū.' The postposition کے *ke* is generally supposed to be, in every instance, merely the inflected form of the genitive affix کا *kā* with one of the postpositions پاس *pās*, تئیں *ta'īn*, or هاں *hān*, understood. It appears however to be more correct to regard it, with the native grammarians, as a distinct postposition, when it is employed in such constructions as اُسکے سخت چوٹ لگي هَي *us-ke sakht choṭ lagī hai*, 'he has received a severe injury,' wherein its signification is precisely that of کو, with which it is no doubt connected (*cf.* § 318 *Rem.*).

239. The following postpositions[1] (and perhaps others besides), when they follow a noun, may optionally govern it in the Formative or the Genitive:

باهِر *bāhir*, 'without,' 'outside' (S. *vahis*).

بغَير *ba-gair*, 'without' (governs the Formative of pronouns and verbal nouns).

پار *pār*, 'on the other side of,' 'across.'

پاس *pās*, 'near,' 'at the side of.'

پِيچھے *pīchhe*, 'behind' (S. *paśchāt*).

تلے *tale*, 'under,' 'underneath' (S. *tale*).

مُوافِق *muwāfiḳ*, 'suitable,' 'according' (to).

E.g. دروازي باهِر *darwāze bāhir* (or دروازہ کے باهِر *darwāze ke bāhir*), 'outside the door;' اُس بغَير *us bagair*, 'without him;' ندي پار *nadī pār*, 'across the river;' بادشاہ پاس *bādshāh pās*, 'near or with the king;' مُجھ پاس *mujh pās*, 'near or

[1] In such constructions as اِس لِيئے *is lī'e*, اِس واسطے *is wāste*, اِس سبب *is sabab*, etc., signifying *for this reason* or *cause*, the pronoun is used as an *adjective* qualifying the postposition in its character of a noun, and hence must necessarily occur in the Formative; but if any other noun, expressed or understood, is qualified by the pronominal adjective, or if the pronoun be *personal*, it must be put in the genitive; as اُس کے لِيئے *us-ke lī'e*, 'for him,' اُس کے سبب *us-ke sabab*, 'on account of him.'

with me;' پيٹھ پيچھے *pīṭh pīchhe*, 'behind (one's) back;' پاؤں تلے *pā'oṅ tale*, 'under foot;' حاجت مُوافِق *ḥājat muwāfiḳ*, 'suitable to (one's) need.'

But if they *precede* the noun, they invariably govern the Genitive: *e.g.* ميري پاس *mere pās*; باهِر دروازي كے *bāhir darwāze ke*; بغير اُسكے *ba-gair uske*; تلے پاؤں كے *tale pā'oṅ ke*; مُوافِق حاجت كے *muwāfiḳ ḥājat ke*.

Rem. When, however, بغَير *ba-gair* governs a verbal noun or an abstract substantive with the force of a verbal noun, this is put in the Formative, even if the postposition precedes: as بغير تحقيق كيے *ba-gair taḥḳīḳ-kiye*, 'without having ascertained,' بغير پروانگي *ba-gair parwānagī*, 'without permission.'

240. The following are the principal *prepositions*, or *postpositions*, which, being *masculine* nouns in the Locative, Ablative, or Accusative case,[1] require the affix كے to be used with the Genitive they govern:

1) Hindī.

آگے *āge*, 'before,' 'in front' (Sanskrit *agre*).

اُوپر *ūpar*, 'on,' 'upon' (S. *upari*).

بھروسے *bharose*, 'in reliance on,' 'trusting to' (S. *bhadra* + *āśā*).

بھل *bhal*, or بل *bal*, 'with—downwards or foremost' (S. *bhara*).

بيچ *bīch*, 'in the midst of,' 'among.'

پري *pare*, 'beyond' (S. *pāra*).

ساتھ *sāth*, 'with,' 'along with' (S. *sārdham*).

سامھنے *sāmhne*, 'in front of,' (S. *sam* + *mukha*).

[1] It will be seen from the examples given that many Persian and Arabic nouns are treated like Hindī nouns, and put in the Locative or Ablative case to form postpositions: *e.g.* حوالے *ḥawāle*, ذريعے *ẕariye*, ذِمّے *ẕimme*, etc. In some instances moreover the Ablative or Locative postposition is expressed.

سِري *sire*, 'at the extremity of,' (S. *śiras*).

سنّگ *sang*, 'along with' (S. *sanga*).

کنے *kane*, 'to,' 'near to' (S. *karṇa*, 'edge').

ماري *māre*, 'on account of,' 'through' (*lit.* 'stricken with,' from *mārnā*).

نِيچے *nīche*, 'under,' 'underneath,' 'below' (S. *nīche*).

هاتھ *hāth*, 'by the hand of,' 'by' (S. *hasta*).

هاں *hāṅ*,[1] 'at or to a place or house' (S. *sthāne*).

2) Persian.

اندر *andar*, 'inside of,' 'within' (= S. *antara*).

برابر *barābar*, 'on a level with,' 'equal to' (*bar* + *ā* + *bar*, 'breast to breast').

بنابر *banābar* or *bināhar*, 'on account of' (Ar. *bina*, 'building' + prep. *bar*, 'upon').

جُز *juz*, 'except,' 'with the exception of,' (contraction of *judā* + *az*).

[1] We must here protest against the use of يہاں *yahāṅ* in place of هاں *hāṅ* by European grammarians. However "idiomatic" it may appear to them, and in spite of the countenance given to it by the usage of the *Bāg-o-bahār*, and other works written about the same time, any one who has lived in India, and attentively observed the speech of the natives, can assure them that *hāṅ*, and not *yahāṅ*, is always used in the sense of *place* absolutely: *e.g.* *fulāne ṣāḥib-ke hāṅ jānā*, 'go to such-and-such a gentleman's place or house.' The following extracts on the use of *hāṅ* are from the *Urdū Grammar* of Maulavī Imām Bakhsh of the Dehlī College: مِثال ظرفِ مکان کے - هاں مُطلق مکان 'Examples of adverbs of place: *hāṅ* of place absolutely;' هاں تنّہا اهْلِ شاهجہان آباد کي زبان میں بہت مُستعمل هَي - جَیسے هم تمهاري هاں گئے تهے - یا وُہ همارے هاں آئے تهے '*Hāṅ* alone is commonly used in the language of the people of Dehlī: *e.g.* *ham tumhāre hāṅ ga'e the*, or *wŏh hamāre hāṅ ā'e the.*

The following passage is extracted from a copy of the 'Alīgaṛh (Allyguṛh) Institute Gazette: *ham musalmānoṅ aur hindū'oṅ donoṅ kī us ātish-bāzī kī nisbat likhte haiṅ jo unke hāṅ shādī meṅ hotī hai.*

We may add that in the matter of this use of *hāṅ*, the people of Lakhnau are at one with their brethren of Dehlī, and hence its uniform usage in all parts of Hindūstān proper.

رُوبرُو *rū-ba-rū*, 'face to face with,' 'facing' (*rū*, 'face' + prep. *ba* + *rū*).

سِپُرد *sipurd*, 'in charge or keeping.'

گِرد *gird*, } 'near,' 'about.'

چوگِرد *chau-gird*, } 'round about.'

نزدیک *nazdīk*, 'near,' 'close to' (frequently corrupted into *nagīch*).

The more common form in which the Persian prepositions occur is that of an inseparable (and genuine) preposition prefixed to a Persian or Arabic noun; the compound in such cases being equivalent to the Hindī ablative or locative case: *e.g.*

از رُوي *az-rū'ĕ*, 'by reason of,' = *rū se* (*lit.* from the face or appearance').

باوُجود *bā-wujūd*, 'notwithstanding' (*lit.* 'along with the existence').

باوصف *bā-waṣf*, 'notwithstanding' (*lit.* 'with the attribute').

بجاي *ba-jā'ĕ*, 'in place of,' 'instead of.'

بجُز *ba-juz*, 'with the exception.'

براي *ba-rā'ĕ*, 'for the sake of,' 'on account of.'

بسبب *ba-sabab*, 'by reason of,' 'on account of.'

بطور *ba-ṭaur*, 'by way of.'

بمُوجِب *ba-mūjib*, 'in accordance with,' 'according to.'

برخِلاف *bar-khilāf*, 'in opposition to,' 'contrary to.'

برعکس *bar-'aks*, 'on the contrary of,' 'in spite of.'

درپَي *dar-pai*, 'in quest of,' 'in pursuit of.'

درپیس *dar-pesh*, 'in front of.'

درمِیَان *dar-miyān*, 'in the midst of,' 'among.'

3) Arabic.

باعِث *bā'iṣ*, 'because of.'

بدلے *badle*, 'in exchange for.'

بعْد *b'ad*, 'after.'

حوالے *ḥawāle*, 'in the charge or care of.'

خِلاف *khilāf*, 'in opposition to.'

ذرِيے *zariye*, 'by means of,' 'through the medium of.'

ذِمّے *zimme*, 'under the charge or responsibility of.'

سبب *sabab*, 'because of,' 'by reason of.'

سِوَا[1] *siwā*, } 'over and above,' 'besides.'
سِواي *siwā'ě*, }

علاوہ *'alāwa*, 'in addition to,' 'besides.'

عِوَض *'iwaẓ*, 'instead of,' 'for.'

قبْل *ḳabl*, 'before.'

قرِيب *ḳarīb*, 'near.'

لائِق *lā'iḳ*, 'suitable for,' 'worthy of.'

مُتعلِق *muta'alliḳ*, 'depending on,' 'connected with.'

مُشابِہ *mushābih*, 'like,' 'resembling.'

مُوجِب *mūjib*, 'because of,' 'by reason of.'

مُطابِق *muṭābiḳ*, 'in conformity to.'

مُوَافِق *muwāfiḳ*, 'agreeable or suitable to' (also governs the Formative).

241. A few of them are compounds, consisting of an inseparable preposition prefixed to a noun in the genitive, or of a preposition following a pronoun: *e.g.*

بدُون *bidūn*, 'without' (prep. *bi* + *dūn*).

بغَير *bigair* (or with pers. prep. *ba-gair*), 'without.'

مابَين *mā-bain*, 'what is between' (from *mā* + prep. *bain*).

ماتحْت *mā-taḥt*, 'that which is under' (*mā* + prep. *taḥt*).

[1] *Siwā* is regarded by native grammarians as an *exceptive* particle, united as *muẓāf*, or determined noun, to another noun. The same is the case with the words ورا *warā* and ماورا *mā-warā*, 'beyond,' 'except.'

242. The following are a few examples of prepositions or postpositions which are originally *feminine* nouns, and hence require the affix کي *ki* with the genitive they govern:

1) *Hindī:* اور *or*, 'towards,' 'in the direction of.'
جگہ *jagah*, 'in place of,' 'in the room of.'

2) *Persian:* بابت *bābat*, 'concerning,' 'for,' 'on account of.'
زباني *zabānī*, 'from the mouth of.'
بجہت *ba-jihat*, 'on account of,' 'by reason of.'
بدولت *ba-daulat*, 'by means of.'

3) *Arabic:* جانِب *jānib*, 'in the direction of,' 'towards.'
جہت *jihat*, 'on account of.'
خاطِر *khāṭir*, 'for the sake of.'
سِمْت *simt*, } 'in the direction of,' 'towards.'
طرف *ṭaraf*, }
طرح *ṭarah*, 'in the manner of.'
معرِفت *ma'rifat*, 'by means of.'
نِسْبت *nisbat*, 'in reference to,' 'in respect of.'

243. The feminine prepositions, when they *precede* the governed noun, require کے *ke* for the genitive affix of that noun: *e.g.* طرف جہاز کے *ṭaraf jahāz-ke*, 'in the direction of the ship' (but جہاز كي طرف *jahāz kī ṭaraf*, when the word *ṭaraf* follows the governed noun): similarly مانِند لڑکے کے *mānind laṛke ke*, 'like a child,' بمدد اُسکے *ba-madad uske*, 'with his help,' مِثْل شیر کے *misl sher-ke*, 'after the likeness of a tiger,' although the words *mānind*, *madad*, and *misl* are feminine. This construction will be more fully noticed in the Syntax.

GENUINE PREPOSITIONS.

244. These are borrowed from the Persian and Arabic.

a) Persian.

از *az*, 'from,' 'by,' 'with.'

بَ or بہ *ba*, 'with,' 'by,' 'in,' etc. (the former being the *inseparable* form).

با *bā*, 'with,' 'along with.

بے *be*, 'without.'

بر *bar*, 'on,' 'upon' (= Sanskrit *upari*).

تا *tā*, 'till,' 'up to,' 'as far as.'

در *dar*, 'in' (contracted from *andar*).

Rem. To these some add پیش *pesh*, 'before,' زبر *zabar*, 'over,' and زیر *zer*, 'below;' but the first is an adverb, and generally takes the prep. *az* after it; as *pesh az īn*, 'prior to this,' 'before this;' and the two last are compounds: *e.g.* *zabar* = *az* or *zi* + *bar*; *zer* = *zi* + *ïr*.

b) Arabic.

245. The Arabic prepositions are of two kinds; *separable* and *inseparable*.

1) Inseparable.

بِ *bi*, 'in,' 'at,' 'by,' 'with,' etc. (*bilā* = *bi* + neg. *lā*, 'not,' = 'without').

لِ *li*, 'to,' 'for,' 'on account of,' (before pronom. suffixes it becomes *la*).

كَ *ka*, 'as,' 'like.'

2) Separable.

إلى *ilā*, 'to.'

حتّى *hattā*, 'till,' 'up to,' 'as far as.'

على *'alā*, 'over,' 'above,' 'upon.'

عن *'an*, 'from,' 'after,' 'for.'

عِنْد *'ind*, 'beside,' 'near,' 'by.'

في *fī*, 'in,' 'into,' 'among,' 'about.'

مع *ma'* or معه *ma'a*, 'with,' 'along with.'

من *min*, 'out of,' 'from.'

246. These prepositions generally occur in Arabic and Persian phrases, but they are occasionally prefixed to Hindī nouns, which are then put in the Formative or the Genitive: *e.g.* پیشاور سے تا کلکتے *peshāwar-se tā kalkatte*, 'from Peshāwar to Kalkattā (Calcutta);' مع ہاتھی کے *ma' hāthī ke*, 'together with the elephant.'

III. CONJUNCTIONS.

247. Conjunctions may be divided into the following classes:

1) Connective.

اَور *aur*, 'and.'	کیا—کیا *kyā—kyā*, 'whether—or.'
بھی *bhī*, 'also.'	نہ—نہ *na—na*, 'neither—nor.'
چاہو *chāho*, 'or;' *chāho—chāho*, 'either—or.'	نِیز *nīz*, 'also.'
خواہ *khwāh*, 'or;' *khwāh—khwāh*, 'either—or.'	و *wa* or *o*, 'and.'
کِہ *ki*, 'that;' 'or.'	یا *yā*, 'or;' *yā—yā*, 'either—or.'

2) Adversative.

امّا *ammā*, 'but,' 'as for.'	تاہم *tā-ham*, 'so also,' 'yet,' 'still,' 'notwithstanding.'
بلکِہ *bal-ki*, 'but rather,' 'on the contrary.'	توبھی *to bhī*, 'even then,' 'still.'
پر *par*, 'but.'	لیکِن *lekin*, 'but,' 'yet.'

3) Exceptive.

مگر *magar*, 'unless,' 'except,' 'save' (= *ma*, 'not' + *gar*, 'if').

اِلّا *illā*, 'except,' 'save' (= *in*, 'if' + *lā*, 'not').

4) Conditional.

اگر *agar*, } 'if.'	نہیں تو *nahīn to*, 'if not,' 'otherwise.'
جو *jo*, } 'if.'	وگرنہ *wa-gar-na*, 'and if not,' 'otherwise.'

5) Concessive.

اگرچہ *agar-chi*, 'although.'	تو *to*, 'then.'
پس *pas*, 'then.'	گوکہ *go-ki*, 'although.'

6) Causal.

ازبسکہ *az-bas-ki*, 'inasmuch as.'	چونکہ *chūṅ-ki*, 'whereas,' 'since.'
بدانکہ *ba-d-āṅ-ki*, 'forasmuch as.'	کیونکہ *kyūṅ-ki*, 'because.'

7) Conclusive.

بنابراں *banā-bar-āṅ*, 'on that account,' 'therefore.'	پھر *phir*, 'then,' 'therefore.'
پس *pas*, 'hence.'	لہٰذا *li-hāẕā*, 'for this reason,' 'therefore.'

8) Final.

تا *tā*, and تاکہ *tā-ki*, 'to the end that,' 'in order that.'

مبادا *ma-bād-ā*, 'lest,' *lit.* 'may it not be.'

IV. INTERJECTIONS.

248. Interjections are mostly sounds or cries expressive of emotion. They may be divided into the following classes:

1) Assent.

E.g. هاں *hāṅ*, or هوں *hūṅ*, 'yes!' اچھا *achchhā*, 'very well!' جي *jī*, 'yes!' (respectful).

2) Approval;

as شاباش *shābāsh* (= شاد باش *shād bāsh*, 'be happy!'), 'bravo!' واہ واہ *wāh wāh*, 'well done!' 'bravo!'

3) Sorrow or Pain;

as اري *are*, 'Oh!' ري *re*, 'Oh!' (always used as an affix); آہ *āh*, 'ah!' ہائے *hā'e*, 'alas!' وائے *wā'e* and واویلا *wā-wailā*, 'woe!' 'alas!' افسوس *afsos*, 'pity!' 'alas!' حَيف *ḥaif*, 'ah!' 'alas!' (chiefly used in poetry).

4) Surprise;

as آها *āhā*, or اوهو *ohō*, 'Ha!' 'Ho!' 'Strange!' واه وا *wāh wā*, 'How fine!' 'strange!' كيا خُوب *kyā khūb*, 'How excellent!' سُبحان الله *subḥān allāh*, 'Good God!'

5) Aversion or Contempt;

as چهي *chhī*, 'fie!' دُر *dur*, 'away!' 'avaunt!' اري *are*, 'O!' ابے *abe*, 'O!' (you fellow).

6) Longing;

as كاشكِ *kāsh-ki*, or كاشكے *kāsh-ke*, 'would that' (*utinam*!).

7) Desire for the Presence or Attention of a Person;

as أي *ai*, 'O!' او *o*, 'O!' هوت *hot*, 'Ho!' (vulgar,—always *follows* the object of address) اري *are*, 'O!' 'Ho!' لے *le*, or لو *lo*, 'there!' 'enough!' 'peace!'

CHAPTER V.

DERIVATION OF WORDS.

249. We purpose, in this chapter, to treat of such Hindī themes as have been derived by modifying forms obtained from the Sanskrit through the Prākrit, as also such as are derived by rules peculiar to the Hindī.[1] With unmodified Sanskrit forms, such as *pālak*, *ānandit*, *balwān*, *gopāl*, etc., which occur in modern Hindī, we have little or no concern. For Persian and Arabic themes we must refer the reader to the section on Persian and Arabic constructions.

250. Derivative words may be classed under the two heads of *primary* and *secondary* formations, according as they are derived from *verbal roots*, or from *nouns*.

I. ABSTRACT NOUNS.

a) Primary Formations.

251. The simple root of a verb is, in many cases, used as an abstract substantive: *e.g.*

مار *mār*, 'beating;' Inf. مارنا *mārnā*, 'to beat.'
لوٹ *lūṭ*, 'plunder;' ,, لوٹنا *lūṭnā*, 'to plunder.'
چمک *chamak*, 'glitter,' 'flash;' ,, چمکنا *chamaknā*, 'to shine,' etc.

[1] Nothing like an attempt to give *all* the themes occurring in Hindī is here made. This would be an almost impossible undertaking, so great is the change which the wear and tear of centuries, so to speak, has effected in most Hindī words. The affixes noticed are mostly those of frequent occurrence, respecting which there can be no doubt, whatever difference of opinion may exist as to the sources from which they are derived. We would observe also that, as in the case of the pronominal series *ab*, *kab*, *jab*, etc., it is highly probable that one derived affix has, in each case, served as a model for others, and that these have been used even with words of non-Aryan origin.

In a few words the root vowel is lengthened: *e.g.*

أتار *utār*, 'descent;' Inf. أترنا *utarnā*, 'to descend.'
چال *chāl*, 'motion,' 'gait,' etc.; „ چلنا *chalnā*, 'to move or go.'
میل *mel*, 'mingling,' 'intimacy;' „ مِلنا *milnā*, 'to mingle,' etc.

252. Other abstract nouns are formed from the root, with or without lengthening the root vowel, by means of the following affixes:

1) ـَا *ā* (=S. affix *a*); as—

پھیرا *pherā*, 'turning,' etc.; Inf. پھیرنا *phernā*, 'to turn.'
جھگڑا *jhagṛā*, 'quarrel;' „ جھگڑنا *jhagaṛnā*, 'to quarrel.'
چھاپا *chhāpā*, 'stamp,' 'print;' „ چھاپنا *chhāpnā*, 'to print,' etc.
میلا *melā*, 'a gathering,' 'a fair;' „ مِلنا *milnā*, 'to meet together.'

Rem. In some instances the *masc.* termination *ā* is changed to the *fem.* *ī*, to express some slight difference of signification; as پھیری *pherī*, 'going about,' 'hawking.'

2) نا *nā*, ـَن *an*, ـَان *ān* (=S. affix *ana*).

The first of these is found in infinitives. Examples of the second are:

چلن *chalan*, 'gait,' 'conduct;' Inf. چلنا *chalnā*.
مرن *maran*, 'dying;' „ مرنا *marnā*.
مِلن *milan*, 'mixing with,' 'meeting;' „ مِلنا *milnā*.

In the third the vowel of the affix *an* is lengthened: *e.g.*

أٹھان *uṭhān*, 'act of appearing;' Inf. أٹھنا *uṭhnā*, 'to rise.'
أڑان *uṛān*, 'act of flying,' 'flight;' „ أڑنا *uṛnā*, 'to fly.'
لگان *lagān*, 'contact,' 'fastening,' etc.; „ لگنا *lagnā*, 'to be in contact.'

Here may also be noticed the affix ـِي *ī*, which is added to the roots of causal verbs to signify 'cost of,' 'expense for,' etc.; for the sister dialects afford proof of this affix being a mere contraction of نِي *nī*, the *fem.* form of the affix نا *nā*: *e.g.*

پِسْوائِي *piswā'ī*, 'price paid for grinding' (پِيسْنا *pīsnā*).
چرائِي *charā'ī*, 'price paid for grazing' (چرانا *charānā*).
دھُلائِي *dhulā'ī*, 'price paid for washing' (دھُلانا *dhulānā*).

3) ت *t*; ــَت *at*; تِي *tī*; (= S. affix *ti*); as—

بچت *bachat*, 'residue;'	Inf. بچْنا *bachnā*, 'to be left.'
بڑھْتِي *baṛhtī*, 'increase;'	,, بڑھْنا *baṛhnā*, 'to increase.'
بھرْتِي *bhartī*, 'filling,' 'completion,' etc.;	,, بھرْنا *bharnā*, 'to fill.'
رنْگت *rangat*, 'colouring,' 'colour;'	,, رنْگنا *rangnā*, 'to colour.'

Rem. The affix *tī*, as will appear further on, is also employed in secondary formations.

4) ــَاٹ *āṭ*, ــَاهٹ *āhaṭ*, ــَاوٹ *āwaṭ*, اؤ *ā'o*.

The original of all these forms is the Sanskrit affix *ātu* (which Bopp traces to the infinitive affix *tu*): the first, though common in the Urdū and Hindī of Southern India, is rarely used in the North, where the second and third (in which *h* and *w* are euphonic) are very common. Examples are:

چمْکاهٹ *chamkāhaṭ*, 'glitter,' 'brilliancy;' Inf. چمکْنا *chamaknā*, 'to shine.'

بِلْبِلاهٹ *bilbilāhaṭ*, 'wailing,' 'moaning;' ,, بِلْبِلانا *bilbilānā*, 'to moan,' etc. (the *ā* of the affix coalesces with final *ā* of the root).

گھبْراهٹ *ghabrāhaṭ*, 'confusion,' 'perturbation;' ,, گھبْرانا *ghabrānā*, 'to be alarmed.'

بناوٹ *banāwaṭ*, 'invention,' 'fabrication;' ,, بنانا *banānā*, 'to make.'

رُکاوٹ *rukāwaṭ*, 'hindrance,' 'obstacle;' ,, روکْنا *roknā*, 'to hinder.'

سجاوٹ *sajāwaṭ*, 'preparation,' 'arrangement;' ,, سجانا *sajānā*, 'to arrange.'

In the case of the affix *ā'o*,[1] the *t* of the affix *atu* has been elided, and the final vowel lengthened. It is an affix of very frequent occurrence. Examples are:

بچاو *bachā'o*, 'protection,' 'defence;' Inf. بچنا *bachnā*, 'to escape.'
چڑھاو *charhā'o*, 'ascent;' ,, چڑھنا *charhnā*, 'to ascend.'
چھڑکاو *chhiṛkā'o*, 'sprinkling;' ,, چھڑکنا *chhiraknā*, 'to sprinkle.'
چھوڑاو *chhoṛā'o*, 'release;' ,, چھوڑنا *chhornā*, 'to let go.'

Rem. a. Many masculines in *ā'o* have corresponding feminines in *ā'ī*, with the same signification; as چڑھائي *charhā'ī*, 'ascent.'

Rem. b. The affix *āhaṭ* (differently derived however) is also employed in secondary formations, as will be shown further on.

Rem. c. The affix *ā'o* often takes the form *āwā* in rustic speech: *e.g.* چھوڑاوا *chhoṛāwā*, 'release.'

Rem. d. Native grammarians add *āp* or *p* to the affixes forming abstract nouns from verbal roots; but we cannot find this termination in any word except *milāp* (the only example adduced by them), and this is in all probability a mere modification of the Sanskrit *melāpaka*.

b) SECONDARY FORMATIONS.

253. Abstract nouns are derived from substantives and adjectives by means of the following affixes:

1) ـي *ī*, ـائي *ā'ī*, (= S. affix *yam*, neuter).

This forms a large class of abstract nouns: *e.g.*

برائي *burā'ī*, 'badness,' 'wickedness,' from برا *burā*, 'bad.'
چوري *chorī*, 'theft,' from چور *chor*, 'a thief.'
ٹھگي *ṭhagī*, 'the practice of a *ṭhag*' (ٹھگ);' 'robbery,' etc.
پنڈتائي *panḍitā'ī*, 'the learning of a *panḍit*,' 'learning.'
گولائي *golā'ī*, 'roundness,' from گول *gol*, 'round.'

[1] This affix is incorrectly written *āw* by some of the grammarians. It is usual in Hindī, no doubt, to represent final *o*, after a vowel, by व, but this is a mere *compendium scripturæ*; the letter is pronounced *o* all the same.

2) تي *tī* (= S. affix *ti*).

This affix, as we have shown, occurs in primary formations; an example of a secondary formation is—

كمتي *kamtī*, 'deficiency,' from كم *kam*, 'less.'

Rem. It is possible however that the origin of this affix is the Sanskrit affix *tā*.

3) ان *ān* (= S. affix *iman*).

This affix is derived by eliding the initial *i* and the *m* of the Sanskrit affix *iman*. It forms abstract nouns from adjectives denoting an inherent quality, but it rarely occurs in Urdū; one example is—

اونچان *ūṅchān*, 'height,' from اونچا *ūṅchā*, 'high.'

Rem. In a few Hindī words the affix *iman* takes the form *mā*: *e.g.* *garimā*, 'weight,' 'importance.'

4) پا *pā*, پن *pan*, پنا *panā*; اٹ *āṭ*, اہٹ *āhaṭ*.

The origin of all these affixes is the Sanskrit affix *tva*; *e.g.* 1) *tva* = *vva* = *ppa* = *pā*: 2) *tva* = Prākrit *tvaṇa* = *vvaṇa* = *ppana* = *pan* and *panā*: 3) *tva* = *tta* = *ṭṭa* = *āṭ*, whence *āhaṭ*, by insertion of *h* for euphony. They are all of frequent occurrence. A long vowel in the base may be shortened, and a final vowel dropped, before the affixes *pā*, *pan*, *panā* are added: *e.g.*

بڑھاپا *buṛhā-pā*, } 'old age,' from بوڑھا *būṛhā*, 'old,' 'an old man.'
بوڑھاپن *būṛhā-pan*, }

چھوٹاپن *chhoṭā-pan*, } 'littleness,' 'infancy,' 'childhood,' from چھوٹا *chhoṭā*, 'little.'
چھٹاپا *chhuṭā-pā*, }
چھٹپنا *chhuṭ-panā*, }

لڑکپن *laṛak-pan*, } 'childishness,' 'childhood,' from لڑکا *laṛkā*, 'a child.'
لڑکاپن *laṛkā-pan*, }

چکناہٹ *chiknāhaṭ*, 'greasiness,' 'smootnness,' from چکنا *chiknā*, 'greasy,' etc.

کڑواہٹ *kaṛwāhaṭ*, 'bitterness,' from کڑوا *kaṛu'ā* or *kaṛwā*, 'bitter.'

Rem. The word لڑکپن is generally pronounced *laṛkpan* by the natives of India; but the dictionaries all give the pronunciation as *laṛakpan.*

5) ـَک *ak* (= S. affix *ika*).

The original affix *ika* is employed in Sanskrit to form adjectives; but in Hindī and Urdū it is occasionally used to form abstract substantives: *e.g.*

ٹھنڈک *ṭhanḍak*, ٹھنڈھک *ṭhanḍhak*, } 'coolness,' *lit.* 'that which makes coolness' (ٹھنڈھ).

6) ـَاس *ās.*

The origin of this affix is probably the Sanskrit noun *āśā*, 'desire.' It is added to a few nouns to form abstract substantives, a long vowel in the base being shortened before the affix is added, and final *ā* coalescing with the *ā* of the affix: *e.g.*

مِٹھاس *miṭhās*, 'sweetness,' from مِیٹھا *mīṭhā*, 'sweet' (S. *mishṭāśā*).
کھٹاس *khaṭās* (or *khaṭṭās*), 'acidity,' from کھٹّا *khaṭṭā*, 'sour.'

II. NOUNS OF AGENCY, ATTRIBUTIVES, POSSESSIVES, APPELLATIVES.

a) PRIMARY FORMATIONS.

1) ـَا *ā*, وَا *wā*, or ہا *hā*; ـَیّا *aiyā*, or وَیّا *waiyā*.

254. The original of these affixes is the Sanskrit affix *aka*; whence by elision of *ka*, and compensatory lengthening of the preceding vowel, the affix *ā* is derived; thence *wā* and *hā* by prefixing *w* and *h* for euphony. Again, by elision of *k*, the form *ayā* is obtained, and this is changed, through the influence of *y*, into *aiyā*, in which *ai* is pronounced more like *aï* than as the diphthong *ai*: from *aiyā*, by prefixing a euphonic *w*, the affix *waiyā* is obtained. They are all added to verbal roots to form *nouns of agency*, and *attributives*: *e.g.*

بهونجا *bhūnjā*, 'a parcher' (of grain), as in بهڑبهونجا *bhaṛ-bhūnjā*, from an obsolete بهنجنا *bhunjnā*, 'to parch.'

گهيرا *gherā*, 'a fence' (S. *grāhaka*, 'inclosing,' etc.), from گهيرنا *ghernā*, 'to surround.'

ديوا *dewā*, 'giving,' 'a giver' (S. *dāyaka*), from دينا *denā*, 'to give.'

ليوا *lewā*, 'taking,' 'a taker,' from لينا *lenā*, 'to take.'

چرواها *charwā-hā*, 'a grazier,' from چروانا *charwānā*, 'to pasture.'

بنٹويا *banṭwaiyā*, 'a sharer or divider,' from بنٹوانا *banṭwānā*, 'to portion out.'

گويا *gawaiyā*, 'a singer,' from گانا *gānā*, 'to sing.'

In a few words the Sanskrit affix is preserved intact: *e.g.* گايک *gāyak*, 'a singer;' گاهک *gāhak* (S. *grāhaka*), 'a taker or seizer.'

2) ـُو *ū*, ـُوا *ū'ā*.

These affixes correspond to the Sanskrit affix *uka*, the *k* of which is elided, and the preceding vowel lengthened by way of compensation. They are used to form *nouns of agency* and *attributives*: *e.g.*

بگاڑو *bigāṛū*, 'a spoiler,' 'a ruiner,' from بگاڑنا *bigāṛnā*, 'to spoil.'

بهلاؤ *bhulā'ū*, 'misleader,' 'misleading,' from بهلانا *bhulānā*, 'to mislead.'

پهسلاؤ *phuslā'ū*, 'a coaxer,' from پهسلانا *phuslānā*, 'to coax.'

کماؤ *kamā'ū*, 'earning much,' 'laborious,' from کمانا *kamānā*, 'to earn.'

ريتوا *retū'ā*, 'a filer,' 'a polisher,' from ريتنا *retnā*, 'to file.'

3) ـاک *āk* or ـاکا *ākā*, ـاؤ *ā'ū*.

The original of these affixes is the Sanskrit affix *āku*, the *k* of which is elided in the last, and the *u* lengthened. They form *nouns of agency* and *attributives*: *e.g.*

پيراک *pairāk*, 'a swimmer,' from پيرنا *pairnā*, 'to swim.'

لڑاک *laṛāk*, }
لڑاکا *laṛākā*, } 'quarrelsome,' 'a brawler,' from لڑنا *laṛnā*, 'to fight.'

14

بِکاؤ *bikā'ū*, 'for sale,' from بِکْنا *biknā*, 'to be sold.'
کساؤ *kasā'ū*, 'astringent,' from کسْنا *kasnā*, 'to bind or tighten.'

4) ـــارِي *ārī*, or ـــاڑِي *āṛī*.

These affixes probably spring from the Sanskrit affix *āru*. They form verbal adjectives (few in number) denoting habitual action or occupation: *e.g.*

پُوجارِي *pūjārī*, 'a worshipper,' from پُوجْنا *pūjnā*, 'to worship.'
کھِلار *khilār*, کھِلاڑِي *khilāṛī*, } 'given to playing,' 'playsome,' from کھیلْنا *khelnā*, 'to play.'

Rem. The affix *ārī* may perhaps be derived from the Sanskrit *kārī* (*kārin*); in which case the above words would be secondary formations from the substantives *pūjā*, 'worship,' and *khel*, 'play.'

5) ـــن *an*, نا *nā* (fem. نِي *nī*).

These affixes, which correspond to the Sanskrit affix *ana*, form *attributives*, or *instrumental nouns*: *e.g.*

بیلن *belan*, بیلْنا *belnā*, بیلْنِي *belnī*, } 'a rolling pin,' *lit.* 'that which rolls.'
اوڑھنِي *oṛhnī*, 'a covering,' 'a veil,' *lit.* 'that which covers.'
جھُنْجھُنا *jhunjhunā*, جھُنْجھُنِي *jhunjhunī*, } 'a rattle,' *lit.* 'that which rattles.'
دھَونْکْنِي *dhaunknī*, 'bellows,' or 'that which blows.'
کترْنِي *katarnī*, 'scissors,' or 'that which clips.'

6) تا *tā* (= S. affix *at*).

This affix is used to form imperfect participles: *e.g.*

ہنْسْتا *hanstā*, 'laughing,' from ہنْسْنا *hansnā*, 'to laugh.'
دیکھْتا *dekhtā*, 'seeing,' from دیکھْنا *dekhnā*, 'to see.'

ـا *ā* (= S. affix *ta* or *ita*).

This is used to form perfect or passive participles: *e.g.*

لِکها *likhā*, 'written,' from لِکهْنا *likh-nā*, 'to write.'

هارا *hārā*, 'lost,' 'overcome,' from هارْنا *hār-nā*, 'to lose,' etc.

b) SECONDARY FORMATIONS.

1) ـِيا *iyā*, or ـِياں *iyāṅ*.

255. The original of this affix is the Sanskrit affix *ika*, the *k* of which is elided, and *y* inserted for euphony. It is used to form *nouns of agency* and *attributives*: *e.g.*

بکهيڑِيا *bakheṛiyā*, 'quarrelsome,' 'a brawler,' from بکهيڑا *bakheṛā*, 'a dispute,' etc.

گڈرِيا *gaḍariyā*, 'a shepherd,' from گاڈر *gāḍar*, 'sheep.'

مکّهنِيا *makkhaniyā*, } 'a butterman,' from مکّهن *makkhan*, 'butter.'
مکهنِياں *makhaniyāṅ*, }

Rem. The Sanskrit affix is preserved intact in the word کهٹِّک *khaṭṭik*, or کهٹِيک *khaṭīk*, 'one who kills and sells game,' (but now generally applied to) 'one who rears and sells poultry.'

2) ـِي *ī*.

This affix, which is one of frequent occurrence, springs from at least three different sources: namely—

a) ـِي *ī* = S. affix *ika*,

forming *nouns of agency*, *attributives*, and *appellatives*: *e.g.*

جهولِي *jholī*, 'a wallet' (S. *jhaulika*).

حلْوائِي *halwā'ī*, 'a confectioner,' from حلْوا *halwā*, 'a sweetmeat.'

قصائِي *kaṣā'ī*, 'a butcher,' (Arabic قصّاب *kaṣṣāb*).

b) ـِي *ī* = S. affix *īya* or *iya*,

forming nouns denoting *origin*, *relationship*, etc.: *e.g.*

بهاگلْپورِي *bhāgalpūrī*, 'of, or made at, Bhāgalpūr.'

سمندري *samundarī*, 'pertaining to the sea' (*samundar*), 'marine.

پهاڙي *pahāṛī*, 'produced in mountains' (*pahāṛ*), 'a mountaineer.'

c) ـِي *ī*=S. affix *in*,

forming *attributives* and *possessives*: *e.g.*

بڑهئي *baṛha'ī*, 'a carpenter' (S. *varddhakin*).

بهاري *bhārī*, 'having weight,' 'weighty,' 'heavy,' from بهار *bhār*, 'a weight,' 'a load.'

بيپاري *baipārī*, 'a merchant,' from بيپار *baipār*, 'traffic.'

تيلي *telī*, 'an oil-man,' from تيل *tel*, 'oil' (S. *tailika* and *tailin*).

مالي *mālī*, 'a gardener' (S. *mālin*).

3) ـُو *ū* or ـُوا *ū'ā*, ـَاو *ā'ū*.

These affixes correspond to the Sanskrit affix *uka*. They are added to substantives to form *attributives* and *nouns of agency*, as in the case of primary formations: *e.g.*

ڈهالو *ḍhālū*, 'slant,' 'sloping,' from ڈهال *ḍhāl*, 'slope.'

مچهوا *machhū'ā*, 'a fisherman,' „ مچه *machh*, 'fish.'

شرماو *sharmā'ū*, 'bashful,' „ شرم *sharm*, 'shame.'

4) ـَا *ā*, S. affix *a*.

This affix forms adjectives from substantives: *e.g.*

پيارا *pyārā*, 'dear,' 'beloved,' from پيار *pyār*, 'affection.'

جهوٹها *jhūṭhā*, 'false,' 'a liar,' „ جهوٹه *jhūṭh*, 'a lie.'

سچا *sachā* or *sachchā*, 'true,' „ سچ *sach*, 'truth.'

5) ـَا *ā*, يَا *yā*, or ـِيَا *iyā*, =S. affix *ta* or *ita*.

This affix is used primarily to form perfect participles; but it is also added to substantives to form adjectives or attributives: *e.g.*

بهوكها *bhūkhā*, 'hungry,' from بهوكه *bhūkh*, 'hunger.'

پیاسا *piyāsā*, 'thirsty,' from پیاس *piyās*. 'thirst.'
دُکھیا *dukhiyā*, 'wretched,' 'afflicted,' from دُکھ *dukh*, 'sorrow,' 'pain.'

6) لُو *lū*, ل *l* = S. affix *lu*:

Forms adjectives or attributives from substantives: *e.g.*

جھگڑالُو *jhagṛālū*, 'quarrelsome,' 'a brawler,' from جھگڑا *jhagṛā*, 'quarrel.'

دیال *dayāl*, 'compassionate,' from دیا *dayā*, 'pity,' mercy.'

7) ـال *āl*, ـالا *ālā*.

This affix, which corresponds to the Sanskrit affix *āla*, is used to form possessives: *e.g.*

بھٹھیال *bhaṭhiyāl*, 'with, or having, the stream' (بھاٹھا *bhāṭhā*).
جوالا *jawālā*, 'grain mixed with barley as food for cattle,' *lit.* 'containing barley' (جو *jau*).
لٹھیال *laṭhiyāl*, 'having a stick,' 'one armed with a stick' (*lāṭhī*).

In a few words the original possessive signification is lost: *e.g.*

گھڑیال *ghaṛiyāl*, 'a gong,' *lit.* 'containing the hour' (*ghaṛī*).

8) لا *lā* = S. affix *ra*.

This affix forms adjectives from substantives: *e.g.*

اگلا *aglā*, 'preceding,' 'former,' from آگا *āgā*, 'the front,' etc.
پچھلا *pichhlā*, 'hindermost,' 'latter,' from پیچھا *pīchhā*, 'hindermost,' etc.
دھُندھلا *dhundhlā*, 'hazy,' 'misty,' from دھُندھ *dhundh*, 'haze,' etc.
ریتلا *retlā*, 'sandy,' from ریت *ret*, 'sand.'

9) ـیرا *īrā*, ـیلا *īlā*, ـیرا *erā*, ـیل *el* or *ail*, ـیلا *elā* or *ailā*.

These affixes, which are of very common occurrence, correspond to the Sanskrit affixes *īrā, īla, ura* (*ula*), or *ūra*.[1] They form *attributives* and *possessives*, often signifying the possession of a quality in an intensive degree: *e.g.*

رسیلا *rasīlā*, 'juicy,' from رس *ras*, 'juice.'
شرمیلا *sharmīlā*, 'bashful,' from شرم *sharm*, 'shame.'
نوکیلا *nokīlā*, 'pointed,' from نوک *nok*, 'a point.'
دنتیلا *dantīlā*, } 'having large tusks,' 'tusked,' from دانت *dānt*,
دنتیل *dāntel*, } 'a tooth' (S. *dantura*).
کمیرا *kamerā*, 'a worker,' 'industrious,' from کام *kām*, 'work.'
بوجھیل *bojhel*, 'loaded,' from بوجھ *bojh*, 'a load.'
دُدھیل *dudhail*, 'giving milk,' 'milch,' from دُودھ *dūdh*, 'milk.'

10) ـول *ol*, or ـوڑ *oṛ*.

The original form of this affix is probably *ula* (*ura*). It is used to form attributives denoting *habit* or *disposition*, and is found in a few words only; *e.g.*

ٹھٹھول *ṭhaṭhol*, 'a jester,' 'a wag,' from ٹھٹھا *ṭhaṭṭhā*, 'fun.'
ہنسوڑ *hansoṛ*, 'facetious,' 'merry,' 'a wag,' from ہنسا *hansā*, 'laughter.'

11) سار *sār*.

The origin of this affix is the Sanskrit adjective *sāra*, which occurs at the end of compounds. It signifies 'full of,' 'pervaded with,' and is employed in both Hindī and Persian to form *possessives* or *attributives*: *e.g.*

[1] The terminations *erā, elā*, etc., are not always affixes; they often result from the elision of one or more letters in an original Sanskrit word, and lengthening of a short vowel on which the accent falls: *e.g. sanperā* (i.e. *sanp-hirā*), 'a snake-catcher,' from the Sanskrit *sarpa-hāra*. The word *banela* or *banailā*, 'wild,' is probably derived in a similar way; it may, however, be formed by adding the affix *elā* to the noun *ban*, 'a forest.' These remarks apply to other terminations also: for example, *āl* in the word *susrāl*, and *ālā* or *wālā* in the word *gwālā*, are not *affixes*, but the result of elision of one or more letters: *susrāl* = Sanskrit *śvaśru* + *ālaya*, 'father-in-law's house;' *gwālā* (i.e. *go'ālā*) = S. *go-pāla*, 'a cowherd,' and not *gau-wālā*, as Mr. Etherington (Hindī Grammar, p. 128) makes it out to be.

مِلنسار *milan-sār*, 'sociable,' 'affable,' from مِلن *milan*, 'mixing with.'
شرمسار *sharm-sār*, 'bashful,' from شرم *sharm*, 'shame.'

12) ـَاشا *āshā*, ـَاسا *āsā* (= S. affix *śa*).

The signification of this affix is 'full of.' It occurs in a few adjectives, some of which are used as substantives: *e.g.*

بتاشا *batāshā*, } 'a kind of sweetmeat,' 'a bubble,' *lit.* 'filled with air'
بتاسا *batāsā*, } (*bāt*).

13) ـَار *ār*.

This affix is derived from the Sanskrit adjective *kāra*, signifying 'making,' 'doing,' by elision of *k*, and is added to substantives to form *nouns of agency*, or nouns denoting *trade* or *occupation*: *e.g.*

سونار *sonār*, 'a goldsmith,' from سونا *sonā*, 'gold.'
لوهار *lohār*, 'a blacksmith,' from لوها *lohā*, 'iron.'
کمّهار *kumhār*, 'a potter,' from کمبھ *kumbh*, 'an earthen pot.'

14) هارا *hārā*, هار *hār*.

This affix also, like the preceding, is derived from the Sanskrit *kāra*. It is added to inflected infinitives and to nouns to form *nouns of agency*, and, affixed to verbal nouns, forms *future active participles* (§ 160, 2): *e.g.*

مرنے هارا *marne-hārā*, } 'one who is dying,' 'one about to die,' from
مرن هار *maran-hār*, } مرنا *marnā*, 'to die.'
لکڑهارا *lakaṛ-hārā*, 'a wood-cutter,' 'a wood-man,' from لکڑ *lakaṛ*, a contraction of لکڑی *lakṛī*, 'wood.'

15) والا *wālā*, or وال *wāl*, or وارا *wārā*.

The original of this affix is the Sanskrit affix *vala*. It is most commonly employed in Hindī and Urdū to form nouns denoting *agency*, *possession*, *origin*, and numerous other relations. Added to infinitives, it often forms *future active participles*: *e.g.*

چلنے والا *chalne-wālā*, 'a goer,' 'one about to go,' from چلنا *chalnā*.

گاڑي والا *gāṛī-wālā*, 'a carter,' from گاڑي *gāṛī*, 'a cart.'

گھر والا *ghar-wālā*, 'the master or owner of a house'(*ghar*).

مکھن والا *makkhan-wālā*, 'a butter-man,' from مکھن *makkhan*, 'butter.'

دِلّي والا *dillī-wālā*, 'an inhabitant of Dillī' (Dehlī).

Rem. Hindī nouns ending in *ā* must be inflected before the affix is added: *e.g.* کپڑے والا *kapṛe-wālā*, 'a cloth-merchant.'

16) واڑي *wāṛī*, واڑ *wāṛ*, or وار *wār*.

This is not so much an affix as the latter part of a compound, signifying, 'place,' 'inclosure,' 'house,' 'garden,' etc. It is derived from the Sanskrit *wāṭī*. Examples are:

پنواڑي *pan-wāṛī*, 'a betel-garden,' from پان *pān*, 'betel-leaf.'

پھلواڑي *phul-wāṛī*, 'a flower-garden,' from پھول *phūl*, 'a flower.'

ستيوار *satī-wāṛ*, 'the place where a *satī* is burnt.'

هڑوار *haṛ-wār*, 'a place where bones (هاڑ *hāṛ*) are laid.'

III. DIMINUTIVES.

256. Diminutives are of frequent occurrence in Hindī and Urdū; in not a few cases, however, though the form is preserved, the diminutive signification is lost. In some instances, moreover, the original from which the diminutive is derived has become obsolete.

257. The idea of diminutiveness is frequently expressed by substituting the feminine termination for the masculine: *e.g.*

اُپلي *uplī*, 'small cakes of dried cow-dung,' from *uplā*.

ٹوکري *ṭokrī*, 'a small basket,' from *ṭokrā*.

رسّي *rassī*, 'a string or cord,' from رسّا *rassā*, 'a rope.'

Various affixes also are employed to form diminutives from nouns, as:

1) ـِيا *iyā.*

This corresponds to the Sanskrit diminutive affix *ka*, the *k* of which is elided, and the final vowel lengthened. The connecting vowel of this affix is always *i*, which takes the place of a final vowel in the base, and a long vowel in the base is shortened before the affix is added: *e.g.*

بِٹِیا *biṭiyā*, 'daughter,' from بیٹی *beṭī*, 'daughter.'

پھُڑِیا *phuṛiyā*, 'a small boil,' 'a pimple,' from پھوڑا *phoṛā*, 'a boil.'

چِڑِیا *chiṛiyā*, 'a bird,' from چِڑی *chiṛī*, 'a bird.'

کھٹیا *khaṭiyā*, 'a small bedstead,' from کھاٹ *khāṭ*, 'a bedstead.' (Sanskrit *khaṭṭika*).

Rem. In the towns, and especially by Mohammadans, the connecting vowel *i* is dropped, and such words are pronounced *phuṛyā*, *chiṛyā*, etc.

2) ـُوا *ū'ā* or *wā.*

This affix, like the last, is derived from the Sanskrit affix *ka*, the difference consisting in the connecting vowel, which in this case is *u* (changeable to *w*); and hence the difference of gender in words formed by means of the two affixes, those with *iyā* being *feminine*, and those with *ū'ā masculine.* A long vowel in the base is shortened before the affix is added: *e.g.*

بٹوا *baṭū'ā* or *baṭwā*, 'a small bag' (original not in use).

بٹوا *biṭū'ā* or *biṭwā*, 'son,' 'dear son,' from بیٹا *beṭā*, 'son.'

مردُوا *mardū'ā*, 'a manikin,' 'a contemptible man' (*mard*).

The Sanskrit affix is preserved unchanged in a few words: *e.g.* ڈھولک *ḍholak*, 'a small drum' (*ḍhol*).

3) را *rā* or ڑا *ṛā*, ری *rī*, ڑی *ṛī*, or لی *lī*, ـیلا *elā*, ـولا *olā.*

These affixes are all derived from the Sanskrit diminutive affix *ra*, *r* and *l* being interchangeable in Hindī. In the first two no connecting vowel is used; but in the last two the connecting vowels are *i* and *u* respectively, which are lengthened to *e* and *o* on account of the accent. A long vowel in the base is generally shortened before the affixes are added. Examples are:

تهكرا *ṭhikrā*, } 'a fragment of an earthen vessel' (original, *ṭhīk*,
تهيكرا *ṭhīkrā*, } obsolete).

تكڑا *ṭukṛā*, 'a small piece,' 'a bit,' from *ṭūk*, 'a piece.'

پلنگڑي *palangṛī*, 'a small bedstead,' from *palang*, 'a bedstead.'

ٹنگڑي *ṭangṛī*, } 'a leg,' from ٹانگ *ṭāng*, 'leg.'
ٹنگري *ṭangrī*, }

كهجلي *khujlī* (for *khajulī*), 'itch,' from كهاج *khāj*, 'itch.'

گهنٹالي *ghanṭālī*, 'a small bell,' from *ghanṭā*, 'a bell.'

مُريلا *murelā*, 'a pea-chick,' 'a pea-fowl,' from مور *mor*, 'a peacock.'

بگهيلا *baghelā*, 'a tiger's cub,' 'a young tiger,' from باگه *bāgh*, 'a tiger.'

كهٹولا *khaṭolā*, 'a small, or rickety, bedstead' (*khāṭ*).

گڑولا *gaṛolā* (for *gaṛholā*), 'a small, or dilapidated, fort,' 'a place with such a fort,' from *gaṛh*, 'a fort.'

گهڑولا *ghaṛolā*, 'a small earthen pot' (*ghaṛā*).

Rem. Some grammarians mention *eṭā*, and *oṭā*, as diminutive affixes, but these are simply contractions of the words *beṭā*, 'son,' and *poṭā* (from *pūt*) 'son,' 'young:' *e.g.* *brahman-eṭā* = *brahman-beṭā*, 'a brahman's son,' 'a young brahman;' *hiran-oṭā* = *hiran-poṭā*, 'a young deer,' 'a fawn.'

IV. COMPOUNDS.

a) Nouns with a Particle Prefixed.

1) Negative Prefixes: ا *a*, اَن *an*, نا *nā*, نِر *nir*, نِ *ni*.

258. The prefix *a* is used with adjectives, *an* chiefly with participles and gerunds, *nā* with adjectives or abstract nouns derived from adjectives. Examples are:

اچل *a-chal*, 'immovable.'	اتها *a-thā*, 'unfordable.'
اچیت *a-chet*, 'thoughtless.'	الگ *a-lag*, 'apart,' 'separate.'
انپڑها *an-paṛhā*, 'unread,' 'illiterate.'	اندیکها *an-dekhā*, 'unseen.'
انجانا *an-jāna*, 'unknowing,' 'ignorant.'	انسنا *an-sunā*, 'unheard.'
ناکارا *nā-kārā*, 'useless.'	ناسمجھ *nā-samajh*, 'unintelligent.'
نِراس *nir-ās*, 'hopeless.'	نِدهڑک *ni-dhaṛak*, 'unhesitatingly.'
نِڈر *ni-ḍar*, 'fearless.'	نِکمّا *ni-kammā*, 'useless,' 'good for nothing.'

Rem. These particles are all of Sanskrit origin, and have the same signification as in Sanskrit, but a slight difference is observable in the use of the particle *an*, it being prefixed in Hindī to nouns beginning with either a vowel or a consonant. For other particles, such as *dur* or *dush*, etc., which rarely occur in Urdū, and in Hindī only in words borrowed directly from the Sanskrit, we must refer the student to the Dictionary.

2) Qualificative Particles: سُ *su*, 'well,' کُ *ku*, 'ill,' 'badly:' *e.g.*

سُڈول *su-ḍaul*, 'well-shaped.'	کُڈهب *ku-ḍhab*, 'ill-shaped.'
سُچیت *su-chet*, 'attentive.'	کُڈهنگ *ku-ḍhang*, 'ill-mannered.'

3) Possessive Particle: سَ *sa*, 'with,' 'having.' (= S. *saha*).

Examples of this affix are not numerous in Urdū; the following are a few:

سویرا *sa-werā*, 'morning,' 'dawn' (= S. *sa* + *vela*, 'time').
ساڑهے *sāṛhe*, 'with a half' (= S. *sa* + *arddha*, 'half').
سچیت *sa-chet*, 'with caution,' 'mindful,' 'cautious.'

259. Compound nouns, though not nearly so numerous as in Sanskrit and Persian, are by no means few in number; but in no instance is a compound formed of more than two nouns. They may be classed under five

heads: Collective (corresponding to the Sanskrit *Dvandva*), Dependent Determinative (the Sanskrit *Tatpurusha*), Appositional Determinative (the Sanskrit *Karmadhāraya*), Numeral Determinative (the *Dvigu* of the Sanskrit), Attributive, or Possessive (corresponding to the *Bahuvrihi* of the Sanskrit).

1) Collective Compounds.

These consist of two words that would naturally be connected by a conjunction: *e.g.*

بھلا چنگا *bhalā-changā*, 'hale and hearty.'
دِن رات *din-rāt*, 'day and night.'
کمتي بڑھتي *kamtī-baṛhtī*, 'deficiency and excess,' 'more or less.'
کہا کہي *kahā-kahī*, 'altercation.'
ما باپ *mā-bāp*, 'father and mother,' 'parents.'

In many instances the conjunction is expressed: *e.g.*

آب وھوا *āb-o-hawā*, 'climate.'
رات ودِن *rāt-o-din*, 'night and day.'
راتورات *rāt-o-rāt*, 'in the middle of the night,' 'all night long.'

And in some cases the place of the copulative conjunction is supplied by the Persian conjunctive particle *ā*: *e.g.*

بِيچا بِيچ *bīch-ā-bīch*, 'in the very middle.'
جھڑا جھڑ *jhaṛ-ā-jhaṛ*, 'heavily' (raining).

Under this head may also be classed the compounds in which one of the words is a meaningless one, used merely to rhyme or jingle with the other: as

ادلا بدلا *adlā-badlā*, 'exchange,' 'alteration.'
اڑوس پڑوس *aṛos-paṛos*, 'neighbourhood.'
اُلٹ پُلٹ *ulaṭ-pulaṭ*, 'higgledy-piggledy,' 'topsy-turvy.'
بھِیڑ بھاڑ *bhīṛ-bhāṛ*, 'crowd,' 'bustle.'

2) Dependent Determinative Compounds.

This class comprises compounds in which the last word governs the first, which is therefore always in the Formative. Such compounds are of frequent occurrence: *e.g.*

انٹّا گھر *anṭā-ghar*, 'a billiard room.'

آنکھ مِچَولي *ānkh-michaulī*, 'blindman's buff,' *lit.* 'covering the eyes.'

انگرکھا *angarkhā* (i.e. *ang-rakhā*), 'a coat,' *lit.* 'body-protector.'

باگڈور *bāg-ḍor*, 'a long rope by which horses are led,' *lit.* 'bridle-rope.'

بھڑبھُونجا *bhaṛ-bhūnjā*, 'a parcher of grain,' *lit.* 'one who parches (grain) in an oven' (*bhaṭ*).

تِل چٹّا *til-chaṭṭā*, 'a cockroach,' *lit.* 'oil (*tel*)-licker.'

دیس نِکالا *des-nikālā*, 'banishment.'

پنچکّي *pan-chakkī*, 'a water-mill.'

ریل گاڑي *rel-gāṛī*, 'a railway carriage.'

بھوجپور *bhoj-pūr*, 'name of a town,' *lit.* 'the city of Bhoj.'

لکھپتي *lakh-patī*, 'rich,' 'a millionnaire,' *lit.* 'owner of a *lac*.'

3) Appositional Determinative Compounds.

In these compounds the first word stands as the predicate of the second: *e.g.*

بھلمنسائي *bhal-mansā'ī*, 'humanity,' 'benignity.'

چوربالو *chor-bālū*, 'a quicksand.'

رتّالو *rat-ālū*, 'a yam,' *lit.* 'a red (or purple) root.'

ماجھدھار *mājh-dhār*, 'midstream.'

مہاجن *mahājan*, 'a banker,' *lit.* 'a great man.'

مہاراج *mahā-rāj*, 'majesty,' 'excellency,' *lit.* 'great king.'

4) Numeral Determinative Compounds.

In these the first word is a numeral, which stands as a predicate of the following noun: *e.g.*

دوپہر *do-pahar*, 'midday,' 'noon.'

دُپٹا *du-paṭṭā*, 'a kind of veil,' *lit.* 'two breadths.'

پچمحل *pach-maḥall*, 'five stories.'

چار آنکھیں *chār-āṅkheṅ*, 'the eyes of two people meeting,' *lit.* 'four eyes.'

چَوماسا *chau-māsā*, 'the rainy season,' *lit.* 'four months.'

چَوراہا *chaurāhā*, 'a cross road,' 'a place where four roads meet.'

5) Attributive or Possessive Compounds.

These always stand as predicate to a subject. The various determinative compounds may be used as possessives by changing them into adjectives. Examples are:

ادھمُوا *adh-mū'ā*, 'half-dead.'

بارہ سِنگا *bāra-singā*, 'a stag,' 'twelve-tined.'

پچمحلا *pach-maḥallā*, 'five-storied.'

ٹوپي پھٹا *ṭopī-phaṭā*, 'having a torn cap.'

دو نالِي *do-nālī*, 'double-barrelled.'

Possessives may also be formed from such compounds as have a particle for the first member: *e.g.*

سلَونا *sa-launā*, 'salted,' 'seasoned,' 'beautiful,' 'piquant.'

کُڈھنگا *ku-ḍhangā*, 'unmannerly,' 'rude.'

PART III.—SYNTAX

CHAPTER VI.

I. OF THE PARTS OF A SENTENCE.

260. Every sentence (جُمْلَه *a sum* or *total* of words) consists necessarily of two principal parts, *the subject*, or that of which something is asserted, and *the predicate*, or that which is asserted of the subject.

261. The subject of a sentence is either a *noun* (substantive, or adjective used as a substantive, pronoun, or infinitive), or *a pronoun implied in the verb;* the predicate is either a verb alone, or a verb with an adjective or substantive annexed as a predicative noun, by which the subject is defined and described: *e.g.*

PREDICATE.	SUBJECT.
كاٹتا هَي *kāṭtā hai,*	کُتّا *kuttā,* 'the dog bites.'
جاؤنگا *jā'ūṅgā,*	مَيں *maiṅ,* 'I will go.'
مريو *mariyo,*	...... 'die!' or 'may you die.'
حاضِر هَي *ḥāzir hai,*	بيمار *bīmār,* 'the sick man is present.'
بُرا هَي *burā hai,*	هنْسْنا *haṅsnā,* 'laughing is bad.'
بيمار تها *bīmār thā,*	وُه *wŏh,* 'he was sick.'

Rem. Urdū grammarians call the predicate of a sentence the مُسْنَد *that which leans upon* (*the subject*), or *the attribute;* and the subject, the مُسْنَد إِلَيه *that upon which* (*the predicate*) *leans*, or *that to which something is attributed.*

262. The verbs which are generally used in connection with a predicative noun subjoined, are هُوں, هَي, etc., and تها, etc., هونا or هو جانا 'to be,' or 'become,' and others which add some modifying idea (as *duration*, *continuity*, *permanence*, etc.) to the simple one of existence: *e.g.* نِکلنا 'to come out,' 'turn out to be;' نظر آنا 'to appear,' 'seem' (to be); رهنا 'to continue or remain;' بَيٹهنا 'to sit down,' 'to be fixed or settled;' ٹهہرنا 'to stay,' 'stand,' 'last,' and such like; as also the passives of verbs which signify to *name*, *make*, *call*, *hold* for anything, etc. (§§ 349, 351), to which the words which denote what a thing is named, what it is made, and for what it is held, are subjoined without any further addition: *e.g.*

وُه بهِي برهمن هو گيا 'even he became an idolater.'

تُو دوست کِسِي کا نهُوا تها 'you did not become any one's friend.'

آخِر وهِي سوچنا ميرا صحِيح نِکلا 'eventually that same thought of mine proved correct.'

زِندگِي دشوار نظر آتِي هَي 'living appears difficult.'

وُه دوپهر بجے تک حاضِر رها 'he was (remained) present till twelve o'clock.'

ميرا منصوبه ٹهيک بيٹها 'my surmise proved correct.'

جِس سے همارا کام عداوت کرنا ٹهہرتا هَي 'whereby our business proves to be bearing enmity.'

گاڑِي کهڑِي کِي گئِي 'the carriage was made stationary.'

نام اُسکا کلّو رکها گيا 'he was named Kallū.'

وُه ايک آيسِي زبان نهِيں سمجهِي گئِي 'it was not considered (held to be) such a language.'

263. Instead of being joined to a predicative noun in the nominative, the verbs هَي, تها, etc., may be combined with some other expression which serves to describe or

define them; as with a genitive, وُہ بڑِي قِيمت کا هَے 'it is of great price;' کلام چار طرح کا هَے 'discourse is of four kinds;' or with a locative case, کِتاب گھر پر هَے 'the book is at home;' or with a postposition and the noun it governs, زَيد کے پاس ايک چِيتا هَے 'there is a leopard in Zaid's possession;' or with an adverb of place, to denote the place or relation in which a thing is, وُہ يہاں هَے 'he is here,' شہر قرِيب تھا 'the city was near;' or with an adverbial phrase which denotes *way* or *manner*, *state* or *condition*, جو بانبِھي کے اندر سے سِر نِکالے تھے 'which were with their heads out of (their) holes.'[1] The following are used impersonally: خَير هَے 'it is well,' اَيسا هُوا 'it happened thus.'

264. The same verbs, as also هونا and the other verbs above cited, may also be used as *self-subsistent* (or *attributive*) verbs: as—

اَوروں پر هَے وُہ ظُلم جو مُجھ پر نہُوا تھا 'on others has fallen (exists) the tyranny which did not fall on me.'

شِکيب کِي جب تلک تھِي طاقت 'as long as the power of endurance existed.'

ناصِح کو سَودا هُوا 'madness has happened to Nāṣih.'

Rem. A sentence of which the predicate is a self-subsistent verb is called by Urdū grammarians *a verbal sentence* (جُملۂ فِعلِيّہ), the subject of which they term فاعِل, *the agent*, and the predicate, فِعل *the action* or *verb*; whereas a sentence whose predicate consists of a

[1] Mr. Dowson (*Urdū Grammar*, page 113) finds fault with this sentence because it is not constructed thus: *jin-ne bāṅbhī-ke andar-se sir nikāle the.* The sentence is, however, quite correct. The mistake is Mr. Dowson's in supposing that the verb *the* is here used as an auxiliary. The phrase *bāṅbhī-ke andar-se sir-nikāle (hū'e)* is the adverbial complement of the verb *the*, and shows the *state* or *condition* (*ḥāl*) of the subject. Numerous examples of the same construction are to be found in the *Khirad Afroz*, as also in more modern works.

non-attributive verb (فِعْل ناقِص *an incomplete* or *defective verb*), is called *a nominal sentence* (جُمْلۂ اِسْمِيّہ), and its subject is termed مُبْتَدا, *the inchoative*, its predicate, خبر *the enuntiative* or *announcement*. An affirmative sentence is called جُمْلۂ فِعْلِيّۂ خبرِيّہ or جُمْلۂ اِسْمِيّۂ خبرِيّہ according as it is a *verbal* or a *nominal* sentence; an imperative or interrogative sentence is called جُمْلۂ اِنْشائِيّہ, *a sentence expressing a command* or *wish*.

265. The predicate may be more accurately defined by adverbs and by substantives (or words used substantively) in certain cases (and by postpositions with their nouns) which denote the *object* of the action asserted, and the circumstances attending it: as—

رعِيَّت کِي داد رسِي ميں خُوب دِل لگاتا '(he) used to apply his mind intently to dispensing justice to his subjects.'

266. A substantive may be connected in a certain relation with another substantive, in order to define it more accurately: *e.g.* خاک کا قالِب 'an earth-mould.' Substantives may also be defined or characterized more closely by adding to them other substantives descriptive of the same person or thing: as—

طائِروں کا بادْشاہ شاہ مُرْغ 'the king of the birds, Shāh-murg.'

حکِيم بيدْپائے برهْمن 'the sage, Bedpā'e, the Brāhman.'

The subjoining of these is called *apposition*, and that which is subjoined, the *appositive* (تابِع 'the follower').

Every substantive may also be defined by having an adjective (participle, or genitive) added to it: an adjective which is immediately connected with the substantive is called *attributive* (اچّها آدمِي 'a good man,' جلْتِي آگ 'burning fire,' ميرِي کِتاب 'my book'), to distinguish it from that which is used as a predicative noun with a non-attributive verb: as كِتاب اچّهي هَي 'the book is good.'

267. If a *determined* noun (اِسْمِ معْرِفہ—*i.e. a proper name, a personal, demonstrative,* or *relative pronoun,* or *a noun governing the genitive of any of these*) and an *undetermined* noun (اِسْمِ نکِرہ) are placed in juxtaposition, a non-attributive verb following, the mere fact of the former being determined and the latter undetermined shows that the latter is the predicate: *e.g.* موهن احْمق هَي 'Mohan is a fool,' ميرا بهائِي بِيمار هَي 'my brother is sick.' But if the two nouns in juxtaposition are both determined, or both undetermined, either may be subject or predicate: *e.g.* يهہ تُمهارِي کِتاب هَي 'this is your book,' or 'your book is this;' آدْمِي اِنْسان هَي 'man is a human being,' or 'a human being is man.'

268. The predicate verb هَي (or the verb and predicative noun) is sometimes omitted, especially in poetry, and in brief proverbial sentences: *e.g.*

نہ کِسِي کو کِسِي کے نفْع سے غرض نہ ضرر سے کام 'no one either has any concern with the benefiting, or anything to do with the injuring, of another.'

همارِي بلا سے (= همارِي بلا سے علاقہ هَي or همارِي بلا کے ساتهہ هَي) 'it rests with (concerns) my evil destiny.'

269. The predicate is also omitted in sentences which contain an imprecation; as—

خاک تيري سِر پر 'may sorrow befal thee' (*lit.* 'dust on thy head').

In such sentences the predicate is generally the Aorist of the verb پڑنا 'to befal,' 'to alight on.'

II. OF THE ORDER OF THE WORDS IN A SIMPLE SENTENCE.

270. The most simple arrangement of the words is this, that the subject, with its adjuncts, stands first, and the predicate follows in such a way that the verb usually stands last, in order to combine the whole proposition (کلامِ تام), while the object and the object of relation, or the predicative noun, with the other definitions of the verb (the ablative or locative case, postpositions with their nouns, adverbs), are placed in the middle, the object generally preceding: *e.g.*

زَید کا بھائِي بڑا عالِم هَي ‘Zaid's brother is very learned.’

وُہ گھرکے اَندر بے خبر سوتا تھا ‘he was sleeping soundly in the house.’

ایک ایک فِقرہ هزار مطلب کو حاوِي هي ‘each single sentence involves a thousand meanings.’

خیانت اَور چورِي کِي بُرائِي دِل پر اَیسِي ثابِت کِي ‘(I) so convinced my mind of the evil of perfidy and dishonesty.’

بھائِي بِرادروں کا خَوف اُنکو تلاش اَور تحقِیق سے مانِع هَي ‘the fear of their brethren prevents them from seeking and ascertaining the truth.’

But if the object be so closely connected with the verb as to form with it a so-called nominal compound, or if the other words used to define the predicate are considered of greater importance, or are first thought of, the object is placed nearest the verb: as—

وُہ رعِیّت کِي داد رسِي میں خُوب دِل لگاتا ‘he used to apply his mind intently to dispensing justice to his subjects.’

همارا عِلم سب کاموں سے همکو مانِع هَي ‘our knowledge hinders us from (progress in) all affairs.’

271. If the verb has two objective complements expressed, one direct and the other indirect (§ 348), the latter generally precedes the former; but if the latter be the antecedent of a following relative, or in any way closely connected with what follows, or any stress be laid on the direct object, this is placed first: as—

مَوْضُوع عِلْم کا أسے کہتے هَیں جِس چیز کا حال أس عِلْم میں بیان کِیا جاوي 'that thing which is treated of in a science is termed (*lit.* they term) the subject-matter of that science.'

وُہ تَهیلِي أسکو دِکھلائي 'I showed him that bag.'

272. The simple arrangement of the words may however be so far departed from that the object may lead off the sentence, and this not only for the sake of emphasis, as is generally supposed, but even where no emphasis is desired: as کلّو کو موهن مارتا هَي 'Mohan is beating Kallū.' This is especially the case if the predicative noun be in the locative, or if a noun in the dative or other case be used with one of the verbs هَي, تہا, etc., to denote possession (§ 340): as—

گهر میں کوئي آدمي هَي 'is there any one in the house?'

ناصِح کو سَودا هُوا 'madness has happened to (possessed) Nāṣiḥ.'

زَید کے پاس ایک چِیتا هَي 'there is a leopard in Zaid's possession.'

The following are examples of a predicative noun, or an object being placed first for the sake of emphasis:

احمق هَي زَید 'Zaid is a fool.'

أن کِتابوں کو تُو کہاں لے گیا هَي 'where have you taken those books to?'

جو تُو کہیگا وهي کرُونگا 'whatever you say, that same (I) will do.'

The relative pronoun however, as objective complement, usually precedes the subject.

Rem. The object may even take the last place in a sentence if that be the most strikingly emphatic, or if it be desired to contrast it (or make it rhyme) with another object in a co-ordinate sentence: *e.g.* جاهِل طلب كرْتا هَي مال كو اَور عاقِل كمال كو 'A fool seeks wealth, and a wise man perfection.' This construction, however, is generally regarded as irregular and feeble, and should not be imitated.

273. The arrangement of the words in an interrogative sentence is not generally different from that in an affirmative sentence: as گهر مين كَون هَي 'who is in the house?' ميرِي كِتاب كهاں هَي 'where is my book?' يِهہ كيا بات هَي 'what matter is this?' The interrogative particle كيا is often placed at the beginning of an interrogative sentence, as كيا توپ دگ گئِي 'what! has the gun fired?' or simply, 'has the gun fired?' But it is more commonly omitted (unless used simply to express *surprise*, *reproof*, etc.), and then, in the absence of an interrogative, the context alone must decide whether the sentence is interrogative or not. In conversation, the tone of the voice is always a certain indication.

Rem. The poetical arrangement of words is distinguished from that followed in prose by a much greater freedom, and also by the circumstance that it is regulated not only by the sense and emphasis, but often by the necessity of the verse. The freedom is shown in the circumstance, that words which are connected together in meaning, and in prose would stand together, are often separated, and words which in prose have a definite place assigned to them, are transposed to another part of the sentence. The following are examples:

هُؤا جب كُفر ثابت هَي وُه تمغائے مُسلمانِي 'when unbelief (what constitutes unbelief) has been proved (impressed on the mind, realized), it is a sign of true belief (Saudā).'

شِكيب كِي جب تلك تهِي طاقت نِباه كا جب تلك تها يارا 'as long as the power of endurance existed, as long as the force of restraint lasted (Mūmin Khān).'

274. A *Substantive* or *Adjective in Apposition* (تابِع *the follower*, or *appositive*) follows the noun to which it refers (the متبُوع, *that which is followed*), and is put in the same number and case, the two nouns being treated as a compound phrase, and the governing postposition (if the nouns be in an oblique case) placed after the last alone: as—

لڑکے سب آئے هَیں 'the boys are all come.'

كلُّو تيرا بهائِي باهر كهڑا هَي 'Kallū, your brother, is standing outside.'

هماري آقا سِنْدْباد نے 'by my (*lit.* our) master Sindbād.'

اُسنے موهن كے بهائِي كلُّو كو مارا 'he beat Mohan's brother, Kallū.'

حكِيم بيدْپائے برهْمن كِي نصِيحت 'the counsel of the sage Bedpā'e, the Brāhman.'

طائِروں كے بادْشاه شاه مُرْغ كے پاس جاكر 'having gone to the bird-king, Shāh-murg.'

275. Similarly if two or more nouns are connected by asyndeton, or by an expressed conjunction, they are regarded as in apposition, and the postposition governing them in an oblique case is placed after the last alone: as—

اُسكِي بُرائِي بهلائِي ميں 'between the evil and the good of it.'

خِيانت اَور چورِي كِي بُرائِي 'the evil of perfidy and dishonesty.'

رِعايا كے خاص و عام كو 'to (both) high and low of (your) subjects.'

276. If the nouns so connected be in an oblique case *of the plural*, the last alone is commonly (but not invariably) put in the Formative plural, the others taking the form of the Formative singular: as—

چھوٹے بڑوں نے خُوشیاں کِیں 'by the small and the great rejoicings were made.'

پہاڑوں کے غار اور وَیرانوں میں 'in mountain caves and desolate places.'

Rem. Urdū grammarians, it may be observed, recognize six kinds of appositives (توابِع): 1) تاکِید *the strengthening* or *corroboration*, which is of two kinds; *a*) تاکِیدِ معنوِي *the corroboration in meaning*, and *b*) تاکِیدِ لفظِي *the verbal corroboration*, which consists in the emphatic repetition of the word itself, whether that word be a noun, verb, or particle. Examples of the first are: زَید خُود آیا, or زَید آپ آیا 'Zaid himself came,' لڑکے سب آئے هَیں 'the boys are all come,' کِتاب کو بِجِنسِہٖ آپ کے پاس بھیجتا هُوں 'I will (immediately) send the book itself to you.' The appositive in this case may be any word that strengthens the idea of totality or of self already contained in the متبُوع or *noun that is followed*. Examples of the second kind are زَید آیا زَید 'Zaid is come, Zaid;' جو جو باتیں 'whatever words;' کیا کیا مُصِیبتیں 'what various misfortunes;' ایک ایک فِقرہ 'each single sentence;' مارا مارا زَید نے 'Zaid beat (him), beat (him);' هاں هاں مَیں نے کِیا 'Yes! Yes! I did (it).'—2) نعت *the description*, or *the qualification*. This may refer to the *matbū'* either directly, in which case it is a simple adjective, or indirectly, in which case it is an *adjective sentence* (a qualificative or relative clause), as وُہ کِتاب جِسکا ورق پھٹا هُوا هَي 'the book, the leaf of which is torn.'—3) بدل *the substitution*, or *permutative*, which is of four kinds; *a*) بدلِ کُل *the substitution of the whole* (for the whole); as کلّو تیرا بھائِي میري هاں آیا تھا 'Kallū, your brother, came to my place;' *b*) بدلِ بعض *the substitution of the part* (for the whole), as یہہ کِتاب مَیں نے اُسکا ورق پھاڑ ڈالا 'this book—I tore a leaf of it;' *c*) بدلِ اِشتِمال *the comprehensive substitution,* as یہہ کِتاب اُسکا جُزدان اچّھا هَي 'this book, its wrapper is good;' *d*) بدلِ غلط *the permutative of error,* as گھر کو مدّرسه کو چلنا چاهِیئے 'we ought to go home, (I mean to say), to school.' The last three kinds of permutatives are common in colloquial speech, and the second and third in poetry also.—4) عطفِ بیان *the explanatory apposition,* which consists in the connection of a substantive with another which it more closely defines, as سِراجُ اَلدِّین بہادُر شاه 'Sirāju'ddīn (alias, or better known as) Bahādur Shāh.'—5) عطفِ بحرف *apposition by means of a conjunction,* as کلّو اَور موهن 'Kallū and Mohan.'—6) تابِعِ مُہمَل *the meaningless appositive,* as روٹِي ووٹِي 'bread,' دَانا دُنکا 'grain.'

277. A *Genitive* may either precede or follow the substantive by which it is governed: as—

اصْل و نفْع اُسکا 'the principal and the profit thereof.'
اخْبار کِي کَیفِیّت 'the character of the newspaper.'

But if emphasis or contrast is desired, the genitive is usually placed before the governing noun; as وُہ میرِي کِتاب هَي 'that is *my* book.'

278. When the governing noun is preceded by an attributive, the genitive may either follow the governing noun or precede the attributive: as—

ظاهِرِي عِبارت اُسکِي 'its apparent wording or tenour.'
موهن کا چھوٹا بھائِي 'Mohan's younger brother.'

279. The genitive may even be separated from its governing noun by other words, as adverbs, interrogative pronouns, etc., so long as they do not make the construction ambiguous or obscure: as—

مَیں تیرا کیونکر اِعتِبار کروں 'how can I believe you?'

تیرا کیا نام هَي 'what is your name?'

تیري اُسمیں کیا مرضِي هَي 'what is your pleasure respecting it?'

اُسکي کھوپڑي کا اِس مَیدان کے درِندوں کے پاني پِینے کا پِیاله بناتا '(I) would have made of his skull a cup for the wild beasts of this desert to drink water out of.'

280. *Adjectives.*—The usual position for an attributive adjective is immediately before its substantive; as ذہِین لڑکا 'an intelligent lad;' اچھا آدمِي 'a good man.' But if the adjective in any way *particularizes* the substantive, it usually follows, especially if other descriptive phrases accompany it: as—

چانول اچھا لانا 'bring *good* rice.'

دسْت آویز پکّي لِکھوالو 'have a sound acknowledgment (of the transfer) written.'

اُس کوچے میں ایک حویلِي بڑي سِي هَي 'there is a very large house in that lane.'

ایک شَي صاف اَور چِکنِي گنبد کِي طرح گول هَي '(Lo!) it was (*lit.* is) an object white and smooth, round like a cupola.'

ایک حبشِي جوان خوبصورت ایک پھینٹا طرحدار سجے هوئے باهر نِکل آیا 'an Abyssinian, young, handsome, with an elegant head-dress nicely arranged, came out.'

281. Similarly the demonstrative pronoun, which usually precedes the substantive, may, for the sake of emphasis, follow it: as طبِیب وہ اچھا هَي جو '*He* is a good physician, who,' etc. (*lit.* '*that* physician is good,' etc.)

282. Great emphasis may be given to an adjective by

separating it from its substantive, and placing it at the end of the sentence, so as to let it produce a more independent impression: as—

ایک پہاڑکا درہ تھا۔ نِہایت عمِیق 'there was a *very deep* mountain gorge.'

283. *Adverbs.*—An adverb which belongs to an adjective or another adverb almost invariably stands before it: as ایک نِہایت عمِیق درہ 'a very deep gorge.' So also an adverb which belongs to a verb usually stands immediately before it: as اُنسے ہنسِي خُوشِي کھیلا کُودا کرتِي '(she) used to romp and play with them right merrily.' But it may be placed, for the sake of emphasis, at the beginning of the sentence, or inserted without emphasis between the more prominent words. If however a whole clause is qualified, it is placed at the beginning: *e.g.*

اور چُونکہ پہلے کبھي اُسکا گُذر وھاں نہُوا تھا 'and inasmuch as his path had never lain that way before.'

ناگہاں ایک جزِیرہ سرسبز اور بہُت خُوبصُورت نظر آیا 'suddenly a verdant and very beautiful island came in sight.'

284. The negative particle, like other adverbs, usually precedes the verb; but if the tense be a compound one, it may also stand between the auxiliary and the participle: as—

میں یہہ نہ جانتا تھا 'I was not aware of this.'

کوئِي سرکارِي قانُون کو سمجھتا نہ تھا 'no one used to understand the Government regulations,' or *lit.* 'any one did not understand,' etc.

The negative is never used *adjectively*, but is always an adverb qualifying the verb in a sentence.

285. *Conjunctions*, as connecting and showing the relation between sentences, naturally precede the members they serve to introduce: as—

مگر اُس میں ظُہور کي قابِلیت تہي 'but still the capacity of manifesting (itself) existed in it.'

لیکِن بعْض عُقلا کِي یِہ بہِي رائے هَي 'but this also is the opinion of certain sages.'

III. CONCORD OF THE SUBJECT AND PREDICATE.

286. The verb of the predicate agrees with the subject in number, person, and gender, unless it be of the form in which personal terminations are found, viz.: the Imperative, the Aorist, and the fragmentary verb هُوں, هَي, etc.; these admit of no change of form to indicate *gender*: *e.g.* میرا باپ جائیگا 'my father will go;' لڑکِي جائیگِي 'the girl will go;' هم پڑهینگے 'we (masc.) will read;' هم پڑهینگِیں 'we (fem.) will read;' مَیں هُوں 'it is I' (masc. or fem.); هم هَیں 'It is we' (masc. or fem.).

Rem. a. Not only are the personal pronouns as subjects often omitted, but a substantive as subject is also occasionally understood: *e.g.* نِہایت فراغت سے گذرْنے لگِي 'life passed in great comfort,' where زِنْدگِي or some similar word is understood.

Rem. b. When a superior addresses an inferior, he frequently speaks of himself in the first person plural: *e.g.* هم هَیں 'it is I;' هم آئینگے 'I will come.' Similarly another is commonly addressed in the second person plural, as in English; *e.g.* تُم کَون هو 'who are you?'

287. The predicative participle or adjective (if this admit of a feminine being formed from it) is regulated by the subject in gender, number and case; and similarly

every adjective (or genitive), whenever possible, agrees with the substantive with which it is connected: as—

شاہزادہ رِوش پر کھڑا هُوا 'the prince stood (became stationary) on the walk.'

سب مکھیاں اُسکي اِطاعت کرتي هیں 'all the bees yield him obedience.'

یہ مُصیبتیں قِسمت میں لِکھي تھیں 'these misfortunes were written in (my) destiny.'

وُہ لِباس بھي مَیلا کُچیلا هو جاتا 'that dress too used to become dirty and tattered.'

جان هر حال میں پیارِی هوتي هَي 'life is dear to one under all circumstances.'

جب خواهش اُسکي پُوري هُوئي 'when his desire was (became) satisfied.'

تُم دِهلي کے رهنے والے هو 'you are (= thou art) an inhabitant of Dehli.'

سب آدمِي ایک سے نہیں هوتے 'all men are not alike.'

Rem. a. When the subject is a noun (pronoun) which has the same form for the singular and plural (as in the last of the above examples), the predicate is a guide to the number of the subject.

Rem. b. Perfect concord in number of the feminine participles in the above examples would require the forms کرتیں, لِکھیں, but such forms are now obsolete. (§ 169, *Rem.*)

288. A plural predicate is often connected with a personal subject in the singular, as a mark of respect or politeness: as—

مهاراج سُنکر بہت خُوش هُوئے 'His Majesty was (became) much pleased on hearing (it).'

حُضور بجا فرماتے هَیں 'your Honour's observation is to the point' (*lit.* 'your Honour observes justly').

Rem. The third person plural is sometimes used without a defined subject to denote a common saying, or the general use of a term, or a general opinion: as کہتے هَیں 'they say or call.' But the noun of Agency of the same verbs may be employed as subject: *e.g.* کہنے والے کہتے هَیں 'the tellers relate.'

289. Some Arabic plurals (*broken* and *regular*), as احوال 'circumstances,' اسباب 'property,' 'articles,' تحقِیقات 'investigation,' وارِدات 'a casualty,' and perhaps a few more, are commonly regarded as singular collectives, and connected with a singular predicate;[1] others, as اَولِیا 'saints,' اکابِر 'great men,' مشائِخ 'elders,' and one or two more, are used both in the singular and plural; in the use of these

[1] Misled by the repeated use in the *Bāg o bahār* of certain Arabic broken plurals with singular verbs, the European grammarians appear to think that all, or nearly all such plurals may be constructed with a singular predicate, or have a singular adjective connected with them. But so far is this from being the case that very few (perhaps not more than six or eight) of these plurals are used as singular collective nouns. In the *Bāg e bahār* we find تختِ طاؤس مین جواهِر جڑوایا - جواهِر خرِیدہ گیا and other instances of broken plurals treated as singular collectives which scholars of the present day by no means approve. The following remarks on the above constructions by a scholar of distinction, M. Shai<u>kh</u> 'Abdullāh of Cawnpore, will show what opinion native scholars hold respecting them: چُونکہ جواهِر جمع هَي جڑوایا فِعلِ مُفرد لانا صحِیح نہِیں هَي - صحِیح جڑوائے هَي - مگر بعضے الفاظِ جمع کو اُردو مین مُفرد بهِي مُستعمل کرتے هَیں - جَیسے لفظِ اَولِیا اَور مشائِخ - شاید نواحِ دِهلِي میں جواهِر کوبهِي مُفرد بولتے هوں - مگراِس طرف مُفرد مُستعمل نہِیں هوتا - نہ کِسِي دِهلِي والے سے سُنا نہ کِسِي کے کلام میں دیکها - مِیر حسن کِي مثنوِي میں ایک جگہ جواهِرجڑا آیا هَي *

Did space permit, we could here add the opinions of distinguished Dehli scholars also. It is to be hoped, however, that the above will suffice to show that the *Bāg o bahār* cannot be safely taken as a perfect representative of the Urdū of the present day.

plural forms the student must be guided by the practice of the best modern writers. Examples are:

جِتّنا اسْباب اُس مکان میں تھا 'as much property as there was in the house.'

میرا یِہہ احْوال هَي 'this is my case' (these are my circumstances).

مَیں رئِیس اور اکابِر اِس شہْر کا هُوں 'I am a chief and a great personage of this city.'

تحْقِیقات هو رهِي هَي 'investigation is taking place.'

ایک وارِدات هُوئِي هَي 'a casualty has occurred.'

Rem. اسْباب is also constructed as a plural, especially when it signifies *causes* or *means*: *e.g.* اِس ترقِّي کے اسْباب کیا هَیں 'what are the causes of this progress?'

290. If two or more subjects of different persons have a common predicate, the subjects are arranged in the order of the persons, beginning with the first, and the predicate is put in the *first person plural* if one of the subjects is of this person, and in the *second person plural* if the subjects are of the second and third persons: *e.g.*

هم تُم دَوڑیں 'let me and you run' (*lit.* us and you).

مَیں اَور وُہ دُوسرا میرا ساتهِي وهاں سے بهاگے 'I and the other (man) my companion fled thence.'

تُم اَور موهن مِلْکر اُسْکو مارو 'you and Mohan together (*lit.* having united) beat him.'

291. Two or more connected subjects of the third person (singular or plural), *when they denote living beings*, usually take the predicate (verb, participle, adjective) in the plural, and the predicate agrees with them in gender,

if they are all of the same gender; but if they are of different genders, the masculine is preferred: *e.g.*

موهن اَور كلّو ميري هاں آئے 'Mohan and Kallū came to my place.'

امِيرن اور نصِيبن مدّرسے كو جاتِي تهِيں 'Amīran and Naṣīban were going to school.'

اُسكے ما باپ مرگئے هَيں 'his mother and father are dead.'

ايكٌ بُوڑها اَور اُسكِي بُڑهِيا وهاں پهنچے 'an old man and his old woman arrived there.'

كهجُور كے درختوں ميں بهِي نرو ماده هوتے هَيں 'male and female are found in date-trees also.'

Rem. If كوئِي , كچهه , سب , دونوں, or any similar word is in apposition to the subjects, the verb of course agrees with it as its proper subject: as زن و فرزند كوئِي ساتهه نه جائيگا 'wife and children, no one will accompany (him).'

292. But if the connected subjects denote *things* or *ideas* (or partly living beings and partly things), the following cases arise:

1) If the subjects are all singular and of the same gender, the predicate agrees with them in gender, and may be put in the singular or plural, but the singular is preferred: as

اُس سے بُزدِلِي اَور كم هِمّتِي اَور بے غَيرتِي وَغَيره پَيدا هوتي هَي or هوتِي هَيں 'from it spring cowardliness, mean-spiritedness, and spiritlessness,' etc.

خُود غرضِي اور طمع غالِب هوتِي هَي 'selfishness and covetousness predominate.'

رُعب اَور وقار جاتا رهتا هَي 'respect and dignity vanish.'

The predicate must however be put in the plural if one or more of the subjects is in the plural: as—

هوش و حواس بجا نہ تہے '(his) senses were not in proper order.'

2) If the subjects are of different genders, the predicate (verb, participle, adjective) usually agrees with the last in gender and number,[1] but it may agree with the masculine even when it is not the nearest subject: *e.g.*

چاروں طرف امن اور آسودگي نظر آتي تهي 'tranquillity and ease were visible on all sides.'

اُسکو نا خوشي اور رنج هوتا هَي 'displeasure and vexation possess him.'

[1] These rules, as also many others laid down in these pages, will be found to differ materially from those of Forbes and other grammarians, who base their rules on the language of the *Bāg o bahār* and other such antiquated works alone, quite ignoring the literature of the present period; as though Urdū had in no way changed or improved since the time of Dr. Gilchrist. Of this we shall have more to say elsewhere. We may here content ourselves with subjoining, in corroboration of what is stated above, the opinion of two distinguished scholars, the one an inhabitant of Dehlī, the other of Lakhnau:

اگر معطوف علیہ مذکر هو اور معطوف مؤنث تو فعل میں علامت مؤنث کي لاحق کرینگے ۔ اور اگر معطوف علیہ مؤنث اور معطوف مذکر هو تو فعل میں علامت مذکر کي لاحق کرینگے (M. Imām Bakhsh, *Urdū Gram.* p. 118.)

جہاں ایک فعل کے کئي فاعل بعضے مذکر بعضے مؤنث هوں فعل کے مذکر اور مؤنث لانے میں متکلم مختار هَي ۔ لیکن اولیٰ و فصیح یہہ هَي کہ کلمہ متصل فعل کا اعتبار کیا جائے (M. Shaikh ʻAbdullāh, Arabic Prof., Cawnpore Zilaʻ School.)

Discussing the following sentence from the *Bāg o bahār* جب حضرت شاه جہاں نے قلعۂ مبارک اور جامع مسجد اور شہرپناه تعمیر کرایا ۔ the last-mentioned scholar remarks عبارت مذکور میں کرائي فعل مؤنث لانا اولیٰ و فصیح هَي *in the above-cited passage it is better and more chaste to use* کرائي, *the feminine verb.*

جابجا مُسافِر خانے اَور عِمارتیں عالِي بنِي هُوئِي هَیں 'houses for travellers and lofty buildings are found constructed here and there.'

زُهْد و قناعت اُس میں اِتْنِي (هي) 'abstinence and content are found in it to this degree.'

نہ معْلُوم کِہ باپ اَور نَوکر اَور اسْباب کہاں گیا 'I have no knowledge as to where father, servants, and property are gone.'

کپْڑي باسن اَور کِتابیں بہُت اچْھِي هَین 'the clothes, plates, and books are very good.'

جِسْکِي اِتْنِي تعْرِیف اَور اِشْتِیاق ظاهِر کِیا 'respecting whom he spoke in so much praise, and evinced such longing.'

بہُت سِي لکْڑیاں اور کانٹے جمْع کِیئے 'many sticks and thorns were collected (by me),' or 'I collected a large quantity of sticks and thorns.'

Rem. The last subject, though singular by form, may be plural in idea, in which case the predicate will be put in the plural; as عقْل و هوش جاتے رهے 'understanding and senses vanished.' And if one idea is expressed in several words, all of the same gender except the last, the predicate may agree in gender with the first subjects, and not with the last; as بعْضے جانوروں مین اِحْتِیاط اَور اٹْکل اَور هوشْیارِي اَور سیانپں اَیسِي پائِي جاتِي هَي 'such foresight, judgment, sense, and knowledge is found in some animals.' If one of the words سب, کُچھ, etc., is in apposition to the subjects, the predicate will agree with it in gender and number; as پوسْت و اُسْتُخواں سب بِکھر جائینگے 'skin and bones, all will be scattered;' مُطْلق طاقت اَور هوش کُچھ باقِي نہ تہا 'absolutely no strength and consciousness, none whatever remained.'

293. If the predicate consists of هونا 'to become,' 'to prove to be,' or one of the verbs mentioned in § 262, and a substantive, the verb is usually regulated in number and

gender by this substantive if it immediately precedes the verb, and is defined by a genitive or an adjective: as—

يِہ تاج و خِلْعت اَور دُرّ و جواہِر ہزار سَوداگر کِي پُونْجِي ہو سکْتِي ھَي 'this crown and robe and (these) pearls and jewels might make up the capital stock of a thousand merchants.'

اِدھر کِي اُدھر باتیں مِلانِي اَور فریب دینا اُسْکِي عادت ہو جاتِي ھَي 'putting together words (concocting stories) from this side and that, and deceiving, becomes his habit.'

294. A declinable adjective which is connected as an attribute with two or more substantives of different genders usually agrees with the masculine if the substantives denote living beings; but if they denote things or ideas, it generally agrees with the nearest: as—

اَیسِي آفتیں اَور خطْرناک مقام 'such calamities and fearful places.'

اِتْنِي تعْرِیف اَور اِشْتِیاق 'so much praise and longing.'

295. An impersonal proposition, by which the existence of an action or relation is asserted, without being referred, as predicate, to any noun for its subject, is formed 1) by the verb چاہِیئے 'it is proper or necessary;' 2) by the verbs ھَي and تھا with one of the adjectives لازِم 'necessary,' مُناسِب 'proper,' واجِب 'right,' 'necessary,' etc., followed in each case by a subordinate proposition to which the assertion refers: as—

چاہِیئے کِہ اُن سے اَیسا برْتاؤ کري 'it is necessary that he so deal with them.'

مناسِب ھي کِہ اِس پر عمل کري 'it is right that he act on this.'

CHAPTER VII.

THE ARTICLE; THE RELATIONS OF SUBSTANTIVES IN A SENTENCE, AND THE CASES.

a) ON THE ABSENCE OF THE ARTICLE IN URDŪ.

296. Urdū, like Sanskrit and the modern Āryan languages, possesses no definite article: thus گهر may be translated by either 'house,' or 'a house,' or 'the house,' according to the context.

297. Some nouns however are in their very nature definite, *e.g.* آفتاب 'the sun,' پُورب 'the East,' etc., and all proper names. Others are rendered definite—

1) by standing in apposition to a proper name; as كراچي بنّدر 'the seaport of Karāchī;' حكِيم بيدْپائے 'the sage, Bedpā'e.'

2) by standing in the relation of governing noun to a proper noun in the genitive, when this is *explicatory* (اِضافتِ بيانِيّه): as زيرْباد كا ديس 'the country of Zerbād;' يُونان كا بادْشاه 'the king of Greece.'

3) by being connected with the demonstrative pronouns, which, in many instances, may be properly rendered by the English definite article: as وُه كِتاب جِسْكا ورق پهٹا هُوا هَي 'that, or the book, a leaf of which is torn.'

Rem. According to the native grammarians not only are all proper names, personal, demonstrative, and relative pronouns, definite or determined (معرف), but a noun which governs any of these in the genitive is also definite; thus موهن كا لڑكا signifies properly 'the child of Mohan,' and not 'a child of Mohan's.'

298. If it be desired to point out a noun as *indefinite*, the numeral adjective ايک 'one, a, an' (called حرفِ تنكير 'the indefinite particle') or the indefinite pronoun كوئي 'some one,' 'a certain one,' is employed for the purpose, with this distinction, however, that the former more commonly particularizes the substantive, implying that only one person or thing is understood, whereas the latter implies that some one out of many, or something not described, is intended: *e.g.*

عِلم ايک اچّهي چيز هَي 'knowledge is a good thing.'

ايک بادشاه نے كِسي زاهِد كو قِيمتِي خِلعت دِي 'a king gave a costly robe to a certain devotee.'

كِسي تالاب كے كِناري ايک بط رهتِي تهي 'a duck used to remain by the margin of some tank.'

299. If some indefinite portion or quantity of a thing is implied, the word كُچه is placed before the noun in the singular or plural; as بازار سے كُچه جُوزا لے آنا 'bring some chickens from the market' (see § 399).

b) THE RELATION OF SUBSTANTIVES IN A SENTENCE.

300. The relation in which a noun (substantive, adjective, participle, pronoun) stands to the other parts of a sentence, is denoted by its case, or by a postposition with its noun.

301. Nouns which stand in the same relation, stand also in the same case: *e.g.*

1) The *appositive* (*tābi'*) and its *matbū'*; as هماري آقا سِنّدباد نے 'by our master Sindbād,' ايکٓ سيرتيل 'a *ser* of oil;' ايکٓ گزکپڑا 'a yard of cloth;' ايکٓ بِيگها زمِين 'a *bīghā* of land;' لاکه گهوڑي 'ten thousand horses.'

Rem. Nouns denoting *measure* or *quantity* are coordinate with the noun denoting the thing of which they form a part. Native grammarians, however, do not regard the two nouns as in *apposition*, but call the second of the two nouns *the specification* (تمِيز) of the first. When a noun is preceded by a numeral adjective (عدد), it is termed معدود or *numbered*. It is wrong to say of such nouns that "they are put in the nominative," for the two nouns may be in any case: *e.g.* دو سير گهِي سے کيا هوگا 'what can be done with two *sers* of *ghī*?'

2) Words which are connected by conjunctions, enumeration, and antithesis; as جاهِل طلب کرتا هَي مال کو اَور عاقِل کمال کو 'the fool seeks wealth, and the wise man perfection.'

3) The word with which a question is put, and that which conveys the answer; as اِس کو کِس نے مارا 'by whom was he beaten?' ('who beat him?'), مَيں نے (مارا) 'by me;' يِه کِسکا گهر هَي 'whose house is this?' موهن کا 'Mohan's;' کس کے لِيئے بناتے هو 'for whom are you making (it)?' فُلانے صاحِب کے لِيئے 'for such-and-such a gentleman.'

I. The Nominative Case.

302. The Nominative is used to denote the subject of which a verb is predicated; مَيں لڑکوں کو پڑهاتا هُوں 'I teach boys,' or 'I am teaching the boys.'

303. The Nominative is also used as the predicative noun, 1) with verbs signifying *to be* or *become*, *to prove*, *issue*, *turn out*; as هَي, هونا, هوجانا, هو سکنا, نِکلنا, etc.; 2) with verbs denoting a *state* or *mode of existence*, as رهنا 'to

remain,' ٹھہرنا 'to stand or last,' etc.; 3) with passive verbs of *naming*, *calling*, *making*, *esteeming*, etc. (*cf.* §§ 262 and 351).

304. The Nominative is often employed absolutely to avoid the use of two or more consecutive nouns in an oblique case, and the case in which these nouns would stand is then taken by a following pronoun or pronominal adjective. This construction is also commonly employed when attention is called to the subject (with which the following pronoun is put in apposition), or when a relative explanatory sentence is inserted between the nominative and the verb: *e.g.*

کِسِي کے کپڑے مِیں عَیب نِکالنا۔ یا کِسِي کِي بد اِعتِقادِي کا ذِکر کرنا اَور عَلیٰ هٰذَا القِیَاس۔ سب غِیبت مِیں داخِل هَي	'to pick holes in any one's dress, or to speak of the untrustworthiness of any one, and so forth—all is comprehended in the word Slander.'
گنوار کا ایک لڑکا جو کھیت کِي نِگہبانِي کے لِیئے وهاں پِھرتا تھا۔ نظر اُسکِي جوں کبُوتر پر پڑِي	'a villager's son, who was moving about there to watch the field—as soon as his eye fell on the pigeon.'
ملِکِ صادِق۔ جو بادشاہ جِنّوں کا هَي۔ تُمهارِي باپ نے اُسکے ساتھ دوستِي پَیدا کِي تِھي	'Malik Ṣādiḳ, who is the king of the Jinn—your father had formed a friendship with him.'
اَور بعض باتیں عربِي اَور فارسِي کِي۔ جِنکا جاننا نَو آموزوں کو ضرورِي اَور مُوجِب هوشیارِي کا تھا۔ وُہ بھِي درج کِي گئِیں	'and certain matters pertaining to the Arabic and Persian, the knowing of which was essential, and a means of enlightenment to young scholars—they also have been introduced.'

305. The Formative plural of nouns denoting *periods of time*, when used *collectively* and *indefinitely*, is used in place of the nominative: *e.g.* برسوں گذر گئے 'years passed away.'

II. THE AGENT.

306. When the verb of a sentence is transitive, such that its perfect participle has a *passive* character, and the tense employed is one which is formed with this participle (the Indefinite Past, the Present Perfect, the Past Perfect, the Past Potential, and one of the forms of the Past Conditional), the structure of the sentence (owing to the nature of the participle) takes a *passive* form, the near or direct object (the Accusative) is made the *subject* of the verb, and the agent of the act is put in the *Agent case*: *e.g.*

مہاراج نے میرا حال پُوچھا 'His Majesty asked after my condition' (*lit.* 'by the king my condition was asked').

اُنھوں نے مُجھکو اچّھي صلاح بتّلائي 'they gave me good advice' (*lit.* 'by them to me good advice was given').

مَیں نے تجارت کي اجناس خريدي تھيں 'I had purchased articles of merchandise' (*lit.* 'articles of merchandise had been purchased by me').

307. A sentence as object (or subject) of a verb is treated as a singular masculine noun; hence—

مَیں نے عہد کِیا تھا کہ پھِر کبھي سفر کا نام نہ لُونگا 'I had vowed that never again would I breathe the word Travel' (*lit.* 'that I will never again take the name of Travel, had been vowed by me').

308. But if, for any reason, the object is constructed with کو, or in other words takes the Dative form, the

concord between it and the verb is broken, and the construction becomes impersonal, the subject, in the form of the pronoun of the *third person singular masculine*, being implied in the verb: *e.g.*

اُنھوں نے سانپ کے سِرکو کُچلا 'they crushed the snake's head' (*lit.* 'as to the snake's head, it was crushed by them').

هم نے اُسکي درخواست کو قبول کِیا هَي 'I have accepted his petition' (*lit.* 'as regards his petition, it has been accepted by us').

مرّدوں کو خُدا نے کمانے کے لِيئے بنایا هَي 'God has made men for the purpose of earning (their livelihood),' or *lit.* 'with reference to men, by God, for the purpose of earning, it has been made,' *i.e.* the act of creating by God, in reference to men, has been with a view to (their) earning.

309. One or two transitive verbs, as بولنا 'to speak,' بھُولنا 'to forget,'[1] the perfect participles of which are regarded as lacking a passive character, are not constructed according to the above rules; as مَیں بولا (not مَیں نے بولا) 'I spoke.'

310. Compound verbs, such as لے آنا (and its contraction لانا) 'to come with, to bring,' لے جانا 'to go away with, to take away,' کھا جانا 'to eat up,' etc., the first member of which (as also the whole verb[2]) is transitive, and the

[1] To these the people of Lakhnau and of Southern India add the verb سمجھنا 'to understand,' 'to think;' whereas Dehlī authors rarely treat this as a neuter verb. In the Khirad Afroz this verb, as also سوچنا, is repeatedly treated as neuter, but *sochnā*, like *bhūlnā*, is sometimes a *transitive* and sometimes an *intransitive* verb. Other verbs, which are added to the above exceptions by some European grammarians —as ڈرنا 'to fear' (to be afraid), چُوکنا 'to fail, to fall short' (of), لڑنا 'to fight' (with), لگنا 'to be in contact' (with), 'to take' (to)—are *essentially intransitive*, and hence cannot possibly take the passive construction.

[2] Forbes's rule—which Messrs. Williams and Dowson repeat—is: When the last member of a compound verb is neuter, the whole verb is neuter, and when it is transitive, the whole verb is transitive. This rule, we may observe, is not based on

second member intransitive, must necessarily be treated as neuter verbs, *i.e.* constructed *actively*, since a *passive* participle cannot be formed from the latter part of the compound, which alone is conjugated: *e.g.* كُتّا سب روٹي كها گيا 'a (or the) dog has eaten up all the bread.'

Rem. In two or more co-ordinate sentences with a common subject, the last of which takes the passive construction with the Agent case, and the other (or others) the active with the Nominative, or *vice versâ*, the Agent or the Nominative (as the case may be) of the last sentence is generally not expressed: *e.g.*

وُه گهوڑي پر سوَار هُوا اَور جنگل كِي راه لِي (اُس نے) 'he mounted the horse and took the road to the jungle.'

ايكٔ خادِم نے ميرا هاتهہ پكڑا اَور (وُه) مُجهه سے كہنے لگا 'a servant seized my hand, and began to say to me.'

This construction serves to show that (as we have already remarked), according to the conception of those who now speak Urdū, the Agent case is simply a modified form of the Nominative, from which it is distinguished by the sign نے, and by its exclusive use with the tenses formed from the perfect participle of transitive verbs. When a Hindūstānī says, for instance, مَيں نے روٹي كهائِي, he means not 'bread was eaten by me,' as the construction implies, but 'I ate bread.'

III. The Genitive.

311. The Genitive of a word denotes that another stands with it in the relation of connection, and is in this

the opinion of native scholars, nor on the practice of standard authors; for the former hold it as absurd to call كهانا *active* and كهاجانا *neuter* as it would be to term *to eat* active, and *to eat up* neuter; and the latter invariably construct the Frequentative and Desiderative compounds actively with the *Nominative*: *e.g.* مَيں تمام دِن اَور تمام رات پانِي ميں هاتهہ پاؤں مارا كِيا 'I kept striking (out) my hands and legs in the water all day and all night.' (*Cf.* § 214, and *note* thereon.)

way defined by it. The genitive serves chiefly to show the relation of the substantive so used to some other substantive (or word used substantively), so that both substantives together express one idea; it is however also connected with some adjectives.

312. The Genitive in Hindūstānī, it should be borne in mind, is, as regards its origin, an *Adjective* (§ 43), and therefore, like other Hindī adjectives terminating in *ā*, it inflects for gender and number so as to agree with the noun it defines.

313. The Genitive may either precede or follow the word by which it is governed (§ 277 *et seq.*).

314. The Genitive after *substantives* is used, generally, to denote dependence of any one substantive upon another: as—

دوستي کا بهانا 'the pretence of friendship.'

صحرا کي راه 'the road of, *i.e.* to the desert.'

آدميوں کا ايک جهاز 'a ship of, *i.e.* laden with men.'

Hence the Genitive depends upon لِئے, واسطے, خاطِر, etc. signifying *for the sake* (of), *on account* (of), and on other postpositions, which are nouns in the Ablative and Locative: as باپ کے لِئے 'for the sake of, or for (my) father,' ميري واسطے 'for me,' 'on my account.' (See § 238 *et seq.*)

Rem. The locative of the Reciprocal Pronoun آپس as governing noun is frequently omitted: *e.g.*

ميري تيری دُشمنیٔ ذاتي هَي 'a natural antagonism exists between me and thee.'

ايک کچهوي اور بچّهو کے دوستي تهي 'a friendship existed between a tortoise and a scorpion.'

كِہ ميري تيري وُهِي بِتا هووي 'so that that same may be a sign between me and thee.'

315. *Genitive of Relation.*—The Genitive is used to denote relationship: as موهن کا بيٹا 'Mohan's son,' لڑکوں کا باپ 'the father of the children.'

316. *Possessive Genitive.*—The Genitive denotes a thing possessed by a possessor, and the possessor of a thing possessed: as گھر کا مالِک 'the owner of a house,' موهن کِي کِتاب 'Mohan's book.'

317. Instead of being joined immediately to the governing substantive, a Possessive Genitive may be connected with it by means of one of the verbs هَی, تها, هونا, etc.: *e.g.*

يِهہ کِتاب موهن کِي هَي 'this book is Mohan's.'

ميرا اُس وقت عجب حال تها 'mine was a strange predicament at that time.'

318. The Genitive of possession in connection with a following verb (هَي, تها, هونا, etc.) often stands without a governing word: *e.g.*

ايک گدها جِسکے دُم نہ تهِي 'an ass which had no tail' (*lit.* 'of which there was no tail').

گدهے کے دل اَور کان نہ تها 'the ass had no heart and ears.'

اُنکے لڑکا نہ تها 'they had no child (their's was no child).'

اُسکے سخت چوٹ لگِي هَي 'he has received (become possessed of) a severe injury.'

پِيادہ کئِي قدم نہ گيا تها کِہ ايک گهوڑي نے اُسکے لات مارِي 'the foot-traveller had not gone many steps when a horse kicked him.'

Rem. In sentences like the first three of the above, it is probable that a postposition, such as پاس or هاں (vulg. يہاں), is understood.

But in the last two the native grammarians, and all native scholars, will not allow that any word is understood; but maintain that the construction is that of the Persian, کے taking the place of the preposition به; *e.g.* بدُو=اُسکے (for به اُو). This is intelligible if the construction occurs in Urdū alone. But we are not sure that it does not occur in Hindī also; and if this be the case, it would seem more probable that کے is here an independent postposition, derived (like کو) from the Sanskrit *krite.*

319. *Subjective Genitive.*—The Subjective Genitive indicates the *subject* of the action expressed in the word on which it depends: as

موهن کا بهاگ جانا 'Mohan's running away.'

هِنّدباد نے جو سِنّدباد کِي محبّت ديکهِي 'when Hindbād perceived *Sindbād's regard* (for him).'

طبيعت کے ساتهه صناعت کا تشبُّه پَيدا کرْنا '*art's producing* a resemblance to nature.'

320. *Objective Genitive.*—The Objective Genitive denotes the *object* of the action, feeling, or notion, expressed in the word on which it depends: as

دُنْيا کِي هوَس 'lust of the world.'

خُدا کا شُکْر 'the thanksgiving of, *i.e.* to God.'

خُدا کا خَوف 'the fear of God.'

اَوروں کِي تکْلِيف 'the sorrow of others.'

اُنکو اِس بات کِي محبّت هَي 'they have *an affection for* this thing.'

ميرا ديکهْنا منْحُوس جانْتے هيں 'they consider *the seeing of me* unlucky.'

Rem. The Objective Genitive is of common occurrence with the so-called nominal verbs, *i.e.* when a substantive in the accusative is added to such verbs کرْنا, رکهْنا, etc., to complete the notion of the verb:

e.g. مَیں جو بَیل کے مارنے کِي کوشِش کرتا هُوں 'the effort which I am making to kill the ox;' کہ ایک پتھر کِي اِتنِي تعرِیف کریں 'that he should make so much praising of (should praise so much) a stone.'

321. *Partitive Genitive.*—The Genitive is used with substantives and words used substantively to indicate the whole of which a part is taken: *e.g.*

آغاز قِصّے کا 'the beginning of the story.'

پہاڑ کِي چوٹِي 'the top of the mountain.'

هِیرِي کا ٹکڑا 'a piece of diamond.'

کھیت کا آدھا 'a half of the field.'

Rem. But if the part taken is a definite *weight, measure, or quantity,* the noun denoting the whole is put in apposition: as تِین سیر دُودھ 'three seers of milk;' ایک گز کپڑا 'a yard of cloth;' ایک بیگھا زمِین 'a *bīghā* of land;' ایک بُوند پانِي 'a drop of water' (*cf. Rem.* § 301, 1).

322. With the Partitive Genitive also are construed nouns expressing the superlative. The Genitive in this case designates the whole out of which some one or something is brought conspicuously forward as its most prominent part: *e.g.*

سب طالبِعلموں کا اچّھا 'the best of all the students.'

حلقے کِي صدر 'the chief seat of the assembly.'

اُنمیں کا چھوٹے سے چھوٹا 'the least of them.'

اعلیٰ درجے کے لوگ 'people of the highest rank.'

عِلم کا اعلیٰ مرتبہ 'the highest stage of knowledge.'

Rem. If it is desired to indicate that an object is the greatest or most distinguished of its kind, the substantive is often repeated in the form of the definite genitive plural. This construction occurs chiefly in Persian and Arabic phrases: *e.g.* خُداوندِ خُدایگاں 'the lord of lords,' *i.e.* 'the supreme lord;' اميرُ الامرا 'the Amīr of Amīrs, the chief Amīr.'

323. *Explicative Genitive.*—The Explicative Genitive, or the Genitive of Definition, is closely connected in signification with the Partitive Genitive. It is used to indicate—

1) *the whole as including all the parts*, the plural کے being employed when the whole conveys *plurality of idea*, or when it is composed of several individual things or persons (masculine): as کھیت کا کھیت 'the whole field;' سب کا سب 'the whole' (of a thing); سب کے سب 'all' (without exception, of a number of objects); جھُوٹھ کا جھُوٹھ 'a lie' (altogether); (*sc.* دُم) ٹیڑھی کی ٹیڑھی 'altogether crooked, as it was before.'

2) *the relation between the material and the form*; as سونے کی گھڑی 'a watch of gold' (a gold watch); کاٹھ کا صنْدُوق 'a box of wood;' فُولاد کا قُفْل 'a lock of steel.'

In this case the Genitive has quite the force of an adjective.

3) the relation between the *species* and the *genus*, and the definition or explanation of a *general* or *universal* by a *special* or *particular*: as—

کھجُور کا درخت 'a date-tree (a tree of the date kind).'

صنْدل کی لکڑی 'sandal wood (wood of the sandal kind).'

زیرْباد کا دیس 'the country of Zerbād.'

کلِمہ مع کا 'the word (of) *ma'*.'

یہ لفْظ کُفْر کا 'this word *kufr*.'

سفر کا نام نہ لُونگا 'I will not breathe the word (of) Travel.'

In the three last examples we should rather have expected a substantive in apposition.

324. *Genitive of Kind.*—The Genitive is also put with words which denote a number, measure, or quantity, to indicate the *kind*, and the thing measured or counted: as—

خادِموں کا ایک گروہ 'a body of servants.'
آدمیوں کا ایک جہاز 'a ship-load of men.'
تِین دِن کا عرصہ 'a space of three days.'

325. *Genitive of Quality.*—The Genitive, generally with an adjective (numeral, genitive), is used to indicate a quality of, or to describe, the noun on which it is dependent: as—

بڑي تعجّب کِي بات 'a matter of great wonder.'
چھوٹے سِر کا آدمِي 'a small-headed man.'
اِس صُورت و قد کا آدمِي 'a man of this form and stature.'
دس برس کا لڑکا 'a boy of ten years.'
بِیس بِیگھے کا کھیت 'a field of twenty *bīghās.*'
چار کوس کا فاصِلہ 'a distance (intervening space) of four *kos.*'
پانچ سیر کا وزن 'two seers of, *i.e.* in weight.'

326. *Genitive of Value.*—The Genitive is also used (generally with an adjective of quantity) to indicate the *value* of a thing, and its *price*, if some word signifying *price* is expressed: *e.g.*

یِہہ کِتنے کا مال ہوگا 'what may be the value of this property?'
اِسکِي بڑي قدر کرتا هَي 'he sets a high value on this.'
اُس نے دس رُوپَے کا کپڑا خرِیدا 'he purchased cloth to the value of ten rupees.'
اِس صندُوق کِي کیا قِیمت هَي 'what is the price of this box?'

Rem. With verbs signifying *to buy* or *sell*, the price of a thing is usually expressed by the Dative, or the Locative; as وُہ گھوڑا کِتنے کو لِیا 'for how much did (you) buy that horse?' يِہہ کِتاب کِتنے میں پڑِي 'how much did this book cost?' (*cf.* §§ 334, and 355, 7.)

327. The Genitive is also used to distinguish a thing to which something belongs as its *contents*, *appurtenance*, etc.: *e.g.*

پانِي کِي صُراحِي 'a gugglet of (*i.e.* containing) water.'
دریا کا پانِي 'water of (*i.e.* contained in) the river.'
تِین دِن کِي خُوراک 'provision for three days.'

328. *Genitive after Adjectives.*—Many adjectives are commonly construed with the genitive. They are chiefly Persian and Arabic active participles, or nouns of agency, and Arabic passive participles, signifying *desirous*, *seeking*, *coveting*, *envying*, *necessitous*, *beloved*, *producing*, *causing*, *requiring* or *exacting*, *following*, *obeying* or *subject to*, *helping*, *opposing*, *hindering*, *fitness*, *capacity*, *similitude*, *guilt*, etc. Some Hindī adjectives also, and nearly all Hindī nouns of agency, are used with a genitive: *e.g.*

اپنے ابنائے جِنس کِي بِہترِي کا دِل سے خواہاں ہو 'be desirous from your heart of the well-being of your fellow-creatures.'
روزِي کا طالِب 'a seeker after subsistence.'
جو آدمِي مال کے حارِص هَین 'those men who are covetous of wealth.'
اُسکے خُون کا پِیاسا 'thirsting for (eagerly desirous of) his blood.'
مَیں مال کا بھُوکھا نہِیں 'I am not hungering for wealth.'
اُنکے حاسِد ہوجاتے هَیں 'they become envious of them.'

وُہ عِبرت کے مُحتاج هَیں 'they (stand in) need (of) warning.'

تاکہ اپنے خُداوند کا پیارا هو 'in order that you may be beloved of your Lord.'

آدمیوں کا محبُوب بن جاتا هَي 'it becomes the object of men's affection.'

اگر خواهِش کِسي اَیسے فِعل کِي مُقتضِي هو 'If desire require (is the demander of) any such action.'

خُداوندِ پاک بهي اُسکا مددگار هوتا هَي 'the Holy God also becomes his helper.'

عِلم کو اُسکا مُخالِف جانتے هَیں 'they consider knowledge the enemy thereof.'

جو امر اُسکے حُصُولِ مطلب کا مزاحِم هوتا هَي 'anything that is an obstacle to the attainment of his object.'

وُہ هتکِ عدالت کا مُجرِم نہِیں هوتا 'he does not become guilty of contempt of court.'

وُہ قتل کا مُرتکِب هوتا هَي 'he becomes guilty (commits the crime) of murder.'

Rem. A number of adjectives are idiomatically constructed with the *inflected* genitive (کے). The most common of these are: برابر 'equal,' تابِع 'obedient,' 'subject,' قابِل 'capable,' قرِیب 'near,' لائِق 'fit,' 'worthy,' مُتعلِق 'adhering to,' 'connected with,' مُشابِہ 'resembling,' مُطابِق 'conformable,' مُوافِق 'like,' موجِب 'rendering necessary,' 'cause,' etc. These adjectives being mostly used as postpositions (§ 240, 3), the same construction has apparently been preserved when they are used as regular adjectives: *e.g.* جب وُہ شہر کے قرِیب پہُنچے 'when they arrived near the city;' چاهِیئے کِہ غُصہ عقل کے تابِع رهے 'anger should be under the control (a follower) of Reason;' اَور تِین

چَوتهائِي نہ کہنے کے قابِل هَي 'and three-fourths (of it) is unfit to be told.'

329. A genitive may be governed by two or more connected nouns, in which case, if these denote *living beings*, and are of different genders, the genitive is usually put in the masculine plural; but if the nouns denote *things* or *ideas*, it generally agrees with the nearest noun: *e.g.*

کلّوکے ما باپ 'Kallū's mother and father.'

اُس شخص کے زن و فرزند 'that person's wife and child (or children).'

اصل و نفع اُسکا 'his capital and profit.'

اُس اخبار کِي کَيفِيَّت اَور دستور اَور طرزِ بیان 'the character, custom, and style of language, of that newspaper.'

Rem. The masculine is occasionally used: *e.g.* جِسکے جاه و حشم کا بیان 'a description of whose pomp and state.' This is especially the case if the nearest noun be one of those the gender of which is not settled: *e.g.* فِکر, جان, etc. (see § 28, 8, *Rem. c*): as تُمهاری جان و مال کو 'your life and property.'

330. If an Urdū genitive is governed by a Persian genitive phrase, one noun of which is masculine and the other feminine, the genitive usually takes the masculine affix: *e.g.*

اپنے ابنائے جِنس کِي بِہتري 'the bettering of his fellow-creatures.'

هماري طرزِ بیان سے 'from the style of our discourse.'

توجّه کا ادائے شُکر 'the repaying of thanks for kindly notice.'

331. A genitive that is governed by a predicative substantive connected with a *singular* (masculine) subject in

the *plural* form, is invariably put in the plural, whether its governing noun admits of a plural form or not: *e.g.*

تم دِهلي کے رهنے والے هو 'you are (=thou art) an inhabitant of Dehlī.'

تم فُلانے صاحِب کے نوکر هو 'you are (=thou art) the servant of such-and-such a gentleman.'

332. If the governing noun denote a person of rank or position who is spoken of, the genitive may be put in the plural as a mark of respect: as جو بادشاه اُس مُلک کے تهے 'who was the king of that country' (*cf.* § 288).

IV. THE DATIVE.

333. The Dative denotes in general that what is asserted by the predicate is done, or holds good *for*, and *in reference to* a certain person or thing. This is indicated by the postposition کو, employed in forming the case, and which signifies originally *for the sake of, on account of, in reference to*: *e.g.*

وُه شیر اُن بیچاروں کو دِکهائِي دیتا تها 'the lion used to appear to those unfortunates.'

جِس بات کا سُننا سُننے والے کو بُرا لگے 'anything the hearing whereof would prove disagreeable to the hearer.'

Rem. In the older literature the place of the Dative postposition is frequently supplied by the postposition تئِیں, with a genitive: *e.g.* کُتّے کے تئِیں دو 'give (it) to the dog.' But the use of this postposition is now almost exclusively confined to the Reflexive Pronoun; as اپنے تئِیں 'to himself,' etc.

334. As the remote object in reference to which an

action takes place, the Dative has the signification of *for*, *for the sake of*, *for the purpose of*, *in return* or *exchange for*, and hence its use with verbs of *selling* and *buying*: *e.g.*

هم تو تیرِي جان کو رو پیٹ کر تجھ سے هاتھ دهو بَیٹھے تھے 'as for us, after weeping and lamenting for your life, we had settled down, giving you up in despair (*lit.* having washed our hands of you).'

میرِي تمام عُمْر کو کافِي هَي 'it is sufficient for my whole lifetime.'

شہْزادہ سَیر کو نِکْلے 'the prince came out for a stroll.'

مَیں مظْلُوم هُوں فرْیاد کو آیا هُوں 'I am the victim of oppression, I am come to complain.'

هاتھ دهونے کو پانِي لاوْ 'bring water to wash the hands.'

اپْنے نزْدِیک میرِي اُترْنے کو مکان دو 'give (me) a house near you for me to put up in' (*lit.* 'to alight').

میں نے دو سَو رُوپَیِ کو اپْنا گھوڑا بیچا 'I sold my horse for two hundred rupees.'

یِہہ کِتاب کِتْنے کو دوگے 'what will you give this book for?'

Rem. The Dative of *motive* or *purpose* (مفْعُول لَہٗ *the object on account of which* anything is done) is generally a verbal noun (*e.g. sair, faryād, utarnā, dhonā*, in the above examples), and may always be rendered in English by the gerund with *to*. The force of the same Dative is very commonly expressed by one of the postpositions خاطِر, واسْطے, لِیئے, etc., and the genitive of a verbal noun: as مرْدوں کو خُدانے کمانے کے لِیئے بنایا هَي 'God has made men to earn (their livelihood);' عالِم هونے کے واسْطے پڑهْتے هَیں 'they study (for) to become learned.' In such sentences the genitive of the verbal noun may be resolved into a clause consisting of کِ or تاکِ and a finite form of the verb: as وي اِس واسْطے پڑهْتے هَیں کِ عالِم هوں 'they study in order that they may become learned.'

335. The Dative is used after verbs implying *motion*: as

خواجہ گھر کو چلا 'the merchant went home (to his house).'

وہ بازار کو گیا 'he went to the bazar.'

کِہ شیر کو رنج نہ پہنچے '(take care) that no annoyance reach the lion.'

336. The Dative is used idiomatically with the verb مِلنا 'to meet, or come in contact with,' to convey the idea of *acquiring*, *finding*: as

اِس لڑکے کو کچھ نہیں مِلا 'this boy has got nothing.'

اُسکو رستہ نہ مِلا 'he did not find a road or way.'

337. The Dative is used after some adjectives signifying *necessary*, *fit*, *agreeable*, and their opposites, when they are employed as predicative nouns: *e.g.*

یِہہ مکان ہمکو درکار هَي 'this house is needed by (in requisition for) us.'

یِہہ بات مُجھکو پسند نہیں 'I do not approve of this matter,' *lit.* 'this matter is not agreeable to me.'

338. The phrases چاهِیئے, مُناسِب هَي, لازِم هَي, etc. signifying *it is necessary*, *proper*, or *right*, govern the Dative: *e.g.*

آدمِي کو چاهِیئے کِہ نیکِي میں سعِي کري 'a man should exert (himself) in doing good,' *lit.* 'it is necessary for a man that he,' etc.

اُسکو لازِم هَي کِہ ایک کِي بات دُوسري سے نہ کہے 'it is necessary for him (it behoves him) that he mention not the words of one person to another.'

339. With the same verbs, and also with the verbs هَي and پڑنا when these imply *intention*, *necessity*, or *constraint*, the Dative is regularly employed before the gerund, the

gerundive, and the perfect participle used as a verbal noun, to denote the subject (*cf.* §§ 415, 426, and 439): as

هم اخبار نویسوں کو سوچنا چاهیئے 'we newspaper-writers should consider,' *lit.* 'for us newspaper-writers considering is necessary or right.'

تم کو ادب سیکھا (= سیکھنا) چاهیئے 'you should learn manners.'

اب همکو ذرہ فکر کرني چاهیئے 'we ought now to consider a bit.'

آیسي مفید باتیں جلد کهني مناسب هیں 'it is right (for you) to mention such beneficial matters without delay.'

اگر همکو گهڑي بناني هي 'if we have to make a watch.'

هم کو اِسي زباں سے اپني تمام ضرورتیں رفع کرني هیں 'we have to provide against all our necessities with this same language.'

سرکار کو اِس میں ضرور دست اندازي کرني پڑیگي 'the government will certainly have (be constrained) to interfere in this matter.'

340. The Dative of the possessor, with هي, تها, هونا, and other kindred verbs, and occasionally with the verb آنا 'to come,' expresses the idea of possession; but the verbs هونا and آنا, with the Dative, more commonly imply *entering into and influencing*: *e.g.*

حضور کو شغل بہت سے هیں 'your Honour has many occupations (many things to occupy you).'

اُس وقت همکو جو گهبراهت اور بے قراري تهي 'the alarm and anxiety which we had (we suffered) at that moment.'

اور جو عقل و شعور اُسے بخوبي نہ هو 'and if he have not sense and understanding in due degree.'

بادشاه کو کچھ تسلّي هوئي 'the king derived some consolation (therefrom).'

شیر کو غیرت آئي 'jealousy possessed the lion.'

مجھکو یقین آیا 'I derived assurance (I became certain).'

بادشاه کو اُنکے حال پر رحم آیا 'pity for their condition possessed the king.'

Rem. Possession may also be signified by the postposition پاس and the *genitive* of the possessor, instead of the Dative: as اُس کے پاس ایک کتا هَي 'he has a dog (there is a dog in his possession);' and, less commonly, by the verb رکھنا 'to keep,' 'have,' with the Accusative of the thing possessed; as کوئي فرزند نہ رکھتا تھا 'he had no child.'

341. The Dative is used to express *time* indefinitely: as

رات کو ڈاکا آیا 'a band of robbers came at night.'

صُبح کو جب وُہ اُٹھا 'in the morning, when he rose.'

Rem. The Dative postposition is often omitted, but in such cases the noun always takes the inflected form, if it is capable of inflection: *e.g.*

صُبح اُٹھتے هِی سوار هوا 'in the morning, as soon as he rose, he mounted (his horse).'

وُہ گھر گیا هَي 'he has gone home.'

وُہ روٹي کھانے گیا هَي 'he has gone to eat his food.

v. The Accusative.

342. The Accusative, in Hindūstānī, occurs only as the objective complement of a transitive verb; as موهن کِتاب پڑھتا هَي 'Mohan is reading a book;' کلّو بدّھو کو مارتا هَي 'Kallū is beating Buddhū.'

Rem. What is predicated of the subject as an action, may be predicated of the object as suffering, so that this takes the place of the subject, and the same verb is predicated of it in the passive. This, as we have already shown (§ 185, 191, *et seq.*), is the usual construction in Urdū when the tenses employed are those formed with the past participle of simple transitive verbs (which is by its nature a *passive* participle), the agent (whether known or not) being generally placed at the head of the sentence in the Agent case: as کُتّے نے روٹي کھائِي 'by the dog the bread was eaten' (= 'the dog ate the bread'); کِسِي نے روٹي کھائِي 'the bread was eaten by some one.' It is important, however, to bear in mind that at the present day this construction is viewed by those who employ it not as *passive*, but *active*, and that when the agent is not known, or it is not desired to mention it, the common passive form (§ 197) is used even in the tenses formed with the passive participle: *e.g.* كوئِي آدمِي مارا گيا هَي 'a man has been killed.'

343. Whether a verb is transitive depends on its signification, and on the circumstance whether an object is at the same time conceived as immediately acted on.

344. Many Urdū verbs have fundamentally a distinct notion from those by which they are commonly rendered in English, and are therefore differently constructed: as مَيں اُس سے اپني کِتاب مانگتا هُوں 'I am asking him for my book' (properly, 'I am wanting my book from him'); وُہ مُجھ سے سبب پُوچھتا هَي 'he is asking me for the reason' (properly, 'he is asking the reason from me'); گھڑي ميں پاني بھرو 'fill water in the pot' ('pour water into the pot till it is full,' and not 'fill the pot with water'); اُسکي آنکھوں ميں آنسو بھري 'tears filled (gathered to the full) in her eyes' (not, as translators render it, 'her eyes filled with tears').

345. Not a few verbs have different significations, so that in one they are transitive and govern the accusative,

while in another they are differently constructed; as وُہ اپنا أسکا هاتھ کھُجلاتا هَي 'he is scratching his hand;' هاتھ کھُجلاتا هي 'his hand itches;' اُس نے مُجھے پُکارا 'he called me;' وُہ پُکارا 'he called out.'

Rem. It is particularly to be observed that intransitive verbs of motion, when compounded with the conjunctive participle of certain transitive verbs, as لينا 'to take,' دينا 'to give,' چھوڑنا 'to leave,' acquire a transitive signification, and are constructed with the Accusative: *e.g.* اُسکو ميري پاس لاؤ 'bring him to me;' وُہ ميري مکان پر يہہ کِتاب دي گيا 'he left (gave) this book at my house on his way;' لڑکے کو يہاں چھوڑ جاؤ 'leave the boy behind here.' This is especially the case when the first member of the compound is the conjunctive participle of the verb لينا (*cf.* § 215 and *Rem.*).

346. The Accusative (مفعُول بِہ) has two forms in Urdū; namely, that of the *Nominative*, and that of the *Dative*. Respecting the employment of one or other of these forms the following general rules may be laid down:

1) If the verb is one which requires a single object (Accusative) alone, the Accusative generally takes the nominative form, so long as there is no possibility of mistaking the object for the subject: *e.g.*

بکري پاني پيتي هَي 'the goat is drinking water.'

سانپ بينگ کهاتا هي 'a snake is devouring a frog.'

ميرا ماجرا سُنو 'hear my history.'

تُمهارِي مُلاقات کِي آرزو رکھتا تها 'I entertained the hope of meeting you.'

جلّادوں نے وونهِيں اُسکا هاتھ پکڑلِيا 'the executioners that instant seized his hand.'

Such is the usual form of the Accusative when the object is inanimate, and the subject either animate or inanimate, and its invariable form when the object is the predicative noun of the verb, as in the so-called Nominal Compounds, *e.g.* اِشْتِیاق کَرْنا 'to form the desire,' اِعْتِماد رَکْھنا 'to place confidence.'

2) If, however, the subject and object denote animate things, the object (Accusative) is generally (in the case of rational beings *invariably*) distinguished by the addition to it of the postposition کو, to obviate the possibility of mistake: as

بھیڑیے نے تُرت بھیڑ کو پھاڑ ڈالا 'the wolf quickly tore the sheep to pieces.'

اگر تُو اِس طرح بَیل کو مار سکے 'if you can kill the ox in such a way.'

بُدّھو کو کلّو مارْتا ھَي 'Kallū is beating Buddhū.'

3) If for any reason it is desired to bring the object conspicuously forward, the Accusative is generally put in the Dative form. This usually takes place when the object has been previously mentioned, and occurs again in connection with a demonstrative pronoun, or other defining word or phrase, or when some particular object is specified, or when two objects are contrasted. But much scope is allowed to individual judgment in this matter: *e.g.*

پھر اُس طبق اَور لگن کو غُلام پِنْجْري کے نزْدِیک لے گئے 'after this the slaves took that dish and platter near the cage.'

جب سانْپ کے پاس پہُنْچے (اُس) زیور کو اُسْکے نزْدِیک گِرا دي 'when you come up to the snake, throw down the ornament near it.'

لومْري نے ایک گُوا کھود کر مُنْہہ کو اسْکے چھپا دِیا تھا 'the fox, having dug a hole, had concealed the mouth thereof.'

ھماري صاحِب شیر کو مارینگے 'our master will kill the tiger.'

347. *Cognate Accusative.*—Intransitive as well as transitive verbs may be constructed with an Accusative of a substantive derived from the same root, or from another root of corresponding signification (مفعُول مُطْلق *the absolute object*). This Accusative can never take the Dative form, and it is generally used in connection with an attributive or an adjective of quantity: *e.g.*

مَیں نے اُسکو بڑي مار ماري 'I gave (*lit.* beat) him a good beating.'

آدمِیوں کِي سِي چال چلو 'conduct (yourself) after the manner of men' (*lit.* 'walk a walking like men's').

هم بھِي سَیکڑوں لڑاياں لڑي 'we also have fought hundreds of fights.'

اِتنِي لاف گزاف بکا 'he prated so much boastful nonsense.'

امِیر کِي بَیٹھک بَیٹھا 'he sat like a gentleman' (*lit.* 'he sat the sitting of a gentleman').

348. *Double Accusative.*—Many verbs (chiefly causatives derived from transitive verbs) take *two objective complements in the Accusative*, generally either both of the person, or one of the person and the other of the thing. In such cases the personal object more commonly precedes the other, and is defined by the postposition کو, the second Accusative being put in the Nominative form: *e.g.*

وُہ اپنِي دفعه کو حِساب پڑھاتا تھا 'he was teaching his class Arithmetic.'

اُسے یِہ کپڑا پہناؤ 'put this dress on him.'

میري خاوِند کو بندِت خانے سے مخلصِي دِلْواتا 'he would have got my lord (husband) released from prison.'

خُدا کے بندوں کو کُتّے کا جھوٹا کِھلانا کِس مذھب میں روَا هي 'in what religion is it permitted to make God's servants eat a dog's leavings.'

Rem. The Nom. form of the Accusative may, under certain circumstances, stand first: as وُہ تَھیلِي اُسْکو دِکھَلائِي 'I showed him that bag' (*cf.* § 271); and occasionally both Accusatives may be defined by کو: as اُس نے اپْنے بھائِي کے حِصّے کو اُسْکِي بیٹي کو دِیا 'he gave his brother's portion to his (the brother's) daughter;' but such examples are of rare occurrence, and must not be taken as a rule: even in this instance it would be perfectly correct to say اپْنے بھائِي کا حِصّہ. In examples like the following, which are cited by Forbes's followers to show that both objects may be defined by کو, the case of the second noun is not the *Accusative* (مفْعُول بِہ), but the *Dative of purpose* (مفْعُول لَہُ): مَیں نے دُوسْرِي کو اُسْکے بُلانے کو رُخْصت کِیا 'I despatched the other to call him;' بادْشاھْزادي کو باغ کِي سَیر کو لیگئے 'they took the prince out to stroll in the garden;' and even in such cases the recurrence of کو is now generally avoided by the use of one of the postpositions لِیئے, واسْطے, etc., with the genitive, in place of the dative: as باغ کِي سَیر کے لِیئے.

349. *Factitive Accusative.*—Verbs signifying *to make*, *appoint*, *call*, *name*, and the like, and those verbs which signify an act that takes place in the mind (افْعالِ قلْب *verbs of the heart*, as the native grammarians term them), such as پانا 'to find,' جانْنا 'to think or deem,' سمجھْنا 'to think or imagine,' and the like, take, besides the object (Accusative) itself, the Accusative of a substantive or adjective which constitutes a *predicate of the object*, and serves to complete the notion of the verb. In such cases the object (or first Accusative) is frequently defined by the postposition کو, and thus the concord between it and the predicative noun (the second Accusative), if it be an adjective or participle, is disturbed, the predicative adjective remaining in the uninflected form of the singular, even

though the object (Acc.) with which it is connected be plural; the verb also (if the tense be one composed of the passive participle) being constructed impersonally (see § 338): as

کِسِي بدِي کو نیکی کا وسِیله کرنا 'to make an evil the means of good.'

اُسے اَیسا تُحفه بنایا هَي 'he has made it such a curiosity.'

مَیں نے اُسکو بهت غریب پایا 'I found him very meek.'

مَیں تُجهے مغمُوم دیکهتا هُوں 'I perceive you (to be) sad.

لازِم هَي کِہ اُس شخص کو بنائے کار کهي 'it is proper that he call that person the builder of the work.'

جِسکو کِسِي مذهب کا عالِم سُنا 'any one whom I heard of (as) a doctor of religion.'

وُه اِس عادت کوچالاکِي جانتے هَیں 'they deem this practice cleverness.'

اِس عَورت کو چنگا کر سکتا هَي 'he can make this woman well.'

اُس نے سب گاڑیوں کو کهڑا کِیا 'he made all the carts stationary.'

350. But both Accusatives may have the nominative form, in which case, if the second is an adjective or participle that inflects, it agrees in gender and number with the first (the object):[1] as

[1] It is noteworthy that Forbes's remarks on this point, although too briefly put, are perfectly sound; and yet succeeding grammarians, who generally follow his teaching without question, have in this instance thought proper to depart from it:—"When adjectives ending in ā are separated from their substantives, they not unfrequently become petrified as it were by being drawn towards a verb, and thus forming with it a sort of compound, lose their capability of change," is the teaching of Professor Monier Williams (*Hindūstānī Grammar*, p. 93).—"Adjectives are often combined with verbs; if the verb is neuter they agree with the nominative: but if active, they remain in the masculine singular," is Mr. Dowson's rule (*Urdū Grammar*, p. 141). Not only are these rules wrong as regards the conception of the adjective spoken of, and its relation to the verb and the object, but they serve clearly to show that both these grammarians have failed to perceive that it is the use of the particle کو with the object that disturbs the concord between this and the predicative adjective.

اُسْکا نُقْصان اَپْنا نُقْصان سَمْجھو 'consider his harm your (own) harm.'

اَپْنا مُنْہ تُونے کالا کِیا 'you have made your face black.'

گاڑِي کھڑِي کر 'stop the cart.'

وُہ مُشْکِل کِسُوکِي اَٹْکِي نہِیں رکْھتا 'he keeps no one's difficulties unremoved.'

وُہ اَپْنِي حاجت پُورِي کرْتا هَي 'he satisfies (makes complete) his wants.'

دُنْیا کِي چِیزیں حاجت سے زِیادہ اِکٹھِي نہ کرو 'do not accumulate (*lit.* make collected, or in one place) more than (is) necessary of this world's things.'

شہْرکے باهر تنْبُو اَور قنات اَور بے چوبے اَور سراپرْدِي اَور کَنْدَلے کھڑِي کرْواکر 'having erected (various kinds of small and large, poled and pole-less) tents outside the city.'

Rem. a. It will be perceived from the above examples that it is the use of the Dative form of the Accusative that disturbs the concord between the object and the predicative adjective or participle. Similarly the concord between an adjective or participle and its substantive is always broken when the substantive is in the Dative form of the Accusative, but in no other case. Of the pronominal Accusatives, both bein g originally Dative forms, the second (مُجھے, تُجھے, اُسے, etc.) would likewise appear to affect the concord similarly to the first (especially if it be the object of a *fe'le kalb*): *e.g.* مُجھے پہُنْچا جان 'consider me (the princess) arrived.' But we also find اُسے کڑِي کرو 'make it (چا the tea) strong,' although the correctness of this seems questionable.

Rem. b. Most of the so-called Nominal verbs come under the class noticed above, and hence the Accusative governed by them is commonly put in the Dative form, and the verb in the Past Tenses (if transitive) is constructed impersonally.

351. In the passive of the verbs of the last class the

direct object becomes the subject, the indirect object remaining in the Dative form of the Accusative: *e.g.*

اگر دونوں کو مُقابله کِیا جاوي 'if the two be compared' (*lit.* 'if comparison be made in reference to the two').

مُناسِب هَي کِہ اُسکو بنائے کار کہا جاوي 'it is right that he be called the builder of the work' (*lit.* 'that builder of the work be said in reference to him').

کِہ مُجھکو تا مُدّتِ اپیل سزا سے محفُوظ رکھا جاوي 'that I be secured from punishment pending the time of appeal.'

VI. THE ABLATIVE.

352. The Ablative postposition سے designates:

1) Departure from a *place*, or from *beside a person*; as دِهلِي سے چلکر 'starting from Dehlī;' کلکتہ سے پیشاور تک تارِ برقِي جارِي هَي 'the telegraph (electric) wire is working from Calcutta to Peshāwar;' وُہ میري سامھنے سے گیا 'he departed from my presence;' آپ همسے اُنکي طرف مُلتفِت هُوئے 'your Honour (you) turned from us to them.' Hence it is used:

a) With verbs (participles, verbal adjectives) that convey the idea of *separation*, *departure*, *being free*, *removing*, *liberating*, *guarding*, *concealing*, *flight*, *caution*, *abstinence*, *avoidance*, *holding oneself aloof* from a person or thing, *frightening away*, *encountering*, *self-defence*, *forbidding*, *hindering*, *depriving*, and the like; and, in general, to express the doing of something *towards* or *in respect to* another; as

وُہ مُجھ سے جُدا هوگیا 'he separated (himself) from me.'

جب هم شهر سے باهِر نِکلے 'when we came out from the city.'

اُس نے میري هاتھ سے پیاله لِیا 'he took the cup from my hand.'

جب وُہ اِس کلام سے فارِغ هوا 'when he finished (ceased from) this discourse.'

کہ آپ قُصُور سے پاک هو جاوي 'in order that he himself should be clear of fault.'

مُجھکو اِس سزا سے محفُوظ رکھِیے 'be pleased to save me from this punishment.'

دوستوں سے بھید چِھپانا دُرست نہیں 'it is not right to keep a secret from friends.'

اُس سے کوئي بات مخفي نہیں رهتي 'nothing remains hidden from him.'

اُنکي خطاؤں سے اِغماض کرنا 'to veil the eyes from (connive at) their faults.'

بُرا کہنے سے اِحتِراض کِیا 'I refrained from evil-speaking.'

هم دونوں وهاں سے بھاگے 'both of us fled from there.'

اِس کام سے پرهیز کرنا مُناسِب هَي 'it is right to abstain from this matter.'

اَیسے شخص سے دُور رهنا لازِم هَي 'it is proper to hold oneself aloof from such a person.'

اَیسِي چِیزوں سے خبردار هونا 'to be on one's guard against such things.'

مَیں اُس سے خُوب لڑا 'I fought with him well.'

جو کوئي اُسکي خواهِش پُوري هونے سے مانِع هوتا هَي 'any one who prevents his desire from being fulfilled.'

چاهِیئے کہ اُنسے اَیسا برتاؤ کري 'he should so deal with them.'

مَیں تجھ سے اَیسا سلُوک کرُونگا 'I will treat you so well (will pursue such a course of conduct towards you).'

مُجھے حِصّے بخري سے کیا کام هَي 'what concern have I with share and portion?'

b) with verbs which signify *revealing*, *knowing*, *informing*, *asking*, and the like; for in these verbs is implied the idea of the removal of a covering, real or figurative: as

یہہ اُسکي بات سے ظاهر هوتا هَي 'it is revealed by (is evident from) his words.'

اِس احوال سے همیں بهي مُطلِع کرو 'acquaint us also with the circumstance.'

اِس بات سے کوئي واقف نہ تها 'no one was cognizant of this matter.'

نہ اُنکو خُدا پرستِي سے کُچهہ خبر 'nor had he any knowledge of the worship of God.'

اِن باتوں سے آگاہ هوکر 'having become acquainted with these matters.'

اُس نے مُجهہ سے کہا 'he said to (or told) me.'

پادشاہ نے وزِیر سے پُوچها 'the king asked the wazīr.'

مَیں حُضُور سے بیان کرُونگا 'I will explain (it) to your honour.'

آپ سے کُچهہ عرض کرنا هَي 'I have something to say (represent) to you.'

Rem. The verbs کہنا and بولنا are also connected with the dative, the latter commonly.

c). With verbs signifying, *giving up in despair*, *abandoning*, *neglecting*, *denying*, *the ability to dispense with a thing*, *disgust*, *satiety*, and other such verbs as imply the notion of *turning away*: as

زِندگِي سے مايُوس هوکر 'having despaired of life.'

اپنِي جان سے هاتهہ دهوکر 'having relinquished hope (washed his hands) of his life.'

اُسکے خُون سے درگذر 'abandon (the idea of shedding) his blood.'

زمانے کِي سختي سے کیُوں غافِل هو 'why are you unmindful of the wrong-doing of the world?'

وي اِس حُکم سے مُنکِر هو جائينگے 'they will refuse to obey (will rebel against) this decree.'

دُنيا کے مال سے مَيں غني تها 'I was able to dispense with worldly wealth.'

اُس سے گهِن کهاکر 'being disgusted with it.'

اَيسِي جلدِي مُجه سے سير هُوئے 'are you so soon weary of me?'

دُنيا کے مال سے نفرت کرنا 'to be averse to worldly wealth.'

d) With verbs signifying *to surpass one*: as

وهاں کے سب سَوداگروں سے سبقت لے گيا 'he surpassed all the merchants of that place.'

Rem. But the Locative is sometimes used: *e.g.* باپ پر بهِي سبقت لے گيا 'he even surpassed his father.'

e) With verbs signifying *coming in contact*, *meeting* and *uniting*, or *connecting*: as

اپنے بدن سے باندهه رکها 'I tied it to my body.'

گهوڑا ميخ سے بندها هُوا تها 'the horse was tied to a peg.'

وُه دماغ سے تعلّق رکهتے هَيں 'they are connected with the brain.'

پتهر سے ٹکر کهاکر 'having knocked against (come in contact with) a stone.'

مَيں اُس سے مِلنے کو يہاں تک آيا 'I came as far as this for the purpose of meeting him.'

کل اُس سے مُلاقات کرُونگا 'I will see (meet) him to-morrow.'

بُقراط نے ايک زبان دراز عَورت سے شادِي کِي 'Socrates married a shrew' (*lit.* 'a long-tongued woman').

2) The *point of time* at which an act or state has *commenced*: *e.g.*

صُبح سے شام تک 'from morn to eve.'

چھٹپن سے اُسکو یہی شوق ہَی 'from childhood he has had this same taste.'

آج کی تارِیخ سے مَوقُوف کرو 'discontinue (it) from this date.'

Similarly, when an expired portion of time is spoken of, it is used to signify *for such-and-such a time*: as

وُہ تِین دِن سے غَیر حاضِر ہَی 'he has been absent for three days.'

ایک مُدّت سے مُجھکو شَوق ہَی 'for some time past I have felt an inclination.'

3) The *origin* and *source* of a thing, and *the reason why* a thing is done: as

وُہ میری حرکت سے حَیران ہُوا 'he was perplexed by my action' ('his perplexity proceeding from, or being caused by, it').

اپنے کہنے سے بہت خجِل اَور نادِم ہُوا 'he became much ashamed in consequence of what he said.'

اِنسان کی زِندگی کھانے پِینے سے ہَی 'Man's life lasts through eating and drinking.'

وُہ ہم سے خُوش ہَی 'he is pleased with us.'

فساد سے جو ضرر پَیدا ہو 'the harm which springs from disorder.'

یہاں سے معلُوم ہوتا ہَی 'hence it is perceived.'

اُنسے کِینہ کرنے لگتے ہَیں 'they begin to bear ill-will towards them.'

راگ سے محظُوظ ہوکر 'having recreated himself with music.'

زمانے کے اِنقلاب سے گھبراکر 'disturbed by the vicissitudes of fortune.'

آپ کے خَوف سے روتا هَي 'he is weeping through fear of you.'

اُنکے جارِي کرنے سے یِہي همارِي غرض هَي 'this alone is our real motive in issuing them.'

4) The relation between the act and the *instrument* with which, or the *means* by which, it is performed: as—

کِسِي اَور کُنجِي سے بھِي نہ کھُلتا 'nor would it open with any other key.'

اپنِي آنکھ سے دیکھِیے 'see with your own eyes.'

کِہ اُنکے وسِیلے سے کِشتکارِي کے آلات بنائے 'that by their means he might make agricultural implements.'

گھڑي کو پاني سے بھرو 'fill the pot with water' (whereas گھڑي میں پاني بھرو implies 'pour water *into* the pot till it becomes full').

When the noun in the Ablative denotes a *person*, and the verb is *neuter* or *causative*, the instrument passes into the *agent*: as

مُجھ سے قُصور هُوا هَي 'I have committed a fault' ('a fault has proceeded from me').

رات کو مُجھ سے کُچھ تدبِیر نہ هو سکِي 'at night-time I was unable to make any arrangement.'

مَولوِي صاحِب سے اپنِي لڑکے کو عربِي پڑھاتا هُوں 'I am having my boy taught Arabic by the Maulavī.'

Rem. In Hindī سے in connection with *passive* verbs also designates the agent of an act; as راون رام سے مارا گیا 'Rāvan was killed by Rām: but this construction is not common in Urdū.

5) It is used with verbs signifying *to barter or exchange*, to indicate that with which exchange is made: as اپنی جنس سے اُس مُلک کی اجناس بدلیں 'I exchanged my goods for articles pertaining to that country' (*lit.* 'with my goods I exchanged articles pertaining to that country').

6) The *mode* or *manner* of an action: as

غور سے مُلاحظہ فرمایے 'be pleased to observe (them) with attention (attentively).'

اِنکِسار سے پیش آتا ھَے 'he conducts himself with humility.'

اِفراط سے پَیدا ہوتا ھَے 'it is produced in great abundance.'

7) The *quality* of a person or thing, in which case it is generally connected with an adjective: as

بدن سے ننگا 'naked of body (naked-bodied).'

ھاتھ پاؤں سے دُرُست 'with sound legs' ('sound as regards the legs').

لین دین سے ہوشیار 'sharp (experienced) in business transactions.'

Rem. The Locative also may be used to indicate a quality: as جِسم میں بڑِی 'big in body (big-bodied);' حرکت میں جلد 'nimble in motion, quick of movement.'

8) The *distance* from, or *proximity to*, a person, place, or thing, and *priority* in point of *time*, after words denoting *distance* or *priority*: as

یہاں سے بہت دُور ھَے 'it is far from this place.'

وھاں سے نزدِیک ایک شیر تھا 'there was a tiger not far from there.'

عقل سے بعِید ھَے 'it is far from (diametrically opposed to) reason.'

اِعْتِدال کے مرتبے سے آگے بڑھ جانا 'to pass beyond the stage (bounds) of moderation.'

شُرُوع کرنے سے پہلے 'before, or previous to, beginning.'

اِس (زمانے) سے پہلے or آگے 'previous to this time.'

Similarly دروازي سے اندر گیا 'he went in through the door;' دروازي سے باهِر نِکلا 'he came out through the door.'

9) The *difference* between two persons or things that are compared with each other: as

کہنے سے اور کرنے سے بڑا فرق هَي 'there is a great difference between saying and doing.'

اِس سے اُس سے کیا مُشابهت هَي 'what resemblance is there between this and that?' ('none whatever; they are quite different.')

Hence the use of the Ablative in forming comparatives and superlatives.

Rem. The Locative may also be used to express the difference between two persons or things: *e.g.* کہنے میں اور کرنے میں بڑا فرق هَي; and similarly, it may be used to form comparatives and superlatives.

10) The relation which subsists between the *part* and the *whole*, the *species* and the *genus*, the *family* or *race* and a *member* thereof: as

هماري گروه سے تُم نہیں هو 'you are not of our body.'

یِہ شخص انگریزوں سے هَي 'this person is an Englishman (one of the English people).'

Rem. The compound postposition میں سے is also commonly employed to express the same relation: as ماں اُسکي عُلمائے دِینِ زردُشت کے خاندان میں سے تھي 'his mother came of the stock of the doctors of the religion of Zoroaster.' Similarly, with the Locative postposition alone: ایک حکیم لقمان کي اولاد میں (موجود) تھا 'a sage of the family of Lŏḳmān was present.'

11) The definition or explanation of a *general* or *universal* by a *special* or *particular*: as

اُنکو خُدانے سب طرح کي فراغت دِي هَي رُوپَي سے پَیسے سے 'God has given him ease in every way,'—*e.g.* wealth, money, etc.

وُہ کِس چیز سے فخر کرتے هَیں زور سے یا شجاعت سے یا دِلیري سے 'in respect of what thing do they pride themselves,—strength, courage, bravery?

Rem. The Locative is often similarly used: *e.g.* تُم کِس چیز میں کم هو زور میں یا زر میں 'in respect of what thing are you wanting—power, money?'

12) *Companionship* or *connection*, being equivalent to the postposition ساتھ with a genitive: as

روٹي سالن سے کھائي مَیں نے 'I ate bread with curry.'

تُم بڑي سامان سے آئے 'you are come with much baggage.'

همارِي بلا سے '(that) is connected with (concerns) my destiny.'

Rem. a. سے is sometimes used in the sense of پر or بعد: as اِس سال کے گذرنے سے 'from (upon, after) the passing of this year (when this year has passed).'

Rem. b. The Ablative postposition, like that of the Dative, is frequently not expressed, especially in idiomatic phrases: *e.g.* اِس طرح 'in this way,' سب طرح 'in every way,' گھر گھر 'from house to house,' هاتھوں هاتھ 'from hand to hand,' نہ آنکھوں دیکھا نہ کانوں سُنا 'neither seen with the eyes, nor heard with the ears;' and similarly after many nouns which are used as adverbial postpositions (*cf.* § 236 *et seq.*).

353. The postposition سے is often combined with the Locative postpositions پر, میں, which then have the force of substantives: as

گھر میں سے باھر نِکلا 'he came out from the inside of the house (he came out of the house).'

گھر میں سے پُکارا 'he called out from inside the house.'

اِنسان کي سب صِفات میں سے سخاوت اشرف اور عُمدہ هَي 'from the midst of (from among, of) all human qualities, generosity is the noblest and the best' (*cf.* § 350, 10, *Rem.*).

وُہ کوٹھے پر سے گِر پڑا 'he fell from (fell off) the top of the house.'

Similarly باھِر سے 'from the outside,' 'from without;' سامھنے سے 'from the front,' 'from before.'

VII. The Locative.

354. The Locative postpositions are میں and پر, which denote, as a rule, essentially distinct relations and ideas, and are therefore better noticed separately.

355. میں shows, in general, that one thing is actually in the midst of another, entirely surrounded by it. Hence—

1) It indicates *rest in a place* or *during a time*, and *motion into a place*: as گھر میں 'in the house;' اِسي سال میں 'in this same year;' وُہ شہر میں گیا 'he went into the city;' وي چھتے میں واپس آتِي هَیں 'they (the bees) return to the hive.' This signification is then transferred to the relation subsisting between any two things, the one of which is regarded as the place in which the other is, or happens, or into which it goes or is put: as

جوانِي کے عالم میں 'in the season of youth.'

اِتنے میں 'in the mean time.'

تھوڑِي دیر میں 'in a little while.'

مشرِقي جانِب میں 'in an easterly direction.'

اُنکِي سِیرت میں کیسِي نرمِي هَي 'what gentleness there is in their disposition!'

وُہ هوش میں آیا 'he came to (recovered) his senses.'

اُسکو پانِي میں مِلاو 'mix it in water' (or, according to our idiom, 'with water').

کِ نجاست وغَیرہ میں آلودہ نہ هوں 'that they will not become polluted (by being mixed up) in filth,' etc.

تُو خُداکے رستے میں خزانہ لٹایا 'you lavished treasure in the path of (for the sake of) God.'

مکّارِي وغَیرہ میں مُبتلا هو جاتے هَیں 'they become entangled in (fall into) deceit,' etc.

اپنے کام میں مشغُول (or مصرُوف) هَیں 'they are occupied in (discharging) their duties.'

کہ اپنے آقا کِي نیکنامِي میں بدِل سعِي کرِي 'that they labour earnestly in (behalf of) the good repute of their master.'

Rem. It is sometimes idiomatically omitted: وُہ غُصّے هُوا 'he got into (a state of) anger (became angry);' وُہ غضب هُوا 'he got into a rage;' اُس سال 'in that year;' اِن دِنوں 'in these days.'

2) It is often used in the sense of the synonymous words بیچ and درمیان, signifying *among*, *between*, and hence occurs in connection with verbs signifying *to unite*, *reconcile*, *separate*, *discriminate*, and the like: *e.g.*

ملِکہ اُن میں نہ تھِي 'the princess was not among them.'

ضرور اُن میں جھگڑے پیدا ہونگے 'dissensions will surely spring up among them.'

اُنھوں نے آدمیوں اور جنّوں میں صُلح کروا دی 'he made peace between men and the Jinn.'

سچ اور جھوٹھ میں اِمتیاز کرو 'discriminate between truth and falsehood.'

اُس میں اور مُجھ میں کیا فرق ہے 'what difference is there between him and me?'

3) It indicates the subject or thought of conversation, that *in* which these move: as

وہ اپنے حال میں لِکھتا ہے 'he writes about (or respecting) himself.'

اِس مُقدمے میں مشورہ کرنا چاہیئے '(you) should consult (some one) about (or in) this case.'

اِس میں بہت سی فِکر کی '(I) thought much about this.'

Hence it is used in stating the subject of a book or chapter: as

حیوانوں کے مشوری میں 'On the consultation of (held by) the animals.'

نیک خوئی کے بیان میں 'On Morality.'

4) It is used (like the Ablative), in connection with an adjective, to indicate the *quality* of a person or thing: as

جِسم میں بڑا 'big in body.'

حرکت میں جلد 'quick or fleet in (of) action.'

5) It is employed in the *comparison* of an object with several others, governing the thing with which comparison is made: as

وہ سب مکھیوں میں بڑا ہوتا ہے 'he is the biggest of all the bees (is big compared with all the other bees).'

ساتوں کواکِب میں نیّرِ اعظم هَي 'it is the greatest luminary of all the seven planets.'

6) It is used *absolutely* with an adjective or substantive (in the manner of the Ablative Absolute of the Latin), to express a *state* or *circumstance*: as

گویا جِیتے جِي بِہشت میں گیا 'as if I entered Paradise alive' (*lit.* 'being in a living state').

In such cases the postposition میں and the participle هوتے are generally understood.

7) It indicates the *price* or *cost* of a thing: as

یِہہ کِتاب کِتنے میں پڑي 'how much did this book cost?' (*cf.* § 326, 334).

8) It is used to define or explain a *general* or *universal* by a *special* or *particular*: as

تُم کِس چِیز میں کم هو زور میں یا زر میں 'in respect of what are you lacking —power or wealth, etc.?' (*cf.* 352, 11, and *Rem.*)

9) It denotes the relation subsisting between the *part* and the *whole*, the *species* and the *genus*, etc.: as

ایک حکِیم لُقمان کے خاندان میں (مَوجُود) تها 'a sage of the house of Lŏḳmān was present' (*cf.* § 349, 10, and *Rem.*).

10) It is commonly used (instead of the Ablative, § 352, *e*) to indicate that one thing is *close by*, or *in contact with* another, and hence it is construed with verbs signifying *to adhere*, *attach* or *connect*: as

گوشت میں هِیري کے ٹکڑي لگ گئے 'the pieces of diamond stuck to the flesh.'

فِعل میں علامت مُذکّر کي لاحِق کرینگے 'they will attach the sign of the masculine to the verb.'

ڈول کو رسّي میں باندهو 'fasten the bucket to the string.'

Rem. The postpositions میں and پر are sometimes interchanged: *e.g.* کِتاب گھر پر هَي 'the book is at home' (where گھر پر = گھر میں); کپڑا بدن میں 'raiment on (his) body' (where مں = پر). Similarly میں is sometimes used in place of سے and کو: as دِرخت میں باندھو 'tie (it) to the tree;' کِتاب کِتنے میں پڑي 'how much did the book cost?' But in such cases the postposition for which میں (or پر) stands may always take its place; nor is it at all necessary that a *verb of motion* should precede the noun governed by میں (or پر). We may say گھر کو گیا, meaning گھر میں گِیا 'he went to his house;' but کو is not used for, and therefore could not take the place of پر or میں, in such sentences as, جب شہر کے دروازي پر گیا 'when he came to the gate of the city;' مجھے ایک حویلي میں لے گیا 'he took me into (inside) a house.'

356. پر (= اوپر), *over*, *above*, *upon*, is used—

1) In its original *local* sense, to denote *higher elevation*: as

چڑیا دِرخت پر بَیٹھي تھي 'the bird was sitting on a tree.'
وُہ گھوڑي پر سوار تھا 'he was mounted on a horse.'
خُدا آسمان پر هَي 'God is in heaven (above).'
مَیں نے دِیوار پر ایک تصوِیر دیکھي 'I saw a picture on the wall.'

The same sense is further exemplified in:

وُہ تالاب کے کِناري پر کھڑا تھا 'he was standing by the side of the tank' (because a person standing by a tank rises *above* the level of it).
مَیں دروازي پر بَیٹھا تھا 'I was seated at the door.'
کوس ایک پر 'at (the distance of) a *kos* or so.'
اگر اُنکے حال پر غور کِیا جائے 'if their condition be reflected on.'
اِعتِدال پر نظر رکھنا 'to keep the eye on moderation.'

اَپنے کاروبار پر خُود توجّہ کرتا هَي 'he attends to his affairs himself.'

اَپنِي جان پر کھیلنا 'to stake life upon something (play for life).'

هماري حال پر رحم کر 'have pity on our state.'

اُسپر عمل نہ کِیا 'he did not act upon it.'

مُجھ پر عجِیب و غریب حوادِث گذري 'wonderful and strange events befell me (passed over me).'

اپني ناداني پر مُطّلِع هوکر 'having become acquainted with my folly.'

وقتِ مُعیّن پر 'at the appointed time.'

2) To indicate an act or feeling directed *against* an object, or *towards* it, with a view to getting possession of it: as

دُشمن پر حمله کِیا 'they attacked the enemy (made an attack *upon* him).'

اُس پر هُجُوم کِیا '(they) rushed upon him.'

وُہ مُجھ پر غُصّے هَي 'he is angry with me.'

تُجھ پر خفگي کا باعِث 'the cause of displeasure with you.'

اُس پر گھوڑا دَوڑایا 'he urged the horse against him.'

اُسکِي کمائي پر قابِض هونا چاهینگے 'they will desire to lay hands on his earnings.'

اِس چند روزکِي زِندگِي پر فریفته هونا 'to be infatuated with this life of a few days.'

اُس پر عاشِق هوا 'he became enamoured of her.'

3) To indicate a *debt* that is due, and a *duty* that is incumbent *upon* one: as

مُجھ پر قرض هَي 'I am in debt (a debt is upon me).'

اُن پر فرض هَي ‘it is incumbent on them.’

جِس چیز کو خُدانے اُن پر واجِب کیا ‘what God has made obligatory on them.’

4) To denote the *distinction* or *superiority* that one thing enjoys *over* another: as

طبیعت صناعت پر مُقدّم هَي ‘Nature precedes (is above) Art.’

اِس دُنیا کِي زِندگِي کو آخِرت پر ترجِیح دیتے هَیں ‘they prefer the life of this world to the life to come.’

5) To indicate the position in which (the ground *on* which) a person or thing stands in respect of *origin*, *custom*, *education*, *business*, etc.: *e.g.*

آدمِي اپنے بادشاهوں کے طرِیقے پر هوتے هَیں ‘men conform to the ways of their kings.’

اِنسان اپنے قَول قرار پر نہیں رهتا ‘man does not abide by his promise.’

سِیاست کا مدار عدالت پر هَي ‘government is based (turns) upon justice.’

هرایک چِیز اپنِي اصل پر جاتِي هَي ‘every individual thing reverts to its original.’

جب خواهِش اِعتِدال کِي حالت پر هو ‘when desire exists in (shall conform to) a state of moderation.’

6) To denote tne *cause of* or *reason for* an action: as

اُسِي طمّع پر ‘on account of (through) that same covetousness (of mine).’

میرِي اِس کہنے پر ‘because of this saying of mine.’

کِس تقصِیر پر اِن غرِیبوں کو مارا ‘for what offence did you beat these poor creatures?’

وُہ میرِي قَول قرار کے نِباهنے پر حَیران رهتِي ‘she used to be perplexed (to account) for my fulfilling my promise.’

7) To show the *rule* or *standard* according to which something is done: as

مُناسِب طور پر 'after a proper manner.'

اپنے معمول پر 'according to his wonted custom.'

حِکمت کے قاعِدي پر 'according to the rules of philosophy.'

8) It is sometimes used as equivalent to the Persian phrases با وُجود, با وصف, = *in spite of*, *notwithstanding*: as

اِتني دانائي پر 'notwithstanding so much wisdom.'

اُسکي اِس خبرداري پر 'in spite of this carefulness of his.'

Rem. a. The postposition ساتھ 'along with' is also employed in this sense, and when so used always *precedes* the pronoun it governs in the genitive: *e.g.* ساتھ اِسکے کِہ وُہ آپ چھوٹا اور ناتواں هو 'notwithstanding this (fact) that he himself be small and powerless.'

Rem. b. پر, like the postpositions of the other cases, is often idiomatically omitted: *e.g.* اِسي وقت 'at this same time;' مَیں اُسکي نظر چڑھ چُکا هُوں 'I have fallen under its (evil) eye (it, the snake, has marked me out for its victim);' وُہ میري سِر هونے لگا 'he began setting upon me' (*lit.* 'falling on my head'). In every instance however of a postposition being understood, the noun governed by it (if capable of inflection) takes the inflected form.

Rem. c. تک or تلک *to, up to, as far as,* is erroneously included by some grammarians among the postpositions of the Locative. It designates, properly, *the limit attained by a thing,* or *an action,* whether that limit be included or not; as پیشاور سے کلکتہ تک 'from Peshāwar to Kalkatta (Calcutta);' میري دُوکان تک آنا 'come as far as my shop;' یہاں تک 'to such an extent, to this degree.' If it be desired to indicate that both limits are actually included, the past conjunctive participle لے signifying *taking, including,* is put after the noun in the Ablative; as ڈال سے لے پات تک 'from the branches to the leaves inclusive.' *Tak* is sometimes used in the sense of کو and کے لیئے: as اور زمین و باغ حاصل کرنے کے لیئے مدتوں لڑي - لوگوں کے حق غضب کیے - جعلسازیاں کیں - فریب دیے - سب آج تک تھے 'and your contending (*lit.* in that you contended) for long days to acquire lands and gardens, (your) violently usurping the rights of (other) people, (your) forgeries, (your) frauds—all were unto (for) this day.'

VIII. The Vocative.

357. The Vocative case indicates the object addressed: it therefore stands in no connection with other words in a sentence. Its position is usually at the beginning of the sentence.

Rem. According to the view of native grammarians however, what we call the Vocative is really the indirect object of a suppressed verb: *e.g.* أي آدمي is regarded by them as equivalent to پکارتا هوں آدمي کو 'I call the man.'

358. The Vocative is often introduced by an interjection: as أي دوست 'O friend!' او لڑکے 'O boy!' but if no particular stress is laid on the address, the interjection may be omitted: *e.g.* لڑکے 'boy!' صاحبو 'gentlemen!' یارو 'O friends!'

359. An adjective (genitive, possessive pronoun) qualifying a noun in the Vocative is also put in the Vocative: as اڑي میري لعل 'O my darling!' أی خداکے بندي 'O servant of God!'

360. Some nouns occur chiefly in the Vocative case: as بھیّا 'brother!' بھینا and بوا 'sister!' مائي 'O mother!' بابا 'father!' میاں 'O friend or master!' The last of these occurs in other cases also: *e.g.* میاں بي بي دونون تھے 'both husband and wife were (there).'

CHAPTER VIII.

ADJECTIVES.

I. THE ATTRIBUTIVE ADJECTIVE.

361. The ordinary rules for the construction of the Adjective have been laid down in the preceding paragraphs (274, 280—282, 291, 292, 294, 349, 350, 359). The following are of a more special character.

362. Two adjectives that are attributives to one substantive are commonly connected by asyndeton, after the manner of substantives and verbs: *e.g.* پهٹے پُرانے کپڑِي 'ragged old garments;' چهوٹے بڑي لڑکوں سے 'from small (and) big boys.'
بڑے

363. An adjective (generally *masculine*) may be used without a substantive to denote things or persons: *e.g.*

زمانے کے بهلے بُري سے 'from the good and evil of the time.'

عقلمندوں کے نزدِيک 'in the opinion of the wise'

بعض بِيماروں کا يِه حال هوتا هَي ہے 'the condition of certain sick persons is such.'

چهوٹے بڑوں نے خُوشِياں کِيں 'small and great made rejoicings.'

364. *a.* The adjective بهر 'full,' approximates closely to the character of a postposition. It governs a noun in the Formative, and either precedes or follows it, more commonly the latter: *e.g.*

مقدورِ بهر (or بهر مقدور = تا مقدور, or حتی المقدور) 'to the utmost (full extent) of one's power, as far as possible.'

عمر بهر (= تا عمر) 'in (for) a whole life-time.'

پیٹ بهر 'a bellyful.'

b. Its signification, when it comes after the substantive, is sometimes that of *as far* or *much as*, or *sufficient for* (= the Persian وار, see § 91, 3, *Rem.*): *e.g.*

کوس بهر 'about, or as far as a *kos*' (whereas بهر کوس would always imply 'a full *kos*').

کہ جهوٹه اُس میں کوڑی بهر نہ هو 'that there be not as much as a *kauṛī* (not a particle) of falsehood in it.'

ٹوپی بهر کپڑا 'cloth sufficient for a cap.'

365. *a.* The adjective سا 'like' is placed *after* nouns (substantives, adjectives, pronouns) to denote similitude, and inflects like the genitive case-sign to agree in gender and number with the object compared: as

شیر سا مرد 'a lion-like man' ('a man bold as a lion').

پری سی لڑکی 'a fairy-like girl.'

کچهہ شَی کالی سی نظر پڑتی هَی 'some black-like (or blackish) object is visible.'

Rem. An attributive adjective or a demonstrative pronoun may precede the substantive, the pronoun (see next para.) being put in the Formative: *e.g.*

مست هاتهی سا 'like a raging elephant;'

اُس سوداگر سا 'like that merchant.'

b. When it follows a pronoun, it governs it in the Formative (*cf.* § 376): *e.g.*

تجهہ سا آدمی عقلمند 'a wise man like thee.'

کہ مُجھ سے مُرّدي کو زِنّدہ کِیا 'that you restored to life a dead man like me.'

تِین دَرْویش تُجھ سے دُکھِیے 'three darweshes afflicted like thee.

c. The Genitive, inasmuch as it possesses the character of (and is by origin) an Adjective, may also be followed by سا, forming with it a kind of compound adjective: *e.g.*

شیر کِي سِي صُورت 'a form like a tiger's' ('a tiger-like form').

اُسکا حال بدنِي رِیاضت کا سا هَي 'its case is similar to that of bodily exercise.'

پاؤں بکرِیوں کے سے 'feet like goats'.'

عقّل و تمِیز همارِي سِي 'understanding and judgment like ours.'

d. The compound with سا may also be employed adverbially and substantively: as

سب آدمِي ایکٹ سے نہِیں هوتے 'all men are not alike.'

تُو بهِي مُرّدہ سا پڑا تها 'you also were lying like a corpse.'

دُور سے ایکٹ شُعّله سا نظر آیا 'something like a light (a light-like) appeared at a distance.'

اُسکا رنگ و رَوغن کُچھ کا کُچھ هوگیا اور کینچلِي سِي ڈال دِي 'his colour and complexion became something quite different, and shed something like the slough of a snake' (*lit.* 'a snake-slough-like').

Rem. In place of سا, the indeclinable adjective سار occurs occasionally in the older literature: *e.g.* تِین دَرْویش تُجھ سار دُکھِیے. We may here point out that instead of تُجھ سار دُکھِیے, the reading of Forbes's *Bāg o bahār* (ed. 1856, page 68) is تُجھ سار رکھے, which is absolutely meaningless. At page 203 also of the same edition we find میرا سا دُکھِیا, which is very extraordinary; for it is evident that the speaker means to say "afflicted like me," and therefore the reading should be مُجھ سا دُکھیا. Some grammarians, strange to say, receive Forbes' version as correct, and translate it "distress like mine." We need hardly point out that دُکھیا can never mean "distress," and that if the speaker had meant to imply "distress like mine," he would have said میرا سا دُکھ.

366. The adverbial affix سا, which is added to *adjectives alone* (most commonly to adjectives of *quantity*), and indicates a *great* or *small degree* of a quality, etc., is generally confounded with the *adjective of similitude*, although the two words are quite distinct both as to origin and signification (§§ 48, 49, and 50, *Rem.*). As both are similarly constructed, it may sometimes happen that the context alone must be looked to, to determine whether *similitude* or *degree* is implied; but this can only occur when the adjective to which سا is joined is one of *quality*: *e.g.* کالا سا may signify *black-like*, or *blackish*, or *very black*, though the last is the more common signification. When however it is connected with an adjective of *quantity*, سا is almost invariably the *adverb of degree*: *e.g.* بہُت سے گھوڑي 'a great many horses;' تھوڑي سے قصُور پر 'for a *trifling* fault;' ذرّہ سي بات 'a *trivial* matter.'

367. *a.* The rules for the formation of comparatives and superlatives, and the various methods of intensifying an adjective, have been laid down in §§ 47 and 48.

b. Persian and Arabic comparatives and superlatives are of common occurrence: *e.g.* بہتر مصلحت 'the better (or best) course;' ادنٰي توجّہ سے 'with the least attention.' The Arabic superlative, whether constructed with a masculine or feminine noun in Urdū, always takes the *masculine* form.

II. NUMERAL ADJECTIVES.

368. The following rules relate to the Cardinal numbers alone; there being nothing special in the construction of the Ordinals beyond what has been already noticed (§ 55 *et seq.*).

369. The cardinal numbers usually precede the noun with which they are connected, and this may be put in the singular or the plural, according to the following rules:

1) If the noun denote *money*, *measure* or *quantity*, *time*, *distance*, *direction*, *manner*, or if it be one which is used as a *collective* numeral (like the English *brace*, *pair*, *head*, etc.), as جوڑا 'a pair,' راس 'a rein,' زنجِیر 'a chain,' قطار 'a string or file,' it is commonly put in the *singular*; but the verb forming its predicate is generally plural: *e.g.*

ایک ہزار اشرفِي 'one thousand *ashrafī* (gold-mohurs).'

چار سَو رُوپَي کِي تھیلي 'a bag of four thousand rupees.'

بِیس گز کا تھان 'a piece (of cloth) of twenty yards.'

دس بِیگھے کا کھیت 'a field of ten *bīghās*.'

دو چار گھڑِي کے بعد 'after two or three *gharīs*.'

دو تِین دِن میں 'in the course of two or three days.'

تِین ہفتے میں 'in three weeks.'

تِین مہینے تلک 'for the space of three months.'

ساٹھ برس تک 'up to (the age of) sixty years.'

تِین طرف سے 'from three sides.'

دو جانِب سے 'from two directions.'

دو طرح سے 'by two means.'

چار قِسم کي 'of four kinds.'

پنْدرہ سَي زنْجِيرِ فِيل 'fifteen hundred chain of elephants' (compare the English "fifteen hundred *head* of cattle").

نَو سَو قطار بارْبرْدارِي کے اُونْٹوں کِي 'nine hundred string (file) of burden-bearing camels.'

دس راس اَسْپِ عِراقِي 'ten rein (*i.e.* ten) 'Irāḳ horses.'

Rem. The plural also is occasionally used when the noun denotes money: as چالِيس اشْرفِياں 'forty *ashrafīs*;' and in this case, when the noun is put in the singular, the verb also is sometimes singular, اڑھائِي سَو اشْرفِي تھِي 'there were (*lit.* was) two hundred and fifty *ashrafī*.'

2) In all other cases the plural is more commonly employed, though the noun may be put in the singular: the predicate however is usually put in the plural: as

لاکھ گھوڑے 'a lakh of horses.'

آدْمِي میں دو چِیز هَیں 'there are two things (*lit.* thing) in man.'

ایکْ سَو ایکْ مرْد سے 'with one hundred and one men.'

دو چار باتیں 'two or three (a few) words.'

چار پانْچ کِشْتِياں 'four or five trays.'

چار چِیزوں کِي تلاش 'quest of four things.'

دو سطرِیں لِکھِیں 'he wrote two lines.'

دو بُونْدیں آنْسُوکِي ٹپکْ پڑِیں 'two drops of tears fell.'

اُنْتالِیس گولِياں (گولِي or) هَیں 'there are thirty-nine bullets.'

370. The higher cardinal numbers, when used as *collective substantives*, are put in the Formative plural, and the noun denoting the things thus vaguely enumerated

follows in the plural or the singular, according to the preceding rules: *e.g.*

سَیکڑوں لڑایاں 'hundreds of fights' (properly, 'fights in hundreds').

ہزاروں ھاتھي 'thousands of elephants.'

لاکھوں رُوپَي کے تُحْفے 'curiosities (to the value) of lakhs of rupees.'

لاکھوں (آدمِي) اُسکے ظُلم سے مرینگے 'lakhs (of men) will die in consequence of his tyranny.'

371. Similarly when the cardinal numbers (generally) are connected with some *definite* or *specific* object, they are used as *collective substantives*, and put in the Formative plural, to indicate that *all* or *the whole of* the objects enumerated are *included*; while the noun denoting these objects may be put in the singular (*cf.* § 369, 2): *e.g.*

چالِیسوں بنْدر 'the whole of the forty monkeys' (before mentioned).

چاروں فقِیروں (or فقِیر) نے 'by all of the four mendicants.'

دونوں بادْشاھوں (or بادْشاہ) میں 'between both of the two kings.'

میري دونوں آنکھوں میں 'into both my (two) eyes.'

دونوں حالتیں خرابِي کِي هَیں 'both of the two states are (states) of evil.'

ساتوں کواکِب میں 'of all the seven planets.'

آٹھوں پہر 'the whole of the eight watches' (into which a day of twenty-four hours is divided, and hence) 'the whole twenty-four hours.'

چاروں طَرَف سے 'from all the four quarters' (the cardinal points), 'from all sides.'

پانْچوں وقْت کِي نماز 'the prayers of all the five (appointed) times.'

Rem. These numeral forms appear to perplex the grammarians in no small degree. Thus we are told by one of our most recent instructors that "in the oblique cases plural, when the numerals are specific, the numeral or the noun, or both the numeral and the noun, are put in the oblique form: (*e.g.*) چالِیسوں دَروازي سے (or) چالِیس دَروازوں سے = 'through the forty doors.' But when the sense is not specific, the noun is put in the nominative plural: (*e.g.*) تِین دِن کے عرصے میں means 'for the space of three days;' but تِینوں دِن کے عرصے میں or تِین دِنوں کے عرصے میں means 'for the space of *the* three days.'" These rules, we may observe, are essentially wrong, and betray a total misconception of the nature of the numeral in the cases compared. In the expressions چالِیس دَروازوں سے and تِین دِن کے عرصے (the signification of which differs in no respect from that of چالِیس دَروازي سے and تِین دِنوں کے عرصے), the numeral is used as an *adjective*; whereas in the expressions چالِیسوں دَروازي (or دَروازوں) سے, etc., the numeral is used as a *collective substantive*, signifying 'including the whole total of forty,' or 'in their whole total of forty,' etc.: thus چالِیس دَروازوں (or دَروازي) سے means 'through forty,' or 'the forty doors,' according to the context; but چالِیسوں دَروازي (or دَروازوں) سے signifies 'through the doors in their whole total of forty,' or 'through all the forty doors.'

CHAPTER IX.

PRONOUNS.

I. THE PERSONAL PRONOUNS.

372. The personal pronouns are not usually expressed when they are the subjects of *personal* verbs, and are even often understood in other instances. But they must be expressed where perspicuity, contrast, or emphasis is required. They generally precede the verb; but they sometimes follow (commonly in the Imperative), especially in poetry: *e.g.*

اُسے چھوڑکر کیونکر جاؤں 'how shall I leave it and go?'

مَیں کروں 'should *I* do (it)?'

دانِشمندوں کا قول یاد کرتا 'I used to call to mind the saying of the wise.'

عجب نادان هَین وُه 'rare fools are they.'

373. Two or more pronouns forming the subjects of one predicate are arranged in the order of the persons (§ 290). The same order is commonly (though not invariably) observed when the pronouns are in an inflected case: *e.g.*

که میري تیري وُهي پتا هووي 'that that same may be a sign between me and thee.'

میرِي تُمهارِي هنسائِي 'the causing (of people) to laugh at me and you.'

But اُس میں اور مُجهه میں کیا فرق هَي 'what difference is there between him and me?'

374. The Genitives of the pronouns are properly possessive adjectives in the Nominative (§ 154), and are inflected accordingly. They are however frequently used as objective genitives: as

تُمھارِي تلاش میں 'in quest of you.'

اُسکِي تلاش میں 'in quest of him or it.'

میرا دیکھنا منحوس جانتے ھیں 'they consider the sight of me unlucky.'

ھماري پکڑنے کو ھاتھ چلائے 'he groped with his hands to catch (for the catching of) us.'

375. *a.* The place of the Accusative of the personal pronouns (including the Demonstrative, when it is used for the pronoun of the *third* person) is supplied by the Dative, either of the two forms of which may be used as a Dative or an Accusative; but the form which takes the postposition کو is that more commonly used for the Accusative: *e.g.*

ھماري آقا سِندباد نے تُجھکو بُلایا ھَي 'our master Sindbād has called thee.'

کپڑا مُنھ سے سرکاکر مُجھکو دیکھا 'she moved the cloth from (her) face and looked at me.'

تُجھکو وھاں پہنچا دِیا 'he went there with you' ('brought you there').

اُنکو کھا گئے 'they ate them up.

فقِیر اُسکو دیکھکر سُن ھُوا 'this *faḳīr* became paralyzed on seeing her.'

تُجھے پہچانکر 'having recognized thee.'

تاکِ مُجھے دیکھیں 'in order that they might see me.'

مُجھے مُوا ھُوا جانکر 'deeming me dead.'

اُسے چھوڑکر کیونکر جاؤں 'how shall I leave it and go?' (*lit.* 'go, having left it').

اُنھیں دیکھتے ھي 'on the instant of seeing them.'

b. If the Dative and the Accusative of a pronoun occur in the same sentence, the Accusative takes the postposition کو, and the Dative the second form: as

اُسکو فُلانے صاحِب نے مُجھے دِیا 'a certain gentleman gave it (or that) to me.'

c. Similarly the second form of the Dative is used for the Dative or Accusative of the pronoun if, in the same sentence, the direct or indirect object of the verb is a noun constructed with کو: *e.g.*

تُمھیں خُدا کو سَونپا 'I have entrusted you to God.'

قاضِي نے لڑکے کو اُسے سِپُرد کِیا 'the Kāẓī made the child over to her.'

376. *a.* When a personal pronoun in any case except the Nominative and Vocative is connected with an attributive adjective, it precedes the same in the Formative, and the case-sign is added to the adjective: *e.g.*

تُجھ کم بخت نے 'by wretched thee' ('thou wretched one').

مُجھ خانه خراب کِي حقِیقت 'the true story of ruined me.'

مُجھِ عاجِز کو 'to lowly me.'

b. Excepting the Agent case and the Genitive, as well as the Nominative, the same construction obtains when the emphatic particle ـِي or هِي (plural ـِیں or هِیں) is added to the pronouns, that of the *third* person included: *e.g.*

تُجھِي کو دِیا 'I gave it to *you*' (and not to any one else).

مُجھِي سے مانگے 'let him ask me' (properly, 'let him ask it from me').

اُسِي کا کام هَي 'it is his work alone.'

But مَیں نے هِي یِہ٭ کام نہیں کِیا 'I alone did not do this.'

میرا هِي طرِیقہ ٹھیک هَي '*my* course is the correct one.'

یِہ مال تیرا هِي هَي 'this property is *yours*.'

c. The Adjective of Similitude سا (as has been shown in § 365) always *follows* the personal pronouns, and governs them in the Formative. It rarely occurs however in connection with the pronoun of the third person. In the pronominal adjectives اَیسا, وَیسا, the pronoun is *demonstrative*, not *personal*, the signification being not *like him*, or *it*, but *like this*, or *that*, *such* (*cf.* § 156 and *Rem.*).

d. The postposition پاس, which governs both the Formative and the Genitive of substantives (§ 239), may likewise govern the Formative or the Genitive of pronouns: *e.g.* مُجھ پاس 'near me,' اُس پاس 'near him.' In both cases however the Genitive is the more common construction.

Rem. The plural pronoun هم is often used for the singular مَیں by persons of rank or position when addressing inferiors; and the plural تُم is commonly employed in place of the singular تُو. These forms being thus used in the singular, their place as plurals is often supplied by the expressions هم لوگ 'we people,' 'we;' تُم لوگ 'you people,' 'you.' The use of تُو 'thou,' though common among the vulgar, is restricted by the educated to the purpose of indicating *contempt, affection* (chiefly in addressing children, or old and trusty servants), or *reverence* (whence its employment in addresses to the Deity). The educated, when conversing with equals, generally use the singular pronouns مَیں and آپ for 'I' and 'you' ('thou'); but تُم may be used instead of آپ, if the two persons are intimate friends. The respectful forms for the third person *singular* in any of the inflected cases except the Agent, are اُنکا, اُنکو, etc.; as اُنکا حُکم 'his order;' but in the case of the Agent the form is اُنہوں نے (*e.g.* اُنہوں نے کہا 'he said'), and not اُن نے, this being now the ordinary form of the singular Agent (*cf.* §§ 140, 141).

II. THE DEMONSTRATIVE PRONOUNS.

377. The Demonstrative pronouns are local adjectives; but, by omitting the object defined, they may be used as nouns: as یے کیا ھَیں 'what are these?' یہہ سُنکر 'hearing this.'

378. There is no personal pronoun of the third person in Hindūstānī: its place is generally supplied by the remote demonstrative وُہ, *that*, *he*, *she*, *it*. But if it be desired to distinguish between a near and a remote object, the pronoun یہہ 'this' is used to indicate the nearer object. When the demonstratives are used as personal pronouns, the case-signs are added immediately to them; but when they are employed adjectively, defining a noun in an inflected case, they are put in the Formative, but the postposition of the case is added to the substantive (*cf.* § 141): *e.g.*

یہہ آدمي کیا کہتا ھَي 'what does this man say?'

وُہ شخص میري پاس بَیٹھا تھا 'that person was seated near me.'

اِس کام سے بازآ 'refrain from this business.'

اُس غارکے پاس 'near that cave.'

وُہ مُجھے دیکھیگا 'he will see me.'

اِسکا کُچھ اِعتِبار نہِیں 'there is no believing him (this man *near*).'

اُسکو میري پاس لاوٗ 'bring him to me.'

Rem. a. The forms یہہ and وُہ are both singular and plural in Urdū (§ 141, *Rem. c.*): *e.g.* وُہ کہتے ہَیں 'they say.'[1]

Rem. b. The rules laid down in §§ 373-376, apply also to the pronoun of the third person.

379. The Demonstrative یہِي 'this same, this very' (= یہہ + the emphatic particle ـِي, or, in the plural, ـِين), refers emphatically to an object close at hand, or just spoken of, or about to be mentioned; وُہِي 'that same, that very,' to a more remote, or a previously mentioned object: *e.g.*

همارے طالِع میں یہِي لِکھا هَي کِہ روز لکڑیاں توڑیں 'this same is written in our destiny (namely) that we shall break (gather) sticks every day.'

اِسِي طرح اشرفیاں کے لالچ سے 'in this same (afore-mentioned) manner, through greed of *ashrafis*.'

هر سال اِنھِیں دِنوں میں 'every year in these same days.'

وُہِي عَورت کہنے لگي 'the same (afore-mentioned) woman began to say.'

نَوکر چاکر اُسِي صاحِب کے 'the servants of the same (afore-mentioned) gentleman.'

اُنھِیں سب تاجِروں کے ساتھ 'along with all those same (afore-mentioned) merchants.'

[1] Similarly in Sindhī هِي 'this' or 'these;' هو 'that' or 'those.' The use of these forms in the plural is termed "ungrammatical" by a recent writer on Urdū grammar. The same thoughtless remark was made some years ago in one of the notes to an English translation of a well-known Urdū work, and happening to fall under the eye of a native scholar in India, called forth the following: "We shall ere long, I suppose, have English gentlemen coming out to India to teach us how to speak and write our own tongue correctly and idiomatically." It may perhaps induce these gentlemen to change their opinion on this subject if they learn that the original plural form of جو also was جے (as it is now in Marațhī and Sindhī), and that this ultimately gave place to جو, as وي, in Urdū, is giving place to وُہ.

380. *a.* In the Accusative, the Demonstratives, when used as adjectives or substantives defining a thing, may take the Nominative forms يِہ, وُہ, if there be no stress laid on them, or the object defined by them has not been previously mentioned; but these forms can never occur when the Demonstratives are used as personal pronouns: *e.g.*

يِہ گٹھڑِي کہاں پہُنچاؤُں 'where shall I take this bundle?'

وُہ مال کِتنے دِن کھاؤُنگا 'for how many days shall I subsist on that money?'

يِہ سُنکر 'having heard this.'

مَیں وُہ تُجھے دُوں 'I will give that (not *it*) to thee.'

b. But if the Demonstratives refer to an animate object, or to a thing which it is desired to bring conspicuously forward (*cf.* § 346, 2, 3), they take the inflected form (§ 378), and the postposition کو is added to the noun defined by them: *e.g.*

اِس لڑکے کو کیُوں مارتے ہو 'why are you beating this boy?'

اِس کُتّے کو لے جاؤ 'take this dog away.'

اُس کِتاب کو مَیں نے پھاڑ ڈالا 'I tore that book.'

c. The use of one or other of the two forms of the Dative-Accusative (viz. اُسے or اُسکو, اُنھیں or اُنکو) of the personal pronouns has been explained in § 375.

Rem. If the Demonstrative defines a noun followed by the adjective of similitude سا, it takes the inflected form (§ 365): as اُس سَوداگر سا 'like that merchant.'

381. The Demonstratives are occasionally used in the sense of the pronominal adjectives اَیسا, وَیسا, derived from them. In such cases an explanatory or descriptive

sentence introduced by the explicatory particle کِ 'that,' generally follows: as

روشني کا يہہ عالم تها کِ شبِ قدر کو وهاں قدر نہ تهي 'such was the state of brilliance that the Night of Power had (would have had) no power (consideration) there.'

III. THE RELATIVE PRONOUNS.

382. There are in Urdū two sorts of relative sentences; namely 1) such as are introduced by the Relative pronoun جو 'who, which, what,' etc.; and 2) such as are annexed to an immediately preceding definite or indefinite noun without the aid of a Relative pronoun. A sentence of the former kind is called جُمْلۂ مَوصُول *a conjunctive sentence*; of the latter kind جُمْلۂ وَصْفِيَّہ or نَعْت *a descriptive* or *qualificative sentence* (see § 276, *Rem.*).

1) The Conjunctive Sentence.

383. The Relative pronoun جو is used both substantively and adjectively: it may moreover be definite or indefinite; as جو آيا 'he who came,' or 'whoever came.'

384. *a.* When the Relative is used as an indefinite substantive, its clause is generally followed by one introduced by the correlative or determinative pronoun سو or وُہ (more commonly the latter, which is often more emphatic than سو), which takes up the Relative, the two pronouns agreeing in gender and number, but each standing in the case

determined by its relation to its own clause. The correlative however is often omitted: *e.g.*

جو هو سو هو 'happen what may' (*lit.* 'whatever shall happen, that (or it) shall happen.'

جِسمیں تُمهارِي خُوشِي هو سو کرو 'do that wherein your pleasure consists' ('do whatever you please').

جو چُست و چالاك تهے وُہ جلدِي سے پنسوئیوں پر کُود کر سوار هُوئے 'those who were smart and active quickly jumped into the boats and went on board (the ship).'

جو آیا (sc. وُہ) مالا مال هوکر گیا 'whoever came went away laden (with treasure).'

Rem. Compare with the Urdū جو ـ سو or وُہ, the Sanskrit यद् *yad*—तद् *tad*, and the Latin *qui—is*, or *idem*.

b. The Relative (and, as the case may be, the correlative) may be repeated for the sake of emphasis (تاکید, see *Rem.* § 276): *e.g.*

جو جو چیزیں مُناسِب اَور فائِدہ مند سمجهیں خرِیدیں 'whatever articles I considered necessary and advantageous (those) I purchased.'

c. The indefinite pronouns جو کوئِي 'whoever,' جو کُچه 'whatsoever,' are also constructed like the Relative; and the place of the following determinative pronoun may be supplied by one of the pronominal adjectives ایسا, وَیسا: *e.g.*

جس کِسِي کو اللّٰه نے بہُت سِي نِعمتیں عطا کِي هَیں اُسکو لائِق هَی کِہ شُکر ادا کرے 'to whomsoever God has given a great many good things, it behoves him to render thanks.'

اُن پھولوں کي پتّيوں سے جو کُچھ چاٹتي هَين وُه لُعاب‌دار شِيره هوکر نِکلتا هَي 'whatever they suck from the petals of those flowers is reproduced in the form of a viscous and sweet substance (called honey).'

جو کُچھ اُسکا فائِده بيان کِيا تها وَيسا هِي ديکھا 'whatever (all that) he had described as its beneficial effects, exactly such I found (it to be).'

385. But if the relative clause is used adjectively (as the صِله) to describe or define a preceding substantive, the construction is similar to that of English: the Relative agrees with its antecedent in gender, number, and person, the concord in gender (since the pronoun has no distinct forms for masc. and fem.) being indicated by the predicate of the relative clause. The case of the Relative is determined by its relation to its own clause: *e.g.*

ايک حکِيم جو پُرانے خط کے پڑھنے ميں هوشيار تها 'a sage, who was skilled in deciphering old characters (or writings).'

يِه ايک اَندهير هَي جسکا کُچھ تدارُک نه هوتا 'this is an outrage for which no punishment is inflicted.'

يِه دَولت خانه سِندباد کا هَي جِسنے جهاں کے تمام درياؤں کا سفر کِيا هَي 'this mansion is Sindbād's, who has made the voyage of all the seas in the world.'

اُنميں ايک پادشاه هوتا هَي جِسکو يعسُوب کهتے هَيں 'there is (they have) a king among them, whom they call Ya'sūb.'

386. *a.* The antecedent, especially if it be an indefinite substantive, is often attracted (in the same case as the Relative adjective) into the relative clause, and the construction is then the same as that explained in § 384: *e.g.*

جو پادشاہ اُن پر عمل نہ کری اُسکي سلطنت همیشہ مُتزلزل رهي 'the king who (= whatever king) does not act upon them, his dominion will ever remain in a tottering condition.'

جو لوگ حاضِر تھے اُن میں سے کوئي اُس خط کو نہ پڑھ سکتا تھا 'none of the people present could read that character.'

جِن تاجِروں کي دِیانت اَور امانت پر اِعتِماد تھا اُنکے ساتھ ایک اچّھے جھاز پر سوار هُوا 'I embarked in a good ship along with some (those) merchants in whose honesty and integrity I had confidence.'

جِس شخص کے سِینے میں کِینہ جم گیا هَي اُس سے بجُز ضرر کے اَور کُچھ فائِدہ حاصِل نہ هوگا 'no benefit—naught but harm (*lit.* no benefit save harm) will be received from the person in whose bosom rancour has established itself.'

جِس نَوکر کو مُقرب بنائِیے اُسکي نِسبت شِکایت نہ سُنِیے 'listen to no complaint against the servant whom you make a favourite (or confidant).'

جِس وقت معلُوم هو کہ فُلاں شخص چُغل خور هَي اُسي وقت اُسکے دفعِیے کي تدبیر کري 'when (*lit.* at which time) it becomes known (to the king) that such and such a person is a tale-bearer, let him immediately (*lit.* at that very time) take steps to remove him (from his place).'

b. If the Relative be connected with a substantive denoting *place*, *direction*, etc., one of the corresponding pronominal adverbs (§ 224) will take the place of the determinative pronoun: as

جِس طرف سے آیا اُدھر هِي کو چلا 'he went in the same direction from which he came.'

جِس درخت کے نیچے تُو کھڑا هَي یہاں ایک آفتابہ اشرفیوں سے بھرا هُوا گڑا هَي ‘a water-pot filled with gold mohurs is buried here under the tree where you are standing.’

387. If emphasis is laid on the Demonstrative clause, it generally precedes the Relative: as

پھر اُس مکھي کو مار ڈالتا جو بدبو اپنے ساتھ لاتي هَي ‘and then he kills the bee that brings the offensive smell with it.’

بے فِکرِي میں وُهِي لوگ زِندگِي بسر کرتے هَیں جو احمق اَور غافِل هَیں ‘those people alone pass their lives in unconcern who are foolish and thoughtless.’

اَور وُہ تدبیر جِس سے مَیں یہاں تک پہنچا اُنکے سامھنے بیان کِیا ‘and I explained in their presence the expedient by (means of) which I got there (*lit.* here).’

Rem. In sentences like the above the native grammarians regard the position of the relative clause as in no wise different from what it is in the sentences noticed under § 386. For example: analyzing the two sentences جو کِتاب کِہ تُم نے لِي تھِي, etc., and وُہ کِتاب جو تُم نے لِي تھِي, they say that, in the first, the *conjunctive noun* (اِسْمِ مَوصُول) is جو کِتاب, and the *conjunctive clause* (صِلہ), تُم نے لِي تھِي; and that, in the second, the conjunctive noun is وُہ کِتاب, and the *ṣila*, جو تُم نے لِي تھِي.

388. *a.* The Relative may be used both as subject and object in one and the same sentence, which then becomes doubly correlative. This construction is always employed in such sentences as in English contain both an indefinite Relative and an indefinite Pronoun. For

example, "*whatever* came into the mind *of any one*," would in Urdū be expressed thus: "*whatsoever* came into the mind *of whomsoever*." In such cases the Correlative pronouns are, one or both, frequently omitted in Urdū: *e.g.*

جو جِس کے هاتھ پڑا اڑا لیگیا 'whatsoever fell into any one's (*lit.* whomsoever's) hands, he carried off.'

جِسکے واسطے جو صُورت مُناسِب جانی عطا کی 'whatsoever form He considered fit for any one soever, He bestowed (it).'

جِسکے واسطے جو کُچھ مُناسِب تها عطا هُوا هَي 'whatsoever was proper for any one soever has been bestowed.'

b. A pronominal adverb derived from the Relative pronoun may even take the place of one of the Relatives: *e.g.*

اَور جهاں سے جو کُچھ پاتے هَیں لے آتے هَیں 'and whatsoever they find any where they bring thence' (*lit.* 'and whencesoever whatsoever they find they bring').

جو جَیسا کریگا وَیسا پاویگا 'as any one does so will he receive.'

Rem. a. This construction, it may be observed, is derived from the Sanskrit: *e.g. yad rochate yasmai*, 'whatsoever is pleasing to whomsoever,' or 'whatever pleases any one;' and, as might be expected, it is found in the Persian also: *e.g.* بهرکِه هرچِه سزاوار بُود بخشِیدنَد 'whatsoever was suitable to any one has been bestowed.'

The Relative is never employed in connection with the Indefinite pronouns, except to form the compound indefinite pronouns جو کوئی (Formative جِس کِسی), and جو کُچھ. If in the first of the above examples we were to substitute کِسی کے for جِسکے, جو would no longer be a Relative pronoun, but a conjunction, and the meaning of the sentence would be "if it fell into the hands of any one, etc." The Relative pronoun however partakes considerably of the character of the Indefinite pronoun, and frequently implies a *condition* also, thus taking the signification of the conjunction جو, 'if;' as جِس صُورت میں (= اگر کِسِي صُورت میں) وُہ لوگ خائِن ھُوئے - اَور بادشاہ کو اُنکے کہنے پر اِعتِماد ھُوا - تو بہُتیري بے گُناہ جان سے جائینگے 'if in any case (*lit.* in the case in which) they turned traitors, and the king had confidence in their statements, then many innocent people would (*lit.* will) lose their lives.'

389. The relative adjectives and adverbs also are used correlatively, in the manner of the relative pronoun: *e.g.*

جَیسا کِیا وَیسا پایا 'as he (or I) did, so he (or I) received.'

جہاں گُل تہاں خار 'where the rose (is) there (also is) the thorn.'

جِتّنا چاھِیئے اُتّنا لے لو 'take as much as is necessary (as you want).'

جب تلک سانس تب تلک آس 'while there is life there is hope.'

2) The Qualificative Sentence.

390. The qualificative or descriptive sentence is annexed to an immediately preceding definite or indefinite noun which it qualifies or describes. It is always introduced by the particle کِہ 'that,' which is simply an *explicatory* particle (called کافِ بیانِیّہ *the kāf of the descriptive sentence*, when preceded by a substantive, and کافِ صِلہ, *the kāf of the conjunctive clause*, when it is preceded by a relative pronoun), and hence may also stand before a sentence beginning with the relative pronoun when such sentence

is descriptive of that which precedes it. The qualificative clause following کِہ contains a pronoun (either expressed or understood, or implied in the verb) which refers to the qualified noun, and connects it with the qualificative clause. This pronoun (the case of which is altogether independent of that of the antecedent) supplies the syntactical place of our relative pronoun. The particle کِہ it should be observed is sometimes omitted and not generally translated: *e.g.*

وزِیر کِہ (*sc.* وُہ) مردِ دانا تھا 'the *wazīr*, who (*lit.* he) was a wise man.'

اَور بہُت سے آدمِي کِہ (*sc.* وي) اُسکِي پُشت پر تھے 'and a great many men, who (*lit.* they) were on its back.'

کِہ کِسِي اَیسے شخص سے مُلاقات ھو جائے کِہ اُسکے ساتھ وطن کو جاؤں 'to the end that I might meet with some such person with whom (*lit.* that with him) I might return to my native land.'

دیکھا (*sc.* کِہ) ایک دُوکان هَي (*sc.* کِہ) اُس میں دو پِنجرى لٹکے هَیں 'I perceived (that) there was (*lit.* is) a shop wherein (*lit.* such that in it) two cages were (*lit.* are) hanging.

وُہ غُلام کِہ جِس نے پرورِش پائي تِھي 'that slave who had been fostered.'

اِتنا مال کِہ جِسکا حِساب نہِیں 'so much wealth of which there is no calculation.'

Rem. The construction with کِہ is borrowed from the Persian, and the explanation here given of its use is taken from the Ḳawā'idĕ Urdū Part IV. *Ki* is neither itself a relative pronoun, nor does it "at the beginning of a sentence with a personal pronoun coming in subsequently represent the Relative;" but it is in all cases a simple particle heading a descriptive or defining clause, which clause, as we have observed above, contains a pronoun that supplies the syntactical place of our relative pronoun. We subjoin the analysis of a sentence by a native grammarian in corroboration of this view. وُہ کِتاب کے گھر پر رکھِي هَي, "the analysis is this—وُہ, *ismĕ ishāra*; کِتاب, *mushārun ilaih*; *ishāra aur mushārun ilaih milkar mauṣūf hū'ā*; کے, *kāf bayān kā*; گھر, *majrūr*; پر, *jārr, aur yĕh donon milkar muta'allik hū'e fe'l, ya'ne* رکھِي هِي *ke, jiskā fā'il ẓamīr hai jo phirtī hai* کِتاب *kī ṭaraf: pas fĕ'l apne fā'il aur muta'allik se milkar, jumla'ĕ fe'līya hokar, ṣifat hū'ī mauṣūf kī: to yahāṅ jumla* گھر پر رکھِي هَي *jumla'e waṣfīya yā na't kahlāwegā.*"

IV. THE INTERROGATIVE PRONOUNS.

391. The Interrogatives are used both substantively and adjectively. As a substantive, the interrogative pronoun کَون 'who?' applies to persons only, and the interrogative کیا 'what?' to things. As an adjective کون applies to things as well as persons, and کیا, when used as an exclamatory word (see § 396, 2, 3), applies to persons as well as things. کَون is declined in the singular and plural (§ 143, IX.); کیا is indeclinable, the Genitive کاهے کا and the Dative کاهے کو belonging properly to the Hindī (Braj) pronoun کہا 'what?' (§ 144, *Rem. b.*): *e.g.*

تُم کون هو 'who are you?'
کِس نے اَیسِي بات کہِي 'who said such a thing?'
وُہ گٹھرِیاں کِس سَوداگر کِي هَیں 'what merchant's packages are those?'
تُمهارا نام کیا هَي 'what is your name?'
کیا کہتا هَي 'what does he say?'
مُجھ سے کیا قُصور هُوا 'what fault have I committed?'

392. The pronouns may be repeated for emphasis (تاكِيد, see § 276, *Rem.*), with a distributive force, or to imply a great number or variety: *e.g.*

كِس كِس طرح 'in what various ways?'

تُجھ میں بہت عَیب ھَیں کِس کِس کو گِنُوں 'you have many faults, which particular ones shall I enumerate?'

اُن سبھوں نے کیا کیا کام کِیئے 'what several works did they all do?'

393. When the question refers to one of two or more, the particle سا (fem. سِي) is generally added to the interrogative: as

کَونْسِي کِتاب میں 'in which particular book?' (out of two or more).

394. The Interrogative like the Relative (§ 388), may be used as both subject and object in the same sentence: *e.g.*

دیکھُوں کَون کِس مرتبے میں ھَي 'let me see in what rank each of you stands' (*lit.* 'who stands in what rank?')

395. The Dative form کاھے کو is used only with the signification of *why*? as کاھے کو اُنکے پاس جاتے 'why do they go near them?' But at the present period the phrase کِس لِیئے or کِس واسْطے 'for what purpose?' 'why?' is more common: *e.g.* یہاں کِس لِیئے بَیٹھے ھو 'why are you sitting here?' تُم سب اِس وَیرانے میں کیُوں آئے ھو 'why have you all come to this desolate place?'

396. *a.* The Interrogative کیا corresponds in nearly all its uses to the English 'what?' It is employed, for example, to express:

1) *Indifference to* or *the ability to dispense with* a thing, or to imply the answer 'no,' 'none whatever:' as

تُجھ بِن بہشت پیاري مَیں لیکے کیا کرُونگا 'what shall I do with Paradise (what is Paradise to me) without thee, darling?'

کھانے میں شرم کیا هَي 'what shame is there in eating?' ('there is no shame,' etc.)

Rem. a. Compare also the use of کیا in the following: آدمي کیا دیو تھا 'a man! nay, he was a demon' (or 'he was no man, he was a demon'); هماري اخلاقِي مُباحثوں پر غَیر کا تو کیا ذِکر هَي خُود هماري هم وطن هِي توجُّه نہیں کرتے 'our very countrymen themselves, not to speak of others, pay no attention to our moral discussions;' آزمائے هُوئے کو پِھر کیا آزماؤں 'to what purpose should I again test that which (or him who) has been tested?'

Rem. b. The interrogative adverbs کب 'when?' کہاں 'where?' etc., are also often used to imply the answer 'no,' 'never:' *e.g.* خُوشامد کب کري عالِي طبِیعت اهلِ دَولت کِي 'when does a noble-minded man flatter the rich?' *i.e.* 'a noble-minded man never flatters,' etc.

2) *Indignation*, or *rebuke*; as

تُم کیا کرتے هو 'what are you doing?' ('don't do that!')

3) *Surprise* or *wonder*: as

کیا هِي نیک مرد هَي 'what a very good man he is!'

b. It may also be used like the English 'how' to denote *extent* or *degree*, etc.: as

کیا خُوب 'how fine or excellent!'

اگر کوئي اُسکے کپڑوں میں گُھس کر کاٹے تو کیا (= گیسا) بے قرار ہوتا هَي 'if one forces its way into his clothes and bites him, how restless he becomes.

397. کیا—کیا like the English *what—what*, and *whether—or*, are used correlatively to connect sentences: *e.g.*

کیا لَیل و کیا نِہار 'what night and what day?' or 'whether in the night or in the day.'

کیا خُوشِي آور کیا تشوِیش میں 'whether in joy or sorrow?'

398. The Interrogatives are used in *indirect* as well as direct questions: in such cases the interrogative clause generally stands as *object* to a preceding negative verb, or an interrogative sentence that is equivalent to a negative: *e.g.*

کیا جانُوں کِہ وُہ کوں (*sc.* شخص) هَي 'what know I (= I don't know) who (what person) he is?'

اُسکو معلُوم نہ تھا کِہ اُس مکان میں کَون رہتا هَي آور وُہ عالِیشان محل کِسکا هَي 'he did not know who lived (*lit.* lives) in that house, and whose that grand mansion was (*lit.* is).'

Rem. a. In such sentences the verb of the governing clause must always be either directly or indirectly negative, otherwise the interrogative cannot be employed; a sentence like مَیں جانتا هُوں کِہ وُہ کَون هَي is unidiomatic and wrong. It betrays a misconception of Urdū idiom to say of sentences like those given above that "the Interrogative is used instead of the Relative."

Rem. b. The interrogative particles آیا 'is it?' 'whether?' and کیُونکر 'how?' are also used in interrogative sentences, the latter commonly:

e.g. آیا یہہ حالت فاعِل کِي بیان کرتا هَي یا مفعُول کِي 'does this indicate the state of the agent or of the object?' تُم یہاں کیُونکر آئے 'how did you come here?'

V. THE INDEFINITE PRONOUNS.

399. The indefinite pronouns کوئي *some, any, a, a certain,* etc., and کُچھ *some, a few, a little,* etc., when used substantively, apply, the former to living beings, the latter to things only; but as adjectives either may be connected with any noun, whether this denote a person or a thing. The pronoun کوئي to a great extent supplies the place of the English indefinite article: it is declined in the singular only, and is not commonly connected with a plural noun (see *Rem.* below), never perhaps with a plural of persons: کُچھ is indeclinable, but it may be connected with a plural denoting either persons or things:[1] *e.g.*

اگر کوئي مُقرّب خِیانت کري یا اَور کِسِي خطا کا مُرتکِب هو 'if a confidential servant commit treachery or be guilty of any other offence.'

جب کوئي مکّهي دُوسري چھتّے کِي آنا چاهتِي هَي 'when a bee of another hive wishes to come.'

هِندُوستان کے کِسِي خِطّے میں ایک راجہ تها 'in a certain region of Hindūstān there was a king.'

کُچھ پانِي لاؤ 'bring some water.'

مُجھکو اِس میں کُچھ شک هَي 'I have some doubt respecting this.'

[1] A recent writer on Urdū grammar terms the use of *kuchh* with a plural noun "uncommon" and "inelegant." We can confidently affirm that it is *commonly* so used by the best native writers, and they are certainly the best judges of the "elegance" of the construction. The same writer doubts the use of *kuchh* in application to persons: that it is so used will be seen from the seventh and eleventh of the above examples.

یہہ اُس سے کُچھ (= کِسِي قدر) بہٖتر هَي 'this is somewhat better than that.

یہہ بہِي کُچھ آدمِي هَي 'he (this man) too is something of a man.'

شاید کُچھ نامُناسِب باتیں میري زبان سے نِکلِیں 'perhaps some improper words escaped my lips (*lit.* tongue).'

اَور کُچھ ٹٹّیاں بناکر درخت کے اُوپر باندھ لِیں 'and having made some screens, I tied (them) upon the tree.'

بچّوں کِي کُچھ هڈِّیاں درخت کے نِیچے اَور کُچھ گِدھ کے کھنڈھلے میں پائِیں 'they found some of the young one's bones under the tree, and some in the vulture's hollow.'

بہُت سے آدمِي کِہ اُسکِي پُشت پر تھے کُچھ پنسوئِیوں پر اَور کُچھ تَیرکر جہاز پر آگئے 'many men who were on its back, some in boats and some by swimming, came on board the ship.'

Rem. a. The inflected form کِسُو of the interrogative کوئِي, though of frequent occurrence in the older literature, is now seldom used.[1]

Rem. b. کوئِي uninflected is sometimes used in connection with a plural substantive denoting a thing; as کوئِي دِن غرِیب خانے میں کرم فرماؤ 'grace for a few days this humble dwelling;' but this construction is not common, کُچھ or چند being more generally used in place of کوئِي 'a few,' and in the sense of *some* or *certain*, the pronominal adjective بعض or بعضے being usually employed with a plural substantive: *e.g.*

بعض مُوَرِّخِین نے لِکھا هَي 'certain historians have written.'

[1] Similarly of the two forms کبھُو, کدھو, and کبھِي, کدھِي, the latter are now commonly used instead of the former.

بعضے جاہِل اَور کمینے لوگوں کي عادت هوتي هَي 'it is the habit of some ignorant and low people.'

بعضِي بعضِي باتیں حُضور میں پُوچھُونگا 'I would question your Highness about certain matters.'

Rem. c. کئِي 'several,' is not the plural of کوئِي, as some grammarians suppose, but a distinct pronominal adjective, derived (like کَي 'how many?') from the Sanskrit कति *kati.*

Rem. d. The particle سا may be added to the indefinite pronouns to intensify the signification: as کوئِي سا 'any one whatever.'

400. In connection with a following negative the indefinite pronouns are equivalent to our 'no,' 'no one,' 'none,' 'none at all:' *e.g.*

مُلک میں کوئِي سرکش نرها 'no (not a) rebel remained in the kingdom.'

اَور کِسِي اَور کُنجِي سے نہ کھُلا 'and it opened with no other key.'

کُچھ فائِدہ حاصِل نہوگا 'no benefit will be derived.'

کُچھ کھانے پِینے کي چِیزیں اِس اطراف میں نہیں مِلتِیں 'no eatables and drinkables are obtainable in these parts.'

Rem. کُچھ in combination with other pronouns and pronominal adjectives has other significations, corresponding to our 'all,' 'ever so much,' etc.: *e.g.* اَور مَیں اُنکے هاتهوں سے یہہ کُچھ دُکھ دیکھُوں 'while I experience all this pain at their hands;' اگر کوئِي ایک دانہ بوتا هَي تو اُس سے کِتنا کُچھ پَیدا هوتا هَي 'if one sows a single seed, what an immense quantity springs from it!'

401. کوئِي—کوئِي, and کُچھ—کُچھ, are equivalent to our *one—another*: *e.g.*

کوئي کُچھ کہْتا هَي کوئي کُچھ 'one says one thing, another (says) another.'

گُناه کوئي کري سزا کوئي پاوي 'one commits a fault, another receives the punishment.'

کوئي تو باپ دادي کِي مِيراث کے طَور پر کِسِي مذهب کا قابِض هَي - اور کِسِي نے دُنْيا کِي دَولت و عِزّت کے واسْطے مُتزلزل دِين اِخْتِيار کر لِيا هَي 'one holds to a religion as an heirloom from his ancestors, another has made choice of an unsound (*lit.* shaky) faith for the sake of worldly wealth and honour.'

Rem. The indefinite pronominal adjectives (*e.g.* فُلاں, فُلانه or فُلانا 'such-and-such,' or substantively, 'so-and-so,' کئي 'several,' etc., § 155), are constructed as ordinary adjectives, and call for no special notice.

VI. THE REFLEXIVE PRONOUN.

402. The Reflexive Pronoun آپ 'myself,' etc., singular and plural (§ 150), is employed as an emphatic appositive (تاکِيد, see *Rem.* § 276) to a noun or personal pronoun (expressed or understood) which forms the subject of a sentence: as

موهن آپ آئيگا 'Mohan himself will come.'

مَيں آپ وهاں گيا 'I myself went there.'

اِس لِيئے (*sc.* وُه) آپ بهي عَيش و عِشْرت ميں بسر کرْتے 'for this reason (he) himself also used to live in ease and enjoyment.'

اور نه (*sc.* وُه) آپ کِسِي کے پاس جائے 'nor shall (he) himself go near any one.'

Rem. The emphatic هِي may be added to آپ : *e.g.* وُه آپ هِي آيا 'he *himself* came;' and instead of آپ the Persian pronoun خُود often occurs: as کِسِي کے واسطے کُوا مت کھود کہ (sc. تو) خُود گِریگا 'dig not a pit for any one, for you yourself will fall.'

403. آپ may also be added emphatically to its own inflected forms, and the word اپنے may even be omitted, as the personal pronoun in the Nominative is (§ 402): *e.g.*

تو اپنے آپ کو ملامت کرنی چاهیئے 'in that case he should blame himself.'

تُو (sc. اپنے) آپ کو بے عیب جانتا هَي 'you consider yourself faultless.'

ایک درویش (sc. اپنے) آپ کو دُنیا کِي زحمت سے بچاکر 'a darwesh, holding himself aloof from the throng of the world.'

Rem. a. The more common form of the Dative-Accusative of آپ is اپنے تئیں: *e.g.* اپنے تئیں کہا 'he said to himself;' اپنے تئیں ملامت کرنے لگا 'I began reproaching myself;' but the form اپنے آپ کو, or its contraction اپنے کو, is also commonly used in writings of the present period: *e.g.* اَور وُہ قَوم همیشه اپنے کو اَوجِ ترقّي پر پہُنچاتِي رهتِي هَي 'and that nation is ever advancing itself to the summit of prosperity;' اِس مُصِیبت سے هم اپنے کو محفُوظ نہیں ٹھہراتے هَیں 'We do not hold ourselves (to be) secure from this misfortune.'

Rem. b. آپ is perhaps never used alone in the sense of 'self,' its original signification. When used without obvious reference to a distinct subject, it commonly relates to an unexpressed pronoun of the first person, or to an indefinite noun understood, and must therefore be rendered *myself*, or *himself*: *e.g.* جو بات (کوئِي شخص *sc.*) اپنے (آپ *sc.*) پر پسند نہ کرے 'a thing which (any one) dislikes (done) to himself.'

404. *a.* The Genitive of آپ, the Reflexive Pronominal Adjective اپنا, is always used in place of the Possessive

Adjectives میرا *my*, تیرا *thy*, etc., when these occur (in connection with a noun in the Accusative or in an oblique case) in the same sentence with the subject to which they refer: *e.g.*

سِنْدْباد نے اپْنے دُوسْري سفر کا حال بیان کرْنا شُرُوع کِیا 'Sindbad began to relate the story of his second voyage.'

مَیں اپْنے چھِپْنے کِي جگہہ سے باھِر نِکْلا 'I came out from my hiding-place.'

اَور هم نے اپْنا اسْباب جا بجا بیچا 'and we sold our goods here and there.'

اِس وقْت تُم اپْنے گھر جاؤ 'do you now go home.'

وي مُجھکو اپْنے ساتھ لے گئے 'they took me along with them.'

b. But if the possessive adjectives occur in a sentence which has a distinct subject, or if they stand in the Nominative, the regular forms میرا, تیرا, etc., are used: *e.g.*

مُجھے اور میري بیٹے کو مارا 'they beat me and my son.'

میرا بھِي جِي للْچایا 'my mind also coveted.'

Rem. a. اپْنا (for *my*, or *our*) is sometimes found in connection with a substantive which is the subject of the proposition, but this is not to be imitated: *e.g.* اپْنا (better میرا) بھِي مِزاج بہک گیا 'my mind also was seduced;' اپْنے (better میري) نَوکر و رفِیقوں نے جب یِہہ غفْلت دیکھِي 'when my servants and my associates perceived this neglect;' اپْنا وقْر اپْنے هاتھ میں هَي (better همارا) 'our (one's) honour is in our own keeping (*lit.* hands).'

Rem. b. اپْنا (as also میرا) is often omitted when no ambiguity can arise therefrom: *e.g.* زبان کو جھُوٹھ بولْنے سے روکا 'I restrained (my) tongue from lying;' غِیبت سُنْنے میں جو مزا آتا تھا اُسْکو دِل سے بھُلا دِیا 'I effaced from (my) mind (*lit.* heart) the pleasure I used to derive from listening to slander.'

405. اپنا is also used substantively to signify *my*, *thy*, etc., *property*, or *kindred*: as

تجھ کو کیا ھوا کہ دوسرا کا مال اپنا بتاتا 'what has possessed thee, that thou callest another's property thine?'

اپنے اور بیگانے میں کچھ فرق نہیں جانتے 'they perceive no difference between their kindred and strangers.'

اپنوں کے پاس آیا 'he came to his own.'

406. The Ablative آپ سے, or emphatically آپ سے آپ, is commonly employed as an adverb: *e.g.*

وہ آپ سے آپ یہاں آیا 'he came here himself, or of his own accord.'

وہ آپ سے آپ اگتا ھے 'it grows spontaneously.'

Rem. In place of آپ سے آپ the Persian phrase خود بہ خود is often used: as

طبیعت خود بہ خود ایسی بے مزا ھوئی 'my mind of itself got so out of tone' (listless, *lit.* insipid).

CHAPTER X.

THE VERB.

a) VERBAL NOUNS AND ADJECTIVES.

I. THE INFINITIVE.

407. The Infinitive is properly a Gerund or verbal noun, and as such can form the subject or object of a verb, or stand in any case (except the Vocative), like any other substantive. It differs however from an ordinary substantive, 1) in being used in the singular number only; and 2) in taking an objective complement after it, if it be derived from an active-transitive verb: *e.g.*

جھوٹھ بولنا بُرا هَے 'to lie (or, lying[1]) is wrong.

ٹھٹّھا کرنے کِي عادت 'the habit of jesting.'

جب کوئِي مکھِي دُوسري چھتے کِي آنا چاهتِي هَي 'when a bee of another hive wishes to come.'

سرزنِش کرنے سے غُصّه پَیدا هوتا هَي 'anger arises from reproaching (= reproach).'

کھانے میں شرم کیا هَي 'what shame is there in eating?'

408. *a.* If only the objective complement of the infinitive (and not likewise the subject) be expressed, it may

[1] The English scholar will not require to be told that *lying* and *to lie* are both infinitive forms.

be put in the Genitive, or either of the two forms of the Accusative: *e.g.*

ایسي بات کے زبان سے نِکالنے میں اُنکو کُچھ خیال نہیں آتا 'they think nothing of uttering such words.'

کُل آلات کا بنانا نِہایت هِي بعِیدُالعقل هَي 'to make (or, the making of) all the implements (required) is highly inconceivable.'

میرا دیکھنا منحُوس جانتے هَیں 'they consider the seeing (= sight) of me unlucky.'

خلق میں اپني نِشانِي چھوڑنا 'to leave his mark in the world.'

آزادِي کو کھو دینا کِسِي حال میں تعرِیف کے قابِل نہیں هوسکتا 'to sacrifice (one's) freedom cannot in any case be deserving of commendation.'

b. But if the subject be likewise expressed, this is usually put in the Genitive, and the objective complement in the Accusative: *e.g.*

طبِیعت کے ساتھ صناعت کا تشبُّه پَیدا کرنا 'Art's producing a resemblance to Nature.'

409. If the Genitive of the Gerund be *subjective*, or if it be governed by one of the postpositions لِیئے, واسطے, etc., it may generally be rendered by the English gerund with *to*: *e.g.*

نہ مُجھ میں قُدرت کہنے کِي اَور نہ تُجھ میں طاقت سُننے کِي رهیگِي 'the power to tell would fail me, and the patience to listen (would fail) thee' (*lit.* 'the ability to tell will not be in me, nor the power to listen in thee').

لکڑِیاں توڑنے کے واسطے 'to break (*lit.* for the purpose of breaking) sticks.'

410. The Genitive of the Infinitive is commonly used in connection with the verbal negative نہیں (§ 148, *Rem.*) to express a strong negative Future: *e.g.*

وُہ نہیں کرنے کا 'he'll not do it, or he is not likely to do it.'

مَیں نہیں رہنے کا 'I shall not (am not likely to) remain.'

411. The Dative of the Gerund occurs after intransitive verbs, and such transitive verbs as govern both a dative and an accusative, and commonly expresses *purpose*; it may therefore be generally rendered in English by the gerund with *to*:[1] *e.g.*

وُہ دیکھنے کو (= دیکھنے کے واسطے) آیا هَي 'he has come to see.'

اپنے نزدیک میري اُترنے کو مکان دو 'give a house near yourself for me to stay in (*lit.* alight).'

Rem. The postposition کو is often omitted: as وي دیکھنے (کو) گئے 'they went to see;' تجھ سے سوال کرنے (*sc.* کو) آئے هَیں 'they have come to examine thee.'

412. The Dative of the Gerund in connection with the verbs هَي and تها expresses the *intention to perform* an act: *e.g.*

وُہ لِکھنے کو هَي 'he is going to write.'

مَیں چلنے کو تھا 'I was going (or was about) to start.'

[1] "It is difficult to distinguish this (*i.e.* the dative of the verbal noun)," a recent writer on Urdū Grammar observes, "from the infinitive; in fact the dative form may always be rendered by an infinitive." On this it is necessary to remark that the dative of the gerund is not the infinitive, although 'to' precedes it. In the expression "he liked to learn," *to learn* is the infinitive, and the object of the verb liked; but in "he came to learn," *to learn* is the *gerund* in the dative, and expresses the *purpose*—"he came *for learning*."

اُسِي وقت کِہ مَیں دریا میں گرنے کو تھا دُور سے ایک جہاز آتا هُوا نظر آیا 'at the very instant that I was going to cast myself into the sea, a ship appeared far off coming (towards me).'

413. The Infinitive in combination with the verb تھا is used to indicate the contemporaneousness of an action with another expressed by a finite verb in a following clause: *e.g.*

جوان کا دروازي پر آنا تھا کِہ ونہیں صاحِبِ خانہ بھي پہنچا 'the young man had but just reached the door when at the same moment the master of the house arrived.'

اَور پانو گوڑي پر دھرنا تھا کِہ گِر پڑي 'and they had scarcely put their feet on the rubbish when down they fell (into the pit).'

414. The Infinitive is often used in the sense of the Imperative, in both affirmative and negative sentences, but generally with more force than the ordinary Imperative. The negative particles employed in this construction are نہ and مت, the latter being prohibitive: *e.g.*

ميري هاں آنا 'come to my place.'

جویے کہیں اُسکو سچ جاننا 'whatever they say, consider it true.'

زِنہار یہہ خیال نہ کرنا 'never think of this!'

آج تُم گھر مت جانا 'don't you go home to-day.'

415. *Gerundive Forms.*—The Infinitive or Gerund, not only of transitive, but also of intransitive verbs, is frequently used as a Gerundive, agreeing in gender and number with its object if the verb be transitive, or with its predicative noun if the verb be هونا. This construction (in

which the Gerund usually occurs in the nominative form as subject or object, but occasionally also in the genitive) is employed in two ways: 1) the Gerund (with its object, if the verb be transitive) in combination with one of the verbs هَي, تها, or one of the tenses of the verbs هونا 'to be or become,' پڑنا 'to fall,' or with such quasi-impersonal phrases as لازِم هَي, مُناسِب هَي, چاهِيئے, etc., *it is necessary*, *proper*, or *right*, is used as an impersonal phrase to denote that a certain action *is to be done* (is settled to be done, should or must be done, is fit, proper, or necessary), the subject of the action (if a definite subject is spoken of) being put in the Dative: or 2) the Gerund with its object (if the verb be transitive), or its predicative substantive (if the verb be هونا), may form the subject, or object, of a following verb without expressing the idea of *duty*, etc: *e.g.*

1) مُجهکو جانا هَي 'I have to go' (*mihi eundum est*).

دوسْت کِي خاطِر رهْنا هُوا	'I had to remain for (my) friend's sake.'
تُم کو لِکهْنا هوگا	'you will have to write.'
اِس غلط فهْمِي کا نتِيجه بهُگتْنا پڑيگا	'we shall have to endure the consequences of this mistake (misapprehension).'
جو کهْنے کِي بات هَي کَونسِي نهِيں کهْتے	'which of those matters that should be spoken of do we not mention?'
اگر تُم کو اَيسِي نا آشْنائِي کرنِي تهِي	'if you had determined to act with such unsociableness.'
جو کام اِنسان کو کرْنے پڑْتے هَيں	'the works which a human being has to do.'
اُسْکے طالِب کو سخْت تکْلِيف اَور مشقّتيں اُٹهانِي پڑْتِي هَيں	'the seeker after it has to endure severe trials and hardships.'

اب همکو ذرّه فِکْر کَرْنی چاهِیئے ‘we should now reflect a little.’

زِنْدگِي میں اَیسے کام کَرْنے چاهِییں ‘we should so act in (our) life-time.’

اُسکو سزا دینِي مُناسِب هَي ‘he should be punished,’ or ‘it is right to punish him.’

2) دُشْمن سے دوسْتِي کِي توقُّع کَرْنِي عقْل کے خِلاف هَي ‘it is unreasonable to expect friendship from an enemy.’

اَور بِیماروں کو دوا دارُو دینِي بهِي اِخْتِیار کِي ‘and I also practised physicing the sick.’

بڑِي بڑِي پتّهر کِشْتِیوں کِي طرف پهینْکنے شُروع کِیئے ‘they began throwing huge stones at the boats.’

اگر نفْسِ ناطِقه کے ٹُکْڑِي هونے مُمْکِن هوں ‘if the divisibility of mind (*lit.* of the rational soul) be possible.’

Rem. The choice between the Gerund and the Gerundive is determined entirely by euphony, or the mere pleasure of the writer. Some writers therefore retain the Gerund (فِکْر کَرْنا) more frequently than others. Dehlī authors exhibit a preference for the Gerundive (فِکْر کَرْنِي). To say, as some grammarians do, that these Gerundive forms are "compounds, like 'fox-hunting,' 'speech-making,'" and that "compounds are occasionally found in which the words do not agree," is simply absurd. Perhaps these writers would say that in *Ars puerorum educandorum difficilis est*, "puerorum educandorum" is a compound, signifying "boy-educating." The Panjābī, we may observe, regularly uses the Gerund as a Gerundive. The Sindhī has a distinct Gerundive, differing however but slightly in form from the Infinitive: *e.g.* Inf. مارِڻُ ‘to beat,’ Gerundive مارِنو *mārino*.

II. The Noun of Agency.

416. The Noun of Agency holds a middle position between the verb and the noun, and partakes of the force

of both, following the government either of the verb or the noun, or of both. If it be derived from a directly transitive verb and have the meaning of the Present or Future, it may take an objective complement in the Genitive or the Accusative; but if it have the meaning of the Perfect, it approaches more nearly to the character of the noun, and is therefore construed with the Genitive alone: *e.g.*

غُصّہ فرو کرنے والے 'those who restrain (or shall restrain) their wrath.'

اَي شہر میں گھروں کے بنانے والے 'O builders of (ye who build) houses in cities!'

اِس خط کے لِکھنے والے کو حاضِر کرو 'bring the writer of (him who has written) this letter to me.'

سِوائے اِس کُتّے کے کوئي میرا رونے والا نہ تھا 'except this dog there was none who mourned for me (I had no mourner).'

417. It is also commonly used as the predicate of a preceding subject to express a *proximate future*: *e.g.*

وُہ دِلّي جانے والا هَي 'he is about going to Dillī.'

وُہ آج کل مرنے والا هَي 'he will die in (the course of) a day or so' (*lit.* to-day or to-morrow).

Rem. The above rules also apply to the Arabic and Persian nouns of agency and verbal adjectives which occur so commonly in Urdū; with this difference however, that when these govern the accusative, they generally stand as the predicate of a preceding subject: *e.g.*

مال و رُتبہ کا خواستگار 'a seeker after rank and wealth.'

نہیں مَیں طالِبِ روزیِ آسماں سے 'I am not a seeker of sustenance from heaven.'

وُہ سب کاموں سے ہمکو مانِع ہوگا 'it will hinder us from (progress) in all works.'

The construction with the genitive however is much the more common of the two, even in the case of the Hindī noun of agency.

III. THE PARTICIPLES.

418. The Participles express the same notion as the verb to which they belong, but (excepting the Past Conjunctive Participle) in the form of an Adjective. They follow the government of the verb from which they are derived.

419. The participles are frequently employed to describe a contemporary, past, or future, action connected with the main action. The relations and circumstances expressed by them must often be expressed in English by subordinate propositions with conjunctions (e.g. *while*, *during*, *when*, *after*, *as soon as*, etc.), or by phrases with prepositions.

a) THE IMPERFECT AND PERFECT PARTICIPLES.

420. The Imperfect and Perfect, or (if it belong to a transitive verb) Passive Participle have so much in common as regards their use and construction that they may be conveniently noticed together. When used adjectively they are usually distinguished by the addition to them of the perfect participle هُوا; but this is often omitted.

421. These participles are frequently used to indicate the *state* or *condition* (حال) of the subject or object of an

action while the action is taking place. Their agreement with the *subject* is in such cases determined by the following rules:

1) If the subject of the participle be likewise that of the finite verb, the participle agrees with it in gender and number: *e.g.*

(*a*). یِہہ کہتي هُوئي چلي گئي 'she went away saying this.'

اُن سے لڑتا بھِڑتا اُس چاہ پر آیا '(the dog) came to the dungeon fighting and struggling with them (all the way).'

گِرتي پڑتي بڑي دِقّت سے یہاں پہُنچِي 'I dragged myself along and (*lit.* falling and lying I) got here with great difficulty.'

ایکبارگي اُسکي ما روتي پیٹتي بیٹي کے گھر میں گئي 'all at once the mother entered her daughter's house weeping and beating (herself).'

(*b*). دسترخواں بِچھا هُوا تها 'the table-cloth was spread.'

کوئي عَورت بَیٹھي هُوئي تھي 'some woman was seated (or sitting).'

داڑھي سُفید چھاتي تک لٹکي هَي 'his beard (which is quite) white hangs (is hanging) down to his breast.'

اُسکے سامھنے دانے پڑي هُوئے هَیں 'grains (of corn) are lying before him.'

یِہہ بھائي لیتا هُوا جاگتا تها 'this brother was lying awake.'

جونہیں رنگ به رنگ کے حِباب اَور گُلابیاں طاقوں پر چُنِیں هُوئِیں نظر پڑِیں 'the moment (that) some wine jars and flagons of various colours (which were) arranged on the shelves fell under my eye.'

مَیں نے هِیرے کے ٹُکڑے پھیلے هُوئے دیکھے 'I saw pieces of diamond strewn about' (*lit.* 'pieces of diamond were seen strewn about by me').

2) But if the subject of the participles is not the same as that of the finite verb, both participles are constructed *absolutely* in the Locative singular, the postposition being suppressed; and the subject of the Imperfect Participle is often omitted: *e.g.*

(*a*). ساري رات تلپھتے کٹي 'the whole night passed in restlessness' (*lit.* 'I being agitated').

مَیں نے روتے بِسورتے کہا 'I said, weeping and sobbing the while.'[1]

(*b*). اُن سے لڑتا بھڑتا روٹي کو بچائے اُس چاه پر آیا '(the dog) fighting and struggling with them came to the dungeon with the bread saved.'

سِر نِیچے کِیئے کھڑا تھا 'I was standing with my head hung down.'

تُم پِیٹھ دِکھائے جاتے هو 'you go showing your back (your back shown).'

غرض پیر زن کو لِیئے هُوئے غار کے مُنھ پر آیا 'In short he came to the mouth of the pit with the old woman (the old woman brought with him).'

مَلِکہ مَیلے کپڑے پہنے باهِر نِکلي 'the princess came out dressed in dirty clothes.'

مَیں اُس جوان کے گلے میں بانھ ڈالے هُوئے بَیٹھي تھي 'I was sitting with my arm thrown round the young man's neck.'

[1] In this example the subject of the verb کہا is the following clause (the مقُولہ or *that which is said*), and the subject of the participle is the pronoun of the first person—*it was said by me* (as follows), *and I was weeping.*

اگر ایک هاتهِي زنجِیر تڑائے هوئے آتا هو ‘if an elephant with his chain broken were (*lit.* should be) coming.’

اُس دري کو مَیں اپني قبر سمجهے هُوئے تها ‘I was under the impression that that defile would prove my grave’ (*lit.* ‘I existed, that defile thought my grave’).[1]

جو بانبهي کے اندر سے سِر نکالے تهے ‘which were with their heads out of their holes.’

ایک مینڈک کو سانپ پکڑي هي ‘a snake is (there is a snake) with a frog caught’ (‘a snake has hold of a frog’).

اژدها جو مُنه پساري هی ‘a (or the) python which is with (has) its mouth wide open.’

Rem. The subject of the participle must necessarily be different from that of the finite verb when the participle is *passive* and, together with its object (Acc.), forms the حال of the subject of the finite verb; for when this object takes the nominative form of the accusative, it stands as the subject of the participle, and when it occurs in the dative form, the construction becomes impersonal (§§ 306, 308). This will become evident if we take the first of the above examples (*b*) and resolve it into the different predications contained in it: *e.g.* ‘the dog came to the dungeon, and he was fighting all the time he was coming, and the bread was saved by him,’ or strictly, ‘it was saved by him as regards the bread.’

[1] We have thought it necessary to multiply examples on this subject, because, firstly, the subject is one of importance; and secondly, its treatment in all existing grammars is most unsatisfactory. One of the most recent actually teaches that لِیئے and کِیئے are not perfect, or rather passive participles, but "irregular forms of the conjunctive participle!" and that in the last two examples above پکڑي هَي and پساري هَي are "forms of the perfect," signifying "has caught" and "has opened;" and no grammar attempts to lay down anything like a rule to guide the student in the use and construction of the participles.

3) If the Participle in either case be repeated for *emphasis*, or to indicate a *lasting* or *continuous state*, or even if such a state be implied without the repetition of the participle, it is always constructed *absolutely*, even though its subject be the same as that of the finite verb: *e.g.*

(*a*). ڈرتے ڈرتے مَیں پاس گیا 'I approached (it) in great fear (fearing much).'

منزِل بہ منزِل چلتے چلتے نَیشاپُور میں پہنچا 'marching on stage by stage I arrived in Naishāpūr.'

ہم گاتے گاتے سِیتے ہَیں 'we keep singing while we stitch.'

(*b*). لیکِن بے کار بَیٹھے بَیٹھے اُکتا گیا 'but I wearied of sitting still.'

تُونے مُجھے بَیٹھے بِٹھایے (= بَیٹھے) ناحق بدنام اَور رُسوا کِیا 'you have unjustly defamed and disgraced me seated quietly (*i.e.* inoffensively).'

وُہ چُپکے بُت کِي طرح بَیٹھے سُنا کِي 'she, continued listening silently, seated like a statue.'

Rem. In sentences like the last but one, where the *passive* construction with نے is used, and the first is simply a *perfect* participle, the second must take the form of its *causative* in order to possess a *passive* character; but the *signification* differs in no respect by this change.

422. *a.* When the participles describe the *state* or *condition* of the *object*, they are somewhat differently constructed. In such cases the object usually occurs in the *dative* form of the accusative, and hence the concord between it and the participle is disturbed: but whereas the Imperfect Participle may be optionally put in the nominative or the locative absolute, the Perfect, or

Passive Participle always takes the form of the nominative: *e.g.*

(*a*). معلوم هُوا کِ دو شخصوں کو چوري کرتے پکڑا هَي 'it appeared that they had (*lit.* have) caught two persons stealing.'

مَیں نے اُسکو چشمے پر سوتا چھوڑا 'I left him sleeping by a spring.'

ایک روز محل میں آتے دیکھ کر اُسے پکڑا 'one day having seen him entering the palace they seized him.'

اُسے روتا دیکھ کر پوُچھا کہ 'seeing him weeping he asked,' etc.

(*b*). گھوڑي کو میخ سے بندھا هُوا دیکھا 'I saw the horse fastened to a peg.'

اُس وقت سے مُجھے مُوا هُوا تصوُّر کرتا هَي 'from that time (forward) he thinks me dead.

وُہ مُجھکو ڈُوبا هُوا جانتا تھا 'he all along thought me (supposed that I had been) drowned.'

b. The construction is the same if the object be a following clause introduced by کِ: as ایک روز کِتاب میں بھِي لِکھا دیکھا کِ 'one day he saw written in a book also, that,' etc.

c. If the object occur in the nominative form of the accusative, the Participle will of course agree with it.

Rem. Of the two forms of the Imperfect Participle, the nominative is perhaps the correct one; at all events it is more in harmony with the construction of the Perfect Participle; and its regular use would moreover have the advantage of removing all ambiguity in sentences which have the passive construction with نے. For example مَیں نے اُسکو تَیرتے دیکھا signifies both 'I saw him whilst I was swimming,' and 'whilst he was swimming;' but if the participle be تَیرتا, the last alone of these significations is admissible.

423. *a.* Distinct from the use of the participles as a حال is their use to indicate that an action takes place *immediately after* or *simultaneously with* another action expressed by the finite verb. The emphatic particle هِي is added to the Imperfect Participle to indicate exact coincidence in point of time in the two actions.[1] In such cases the participles are always constructed *absolutely.*

The subject of the Imperfect Participle may be the same as that of the finite verb (whereby, as also by the participle not taking the *adjective* form with هُوا, it is distinguished from the اِسْم حالِيہ), or it may be different. In the latter case, if the subject is expressed, it is put in the Formative or the genitive, the latter being the more common when the subject is *animate.*

The subject of the Perfect Participle is usually different from that of the finite verb, and is put in the Formative: *e.g.*

(*a*). فَجْر هوتے وُہ رُخْصت هُوا 'he took his departure on dawn appearing.'

حُكْم هوتے وُہ كهودْنے لگے 'on the order being given they commenced digging.'

خواجہ نے ديكهتے هِي خاطِر دارِي كِي 'as soon as the merchant saw (this), he ministered consolation.'

مُجهے سُنْتے هِي غُصّہ چڑهہ آيا 'immediately on hearing this, anger overcame me.'

[1] Some grammarians mistakenly suppose that the imperfect participle must always be inflected when the particle هِي is added to it, and hence pronounce this sentence ungrammatical: مُجهے جِيتاهِي زمِيں كا پَيوَنْد كردو 'Thrust me into the ground alive (as I am).' The sentence is however quite grammatical; جِيتا is not the so-called "adverbial participle," but the *ḥāl* of the object *mujhe.*

میري الگ هوتے هِي وُه ایک اژدهے پر جاکر گِرا 'I no sooner became detached than it swooped down upon a boa-constrictor.'

(*b*). کیوں اِتني رات گئے تم آئے 'why have you come at this late hour of the night?' ('when so much of the night is gone').

پهر دِن چڑهے (مَیں) اُترا 'when one (the first) watch of the day was reached (when day had risen to one watch), I came down.'

b. If the Imperfect Participle has an objective complement expressed, this is put in the accusative or the genitive: *e.g.*

اُنهیں دیکهتے هِي هم سب بهاگے 'we all fled on the instant of seeing them.'

جوان اُسکے دیکهتے هي آیسا خُوش هُوا جَیسے دُنیا کِي نِعمت مِلي 'the young man became as delighted at the sight of her as if he had obtained the wealth of the world.'

Rem. The use of the objective complement in the genitive serves to show that the participle in such cases partakes of the character of the *noun* as well as that of the verb.'

424. In its *adjective* form either participle may be employed, 1) as an adjective defining a noun (either with the signification of a relative periphrasis, or to express a quality or state in general); and 2) as a substantive, concrete or abstract. As an abstract substantive the Imperfect Participle is equivalent to the Gerund: *e.g.*

1) As an adjective:

(*a*). سب میں نادان وُه هَي کہ سوتے هُوئے فِتنے کو جگاوي 'unwisest of all is he who rouses slumbering strife' (*cf.* § 47, *Rem. b.*).

ایک بولتي هوئي مَینا 'a talking *mainā*.'

چلتي چکّي دیکھ 'having seen a revolving millstone.'

اگر حُکم کرو تو جلتي آگ میں کود پڑوں 'if you bid (me), I will leap into burning fire.

(*b*). جما هُوا عرق کافور کہلاتا هَے 'the congealed juice is called camphor.'

ایک لِکھا هُوا کاغذ 'a written paper, or a paper with writing on it.'

کوئي مُوا جانور هوگا 'it may be some dead animal.'

2) As a substantive.

(*a*). ڈُوبتے کو تِنکے کا آسرا بہُت هَے 'the support of a straw is ample for a drowning man' ('a drowning man clings to a straw').

مُجھے سوتے سے جگایا 'he awoke me from sleeping (= sleep).'

اسباب هوتے (= هونے پر) توکّل خُوب نہیں 'to be confident because of possessing (= the possession of) property is not well or becoming.'

(*b*). آزمائے کو پھر کیا آزماؤں 'to what purpose should I again test what has been tested.'

سانپ کا بھیجا هُوا آیا هُوں 'I am come as the emissary of the snake.'

اپنے کِیئے سے پچھتاتا هُوں 'I am suffering remorse in consequence of my deed.'

راہ میں هزیمت کھائے هُوؤں کا ایک گروہ پہُنچکر 'a band of those who had experienced defeat having arrived on the road.'

Rem. This use of the participles corresponds to that of the Active and Passive Participles—the إسمِ فاعِل and إسمِ مفعُول—of the Arabic.

425. The Perfect or Passive Participle is commonly used for the Infinitive, chiefly in connection with the quasi-impersonal verb چاہِیئے: *e.g.*

جو کام آج کِیا (=کرنا) چاہِیئے 'the work which (you) ought to do to-day.'

دُشمن کي مَوت سے خُوش نہ ھُوا (=ھونا) چاہِیئے 'we should not rejoice at (in consequence of) the death of an enemy.'

426. The Perfect or Passive Participle is also used as an abstract (verbal) substantive in combination with the verb جانا, when this is equivalent to هو سکنا, and in the Frequentative and Desiderative Compounds (§ 24 and *Rem.*): *e.g.*

مُجھ سے ڈُوبا نہ گیا 'I could not drown myself' (*lit.* 'drowning was not possible by me').

تقدِیر سے لڑا نہیں جاتا 'there's no fighting against fate.'

مَیں دِن بھر اُس جنگل میں پھِرا کِیا 'I kept wandering about (*lit.* I did or made wandering) in that jungle the whole day.'

Rem. Observe also the following: میرا کہا مان 'mind what I say' (*lit.* 'my saying—what I shall say, or am about to say').

427. The Passive Participle, when governed by one of the postpositions بِن, بے, or بغَیر, has in some instances an *active* signification: *e.g.*

کِہ بے میري کہے میري ساتھ کھانا کھاتا هَي 'that without my bidding (thee) thou eatest food with me.'

بغَیر کھائے کیُونکر زِندہ رہ سکتا هَي 'how can he keep alive without eating?'

b) The Past Conjunctive Participle.

428. *a.* The Past Conjunctive Participle is very often used in Urdū so as to avoid the use of conjunctions where several predications are united in the one sentence: *e.g.*

یہہ کہکر چلا گیا 'having said this, he went away.'

کچہہ بات بناکر اور جواہر اور پوشاک لیکر اور قیمت اُسکي دیکر رُخصت چاہي 'having invented some pretext, and having taken the jewels and dress, and having given the price thereof, I requested permission to go' (*i.e.* 'I invented some pretext, and after taking the jewels and dress and paying for them, I requested,' etc.).

b. We sometimes find a preceding verb repeated in the participle: as

وہ اُٹھا اور اُٹھکر باہر گیا 'he rose, and having risen went out.'

عرق بہہ کر ایک برتن میں جمع ہوتا هے اور جمع ہوکر جم جاتا هے 'the juice having flowed (out), collects in a vessel, and having collected, congeals.'

429. The participle most commonly refers, as in the above examples, to the subject of the finite verb, or, if the construction be passive, to the Agent. In the latter case, when the participle is ہوکر, and a predicative adjective or participle is joined to it, this, if capable of inflection, is always put in the inflected masculine singular: *e.g.*

اُس جوان نے رُوکھے پھیکے ہوکر کہا 'the young man became cool and constrained, and said.'

اور کھسیانے هوکر فرمایا کہ 'and having become angry, I ordered that,' etc.

بعد اسکے کهڑي هوکر یہہ خطبہ پڑها 'after that, having stood up, he read this discourse.'

430. But the participle may refer to the object (dative, accusative); and in the same sentence one participle may refer to the subject, and another to the Agent: *e.g.*

یہہ بات سنکر مجھے بهي غیرت آئي 'having heard this, jealousy possessed me also.'

خدا کے حکم سے بهاگ کر جانے کے لیئے کہیں ٹهکانا نہیں 'there is no assured refuge anywhere to flee to from God's decree' (*lit.* 'having fled, or fleeing from, God's decree, there is no assured refuge for you to go to').

آخر وعده ان چیزوں کو پہنچا کر میري پهر آنے کا لیکر اور قسم کهلاکر رخصت کیا 'at last, having made me promise and swear that I would return after leaving those things (at home), he let me go.'

(شہزادي *sc.*) خوش هوکر (کشتیاں *sc.*) خانساماں کے حوالے هوئے اور فرمایا 'the princess having become pleased, the trays (of jewels, etc.) were made over to the steward, and she said.'

431. The participle may even be used absolutely, without reference to a subject, as is the case when the finite verb is in the passive voice: *e.g.*

وه کهود کر جیتا نکالا گیا 'he was dug out alive' ('they having dug, he was taken out alive').

432. The participle is often repeated for the sake of *emphasis*, or to indicate a *repeated* or *continued* action: as

میوي توڑ توڑ کر جمع کرنے لگے 'we kept breaking the fruits and collecting them.'

پتھر مار مار کے سب کِشتیاں ڈُبو دِیں 'having kept on throwing stones, they sank all the boats.'

433. In some instances the Conjunctive Participle has all the force of an adverb, and would appear to be used as such: *e.g.*

اُس نے جان بُوجھ کر یِہہ کام کِیا 'he did this wittingly.'

وُہ کِھلکِھلا کر ھنسا 'he laughed aloud.'

چھپا کر وُہ کِتاب اَور کِتابوں کے ساتھ اُس کے حوالے کِي 'I made that book over to him secretly along with others.'

اُسے مضبُوط کرکے باندھا 'I tied it tight.'

وُہ لنگڑا کر چلتا هَي 'he walks lame.'

b. THE INDICATIVE AND ITS TENSES.

I. THE AORIST.

434. The Aorist, though more commonly employed in the Subjunctive Mood, is also used in propositions, both leading and subordinate, which deal with *facts*, whether actual or assumed for the purpose of argument; in other words, it occurs in the *Indicative Mood.*

The Aorist does not in itself express any idea of time; it merely indicates a *begun*, *incomplete*, *enduring* existence either in *present* or *future* time. Hence it has the signification of the English *Present*, as well as that of the *Future Indefinite*: *e.g.*

خُدا جانے 'God knows.'

اب مَیں جو کہوں سو کر 'now do what I tell (am about to tell) you.'

خُوشامد کب کري عالي طبیعت اہلِ دَولت کي 'when does a noble-minded man fawn upon the rich' (*i.e.* 'a noble-minded man never fawns upon the rich').

دِل میں آیا کِہ پھِر سفر کرُوں 'It came into my mind "I will travel again."'

جب مَیں مر جاؤں گاڑداب دِیجو 'when I die (shall die), bury me out of sight.'

تُم یہاں بَیٹھو مَیں جاکر خبر کرُوں 'you sit here, I will go and announce (your arrival).'

اُس نے کہا چلو آج تُمھیں پادشاہ پاس لے چلوں 'he said: Come, I'll take you to the king to-day.'

435. The Aorist is commonly used in proverbs: *e.g.*

کم بخْتِي جو آوي اُونٹ چڑھے (*sc.* کو) کُتا کاٹے 'when misfortune comes, a dog bites one (who is) mounted on a camel.'

گُناہ کوئي کري سزا کوئي پاوي 'one commits the fault, another is punished for it.'

436. To render the idea of *present* time still more distinct, the auxiliary verb ہُوں, ہَي, etc., is added to the Aorist: as

آنکھیں ملکرکے جو دیکھُوں ہُوں 'when I rub my eyes and look.'

آتِشِ عِشق سے جلے ہَي دِل 'my heart burns with love's fire.'

گہ کري ہَي برگِ گُل مرکب 'now it makes the leaf of the rose its steed' (*i.e.* 'one moment it mounts the rose, another it,' etc.).

But this form of the Present,[1] though once very common, is now rarely used in Urdū (see § 189, *Rem.*).

437. As a present tense the Aorist is employed in narrative for a past (the *Historical Present*): *e.g.*

آگے جاکر جو دیکھوں (= دیکھا) تو مِلِک هَي 'when I went forward and looked, lo! it was the princess' (*lit.* 'when, having gone forward, I look, lo! it is the princess').

جِي ميں آوي كِ يا اِلٰهي يِه دمِ جان نِكل جاوي تو بهتر هَي 'it came (was coming, *lit.* comes) into my mind, "O God! if this breath of life depart, it is better."'

438. The Aorist often occurs in a form identical with that of the Precative[2] (§ 176) in the three persons of the singular, and with nasal *n* added to that form in the plural: *e.g.*

[1] Most European grammarians ignore this tense altogether, and those who do notice it wrongly term it "a perfect," and generally mistake for it the perfect participle when this is used as a *ḥāl* in connection with a subject that has for its predicate one of the verbs هَي or تها. For example, in the sentence *ek meṅḍak ko sāṅp pakṛe hai*, they call *pakṛe hai* "a perfect," and translate, "the snake has caught a frog;" whereas *pakṛe* is a *ḥāl*, and the translation should be *a snake is* (there is a snake) *with a frog caught*. As a finite verb *pakṛe hai* would signify "catches," not "has caught."

[2] It does not follow that because this form is identical with that of the precative, therefore this, or, as the grammarians phrase it, "the respectful imperative," is used for the aorist. In the use of these precative forms the Hindī and Urdū follow the Prākṛit pretty closely, and the following extracts from the *Prākṛita-Prakāśa* (ed. Cowell, sect. vii. 20, 21) show that they are not used the one for the other, but that, though connected both in form and signification, they are yet distinct: "*Jja*, *jjā* are optionally substituted for the proper affixes of the present and the definite future, and also when command, etc., are implied: *e.g.* *hojja*, *hojjā*, or *hoi*, 'he is;' *hasejja*, *hasejjā*, or *hasaï*, 'he laughs;' (and the same form applies to the three persons in both numbers;) future *hojja*, *hojjā*, *hohii*, 'he will be;' and similarly in the sense of the imperative." "*Jja*, *jjā* are also optionally inserted between the root and the affixes" in the same tenses; "as (present) *hojjaï*, *hojjāi*; (future) *hojjahii*, *hojjāhii*; (imperative) *hojjaii*, *hojjāu*;" this however only occurs "when the root ends in a vowel, and is therefore monosyllabic."

میري دِل میں یِہ خِیال گذرا کِہ اَبکِي دفعه اَنگور لگائِیے (= لگاؤں) '(when I reached the garden), the thought entered my mind, This time I will plant a vine.'

کیا کہیئے اُن لوگوں کو جو نافرمانِي کرکے ناحق اُس سے برگشته هوتے هَیں 'what shall I say respecting those people who, having rebelled, unjustly turn away from Him ?'

Rem. Additional examples of this form of the Aorist will be found under the Subjunctive Mood, in which it more commonly occurs.

439. The Aorist چاهِیئے is commonly used as a phrase in the sense and after the manner of *opus, necesse, est*, 'it is necessary,' *debet*, 'it is proper or right,' *oportet*, 'it behoves,' with an infinitive, or a gerundive and its substantive, or a perfect participle used as a gerund (§ 425), as the subject, the true subject or agent of the act usually preceding in the Dative, if a definite agent is implied; the agent, however, is not always expressed—rarely so if the idea of *duty*, etc., implied in the phrase *chāhiye* is of general application, or if the infinitive is accompanied by an object in the dative form of the accusative: *e.g.*

جو صاحِب کو چاهِیئے سب مَوجُود هَي 'whatever the master wants is ready (to be had).'

اِن لوگوں کو مغلُوب رکھنا چاهِیئے '(the king) should keep these people under subjection' (*lit.* 'to keep these people under subjection is necessary for the king').

اب همکو ذرّه فِکر کرنِي چاهِیئے 'we should now consider a little.'

زِندگِي میں اَیسے کام کرنے چاهِییں 'one should perform such acts in life.'

ایکٔ دفعه وهاں بهي چلا (= چلنا) چاهیٔے 'I ought to go once there also.'

تفسیر اِسکي عالِموں سے پُوچها چاهیٔے 'the explanation of this should be asked of the doctors of religion' (*lit.* 'asking the explanation of this of the doctors is necessary').

Rem. a. The agent of the act is sometimes put in the genitive in construction with an Arabic *nomen actionis*; as فقیرکا عمل اُن پر چاهِیٔے 'a *faḳīr* should act upon them.' And if the thing *necessary* or *requisite* be a *quality*, or that which should be found *in* some person or thing, the locative is generally used instead of the dative: *e.g.* وي کونسي خصلتیں هَیں کِہ قاصِد میں چاهِییں 'what special qualities are those which a messenger should possess?' ('which are requisite in a messenger').

Rem. b. چاهِیٔے is also very commonly used in the Subjunctive Mood: the infinitive is then replaced by the ordinary Aorist, which follows چاهِیٔے, and is preceded by کِہ (= Latin *ut*), the agent of the act either preceding *chāhiye* in the dative, or following it in the nominative: *e.g.* پادشاه کو چاهِیٔے کِہ اِن لوگوں کو مغلوب رکهے, or چاهِیٔے کِہ پادشاه اِن لوگوں کو مغلوب رکهے 'the king should keep these people under subjection.'

Rem. c. The phrases مُناسِب هي, لازِم هَي, ضرُور هَي, *it is necessary, right,* or *proper,* are used in the same way as چاهِیٔے, chiefly in the Subjunctive.

Rem. d. According to some European grammarians any "Respectful Imperative," as they term it, may be used "with a sense of obligation, and may be translated *ought, should,* or *must.*" This however is not correct; *chāhiye* alone can, of itself, be so used. The examples given by them are such as the following: اِس سے دریافت کِیجِیے 'learn from, or let one learn from, this' (not "from this one *ought* to learn"); اِس جنگل میں رهِیے اَور پاسبانِي کِیجِیے 'let us remain in this jungle and watch' (not "we *must* stay in this wood and keep watch"); آنکھیں دروازي کي طرف لگ رهي تهیں که دیکهیے کیا ظاهر هوتا هَي '(my) eyes were kept fixed on the door to see (*lit. saying* to myself "Let me see") what was (*lit.* is) about to appear' (not "my eyes were fixed on the door, and I said I *must* see," etc.).

440. To imply that an act should or ought *to have been done*, the phrase چاهِئے تها is employed: as

تیرا گهونسلا ایک کانٹے کے درخت میں یا کِسي دِیوار کے اوپر چاهِیے تها نه بادشاه کي محل سرا میں 'thy nest ought to have been (built) in some thorny bush or on the top of a wall, (and) not in the king's palace.'

Rem. The same phrase is used in the Subjunctive also (§ 467, *Rem. c*).

II. The Future Indefinite.

441. Although the Aorist itself has the signification of the simple Future, yet to render the futurity of the act quite distinct, the perfect participle گا (see § 187) is added to it; and thus the Future also derives the signification of an *Intentional* and a *Desiderative*: *e.g.*

مَیں دیکهونگا 'I shall see,' and 'I wish to, or would, see.'

آخِر مر جاؤنگا تب خُدا کو کیا جواب دُونگا 'eventually I shall die, and what answer shall I then give to God?'

بعضي بعضي باتیں حُضُور میں پُوچهُونگا 'I would question Your Highness about certain matters.'

442. The participle گا is also added to the Precative form of the Aorist to form the Future: *e.g.*

آپ اُس شخص کو پَیدا کِیجِیگا جو رُوئِ زمِیں پر فساد اور خُون ریزِي کري 'wilt thou (wouldst thou, is it thy intention to) create a being who will work mischief and shed blood on the face of the earth?'

جو یُوں کھینْچِیگا مغْز کے گُودي کو نہ چھوڑیگا 'if you pull (will pull) so (*i.e.* as you are going to do), it will not leave hold of the pulp of the brain.'

Rem. The Future and the Aorist being thus intimately connected, we often find the one used for the other, especially in conditional and hypothetical sentences, where in English the Present Indicative, or the Present or Future Subjunctive, is used; as اگر دیر لگاؤنگا تو وي اِس پِیرِي میں روتے روتے مرجائینگے 'if I tarry long, he in this state of old age will weep himself to death;' اگر اُسکے نزْدِیک جاؤگے تو گُنہگار هوگے 'if you go near it you sin' (*lit.* 'will become a sinner'); کِہ نہ مُجھ میں قُدْرت کہنے کِي اور نہ تُجھ میں طاقت سُنْنے کِي رهیگِي 'for (were I to attempt it), I should not have the power to tell, nor you the patience (*lit.* power) to listen.'

III. The Present Tense.

443. The Present Tense is used to indicate an act which *is now taking place*, or a *repeated*, *habitual*, or *enduring* act; it also commonly expresses a *universal truth*, *e.g.*

وُہ کیا کرْتا هَي 'what is he doing?'

کیا دیکھتے هو 'what are you looking at?' or 'what do you see?'

جو کُچھ تُو کہْتا هَي مَیں یِہ سب سمجھْتا هُوں 'I understand all this that you are saying.'

آدمي اپنے بادشاهوں کے طریقے پر هوتے هیں 'men conform to the ways of their kings.'

رات دِن یہہ مِہر و ماہ پِهرتے هیں 'this sun and moon are revolving night and day.'

Rem. a. An act which is now taking place may also be expressed by using the perfect participle of a verb compounded with رهنا in place of the imperfect participle, for in both cases the participle is used as a *ḥāl*: *e.g.* صاحِب سو رها (= سوتا) هَي 'the master is sleeping;' عَورت نہا رهي (= نہاتي) هَي 'the woman is bathing.'

Rem. b. The auxiliary, both in this tense and the Perfect, occasionally takes the form هَیگا, which is generally more emphatic than هَي; as وُہ مارتا هَیگا 'he is (or I am sure he is) beating.' The auxiliary may also take this form when used independently; as آیا یِہہ کَون هَینگے 'alas! who *are* these?'

444. The auxiliary is often omitted, chiefly in negative sentences (*cf.* § 148, *Rem.*), and the Present then assumes the form of the Past Conditional, but the two tenses must not be confounded: *e.g.*

قافِلے کے آدمي اِس لِیئے نہیں کہتے کِہ تُو شرمِندہ هوگا 'the people of the caravan do not mention (it), because you would be ashamed.'

کوئِي آپ سے کُوئے میں نہیں گِرتا 'no one falls into a well of himself.'

And in two co-ordinate sentences, the verbs of which are both in the Present, the auxiliary of one may be omitted, unless emphasis requires it to be repeated: *e.g.*

وُہ نہ هِلتِي هَي نہ ڈُلتِي 'she neither moves nor stirs.'

445. The Present Tense is commonly used in narrative for a past for the sake of greater vividness (the *Historical Present*): *e.g.*

آنکھیں ملکر جو دیکھتا ھوں تو اُس مکان میں نہ وُہ بُوڑھا ھَي نہ کوئِي اَور ھَي 'when I rubbed my eyes and looked (*lit.* when, having rubbed my eyes, I look), lo! neither that old man nor any one else was (*lit.* is) in that house.'

پھر رونے لگے اَور فرّیاد اَور زارِي کرنے لگے مگر کیا ھوتا ھَي اَور کَون سُنتا ھَي 'thereupon we began to weep and to cry aloud and wail, but what comes of it? and who hears?' (*i.e.* nothing came of it, etc.).

446. The Present Tense is also frequently used for the Future to indicate that an action will take place forthwith, or shortly after the time of speaking: *e.g.*

تُم چلو مَیں بھِي چلتا ھُوں 'you go, I also am coming (immediately).'

مَیں ابھِي حُکم کرتا ھُوں 'I will this instant give the order.'

جلد پھِر آتا ھُوں 'I shall speedily return.'

447. The Present Tense is occasionally employed in conditional sentences as a Future Subjunctive: as

اگر مَیں بھِي منع کرتا ھُوں تو ابھِي مَینا کِي طرح سے مارا جاتا ھُوں 'if I too forbid (her), I shall be instantly killed as the *mainā* has been.'

اگر مَیں اپنِي بانِي پر آتا ھُوں تو اُسکِي سلطنت کو خاک میں ملادیتا ھُوں 'if I come according to my plighted word,[1] I will mingle his kingdom with the dust.'

[1] That is to say, "if I say I will come and do come." We know of no authority for the meaning of "one's own might," which is given to the word *bānī* in the vocabulary of the *Totā Kahānī*. The word means simply 'speech,' 'word,' and the phrase *bānī par ānā* is explained by Urdū scholars as we have translated it.

Rem. An act which *it is intended to perform* (the Present Intentional) is expressed as in English: *e.g.* وُہ لِکھنے کو ھَي 'he is going to write' (see § 412.)

IV. The Past Imperfect Tense.

448. The Past Imperfect Tense indicates an action which was going on at some past time spoken of: as

ہر طرف دیکھتا پھِرتا تھا 'he was wandering about, looking around him.'

ھوَا نرم نرم بہتِي تھِي 'a very soft breeze was blowing.'

Rem. The same idea is expressed by using the perfect participle of a verb compounded with رھنا in place of the simple imperfect participle; وُہ نہا رھِي (= نہاتِي) تھِي 'she was bathing;' مَیں آھِستہ یِہہ شِعْر پڑھ رھا تھا 'I was repeating this verse in a very low voice.'

449. In many cases this tense must be rendered by the English Past Indefinite: as

جو یِہہ کہتے تھے سو کرتا تھا 'he did whatever they told him (at the time).'

ازبسکِہ خیر خواھِي اَور تدبیر اَور جان نِثارِي اُسکِي جانتے تھے 'inasmuch as he was aware of his loyalty, judgment, and devotion.'

450. The auxiliary is often omitted[1]: *e.g.*

جو کوئِي آدمِي میرِي نظر پڑتا منع کرتا 'every one I saw (at the time) forbade me.'

[1] As this tense then assumes the form of the Past Conditional, it is very generally mistaken for the latter by European grammarians. The two tenses, however, are essentially different, the one occurring in the Indicative Mood alone, the other only in the Subjunctive, and never admitting of the auxiliary تھا after it, as the Imperfect Indicative does. Nor can either of these tenses ever have the signification of the *Present*, as the grammarians affirm.

اگر وُہ پانِي نہ لاتِي تو یِہہ اُسکے باسن پھوڑ ڈالتا 'if she did not bring water, he (the dog) broke her vessels.'

Rem. In two coordinate sentences, the verbs of both of which are in the Past Imperfect, the auxiliary is usually expressed with the last alone: as وُہ شُکرِ خُدا کا کرتا اَور کُوچ درکُوچ چلا جاتا تھا 'he was thanking God and going on stage by stage.'

451. The Past Imperfect is frequently used to indicate an act that *was wont* to be done, and the auxiliary is then often omitted: *e.g.*[1]

اُس کُوئے کا نام زِندانِ سُلَیمان کہتے تھے 'they used to name that pit Solomon's Prison.'

غِیبت سُننے میں جو مزا آتا تھا اُسکو دِل سے بھُلا دِیا 'I effaced from my mind the pleasure I was wont to derive from listening to slander.'

اَور وُہ رنگ جو کُندن سا دمکتا تھا هلدِي سا بن گیا 'and that complexion (or colour) which used to glisten like bright gold became like turmeric.'

جِس وقت سفر سے آتا هر ایک مُلک کا تُحفہ بہ طرِیقِ سَوغات لاتا اَور مُجھے دیتا 'when he used to return from his travels, he was wont to bring curiosities of each country (he visited) as presents for me' (*lit.* 'and used to give them to me').

v. The Past Indefinite Tense.

452. The Past Indefinite Tense indicates an action completed at some past time, and is commonly employed in narrating past events which do not involve the idea of *duration.* Its *passive* construction (when the participle

[1] See note on preceding page.

is *passive*), as also that of the other past tenses composed of a passive participle, has been explained in § 185, 191, etc.: *e.g.*

وُہ میري مکان پردي گیا 'he left it at my house on his way.'

اُس نے صحّرا کِي راہ لِي 'he took the road to the desert.'

453. *a.* After the conditional particles اگر, جو, 'if,' and after other particles (*e.g.* جب 'when,' etc.), which imply the conditional meaning of اگر, the Past Indefinite often takes a *future* sense, the condition being represented as already fulfilled; but it may be rendered in English by the Present: as

اگر یِہہ راز فاش هُوا تو تیري حق میں بہُت بُرا هَي 'if this secret is (*lit.* was, or became) divulged, it will be (*lit.* is) very bad for you.'

لیکِن ایک کام همارا هَي - اگر وُہ اِس سے هو سکا اَور خِیانت نہ کِي اَور بہ خُوبِي انجام دِیا اَور اِس اِمتِحان میں پُورا اُترا - تو مَیں قَول قرار کرتا هُوں کِہ زِیادہ پادشاہ سے سُلُوک کرُونگا 'but I have a work (for him to do), if that can be done by this (youth), and he practises no treachery, but accomplishes it satisfactorily, and comes out perfect in this ordeal, then I promise that I will deal with him better than any king.'

b. The verbs of the *principal* clauses in the above sentences are in the Present and Future, but the Past Indefinite is also employed to indicate an act, the occurrence of which is so certain, that it may be described as having already taken place: as

اگر پادشاه ایسے لوگوں کي جھوٹھ سچ باتیں سُننے لگا اور اصل حال کي تحقیق پر اِلتِفات نہ کي - تو طرح طرح کي خرابیاں پیدا ھوئیں 'if the king begins to listen to the misrepresentations (*lit.* false and true words) of such persons, and does not attempt to inquire into the actual facts of the case, various kinds of evils will result (*lit.* have resulted).

VI. The Present Perfect Tense.

454. The Present Perfect (or Past Proximate) Tense indicates an act which at the moment of speaking has been already completed, and remains in a state of completion: *e.g.*

وہ کانھپور گیا ھَي 'he is gone to Kānhpūr (Cawnpore).'

راجہ صاحِب نے شیر مارا ھَي 'the Rāja Ṣāḥib has killed a tiger.'

455. The auxiliary is often omitted, or in other words the Past Indefinite is used for the Present Perfect: *e.g.*

یِہہ چار باتیں جو اوپر بیان ھوئیں 'these four things that have been mentioned above.'

جِس شخص کے سِینے میں کِینہ جم گیا (*sc.* ھَي) اُس سے بجز ضرر کے کُچھ فائِدہ حاصِل نہ هوگا 'naught but injury can proceed from him in whose breast hatred has established itself.'

Rem. In the colloquial the Present Perfect is frequently used for the Present in the sense of the Proximate Future, and in such cases the auxiliary is generally omitted: *e.g.* (Master *loq.*) همارِي ٹوپِي اَور چھڑِي جلد لاؤ 'bring my hat and stick quickly;' (Servant) لایا صاحِب 'I am bringing it, Sir' (*lit.* 'I have brought').

VII. The Past Perfect Tense.

456. The Past Perfect (or Past Remote) Tense indicates that an act *had taken place* at the time spoken of, or anterior to some other past event spoken of or implied: *e.g.*

وُہ دُور سے چلکر آیا تھا 'he had come walking from a distance.'

مَیں نے اَیسِي بات کبھِي نہ سُنِي تھِي 'I had never heard such a thing.'

But the auxiliary is often omitted, or in other words the Past Indefinite is used for the Past Perfect. It must however be rendered in English by the Past Perfect: *e.g.*

مَیں نے زَید کو بہُت سمجھایا (*sc.* تھا) 'I had reasoned a great deal with Zaid.'

457. The Past Perfect is often used where in English we use the Past Indefinite; usually so when the action is regarded by the narrator as completely past, so that its results have already become manifest at the time spoken of; or when it is implied that since the occurrence of that action, another, in some way connected with it, has occurred: *e.g.*

اَور جب شیرنے میري تئِیں تیري لانے کو بھیجا تھا جو کُچھ مَیں نے عہد و پَیمان کِیا تھا 'and whatever I (had) promised when the lion (had) sent me to bring thee.'

بِلِّي آئِي تھِي مَیں نے اُسکو ٹٹولا تھا بھیگِي تھِي 'the cat came (*lit.* had come), (and) I (had) felt her, and she was wet (and so I knew it was raining).'

Rem. The Past Perfect Indicative is sometimes used for the Past Conditional, for the sake of greater vividness: as اُس دوست نے مُجھے ہلاک کِیا تھا ۔ اگر یِہ دانا دُشمن نہ ہوتا توکام میرا ہاتھ سے جا چُکا

تها اَور جان میرِي اِس خیال میں تمام هُوئِي تهِي 'that friend well nigh destroyed me: if it had not been for this wise enemy, my work was well nigh gone from my hands, and my life brought to a close in this vain idea.'

c. THE IMPERATIVE.

458. The Imperative has only the second person singular and plural; the other persons are supplied by the aorist. It has two forms, the Imperative proper, which is used in giving *orders*, *directions*, or *advice*, and the Precative (§ 176), which implies simple *request*, *advice*, *entreaty*, or *exhortation*.

Rem. The second of the Precative forms, however, often has the force of a command, as will be seen from the examples given below.

459. The Precative again has two forms, one ending in ـِیے, the other in ـِیو, both of which are used in either the singular or plural, the former always in connection with the *pronomen reverentiæ* آپ, expressed or understood, the latter with the personal pronouns تُو 'thou,' and تُم 'you.'

460. The Imperative, and the Precative ending in *iye*, are used with reference to the immediate present, or without reference to any definite time; the Precative ending in *iyo* most commonly refers to the Future. The addition of گا to the Precative ending in *iye* imparts to it also a future signification, but the form is not very common: *e.g.*

میرا کہنا مان اَور اِس بیہُودہ آرزُو کو دِل سے نِکال 'mind what I say, and chase this vain desire from thy mind.'

تُم یہاں بَیٹھو 'you sit here.'

جو کُچھ درکار هو اِس خانہ زاد کو کہیے 'mention to this slave anything you may require.'

اِس کو کھا پیکر پھِر آئیو اَور جو مانگیگا لیجیو 'come again when you have spent this, and take whatever you want.'

جب تیرا احوال پُوچھے تُو کہیو مَیں عجم کا رهنے والا هُوں 'when she asks thy story, thou shalt say: I am an inhabitant of Persia.'

نہیں تو جو جِي چاهیگا سو مُجھے کِیجِیگا 'and if not, do (*i.e.* you shall do) unto me whatever you please.'

Rem. The English Imperative being used to express a *request* as well as an *order*, it is not at all necessary to employ such phrases as "please to do," or "you will be pleased to do," etc., in rendering the Precative forms; nor indeed do these phrases at all represent the idea in a native's mind when he uses a Precative. We have repeatedly observed, that when a native scholar well acquainted with English is asked to render in Urdū such an expression as "please do this," he invariably uses the phrase *az rāhĕ mihrbānī isko karo* or *kījiye.* It is evident too that in not a few cases the phrases "please to," etc., cannot be applied: as for example in the following sentence, in which the speaker is soliloquizing: کِہ اگر پھٹکري اَور گندھک کو چراغ میں بتّي کے آس پاس چھِڑک دِیجِیے تو کیسي هِي هوَا چلے چراغ گُل نہ هوگا 'for if you sprinkle alum and sulphur in a lamp, round about the wick, no matter how strong a wind blow, the lamp will not be extinguished.'

461. The Precative ending in *o* is also employed in benedictions and imprecations: *e.g.*

خُوش رهِیو 'may you be happy!'

خُدا کي لعنت کافِروں اَور مُشرِکوں پر هُوجِیو 'may the curse of God be upon infidels and believers in a plurality of gods!'

462. The negatives نہ and نہیں in connection with the Imperative usually express a *strict negation*, but the former is occasionally prohibitive (especially in connection with the Precative ending in *iyo*); the negative مت is used in a prohibitive sense, and hence occurs with the Imperative or Precative alone: *e.g.*

تُو ڈر نہیں 'be not afraid.'

آخِرت کے سامان کرنے میں غفلت نہ کر 'neglect not to make preparation for the world to come.'

آج گھر مت جاؤ 'don't go home to-day.'

اُن کی آشنائی کا اِعتماد نہ کریے 'rely not on their friendship.'

اِس درخت کے پاس نہ جائیو 'you are not to approach this tree' (or 'thou shalt not go near this tree').

بھولیو مت 'you will not forget' ('take care that you don't forget').

Rem. As the negative نہیں does not occur in the *Bāg o bahār* in connection with the Imperative, therefore, we suppose, the European grammarians say, that it "is not used with the Imperative." That it is so used will be seen from the first of the above examples, and we may add that (though not so common as نہ) it is by no means uncommon in such cases.

463. The Aorist, which is connected with the Imperative both in form and signification, is used instead of it in the first and third persons, but usually with less authority than the Imperative: *e.g.*

وُہ کیا بات تھی؟ ذرا میں بھی سُنوں 'what was it that he said? let me also just hear.'

دیکھیں اِس کے نصیبوں میں کیا لِکھا هَي 'let us see what is recorded in her destiny.'

تُو خبردار رهِیو اَیسِي حرکت نہ کري جو ٹانکے ٹُوٹ جائیں 'you will be careful: let her not move so that the stitches give way.'

کوئي میري پاس نہ آوی 'let no one come near me' (not, "no one *must* come near me:" see *Rem. d*, § 439).

لیکِن ملِکہ اِس کا قَول قرار کریں کہ اَپنے کہنے سے نہ پھریں 'but let the princess promise this, to wit, that she will not withdraw from what she has said' (not, "the princess *must* promise, etc.").

کمال نہ حاصِل کرنے کے لِیئے عُمر کي زِیادتي کا عُذر نہ کري 'let no one plead advanced age as an excuse for not acquiring (not trying to attain to) perfection.'

464. Reversely, the Imperative is occasionally used for the second person singular of the Aorist, usually in the first of two correlative clauses which follow a particle implying a condition or the relative pronoun, when the second clause contains an Imperative: *e.g.*

جو مُناسِب جان (= جانے) سو کر 'do whatever you think proper.'

Rem. The use of the Imperative for the Aorist is not so common as the grammarians suppose; it occurs, we believe, only in sentences of the description mentioned above. In the following examples the last verb is not "an Aorist in the Imperative form," but a simple Imperative: اَیسا کام کرکہ شہزادي کو فریب سے مار ڈال 'do so (or act in this wise): kill the prince by stratagem' (not, "act *in such a manner as to* kill, etc.," for کہ here is simply *explicative*, and does not denote the *purpose* or *object* of the verb in the first clause); جب تئيں تو پار چلنے كي كچھ تدبير كر 'in the mean time you make some arrangement to cross over' (not, "*whilst thou formest* some plan, etc.").

465. The Imperative, singular and plural, of the verb لينا 'to take,' is often used as an interjection, signifying *there* or *there now! enough! peace!* etc.: *e.g.*

لے اپنا كام كر 'enough! go on with thy work.'

لے ميں نے اپني حقيقت سب سنائي 'there now! I have told you my whole history.'

لو مجھے ديكھا خاطر جمع هوئي 'there! you have seen me; is your mind relieved?'

ميں نے كہا لو اب بہت مكر چكر كيا 'I said: Now have done! you have tried subterfuges enough.'

d. THE SUBJUNCTIVE AND ITS TENSES.

I. THE AORIST.

466. The Aorist is used in the Subjunctive Mood, as a Present or Future, in correlative conditional clauses that depend upon اگر, or any particle having the sense of اگر. The conditional clause commonly precedes the principal clause (but it may follow it), and is separated from it by the جوابِ شرط, or *correlative* particle, تو, which is generally not translated. The Aorist is used in one or both clauses, according to the following rules:

1) *a.* If both the conditional and the principal clause imply *uncertainty*, *doubt*, *possibility*, or *indefiniteness*, the Aorist is used in both: *e.g.*

اگر وہ آجاوي تو کيا کروں 'if he should come, what am I to do?'

اگر اجازت هو تو اُنکا حال تمهاري رُوبرُو بياں کروں 'if permission be granted, I will state their case in your presence.'

حنظل سے شهد ٹپکے جو لگے نشترِ زنبورِ عسل 'honey would drop from the colocynth-gourd if the sting of the honey-bee were to touch it.'

b. The Present Potential occasionally occurs in place of the Aorist in the principal clause: *e.g.*

اگر ملِکہ کي سلطنت پر نِگاہ کِيجِيے تو اُسکي آمد فقط باورچي خانے کے خرچ کو بهِي کِفايت نہ کرتي هوگي 'if one look at the princess's dominion, its revenue probably does not suffice (may not be sufficing) for the expenditure of the cuisine alone.'

c. And an Imperative may take the place of the Aorist in the conditional clause: as

تهوڑا پاني گرم کردي تو نهاؤں 'warm a little water and I'll bathe.'

ايک بيٹا جِيتا جاگتا مُجهے دي تو ميرا نام اَور اِس سَلطنت کا نِشان قائم رهے 'bestow on me a living son, then will my name and the trace of this empire endure.'

Rem. The Aorist of the conditional clause may often be rendered in English by the Past Imperfect, as in the third of the above examples.

2). If the condition be regarded as *uncertain*, or only *possible*, etc., while the conditioned is regarded as *certain* and *positive*, the Aorist is employed in the conditional, and the Present or Future Indicative in the principal clause: as

اگر چلو تو اچّها هَي 'if you come, it is well.'

اگر بن آوي تو بڑي بات هَي 'if it succeed, it is a great matter.'

جو کوئِي دعْوىٰ کري اِسْکا بڑا نادان هَي 'any one who pretends to this is a great fool.'

شرافت أسِي کو حاصِل هوگي کِہ جِس پر بادْشاہ نظرِعِنايت کِي فرْماوي 'honour will be obtained by him alone on whom the monarch shall look with favour.'

Rem. a. The Relative Pronoun, implying as it often does a virtual hypothesis, is commonly followed by the Subjunctive, as in the last of the above examples. (*cf.* § 388, *Rem.*)

Rem. b. The Future is often used in the conditional clause also, and occasionally where the idea of certainty is, to say the least, not very prominent (see § 442, *Rem.*); but wherever this idea is prominent, the Indicative is used in both clauses: *e.g.* اگر جلْد آؤگے تو مُجھے جِيتا پاؤگے 'if you come soon (as I expect, or am sure, you will), you will find me alive.'

467. The Aorist is also employed in subordinate clauses with one or other of the conjunctions جو 'that,' کِہ (= Lat. *ut*), تاکِہ 'in order that' (= Lat. *quo*), بشرْطيکِہ 'on condition, or provided, that,' شايد کِہ 'it may be that, perchance,' etc., to express an *object or purpose*, *effect or consequence*, *resolution*, *hope*, *desire*, *disinclination*, *order*, *advice*, *necessity*, *duty* (as signified by the phrases لازِم هَي, چاهِيئے, etc. see § 439 and *Rem. b.*), *effort*, *permission*, *fear*, etc.:[1] *e.g.*

قصْد کِيا کِہ أس راہ سے چلوں 'I determined to go (that I would go) by that road.'

آدْمِيوں کے واسْطے يِہ بِہْتر معْلوم هوتا هَي کِہ گوشہ نِشِيں هو جائيں 'it appears better for men that they become recluses.'

[1] This construction, which is found in the Persian also, would appear to be derived from the Arabic.

پادشاہ کو چاهيئے کہ اُمرا اور ارکانِ دولت سے اَيسا برتاو کري کہ اُنکو پادشاہ کي مُوافقت اَور نيک‌خواهي کا يقين هوجائے 'the king should so treat his lords and nobles that they may be assured of His Majesty's sympathy and good-will.'

چاهيئے کہ قاصِد فاضِل هو 'a messenger (or emissary) should be one possessed of learning.'

اگر تُجهے آرزو کمال هَي کہ يهہ ماهيّت دريافت کري 'if you have great desire to know this matter.'

مَيں ڈرتا هوں کہ شايد دُعائے بد نہ کري 'I am afraid that he may not perhaps curse me (or, according to an idiom of the language, 'that he may curse me').

بُقراط نے ايک زبان دراز عَورت سے شادي کي تاکہ اپني قوّتِ غضبي کو مغلوب کري 'Socrates (or, according to Johnson's Dictionary, Hippocrates) married a shrew in order to subdue his passion of anger.'

بشرطيکہ جهوٹه اِس ميں کَوڑي بهر نہ هو 'provided there be not as much as a *kauṛī* of untruth in it.'

شايد (*sc.* کہ) اُس کا هاته راس آوي 'perhaps his hand (treatment) may prove successful.'

Rem. a. In sentences signifying *purpose, resolution, wish,* etc., the Aorist may generally be rendered in English by the gerund with *to,* since this corresponds to the genitive (subjective) or the dative of the Urdū gerund, and this may in most cases be substituted for the construction with the Aorist: *e.g.* the first of the above examples may also be constructed thus: مَيں نے اُس راہ سے چلنے کا قصد کيا; and the fifth thus: اگر تُجهے اِس ماهِيّت کے دريافت کرنے کو آرزو کمال هَي.

Rem. b. The *direct oration* often occurs in such subordinate clauses as express *purpose* or *resolution*: اَور قصد کِیا کِہ بہن کے پاس چلِیے 'and determined to go to my sister' (*lit.* 'that I will go'); آنکھیں دروازي کِي طرف لگ رهِي تهِيں کِہ دیکھِیے کیا ظاهِر هوتا هَي 'my eyes were kept fixed in the direction of the door to see what was going to appear' (*lit.* 'saying to myself, Let me see what is going to appear').

Rem. c. The phrases لازم هَي, چاهِیئے, etc., may also be constructed with the infinitive (§ 439, and *Rem. b.* and *c*). In reference to past time these phrases take the forms لازِم تها, چاهِیئے تها, and are followed by کِہ with the Past Perfect Subjunctive (the Past Conditional): *e.g.* چاهِیئے تها کِہ مہاراج اپنے غضب پر غالِب رهتے 'Your Majesty ought to have subdued your wrath.'

468. The Aorist is used to express a wish which, generally speaking, is regarded as attainable: as

عُمر تیرِي بڑهے دَولت دُو چند هووي 'may your life be prolonged! your wealth be multiplied!'

جب تلک یِہ زمِین و آسمان برپا هَي تُمهارِي تاج و تخت قائِم رهي 'may your crown and throne (your sovereignty) endure as long as this earth and heaven last!'

469. The Aorist is used in questions indicating doubt or perplexity: as

اِلٰهِي اب کیا کرُوں 'O God! what am I to do now?'

کیا کہُوں اَور کِسکا شِکوہ کرُوں 'what should I say? and of whom should I complain?'

اِندر کا اکھاڑا کہُوں یا پرِیوں کا اُتارا 'should I call it Indra's court, or a descent of fairies?'

470. The second person, singular and plural, of the Aorist is used as a disjunctive conjunction: *e.g.*

مَیں نہیں کہتا رہو چاہو جاؤ 'I say nothing: remain or go (as you please).'

II. The Present Potential.

471. The Present Potential, as its name implies, occurs chiefly in potential propositions, with a definite or indefinite subject, and indicates that a thing *may*, *might*, or *must be happening*: it corresponds therefore to the English Present Imperfect Subjunctive. It stands to the Aorist in the same relation as the Present Imperfect Indicative to the Present Indefinite; and hence the Aorist is often used in its place. Of the two forms in which it occurs, that in which the *future* of the verb ہونا is used may occasionally be rendered in English by the Future Imperfect Indicative; but those who speak the language recognize no distinction between the two forms. The following are examples of its use:

وُہ اپنے جِي میں کیا کہتا ہوگا 'what must he be thinking?' (*lit.* 'saying in his mind').

شاید تُو جانتا ہوگا کِہ مُجھکو یِہ سب فراغت اَور دَولت بے مشقّت حاصِل ہوئي 'perhaps you think (*lit.* may be thinking) that I have become possessed of all this comfort and wealth without trouble.'

ایسے غرِیب ہزاروں تُمھاري مُلکوں میں آتے جاتے ہونگے 'thousands of such poor people must be constantly passing through (*lit.* may be coming and going in) your dominions.'

وُہ حاکِم اَیسا ہونا چاہِیئے کِہ سِیاست کے قاعِدي خُوب جانتا ہو	'that ruler ought to be well acquainted with (*lit.* such as may be knowing well) the laws of government.'
اَور جو بادشاہ بیدار ہو سلطنت کے کارو بار پر توجُّہ کرتا ہو تو کِسِي طرح سلطنت میں خلل نہیں آتا	'and if the king look (*lit.* be looking) watchfully after the affairs of his kingdom, no disturbance by any means enters the realm.'
اُسکے کلام میں کوئِي فِقرہ اَیسا نہیں ہَے جِس سے کِسِي کِي بد خواہِي ثابِت ہوتِي ہو	'there is no such sentence in his discourse whereby malevolence towards any one may be proved.'

III. The Past Potential.

472. The Past Potential is employed when it is indicated that a thing *may*, *might*, or *must have happened.* It has two forms, corresponding to those of the Present Potential, but no distinction is generally made between them: *e.g.*

آپ نے یِہہ بَیت سُنِي ہوگِي	'Your Majesty may (or must) have heard this couplet.'
خُدا جانے اُنکِي کیا حالت ہُوئِي ہوگِي	'God knows what their state may have been.'
جِس وقت تیّارِي اِس کِي (ہُوئِي .sc) ہوگِي کیا ہِي مکانِ دِل‌چسپ بنا ہوگا	'what a very charming residence must have been made when it was first constructed' (*lit.* 'when its preparation may have taken place').

اپنے اور اپنے بزرگوں کے احسان جو دوسري شخص يا اسکے بزرگوں کي نسبت هوئے هوں بيان کرتا هَي ‘he mentions the kindnesses which he or his forefathers may have done to another or to his forefathers.’

تيري گروه نے جو ظلم آدميوں کے هاتھ سے اٹھايا هو تو بهي کهہ ‘do you also mention whatever oppression your tribe may have suffered at the hands of men.’

Rem. The third of the above examples is thus rendered in Prof. Monier Williams' Hindūstānī Grammar (p. 136, § 510): "When it shall be repaired, what a charming place it will be made." But although this tense may sometimes be rendered in English by the *Future Perfect*, it is never used in the sense of, and can certainly never be rendered by, the *Future Indefinite.*

IV. The Past Conditional.

473. The Past Conditional corresponds to the English Past Perfect Subjunctive. It has two forms, the one (which is that most commonly used) consisting simply of the imperfect participle of a verb; the other of the perfect participle in combination with the imperfect participle of the verb هونا.

474. The Past Conditional is used in correlative conditional clauses that depend upon اگر, or any particle having the sense of اگر. In the leading clause it may generally be rendered in English by the Future Perfect Subjunctive: *e.g.*

اگر تو وه ديکهتا جو مَيں نے ديکها هَي هرگز اُنکے پاس نہ آتا ‘had you seen what I have seen, you would never have come near them.’

جو مُجھے مُرید کرنے کِي خواهِش نہ هوتِي تو مَیں چورکِي چرب زبانِي سے فریب نہ کھاتا 'if the desire to make a disciple had not possessed me, I should not have been deceived by a thief's oiliness of speech.'

اندھا بیٹا تُمھاري کِس کام آتا ؟ جو کُچھ بیٹا کرتا مَیں بھِي کر سکتا هُوں 'of what use would a blind son have been to you? I too can do whatever a son would have done.' (The condition اگر هوتا is here understood in both sentences.)

تا کِہ اُسکے فساد سے جو ضرر پَیدا هوتے نہ هونے پائیں 'so that the evils which would result (*lit.* would have resulted) from his mischief (were he permitted to practise it) be not allowed to happen.'

اگر کِسِي اَور نے یِہہ حرکتِ بےمعْنِي کِي هوتِي اُسکِي بوٹیاں کٹوا چِیلوں کو بانٹتِي 'had any one else committed such senseless impropriety of conduct, I would have had him cut into mince-meat, and portioned it out to the kites.'

تُو ناحق مارا گیا هوتا پر بچ گیا 'you would have been unjustly (or needlessly) killed, (had you been killed), but you (have) escaped.'

Rem. a. The condition, as we have shown in some of the above examples, is sometimes omitted. It is occasionally implied in a negative clause preceding the principal clause: *e.g.* مَیں نے اُس میں کُچھ شُکوہ نہ دیکھِي جو زور اُس کا دریافت کرتا 'I perceived nothing grand in him to make me test (*lit.* that I should have tested) his strength.' This sentence is taken from the Khirad Afroz (p. 62), and the following note upon it by the editor of the work serves to show how completely the Past Conditional Tense is misunderstood by European grammarians: "The aorist instead of the present here, and a neuter verb instead of an active, might well be expected. As it is, the sentence is quite ungrammatical."

Rem. b. As it is sometimes necessary to render the Past Perfect Indicative of the Urdū by the English Past Imperfect, so the Past Conditional has occasionally to be rendered in English by the Past Imperfect Subjunctive. Such is the case in the fourth of the above examples. (*cf.* § 457.)

475. Instead of the Past Conditional, the Past Perfect Indicative is occasionally used in the principal clause, for the sake of greater vividness; but it may be rendered in English by the Past Indefinite; as

اگر یِہہ دانا دُشمن نہ هوتا تو کام میرا هاتھ سے جاچُکا تها اَور جان میرِي اِس خیال میں تمام هُوئي تهي 'had it not been for this wise enemy, my work was well nigh gone from my hands, and my life brought to a close in (pursuit of) this idea.'

476. The Past Conditional is also used to express a wish for a thing that is regarded as unattainable, and is then commonly preceded by the conjunction کاشکِ or کاشکے 'O that!' 'would that!' *e.g.*

کاشکے اُنکو وهاں نہ چھوڑ آتے 'would that I (*lit.* we) had not left them behind there!'

کاشکے تُمهارِي خِدمت میں بنّدگي پَیدا نہ کِي هوتي اَور یِہہ شفقت جو صاحِب میري حق میں کرّتے هَیں نہ کرّتے 'would that I had not cherished a devoted attachment to you, and that you (*lit.* the master) had not shown for me the tenderness which you have shown and still show (*lit.* which you are showing)!'

Rem. The use of کاشکے however is not always necessary; a wish may be implied even in a conditional sentence: *e.g.* اگر زَید هوتا تو کیا خُوب هوتا 'If Zaid were (or, had been) here, how nice it would be (or, would have been)' = 'I wish Zaid were (or had been) here.'

e. THE PASSIVE VOICE.

477. When the agent of an act is to be named, the Active Voice must be employed (except in such tenses as are composed of a perfect participle of directly transitive verbs, which are undoubtedly passive in construction, though regarded as active by those who speak Urdū). But the subject of a sentence is frequently not specified, either because it is not known, or it is not desired to mention it. The speaker, however, has the option of expressing himself personally by such forms as کہتے هَیں or لوگ کہتے هَیں 'people say' (Fr. *on dit*), کہلاتا هَي 'one calls' (or 'it is called'), or کہنے والا کہتا هَي 'one says, or one who is in a position to say, says;' or by means of the Passive Voice used impersonally, in the third person singular masculine; as دیکھا جائیگا 'it will be seen to;' or personally as explained in the next paragraph.

478. The personal passive is commonly used in Urdū; the direct object or accusative of the active voice becoming the subject of the passive: *e.g.*

جب ایک گز عمیق گڑھا کھودا گیا 'when a hole a yard deep was dug.'

حِکمت کِي کِتابوں میں یہہ بات ثابِت کِي گئِي هَي 'it (the following fact) has been proved in philosophical works.'

جب جھوٹي بات کِسي کي نِسْبت عَیب نِکالنے کے واسطے بیان کي جائے ‘when a lie is told regarding any one to make it appear that he has faults.’

تُو ناحق مارا گیا هوتا پر بچ گیا ‘you had been unjustly killed, but you escaped.’

Rem. If the accusative in the active voice be constructed with کو, the same form may be retained in the passive; but the passive then becomes *impersonal*: *e.g.* یادگار کے لِحاظ سے اگر اُسکو بهي دیکها جاوي ‘if it too be viewed as a memorial;’ *lit.* ‘if it be looked at in reference to it also as a memorial.’

479. If the verb in the active voice governs two accusatives, that which has the nominative form, or which is next to the verb, becomes the nominative to the passive: as

اگر دونوں کو مُقابله کِیا جاوي ‘if the two be compared;’ *lit.* ‘if comparison in reference to the two be made.’

مُناسِب هَي کِہ اُس شخص کو بنائے کار کہا جاوي ‘it is right that that person be called the architect of the work;’ *lit.* ‘it is right that architect of the work be called or said in reference to that person.’

Rem. a. As the perfect participle is often used as an abstract (verbal) substantive, and the verb جانا is also employed in other constructions than that of the passive voice, many expressions which are not passive are mistaken for such by European grammarians: *e.g.* مُجھ سے دیکھا نہیں جاتا ‘I cannot bear to see (it),’ *lit.* ‘seeing, or seeing it, by me is impossible’ (not, “it is not seen by me:” *cf.* § 426).

Rem. b. Whether the passive be personal or impersonal, it is termed by Urdū grammarians مَا لَمْ يُسَمَّ فَاعِلُهُ *mā lam yusamma fā‘iluhu,* ‘a verb of which the agent is not named.' In the case of a personal passive, the subject is called قائِم مقامِ فاعِل 'that which stands in the place of the agent.'

Rem. c. Impersonal actives, like our *it rains, it snows*, etc., are as a rule expressed personally in Urdū: *e.g.* پانِي پڑتا هَي, or مينہ برستا هَي 'it rains,' *lit.* 'rain, or water, falls, or rains;' but the expression برستا هَي, alone, is also used.

f. CAUSAL VERBS.

480. The construction of causal verbs has been explained at length in § 199, *et seq.* If the primitive verb is intransitive, the causal is simply a transitive verb, and is constructed like other simple transitive verbs that take a single objective complement in the accusative; as اُس نے ميز هِلائِي or اُس نے ميز کو هِلايا 'he shook the table;' ميز کو کَون هِلاتا هَي 'who is shaking the table?' But if the primitive verb is transitive, the causal takes two objective complements in the accusative, which are constructed according to the rules laid down in § 348 and *Rem.*: *e.g.* مُجھے پانِي پِلاؤ 'give me water to drink;' مَيں نے وُه تَھيلِي اُس کو دِکھلائِي 'I showed him that bag.' Both the objective complements, however, are not always expressed; as سب فقِيروں کو کِھلايا 'he fed all the beggars.'

g. COMPOUND VERBS.

481. Compound Verbs are of seven[1] kinds; namely, Intensives, Potentials, Completives, Continuatives formed with an imperfect participle, Frequentatives or Con-

[1] By an oversight the Continuatives formed with imperfect participles, and Transitives formed with conjunctive participles, have been omitted in the enumeration of the compound verbs in § 218. The oversight has been noticed in the errata, and the reader is requested to make the corrections there pointed out.

tinuatives formed with a perfect participle, Desideratives, and Transitives formed with a conjunctive participle. To the remarks already made concerning these (see § 208, *et seq.*) we may here add the following:

1) *Intensives.*—The intensifying verb may be transitive or intransitive; if the former, the *passive* construction, as in the case of simple transitive verbs (§ 306, *et seq.*), is employed in all the tenses composed of the perfect participle: *e.g.* اُس نے بچھو کو مار ڈالا 'he killed the scorpion;' but if the intensifying verb is intransitive, this construction becomes impossible, since a *passive* participle is needed for it, and such a participle cannot be formed from the intransitive final member of the compound. This however does not convert the compound verb into a "neuter," as is generally supposed; for in Urdū, as in English, a verb is transitive if it takes an objective complement in the accusative (not the *cognate* accusative); hence, although a native grammarian must say وُہ روٹی کو کھا گیا instead of اُس نے روٹی کو کھا گیا 'he ate up the bread,' he still parses کھا گیا as a *fe'lĕ muta'addī ba yak maf'ūl,* 'a transitive verb with a single objective complement.'

Rem. In some intensive compounds, the verb which indicates the act is placed last and conjugated, the intensifying member preceding it and remaining unchanged: *e.g.* مار دیا = دي مارا 'I (or he) laid on to (him);' پٹک دِیا = دي پٹکا 'I (or he) threw or dashed (him or it) down.'

2), 3) *Potentials* and *Completives* must always be constructed *actively* in the tenses composed of the perfect participle, as in the other tenses, since the verbs سکنا and چُکنا are intransitive: *e.g.* هم (not هم نے) سُن چُکے هَیں 'we have already heard.'

Rem. For the idiomatic use of the Past Indefinite Tense of verbs compounded with چُکنا, see § 210.

4) *Continuatives,* formed with an *inflected* imperfect participle, and one of the verbs جانا or رهنا, cannot but take the *active* construction

in all the tenses, as جانا or رهنا are intransitive verbs (*cf.* § 481, 1): *e.g.* وه اِسِي طرح بکتے رهتِي (or جاتِي) هَي 'she keeps on (or is always) prating in this same way.'

Rem. The participle in these compounds must always be inflected (see § 212, as also the *Rem.* on § 213). In the following examples, which are given under the head of Continuatives by European grammarians, there is nothing of the nature of a *continuous* or *repeated* act implied in the verb; the participle has the force of a finite verb, and very properly agrees with the subject of the sentence: تُمهارِي هاته سے مال جاتا رها 'your wealth *has gone for good* from your hands' (here جاتا رها = گیا اَور رها); فِکر دِل سے اُس کے جاتِي رهیگِي 'care will *vanish for ever* from his heart' (here جاتِي رهیگِي = جائیگِي اَور رهیگِي). In examples like the following, again, the *continuity* of the action is implied in the verb itself (which must always be *rahnā*), the participle being used as a *ḥāl*, and agreeing in gender with the subject: آدمِي کو چاهِیئے کِہ اَپنے عَیبوں کِي جُستجُو میں بہُت سعي کرتا رهے 'it behoves a man to be ever diligent in finding out his defects.'

5), 6) *Frequentatives* or *Continuatives*, and *Desideratives*, are always *actively* constructed in the tenses composed of the perfect participle, since the participle which forms the first member of these compounds is used as an *abstract* (verbal) *substantive in the accusative* (§ 214), to which the act signified by the following verb (کرنا or چاهنا) is regarded as adhering. These compounds may take an objective complement in the accusative when the participle which forms the first member is derived from a transitive verb, but not otherwise; for the objective complement is properly that of the participle or verbal noun: *e.g.* سب کهڑي دیکها کِیئے 'all kept looking on, standing the while;' مَیں دِن بهر اُس جنگل میں پهرا کِیا 'I wandered about in that jungle the whole day long;' وه چُپکے بُت کِي طرح بَیٹهے سُنا کِي 'she, seated silent like a statue, continued to listen;' ایک مُدّت تلک اُس غم میں رویا کِیئے 'we continued to mourn for a long while under that affliction;'

مَیں تمام دِن اَور تمام رات پانِي میں هاتهہ پاؤں مارا کِیا 'I kept striking (out) my hands and legs in the water the whole day and the whole night.'—*Continuatives* are also formed by prefixing an *inflected* perfect participle to the verb جانا (see § 214, *b*): *e.g.* جو هم کهیں سو بِلا عُذر کِیئے جائِیو 'go on doing what I say without demur.'

Rem. We must here repeat that whenever a verbal substantive in any form is compounded with a transitive verb, the compound verb is *actively* constructed in *all* the tenses of the active voice: *e.g.* آدمِي کِي آواز سُنائِي دِي 'a man's voice was heard' (*lit.* 'gave a hearing,' *i.e.* 'made itself heard'); دو آدمِي دِکهائِي دِیئے 'two men showed themselves, or appeared.'

7) *Transitives formed with a Conjunctive Participle* cannot in any case be *passively* constructed, for the reason given in § 481, 1: *e.g.* کِتاب کو اپنے ساتهہ لایا هُوں 'I have brought the book with me;' اُن چیزوں کو کَون (کِس نے not) لے گیا 'who took away (went with) those things?' لڑکے کو یہاں چهوڑ گیا 'he left the boy behind here.'

Rem. Although the participle which most commonly occurs in these compounds is that of the verb لینا 'to take,' there is nothing in the nature of the construction to restrict it to this participle: چهوڑ جانا 'to leave behind,' دي جانا 'to leave, or give on (one's) way,' etc., are compounds just as much as لے آنا and its contraction لانا 'to come with, to bring' are; and in the mouth of a native the former no more signify "having left, to go," and "having given, to go," than the latter signifies *having taken, to come.*

482. *Nominals*, *Staticals*, *Inceptives*, *Permissives*, etc., are not compound verbs (see §§ 205, 213, 216). Of the Nominals we shall have more to say further on. The construction of the participles in statical forms has been fully explained in § 421, *et seq.* The Inceptives, etc., call for little notice beyond a few examples of their use:

1) *Inceptives.*—A gerund in the locative case, with the governing postposition suppressed, is used in connection with the verb لگنا, which usually (though not invariably) follows the gerund, and in this construction takes the signification of *to begin*: as اُسکے هاتھ پکڑ کر کہنے لگا 'he took hold of his hand, and began to say;' اپني بدنصيبي پر اَور لگا اُس کا افسوس کرنے لگا 'he began lamenting his ill-luck;' مُنہہ دیکھ دیکھ بے قرار هو رونے 'and repeatedly looking at his face, he became agitated and began weeping.'

2) *Permissives.*—An infinitive in the dative form of the accusative, with the postposition کو suppressed, is constructed with the verb دینا, which in this construction has the sense of *to allow* or *permit*: as حویلي میں رهنے دو 'let (him) remain in the house;' اگر پاک صاف پاتے هَیں تو اندر جانے دیتے هَیں 'if they find (them) unpolluted, they permit (them) to enter.'

3) *Acquisitives.*—The same construction is employed as in Permissives, the verb پانا, in the sense of *to get* or *obtain permission*, or *a chance* or *opportunity*, *to be allowed*, taking the place of دینا: as آسمان کي طرف نِگاه نہ کرنے پاوي 'let him not be allowed to look towards the sky;' نہ مُجھے کوئي دیکھنے پاتا تھا 'nor was any one permitted to see me.'

4) *Desideratives.*—In these an infinitive constructed as in the Permissives, etc., is used in connection with the verbs چاهنا and مانگنا, 'to wish, or want;' as آپ کا گھوڑا دیکھنے چاهتا هوں 'I wish to see your horse;' وہ گھر جانے مانگتا هَي 'he wants to go home.' With the verb چاهنا however, the infinitive more generally takes the *nominative form* of the accusative: as جب کوئي مکھي دُوسري چھتے کي آنا چاهتي هَي 'when a bee of another hive wishes to come;' مِحنتیوں کي کمائي پر بے اِستحقاق قابِض اَور مُتصرِف هونا چاهینگے 'they will unjustly desire to seize and apply to (their own) use the earnings of others.'

483. *Nominal Verbs.*—The so-called Nominals are commonly, though incorrectly, regarded as Compound Verbs. They consist simply of a verb and a predicative substantive or adjective, which is in the nominative case if the verb is a neuter one denoting existence (either simple or modified), and in the accusative (the nom. form) if the verb is transitive. In the first of these cases the verb agrees with its proper subject (unless the predicative substantive is defined by a genitive or adjective, § 293); and a predicative adjective, if it be declinable, also agrees in gender and number with the subject: as

اگر یِہہ میري رُوبرُو ترْبِیَت نہ هوگا 'if he shall not be reared in my presence.'

یہے ساتوں لڑکِیاں کھڑِي تھِیں 'all these seven girls were standing.'

کِہ اِنْکے اخْلاق دُرُست هو جائیں 'that their morals become correct.'

أور إعانت ایکْ دُوسْري کِي جب تھي هوسکْتِي هَي کِہ اِکٹھے رهیں 'and one's helping another is possible only when they dwell together.'

Rem. a. The predicative noun most commonly comes immediately before the verb, as in the above examples; but it may also follow the verb, as is frequently the case in poetry: *e.g.* أیسے مِہْمان کِي تو لازِم هَي کِہ خاطِر هو عزِیز 'the heart of such a guest ought indeed to be (esteemed) precious.'

Rem. b. Even what are clearly *phrases* are erroneously classed by European grammarians among what they term "Nominal Compounds." Now in phrases the substantive and verb stand to each other in relations distinct from those specified above, the substantive being either in the nominative as the *subject* of the verb, or in an oblique case: *e.g.* أن کو یاد آیا 'they remembered' (properly, 'recollection came to them'); مُجھ کو تُجھ پر افْسوس آتا هَي 'I feel (am possessed with) pity for you' (for the use of آنا with the Dative of the possessor see § 340); پيٹ ميں آگ لگي 'the fire (of hunger) kindled in (my) stomach;' مجھے بھي وزير کا کہنا ياد (sc. ميں) آيا 'I also called to mind what the *wazīr* had said' (properly, 'to me also the *wazīr's* saying or remark came into recollection'); کہ وقت پر کام (sc. ميں) آتا ھے 'so that on occasion it comes of use' (properly, 'into use').

484. In the case where a predicative noun in the accusative is added to a transitive verb, the verb may be one which requires a single objective complement alone, or it may be a *factitive* verb (see § 349). In the first of these cases the predicative substantive necessarily becomes the *subject* of the verb in those tenses which are passively constructed with the Agent case: *e.g.* اس نے ڈبکي ماري 'he dived (a dive was taken, *lit.* struck, by him).' In the second, the construction of the verb in the same tenses depends upon the accusative of the *object*: if this be in the *nominative* form, the verb (as also a predicative adjective, if it be declinable) agrees with it; but if it be in the *dative* form, the verb (as also the adjective) is impersonally constructed (see §§ 348—350): *e.g.*

ھرچند اس قفل کي کنجي تلاش کي نہ ملي 'much as they searched for the key of that lock, it was not found' (properly, 'much as the key of that lock was made search for by them,' etc.).

ديو کو رخصت کيا 'he dismissed the demon' (properly, 'there was performed by him the act of dismissing in reference to the demon').

گاڑي کھڑي کي 'he made the cart stationary' ('the cart was made stationary by him').

گاڑِي کو کھڑا کِي 'he made the cart stationary' (properly, 'it was made stationary by him in respect to the cart').

Rem. a. The only instances in which a factitive verb (in the passively constructed tenses) can agree with the complementary accusative are those in which by a change of construction this becomes really or virtually the only accusative in the sentence: *e.g.* 1) when a sentence following the verb takes the place of the object; as أس نے عرض کِيا کِہ 'he made representation, saying;' (here however some writers would put the verb in the masc. sing. عرض کِيا, to agree with the objective clause (see § 307); 2) when the place of the object is supplied by a substantive which is governed in the genitive by the predicative substantive; as بادشاہ نے أسکِي تعرِيف کِي 'the king praised it' ('the act of praising was performed by the king in respect of it'); 3) when the factitive verb is connected by أور 'and,' with another verb that stands nearest to the common object of the two verbs, this object being in the dative form of the accusative; as پِيادوں کو ڈانٹا أور تنبِيہ کِي 'he reproved and admonished the magistrate's peons.'

Rem. b. If the predicative substantive is determined by a genitive, it may be separated from the verb by one or more words; as إِس قُوت کا إِظہار چِلانے أور رونے و غَيرہ سے کرتا هَي 'it (a child) manifests this faculty by screaming and crying.'

CHAPTER XI.

PARTICLES.

I. ADVERBS.

485. The rules for the construction of adverbs are given in § 283, *et seq.* Sentences like the following are in nowise opposed to those rules, since نہیں is both a negative adverb and a negative verb (= نہ ہے, see § 148, *Rem.*), and in the latter sense therefore may stand last in the sentence:

ایک کی سجدھج سے دوسری کا ڈیل ڈول ملتا نہیں 'the form and fashion of one agrees not with the shape and figure of another.'

اس وقت دروازہ کھولنے کا حکم نہیں 'there is no order to open the gate at this time.'

486. The particle تو, which has both a conditional and an emphatic force, is often added to the negative نہیں, forming in the one case an alternative conjunction (see § 499), in the other an emphatic adverb signifying *no indeed.*

Rem. The adverb تو is often used idiomatically in Urdū, and is untranslateable: *e.g.* کر تو سہی 'just do it.' After the verb دیکھنا 'to see,' it may generally be rendered by the phrase 'and lo!' as دیکھا تو

سب اپنے اپنے کام میں مصرُوف هَیں 'he looked, and lo! they were all engaged in their respective tasks.'

487. The adverb کہاں 'where?' is idiomatically joined to two different subjects to indicate a *very great difference*, *marked contrast*, or *incompatibility*, between them or their circumstances: as

نہیں تو مَیں کہاں اَور تُو کہاں 'otherwise what possibility was there of our meeting?' (*lit.* 'where I and where thou? our paths lay so wide apart that we could never have met, but for this accident').

تُو کہاں اَور یِہہ بات کہاں 'this speech is quite unsuitable to thy position.'

کہاں راجا بھوج کہاں گنگا تیلي 'there is no comparison between King Bhoj and Gangā the oilman.'

Rem. Compare with this use of کہاں—کہاں that of क्व—क्व *kva—kva* in Sanskrit.

488. The adverb هِي (or ـِي) may be added for emphasis to any part of speech, and may generally be rendered in English by *very*, *the very same*, *but*, *alone*, etc., though sometimes simple stress upon the word to which it is joined (shown in writing by the use of italics) is sufficient: *e.g.*

دِل هِي جانتا هَي '(my) heart alone knows.'

ایک هِي حملے میں 'in one single (or in but one) assault.'

وُهِي جوان آیا 'the very same young man came.'

لیکِن اُس کے دم میں آهِي گئي 'but (after all) she *did* yield to her cajoling.'

II. PREPOSITIONS AND POSTPOSITIONS.

489. Prepositions and Postpositions serve to show the relation of one substantive to another, or to some other word in the sentence.

490. Some postpositions govern a noun in the Formative only, some in the genitive case only, some take the governed noun in the Formative or the genitive. Lists of the prepositions and postpositions together with the case they govern are given in §§ 236–240. The following are a few that have special significations or uses in addition to those specified in the lists :

1) آگے 'before,' is used of *comparison*: *e.g.*

عکسِ گُلشن یہہ زمین پر هَي کِہ جِسکے آگے ـ کارِ نقّاشيِ ماني هَي دُوم وُہ اوّل 'such is the reflection of the flower-garden on the ground that, compared therewith, the painting of Mānī (Manes) stands second, it first.'

Rem. The postposition سامھنے 'in front,' may be used in the same sense.

2) ساتھ, which as a postposition signifies 'with,' 'along with,' as a *preposition*, with a demonstrative pronoun following, usually signifies *in addition to*, *notwithstanding* or *although* (= the Persian باوُجُود or باوصف): *e.g.*

موھن زَید کے ساتھ اِلٰہ آباد چلا گیا 'Mohan went away to Ilāhābād (Allahabad) along with Zaid.'

ساتھ اُس کے عُمْر مِحنت کے ساتھ کٹیگي 'in addition to that life will pass with trouble (or difficulty).'

ساتھ اُسکے کِہ وُہ آپ چھوٹا اور ناتُواں ہو اور دُشمن اُسکا قوِي تب بھِي فتح کِي اُمید هَي 'notwithstanding that (or although) he himself be small and feeble and his foe powerful, there is still hope of victory.'

3) طرف 'towards,' 'to,' is used both of *local* direction and of *feeling* or *conduct*, generally preceding, in this sense, an Arabic verbal noun: *e.g.*

بازار کِي طرف گیا هَي 'he is gone towards (or to) the market;' (the corresponding Hindī postpositions in this construction are تک and کو).

میرِي طرف سے سلام کہہ دینا 'tender compliments from me' (*lit.* 'from my side' = Fr. de ma part).

بُرِي بُرِي باتوں کِي طرف مَیلان هوتا هَي 'he becomes inclined to (fond of) very evil things;' (the corresponding Hindī postposition in this sense is پر).

کِسِي شخص کِي طرف سے بدگُماں هو جانا 'to become suspicious of (*lit.* towards) a person.'

کئِي شخصوں کے کاموں کِي طرف اِحتِیاج هَي 'he needs the labours of several persons.'

Rem. In both the above senses the postposition طرف is the Urdū rendering of the Arabic preposition اِلیٰ; and the idiom in sentences like the last three of the above is borrowed from the Arabic. The postposition جانِب 'side, direction,' is rarely used of *feeling* or *conduct*.

4) نزدِیک 'near,' as a postposition, is often used in the sense of *in one's opinion* (like the Lat. *apud*, and the Fr. *chez*), a sense in which قریب and پاس do not occur: *e.g.* عقلمندوں کے نزدِیک 'in the opinion of the wise.'

491. A feminine *postposition* requires the noun it governs in the genitive to be constructed with کي in agreement with itself; but if the postposition be used as a *preposition*, i.e. *precede* the noun it governs (which can only occur when it is a Persian or Arabic word), the genitive of the governed noun will be constructed with کے (see § 243): *e.g.*

تاري کي مانند, but مانند تاري کے, 'like a star.'

أس کي بابت, but بابت أس کے, 'concerning him or it.'

مِثل طبيب و نجومي کے هين, 'they are like physicians and astrologers.'

بمدد عقل کے, 'by the aid of the understanding.'

تمهاري بموجب فرمانے کے, 'in accordance with (or according to) your ordering (= order).'

In the first of these cases the construction is that of the Hindī, in the second that of the Persian (whence the occurrence of none but Persian or Arabic prepositions in the construction).[1] The use of the genitive affix کے is due to the influence of a Persian preposition (most commonly به), which governs the postposition in the genitive. This preposition, though not expressed in the case of بابت, مانند, etc., is implied in the construction, and, being originally a masculine noun, requires the use of the affix کے with the genitive of the governed noun. The same

[1] This construction is not only employed with "some of the feminine prepositions," as European grammarians say, but with all such as are Persian or Arabic words. Nor is it "arbitrary": no Urdū scholar would, we are assured, say or write مانند پروانے کي *mānind parwāne kī*, 'like a moth;' but as no distinction is usually made in writing between *majhūl* and *ma'rūf ye*, it is quite possible for an Englishman to mistake کي for *kī*, when the writer intends it for *ke* (کے).

construction occurs with the preposition بے, 'without:' *e.g.* بے مرضي حضور کے, *without her highness' pleasure*; بے صلاح و مشورت کے, *without advice and counsel.* It is true that we also meet with such constructions as اُسکي بے مرضي (*sc.* سے), *with his or her displeasure*; but in such cases بے is a *prefix*, not a separate preposition, and the words بے مرضي, etc., are treated as simple Hindī postpositions.

Rem. If the preposition به is expressed, even a *preceding* genitive is constructed with the affix کے: as قادرِ مُطلق خُدا کے بنِسبت آدمي کِتنا کُچھ ناچِيز هَي, *how very insignificant is man compared to the Almighty!* And not only does به, expressed or implied, require the genitive to be constructed with کے, but, according to the native grammarians, کے is in some instances used as the equivalent of به (see § 318, *Rem.*).

III. CONJUNCTIONS.

492. The combination of coordinate and subordinate propositions is effected by means of conjunctions.

Rem. Lists of some of the principal conjunctions are given in § 247.

493. *Coordinate Combination.*—The conjunctions used in coordinate combination are the Connective (Copulative, Disjunctive, Alternative, Negative), Adversative, Exceptive, and Conclusive.

494. The Connective conjunctions do not affect the structure of a sentence. اَور (or و), 'and,' is the one most used simply to connect words and sentences. But the omission of it (Asyndeton) is of frequent occurrence (see §§ 217, 275, 362).

495. اَور is also used idiomatically to denote:

1) The almost simultaneous occurrence of the acts indicated by the verbs in two propositions which it connects; as تُم اُٹھے اَور خرابِي آئِي (= بفَور تُمهاري اُٹھنے کے خرابِي آئِي), *you rose and evil came* ('no sooner did you rise than evil ensued').

2) Inseparable connection of two subjects; as مَیں هُوں اَور تُم هو (= تُمهارا ساتھ نہ چھوڑُونگا), *I am and you are* (*i.e.* 'where you are I will be,' or 'I will stick to you wherever you are').

3) Defiance or threat; as پھِر مَیں هُوں اَور تُم هو (= مَیں تُمْکو خُوب سمجھُونگا), *then I am and you are* (*i.e.* 'now I will settle accounts with you'); اب تُو جان اَور بڑا بُت جانے, *now you know and the great idol will know* ('the great idol will settle accounts with you').

496. The negative نہ, repeated, has the signification of our *neither—nor*; but the conjunction اَور is often prefixed to the second نہ: *e.g.* نہ ایک کو دُوسْري سے تکْلِیف نہ اُسْکو اِس سے رنْج, *neither does one suffer inconvenience from another, nor that annoyance from this*; تِیسْري وُہ کلام هَي کِہ اُس میں نہ تو ضرر هو اَور نہ نفْع, *the third is that speech wherein there is neither harm nor benefit.*

497. The disjunctive conjunction یا 'or' (as an alternative یا—یا 'either—or'), is used in the sense of both the Latin *vel* and *aut*: *e.g.* کوئِي مهاجن یا بَیپارِي اُنْکے برابر نہ تها, *no merchant or trader came up to him*; جو کوئِي مُسافِر فقِیر یا دُنْیادار اِس شہْر میں آوے, *any traveller*, (whether) *a devotee or a man of the world, who enters this city.*

Rem. يا—يا is sometimes used to indicate a remarkable contrast arising from a sudden change; as يا وُہ رَونق تهِي يا سُن سان هوگيا, *but now there was that* (such) *display, and the next moment all became desolate.*

498. The conjunction كِہ, which more commonly occurs in subordinate clauses, is also used as a disjunctive, signifying 'or:' *e.g.* وهاں تُم جاؤگے كِہ مَيں, *will you go there or shall I?* تُم نے كُچه عِلم منّطِق كا بهِي سِيكها هَي كِہ نہيں, *have you learned anything of the science of logic also or not?*

499. The compound conjunctions نہيں تو and ورّنہ, 'otherwise,' 'or else,' are used in stating an alternative; as تب ميرا كليجا ٹهنّڈا هو نہيں تو اِس غُصّے كِي آگ ميں پهكٹ رهِي هُوں, *then* (perhaps) *my heart* (*lit.* liver) *will be quieted, otherwise I am burning* (shall continue to burn) *with the fire of this wrath;* وُہ حاكِم آيسا هونا چاهِيئے كِہ سِياست كے قاعِدي خُوب جانّتا هو ورّنہ سلّطنت ميں زوَال آجائيگا, *that ruler should be such a one as is well acquainted with the laws of government, or else decline will overtake the state.*

Rem. The following are examples of some of the remaining disjunctive conjunctions: تُمّكو جانے نہ دُونّگا بُرا مانو خواہ بهلا, *I will not let you go,* (whether you) *take it ill or well;* مَيں نہيں كہّتا چاهو رهو چاهو جاؤ, '*I say nothing; either go or remain,* as you please.' For examples of كيا—كيا see § 397.

500. The Adversative conjunctions are مگر, لیکِن, پر (which however is more commonly *exceptive*), بلّكِہ, etc., signifying *but, yet, still, but rather, on the contrary.* They are used in stating a proposition which alters, limits, or sets aside what has preceded, and do not affect the struc-

ture of a sentence. The first three of those mentioned above are often used correlatively with the Concessive conjunctions اگرچه, گو, 'although,' 'even if:' *e.g.* اور سب نام چاہتے ہیں پر ویسا کام نہیں کرتے, *and all desire the name* (Generous), *but do not perform such acts*; غرض کے وقت سب کچھ کہتا لیکن یاد نہیں رکھتا, *he says anything and everything when he has an object* (to gain), *but does not keep* (his promise) *in mind*; اِس میں ہرگز خلل نہیں بلکہ افزوں ہے, *there is no defect at all in this, but rather there is excess*; اگرچہ تیرا باپ بادشاہ ہے لیکن تیری قسمت میں یہہ بھی بدا تھا, *although your father is a king, yet this also was decreed in your destiny.*

501. The Exceptive conjunctions are مگر, اِلّا, and sometimes لیکن, signifying *only*, *but*, *but not*, *except*. They are used to exclude the case in which the assertion does not hold good: *e.g.* سب برادری کے آدمی آئے مگر (لیکن or) موہن نہیں آیا *all the brotherhood came, but Mohan did not come* ('all came except Mohan'). The thing excepted may be totally different in kind from the general term; as سب شہزادے آئے تھے اِلّا سپاہی, *all the princes came* (*lit.* had come), *but not their troops.*

Rem. مگر is sometimes used, as in Persian, in the sense of شاید, 'perhaps:' as اِس بے درد شوہر نے میری مگر اُسکو گھر کے دروازے پر دیکھا, *this feelingless husband of mine perhaps saw him at the door of the house.*

502. The Conclusive or Illative conjunctions are اِس لیئے, پھر, سو, پس, چنانچہ, لہٰذا, etc., which may be translated *therefore*, *wherefore*, *accordingly*, *consequently*, etc. The

following are examples of their use: زباں سے بہت سي خرابياں پيدا هوتي هيں اور اُن سے بچنا دشوار هي - اس ليئے مصلحت يہہ هي کہ آدمي خاموشي اختيار کري, *many evils spring from the tongue, and to avoid them is difficult, it is therefore advisable that a man observe silence*; راجہ نے حکم ديا کہ خزانوں کے دروازي کهول ديں چنانچہ آيسا هي هُوا, *the king ordered that they should open the doors of the treasuries, and such was accordingly done*; کئي باتيں خيال ميں گذريں لہذا فدوي مُتبسِم هُوا, *several things passed through his mind, and consequently your devoted slave smiled.*

503. *Subordinate Combination.*—The conjunctions employed in subordinate combination are the Hypothetical, Temporal, Concessive, Comparative, Causal, and Final.

504. The Hypothetical conjunctions are اگر, جو 'if,' جب 'when,' etc. These are construed with the Indicative or the Subjunctive, as shown in § 466, 1) *a*, and 2), *Rem. b.* The regular correlative of the first two is تو; that of the third تب. But the correlatives are not always expressed; and even the hypothetical particle is occasionally omitted, as in the following sentence: اُس کي خوشي يُوں هي هُوئي تو کيا کرُوں, *when, or if, her pleasure took this course alone, what could I do?*

505. The correlatives تو and تب being synonymous, the one is sometimes used for the other; as اور اگر يہہ سب سامان مُيسّر بهي هو تب بهي ظاهر هي, *and even if all these pliances be obtained, then even it is evident*, etc.; جب آدمي کو آيسا علم حاصل هو تو اُس سے حکمت حاصل هو سکتي هي, *when a man acquires such knowledge, wisdom may thereby be attained.*

Rem. تو is now commonly used instead of تب as the correlative of جب.

506. The conjunction جو is sometimes used in the sense of جب ; as جو اُسکو کھولکر دیکھا تو وُہ جوان اَور اُسکي رنڈي سِرکٹے پڑي ھَیں, *when he opened it and looked, lo! that young man and his paramour were* (*lit.* are) *lying beheaded.*

507. جب is occasionally used in the sense (1) of اب جو 'now that,' and (2) of تب, in which case the conditional clause, if expressed, may follow, being introduced by the conjunction کِ in the sense of جب ; as جب معلوم ھُوا کِ تُم اُنھوں کے احوال سے مُطلِع ھو شُکر بجا لاکر یہی کہتا ھُوں, *now that I know that you are acquainted with their history, I give thanks and say this,* etc.; سخت مِحنت کرني پڑتي ھَي جب کُچھ آتا ھَي, *one has to work hard, then something is acquired*; اِعانت ایک دُوسري کي جب ھِي ھو سکتي ھَي کِ اِکٹھے رھیں, *then alone is mutual help* (*lit.* the helping of one another) *possible, when they dwell together.*

508. جب in combination with the postpositions تک (or تلک) and لگ (which however rarely occurs in modern Urdū), forms *temporal* conjunctions, signifying *whilst, until, as long as*; and the same postpositions are repeated after the correlative تب when this is expressed. These conjunctions are construed with the Indicative or the Subjunctive (the Aorist, which is however rendered in English by the Present Indicative), according as simple fact or contingency (design, etc.) is indicated. They are often followed by the negative نہ (or نہیں), and may then be generally translated 'as long as,' 'so long as:' *e.g.* جب تک

آونگا دِل یہیں لگا رهیگا, *until I come* (back) *here alone will my heart be fixed*; جب تلک اُسکا دم نہیں نِکلتا دم نہیں لینے دیتے, *as long as his breath* (life) *does not depart, they give him no peace* (*lit.* 'do not let him take breath'); جب لگ کِہ اُسکا نقصان نہ هوگا تب لگ میري قدر نہ جانیگا, *so long as he suffers no harm, he will not know my value*; جب تک جوان نہ هو باهِر نہ نِکلے, *let him not come out* (of the harem) *as long as he is not a man* (shall not have attained to manhood); یہاں رهو جب تک تُمهارِي آرزو بر آوي, *remain here till your desire is fulfilled.*

509. The Concessive conjunctions are اگرچِہ, گو or گوکِہ, etc., 'although,' 'even if.' The latter is usually construed with the Subjunctive (the Aorist); the former with the Indicative or the Subjunctive, according as a simple fact is expressed or not: *e.g.* اگرچِہ طاقت بولنے کِي نہ تهِي آهِستے سے کہا شُکر هَي, *although she had not the strength to speak, she said faintly, Thank God!* مَیں بهِي اُنکِي داد کو پہنچتا هُوں اگرچِہ وي کافِر هوں, *even I dispense justice to them, although they be unbelievers*; اور گو سب عادتیں اچّهِي نہ هوں جِس قدر اچّهِي هوسکیں اُنکے دُرُست کرنے میں دِل لگائے, *and even though all* (his) *habits may not become good, let him labour earnestly to correct them to the extent that it is possible for them to be good.*

510. The Comparative conjunctions are those which express a resemblance. They are جَیسا 'as,' گویا 'as if:' *e.g.* جَیسا رائے دابِشلِیم کا مُلک آسوده اور رعِیّت فارِغ بال تهِي, *as Rāe Dābishlīm's kingdom was tranquil, and his subjects contented*; هرگِز هوا اُسکو نہیں لگتِي گویا فانُوس اُسکِي آسمان هَي,

the wind never touches it; (it is) *as if the sky is its shade.*

511. The Causal conjunctions are those which are used in stating a reason. They are جو, کہ, and others which are compounds formed with کہ, as اِس واسطے کہ, کیونکہ, چونکہ, etc. They may mostly be translated *for*, *because*, *since*, *seeing that*, *inasmuch as*, etc. The following are examples of their use: اِسکے دِل میں تو محبّت اب تلک باقی ہَے جو اِس جان‌کندنی کی حالت میں اُسکو یاد کرتی ہَے, *in her heart indeed affection still lingers, seeing that she remembers him in this death-agony*; میری پکڑنے کی خاطِر جو قبول کیا ہَے پورا کرو کہ ساری ڈِیل میں زباں حلال ہَے, *fulfil what you agreed to for my capture, for in the whole body the tongue is* (the only) *free* (and therefore responsible member); اُسکی بات کا اِعتِبار نہ کری اِس واسطے کہ چغل‌خور اکثر اِعتِبار کے قابِل نہیں ہوتا *let him put no faith in his statement, for a tale-bearer, generally speaking, is not deserving of credit*; زر و جواہِر پر فریفتہ ہونا دانِشمندوں کا کام نہیں کیونکہ وہ کِسی کے پاس نہیں رہتے *it is not the work of the wise to be infatuated with gold and jewels, since those* (things) *abide with no one.*

512. Final conjunctions are used to denote the purpose or consequence of an action. They are constructed with the Subjunctive, as shown in § 467. To the examples there given may be added the following: شاہِ بندر کے خوف سے کہ مبادا چھین لے کنیزکوں کو صندوقوں میں بند کیا, *through fear of the harbour-superintendent, they locked up their slave-girls in* (their) *chests, lest he should take them by force.*

Rem. The particle کِہ has other significations and uses besides those noticed above (§§ 498, 507, 511, 512). It is sometimes used (as in Persian) in the sense of از 'than;' but this can only occur in Persian construction: as ایک آدمي مري بہترکِہ تمام شہر, *better one man perish than the whole city.* It is of frequent occurrence as a simple explicatory particle: 1) at the head of an adjective (qualificative, descriptive), or conjunctive clause, as exemplified in § 390; 2) at the head of a saying or speech (مقُول), which stands as the object of a preceding verb, or, generally, at the beginning of an objective clause: as اُس نے پُوچھا کِہ یہ کیا کر رہے ہَیں, *he asked, What are these doing?* In such cases it may sometimes be rendered by 'that,' 'saying,' 'namely,' etc., but it is often untranslatable.

CHAPTER XII.

ON THE DIRECT ORATION.

513. The indirect oration is rarely employed in Urdū. The words and thoughts of a person are usually expressed in the direct oration, introduced by the particle کِہ, which however is frequently omitted (*cf.* also § 445): *e.g.*

اہلِ جہاز سے معلوم ہُوا کِہ اُس جزِیرے میں دجّال رہتا ہَے 'I learned from the people of the ship that the Antichrist dwelt in that island' (*lit.* 'I learned from the people of the ship "Antichrist lives, etc."').

اگر یِہ قصد ہَے کِہ شہر میں جاؤں 'if it is your intention to enter the city' (*lit.* 'if this is thy intention: "I will enter, etc."').

اُس نے مُجھ سے کہا تیری بہِن بِیمار ہَے 'he told me my sister was sick' (*lit.* 'he said to me, "Thy sister is sick"').

فِکر میں گیا کِہ کِس صُورت سے اُن لعلوں کو لے جاؤں 'he pondered how he should carry away those rubies' (*lit.* 'how shall I carry away, etc.').

مَیں نے اُن سے کہا تمھاری ساتھ مَیں بِھی چلُونگا 'I told them that I also would accompany them' (*lit.* 'I said to them, "I also will accompany you"').

APPENDIX.

ON THE CALENDAR.

The following remarks on the Musalmān and Hindū Calendars are mostly taken from Forbes's Hindūstānī Grammar.

THE MOḤAMMADAN CALENDAR.

"The Musalmāns reckon by lunar time, their era called the *Hijra* commencing from the day on which Moḥammad retreated from Mekka to Medīna; which, according to the best accounts, took place on Friday, the 16th of July (18th new style), A.D. 622. Their year consists of 12 lunations, amounting to 354 days and 9 hours, very nearly; and hence their New Year's Day will happen every year about eleven days earlier than in the preceding year."

"To find the Christian year corresponding to that of the Hijra, apply the following rule:—From the given number of Musalmān years deduct *three per cent.*, and to the remainder add the number 621·54; the sum is the period of the Christian era at which the given current Musalmān year ends. This rule is founded on the fact that 100 lunar years are very nearly equal to 97 solar years, the difference being about eighteen days only."

"When great accuracy is required, and when the year, month, and day of the Moḥammadan era are given, the precise period of the Christian era may be found very nearly, as follows:—Express the Musalmān date in years and decimals of a year; multiply by ·97; to the product add 621·54: and the sum will be the period of the Christian era."

"The Moḥammadan or lunar months are made to consist of thirty and twenty-nine days alternately, but in a period of thirty years it is found necessary to intercalate the last month eleven times, so as to be reckoned thirty days instead of twenty-nine. The months retain their Arabic names in all Moḥammadan countries, as follows:"

LUNAR MONTHS.

		DAYS.			DAYS.
مُحرّم	*mŏḥarram*	30	رجب	*rajab*	30
صفر	*ṣafar*	29	شعْبان	*sha'bān*	29
ربیعُ الاوّل	*rabī'u 'l-awwal*	30	رمضان	*ramaẓān*	30
ربیعُ الثّانی	*rabī'u 's-ṣānī*	29	شوّال	*shawwāl*	29
ربیعُ الاخِر	*rabī'u 'l-ākhir*		ذِی القعْدہ	*zi 'l-ka'da*	30
جُمادَی الاوّل	*jumāda'l-awwal*	30	ذِی قعْدہ	*zī ka'da*	
جُمادَی الثّانی	*jumāda's-ṣānī*	29	ذِی الحِجّہ	*zi 'l-ḥijja*	29
جُمادَی الاخِر	*jumāda'l-ākhir*		ذِی حِجّہ	*zī ḥijja*	

The following are the days of the week in Urdū, Hindī, and Persian:

	URDU.	HINDI.	PERSIAN.
Sun.	اِتْوار *itwār*	رِبیبار *rabī-bār*	یکْشنْبہ *yak-shamba*
Mon.	پیر (or سومْوار) *pīr*	سومْبار *som-bār*	دُو شنْبہ *du-shamba*
Tues.	منْگل *mangal*	منْگلْبار *mangal-bār*	سِہ شنْبہ *sih-shamba*
Wed.	بُدھ *budh*	بُدھْبار *budh-bār*	چہار شنْبہ *ohahār-shamba*
Thurs.	جُمْعہ رات *jum'a rāt*	برِھسْپتِبار *brihaspati-bār*	پنْجْشنْبہ *panj-shamba*
Fri.	جُمْعہ *jum'a*	سُکْربار *sukra-bār*	آدِینہ *ādīna*
Sat.	سنِیچر *sanīchar*	سنِیبار *sanībār*	شنْبہ or ھفْتہ *shamba* or *hafta*

The Hindūs regard the day as commencing at midnight, as we do; but the Moḥammadans regard it as commencing at the preceding evening, so that 'the night of a certain day,' in the mouth of a Musalmān, signifies 'the night of the previous day.' For example جُمعے كي رات 'Friday night,' is really 'Thursday night' according to our way of reckoning

THE HINDU CALENDAR.

The Hindū year is divided into twelve equal portions which nearly correspond to our solar months. The month again is divided into two parts, each called *pakh*, 'lunar fortnight.' The first *pakh* extends from new to full moon, and is called *sudī*, 'the light fortnight;' the second extends from full to new moon, and is called *badī*, 'the dark fortnight.' "All festivals and dates are reckoned, not by the solar months, but by the duration of the moon which terminates in each. Hence although the month *Baisākh* begins *de jure* about the 11th of April, it may have commenced *de facto* from one day to twenty-eight days sooner. When two new moons occur during one solar month, which happens once in three years, there is an intercalary month, and the month so intercalated receives the name of the one which preceded it, that is of the solar month within which the two new moons may happen."

The era however which is commonly used by the Hindūs of the northern half of India is that called *sambat* (Sanskrit *samvat*, 'year'), which dates from the month *Kātik* of the year 57 B.C. when king Vikramāditya is supposed to have ascended the throne of Ujjain.

Another common era, especially in Southern India, is that of Śālivāhana. It is called *śāka*, and dates from the month *Chait* of the year 78 A.D.

The following are the names of the Hindū solar months:

بَیساکھ *baisākh*, April—May.	کاتِک *kātik*, } Oct.—Nov.
جیٹھ *jeṭh*, May—June.	کارتِک *kārtik*, } Oct.—Nov.
اساڑھ *asāṛh*, June—July.	اگھن *aghan*, Nov.—Dec.
ساون *sāwan*, } July—Aug.	پُوس *pūs*, Dec.—Jan.
سراون *srāwan*, } July—Aug.	ماگھ *māgh*, Jan.—Feb.
بھادوں *bhādoṅ*, Aug.—Sept.	پھاگن *phāgun*, Feb.—March.
کوار or آسِن *kū'ār* or *āsin*, Sept.—Oct.	چَیت *chait*, March—April.

These are in common use among both Hindūs and Musalmāns. But the names of the English months are also often used at the present time especially in official correspondence.

THE END.